Europe's Coherence Gap in External Crisis and Conflict Management

Bertelsmann Stiftung (ed.)

Europe's Coherence Gap in External Crisis and Conflict Management

Political Rhetoric and Institutional Practices in the EU and Its Member States

| Verlag BertelsmannStiftung

Bibliographic information published by the Deutsche Nationalbibliothek

The Deutsche Nationalbibliothek lists this publication in the
Deutsche Nationalbibliografie; detailed bibliographic data
is available on the Internet at http://dnb.dnb.de.

© 2020 Verlag Bertelsmann Stiftung, Guetersloh
Responsible: Stefani Weiss
Copy editor: Josh Ward
Production editor: Christiane Raffel
Cover design: Elisabeth Menke
Cover illustration: © Shutterstock/Thomas Dutour
Illustration pp. 372, 376, 377: Dieter Dollacker
Typesetting: Katrin Berkenkamp
Printing: Hans Gieselmann Druck und Medienhaus
GmbH & Co. KG, Bielefeld
ISBN 978-3-86793-911-9 (print)
ISBN 978-3-86793-912-6 (e-book PDF)
ISBN 978-3-86793-913-3 (e-book EPUB)

www.bertelsmann-stiftung.org/publications

Contents

Introduction

Stefani Weiss

The end of the Cold War initially relaxed the security situation in Europe and enabled the European Union to press ahead with its effort to peacefully unify the continent. Almost everywhere (with the exception of the Balkans), hopes were flying high that a new era would dawn in which human rights and democracy could triumph and usher in a lasting era of peaceful, prosperous development. The EU, in particular, was confident that its soft power would enable it to export its own 'peace-through-integration' model. In fact, nothing less was expected than that the EU would soon be surrounded by a ring of well-governed democratic states that shared its values of rules-based, non-violent conflict resolution in internal and foreign affairs.

Today, we know that history took a different course. Geopolitics is back, and the growing superpower rivalry between the United States and China – not to mention Russia's new hegemonic policy – do not bode well. In response to these developments, many democratic reform processes that the EU and its member states were engaging in slowed down, suffered setbacks or failed to materialise at all. Accordingly, intra- and inter-state crises and conflicts continue to haunt international affairs – and this worrying situation is only exacerbated by climate change. In fact, the 2019 annual report of the United Nations High Commissioner for Refugees says that there was a record number of forcibly displaced persons worldwide in 2018, a staggering figure of over 70 million.

The impact of the deteriorating security environment is becoming increasingly tangible in Europe itself, and threatens both security and political stability within the EU. As with 9/11 in the US, the large-scale attacks by Islamist-motivated terrorists in Brussels, Paris, London, Berlin and elsewhere have left European citizens feeling extremely vulnerable and insecure. Russia's 2014 annexation of Crimea and the hybrid warfare it is engaged in in eastern Ukraine have broken with the post-Cold War security order that the EU has trusted in and relied upon. Furthermore, hundreds of thousands of people who were seeking refuge in Europe following the still-ongoing war in Syria and the wider region have heightened Europeans' anxieties about cultural alienation and a loss of social status, leading to increased support for extremist parties.

Given these circumstances, the EU is being called upon – and perhaps even more so than ever before – to maintain its influence as a force for peace and to become the responsible global actor it expressly desires to be. Unfortunately, we repeatedly see that both the EU and its member states are failing to live up to their aspirations. In sad fact, more often than not, the EU's response to crisis is 'too little, too late'. For example, the Union is largely absent from Syria and the rest of the Middle East; France and Italy have torpedoed each other's and the EU's policies in Libya; and only France and Germany have been making overt efforts to persuade Russian President Vladimir Putin to end the war in the Donbas region. What's more, though they are all well-intended, EU crisis- and conflict-management missions in the Sahel region and other parts of Africa often lack the military clout needed to have a significant and/or lasting impact.

Arguably, the EU is the only instrument that its member states – and even the biggest among them – have at their disposal to make a difference on the international stage. Nevertheless, we see that the EU rarely speaks with one voice, and that national interests prevail over joint actions. This results from the fact that the EU's foreign and security policy has predominantly remained the domain of its member states. In principle, this could only be changed if member states were to transfer the exercise of their sovereign powers and allow for foreign and security policy to be (to use a good EU word) communitarised. Unfortunately, the chances that this will happen anytime soon are exceedingly slim.

The policy coherence agenda

Before thinking about any major treaty reforms that a truly 'common' foreign and security policy would require, it is worth reflecting on whether there are other incremental reforms that could be made to the existing system to enhance the capabilities of the EU and its member states to effectively respond to and manage external crises and conflicts.

Already in the early 1990s, there was a growing awareness that the complex and interlinked problems of human security, social and economic underdevelopment, and bad governance – factors that underpinned and kept fuelling many of these conflicts – required entirely new policy approaches if there were to be any chance of achieving a successful peace policy. A first step in this direction was taken in 1992 with the release of the UN report 'An Agenda for Peace'. The Agenda, which acknowledged the nexus between development and security, prompted a reorganisation of the UN's peacebuilding architecture. Its aim was to achieve greater policy coherence across the political, military, humanitarian and development realms by improving coordination and by pooling the responsibilities spread out among multiple departments and agencies, on the one hand, and the instruments that played a role in peacebuilding, on the other.

Since then, there have been ongoing discussions about the need for a new approach to foreign, development and security policy. In addition to being subject to a broad concept of security, this approach is meant to align short-term responses focused on security and stability with the long-term development concerns set forth in the Sustainable Development Goals adopted by the UN in 2015. Under various names –such as '3D', for the interaction of diplomacy, development and defence, or 'integrated approach', as most recently in the EU Global Strategy of 2016 – this holistic policy approach has been further developed and refined.

The concept has repeatedly been given fresh impetus by organisational theory, which deals with complex, interdependent and rapidly changing problems in a wide range of policy areas. This theory has formed the theoretical basis for whole-of-government approaches (WGAs), which aim to foster vertical and horizontal coordination of various government departments and public institutions (see, e.g., Christensen and Laegreid 2007; Bouckaert, Peters and Verhoest 2010;

Colgan, Kennedy and Doherty 2014; Tosun and Lang 2017; Gray and Purdy 2018; Trein, Meyer and Maggetti 2019). A WGA has two basic elements: first, joint conflict analysis; and, second, jointly elaborated strategies that are coordinated and deconflicted at a minimum and ideally integrated to enable responses that align interests, avoid duplications and reduce costs.

Roughly speaking, four WGA enablers can be identified in the organisational literature (see, e.g., Ling 2002; Hunt 2005; ADE 2010; Colgan, Kennedy and Doherty 2014). First, adaptations to institutional setups and structures (e.g. the creation of specific units or inter-departmental structures of coordination) are attributed with facilitating coordinated and coherent approaches. Second, the presence of WGA-specific human resources (including specialised staff or resources and specific trainings) may enable successful WGA implementation. Third, political and administrative leadership is identified as playing an important role in actively pushing for a WGA. And, lastly, the establishment of specific instruments and tools (e.g. joint financial instruments, early warning, country/regional/sectoral strategies, joint analysis, and guidelines or rules of procedure informing the WGA conduct) can also contribute to successful whole-of-government action.

By now, it is widely recognised that meaningful responses to the wide range of security challenges fuelling many of today's crises and conflicts require new forms of inter-institutional coordination and cooperation. This certainly applies to the EU member states, as they have all subscribed to the EU's Global Strategy and its integrated approach. Accordingly, efforts have been made to implement such a WGA not only among those ministries that have traditionally been in charge of security, but also among ministries and agencies that gradually came to be seen as indispensable partners in efforts to forge effective and coherent responses to crises and conflicts. These additional ministries and agencies come from a broad range of policy fields, including the economy and social affairs, justice and home affairs, trade, environment, agriculture, finance, transport and infrastructure, education, information and communication, and health.

Walking the talk

Nowadays, WGAs have become ubiquitous on paper and in political rhetoric. However, one should stay alert and ask whether the practice has followed accordingly – that is, whether deeds have followed words. Thus, this book is dedicated to answering one overarching question: Have both the EU and its member states gotten serious about implementing WGAs? It aims to assess whether and, if so, how and with what degree of success the EU and its member states have opted to overhaul their respective governance and to adapt their individual policies, strategies, instruments and procedures related to responding to and managing external crisis and conflicts so as to ensure greater policy coherence. However, the reader should be aware of one significant caveat, namely, that this volume only deals with WGAs on the headquarters level. This implies that the research does not assess whether any of the institutional, structural and procedural changes that have accompanied the implementation of WGAs might also have improved the related outcomes. In other words, it deliberately does not explore whether it can be shown that the EU and its member states have actually and verifiably become better actors when it comes to preventing crises and managing conflict on the ground.

Much has already been written on the subject of policy coherence in conflict transformation and peacebuilding, especially as regards fragile and precarious statehood. However, such scholarship is limited to select international organisations, the EU or larger member states, or it focuses on individual fields of action (see, e.g., OECD 2006; Hauck and Rocca 2014; Tardy 2017). What has been missing so far is a comprehensive overview and analysis of the policy coherence policies of the EU and its (currently) 28 member states. This book aims to fill this gap in the literature for the first time. Our hope is that the new material will help decision-makers in the EU to hone their respective WGA approaches after learning about the best practices of other countries. Likewise, we hope that scholars will use our rich data to further develop the theoretical basis of WGAs to external crisis and conflict management.

Research design

This anthology is the result of a project of the Bertelsmann Stiftung's 'Europe's Future' programme. The project follows on from an earlier study by the Bertelsmann Stiftung, the results of which were published in 2010 under the title 'Diplomacy, Development and Defense: A Paradigm for Policy Coherence' (Weiss, Spanger and van Meurs 2010), which supplied a comparative analysis of the WGA strategies of that time in the EU, Germany, the Netherlands, the United Kingdom and the United States. Ten years on, we deemed it time to take a second look at how the policy coherence agenda has advanced in the intervening period. The research plan was developed in cooperation with the Brussels-based Centre for European Policy Studies (CEPS). The research for the studies was jointly conducted in 2019 and completed on 1 December 2019. Thus, it predated Brexit and took place before the new set of EU leaders took office. What's more, it naturally only reflects the state of affairs at that time.

Methodologically, the research assumes that the organisation of political coherence through a WGA is a necessary though insufficient condition for success in crisis and conflict management. The project is also based on the assumption that any country that claims to have adopted a WGA must necessarily have undergone changes in its method of cooperation – both within and between its institutions on the national level as well as with the EU or other international organisations – and that these changes can be observed and described. The same also applies to the EU and its implementation of an integrated approach, which is described in what follows as a 'whole of governance' rather than a 'whole of government' approach'.

The research is based on a semi-structured questionnaire that inquired into the institutional or procedural changes – or 'enablers' – described above (limited to the headquarters level). The questionnaire, which is included in the Annex, centred on three inter-related sets of questions: (1) What WGA policies have been designed? (2) Who are the actors involved in these WGA policies? And (3) how has the WGA been institutionalised?

The group of individuals conducting this research included experts from all EU member states. Some of them were current or former diplomats, military officers or government officials involved in development cooperation, but all of them have worked for or with their respective governments and therefore have first-hand knowledge of the organisation and procedures of governmental practice. The research was also supported by numerous interviews with representatives of the relevant bureaucracies.

The reports condense the results of the questionnaire. In order to make the country reports more easily comparable, a uniform structure was applied and the titles of the individual chapters in the respective country reports were standardised. The following questions guided the research under the following headings:

Starting Point: Briefly reflect about when and why a WGA has/ hasn't been introduced in your country. In what ways does a WGA in your country reflect the country's specificities (e.g. in relation to its institutional and constitutional setup)?

Policies on Paper: Discuss both explicitly formulated WGA policies and more implicit references to a WGA in your country. You may, for example, describe and assess the scope and quality of official or semi-official policies or discuss the country's obligations under international and EU agreements.

Players and Interplay: Who are the main actors that cooperate in a WGA-like fashion in your country? At what levels do you see cooperation and coordination, whether in a formal or informal manner, taking place in your country's dealings with external crises and conflicts?

Policies in Action: What administrative structures and processes are in place to back up the policies described in the previous section? How does your country operationalise a WGA, and with what success? What are the key operational 'enablers' and 'disablers' of a WGA in your country?

Progress Report: Overall, in what ways and with what success has your country implemented a WGA? What would you consider the success factors underpinning a WGA in your country?

The careful reader will note a few anomalies: first, that subjects covered in specific sections of one report can occasionally be found in different 'silos' of others; and, second, that information is sometimes repeated in different 'silos' within individual reports (which only underlines how difficult it is to overcome fragmentation). Nevertheless, we have determined that using this structure is the most prudent path to follow when collecting data providing for a comparison of the state of affairs in the EU and its 28 member states. In the process, we took into account that the various histories, geographies, institutions and experiences of individual EU member states have sometimes led them to be less amenable to a 'one-size-fits-all' system of categorisation – and, therefore, schematisation. We therefore decided – both for describing complex causal and institutional interconnections and providing the reader with an easy-to-grasp, all-in-one-place explanation – that it is sometimes preferable to opt for repetition over crispness.

All reports will be made available online at https://www.wga-pro ject.eu. This platform will enable a simple and direct comparison of the 28 countries and the EU via various applications.

The final part of this volume has two purposes. First, it summarises the findings of the country studies. And, second, it attempts to classify and group together the 28 member states based on success factors or enablers in order to highlight best practices and to point out where there might be room for improvement.

Reference list

ADE (2010). Thematic Evaluation of European Commission Support to Conflict Prevention and Peace Building: Concept Study. Brussels: Particip. https://ec.europa.eu/europeaid/sites/devco/files/ evaluation-cooperation-ec-conflict-ppb-1277-main-report-201009_ en_3_0.pdf.

Below, Alexis, and Anne-Sophie Belzile (2013). Comparing Whole of Government Approaches to Fragile States. Brandenburg Institute for Society and Security (BIGS) Policy Paper No. 3. May 2013. www.bigs-potsdam.org/images/Policy%20Paper/BIGS%20Policy %20Paper%20No.%203%20Fragile%20States%20Bildschirmvers ion.pdf.

Bouckaert, Geert, B. Guy Peters and Koen Verhoest (2010). *The Coordination of Public Sector Organizations: Shifting Patterns of Public Management*. Hampshire, UK: Palgrave MacMillan.

Christensen, Tom, and Per Laegreid (2007). "The Whole-of-Government Approach to Public Sector Reform." *Public Administration Review* (67) 6: 1059–1066.

Colgan, Anne, Lisa Ann Kennedy and Nuala Doherty (2014) A Primer on Implementing Whole of Government Approaches. Dublin: Centre for Effective Services (CES). www.effectiveservices.org/do wnloads/CES_Whole_of_Government_Approaches.pdf.

Gray, Barbara, and Jill Purdy (2018). *Collaborating for Our Future: Multistakeholder Partnerships for Solving Complex Problems.* Oxford: Oxford University Press.

Hauck, Volker, and Camilla Rocca (2014). Gaps between Comprehensive Approaches of the EU and the EU Member States: Scoping Study. European Centre for Development Policy Management (ECDPM). December 2014. https://ecdpm.org/wp-content/uploads/Gaps-Between-Comprehensieve-Approach-of-the-EU-and-EU-Member-States.pdf.

Hunt, Sue (2005). "Whole-of-government: does working together work?" Asia Pacific School of Economics and Government Discussion Paper 05-01. https://openresearch-repository.anu.edu.au/bitstream/1885/43012/2/PDP05-1.pdf.

Ling, Tom. (2002). "Delivering joined-up government in the UK: Dimensions, issues and problems." *Public Administration* 80: 615–642.

OECD (2006). *Whole of Government Approaches to Fragile States.* Paris: OECD.

Post, Svenja (2014). *Toward a Whole-of-Europe Approach: Organizing the European Union's and Member States' Comprehensive Crisis Management.* Wiesbaden: Springer VS.

Stepputat, Finn, and Lauren Greenwood (2013). Whole-of-Government Approaches to Fragile States and Situations. Danish Institute for International Studies (DIIS) Report 2013: 25. https://pdfs.semanticscholar.org/ffc5/3c1403ebd1db067ed72541fe84b10aa4381a.pdf.

Tardy, Thierry (2017). *The EU: from comprehensive vision to integrated action.* European Union Institute for Security Studies (EUISS) Brief Issue 5 (February 2017). www.iss.europa.eu/sites/default/files/EUISSFiles/Brief_5_Integrated_Approach.pdf.

Tosun, Jale, and Achim Lang (2017). "Policy integration: mapping the different concepts." *Policy Studies* (38) 6: 553–570.

Trein, Philipp, Iris Meyer and Martino Maggetti (2019). "The Integration and Coordination of Public Policies: A Systematic Comparative Review." *Journal of Comparative Policy Analysis: Research and Practice* (21) 4: 332–349.

Weiss, Stefani, Hans-Joachim Spanger and Wim van Meurs (eds.) (2010). *Diplomacy, Development and Defense: A Paradigm for Policy Coherence.* Guetersloh: Verlag Bertelsmann Stiftung.

Reports

EU

Loes Debuysere and Steven Blockmans

1 | Introduction

To respond to security challenges posed by fragile states in its neighbourhood and beyond, the EU and its institutions have sought to develop 'whole-of-governance' approaches – as opposed to the 'whole-of-government' approaches of its member states (both referred to as WGAs) – to external conflicts and crises since the mid-1990s. The EU's WGA policies have gradually evolved in parallel to those pioneered by Denmark, the Netherlands and the UK. Similarly, other multilateral actors (e.g. the UN, NATO and the OSCE) have been developing WGAs in parallel to the EU (Debuysere and Blockmans 2019a). This has inevitably led to conceptual exchanges and interactions among these organisations.

Concretely, the EU's WGA policies have evolved from a minimal definition based on the security-development nexus to a full-fledged and ambitious 'integrated approach to conflict and crisis' (IA) that incorporates non-traditional security concepts. The rationale behind the IA is outlined in the EU's Global Strategy (EUGS) issued in 2016 (EEAS 2016: 28):

"We increasingly observe fragile states breaking down in violent conflict. These crises, and the unspeakable violence and human suffering to which they give rise, threaten our shared vital interests. The EU will engage in a practical and principled way in peacebuilding, concentrating our efforts in surrounding regions to the east and south, while considering engagement further afield on a case-by-case basis. The EU will foster human security through an integrated approach."

While policy documents of the past two decades have highlighted the EU's commitment to an integrated approach, a few crucial questions remain unanswered: Has this commitment (words) truly become a working methodology (deeds)? And, if so, how has it been institutionalised and 'operationalised' at the headquarters level to increase the coherence of responses to external conflicts and crises? This chapter, which is based on a longer report (Debuysere and Blockmans 2019b), intends to investigate these questions.

2 | What policies have been developed to further policy coherence?

For the past two decades, the EU has aspired to contribute to conflict prevention, crisis management and post-conflict peacebuilding through civilian and/or military means. In 2001, an 'integrated approach' was introduced in a Commission communication that identifies 'conflict prevention' as the most effective effort to counter human suffering caused by violent conflicts (EC 2001). The 2003 European Security Strategy (ESS) (Council of the European Union 2003), while not mentioning the concepts of 'comprehensiveness' or 'integration', stressed the need for using EU policies and instruments in a more coherent and coordinated manner to respond to interconnected security and development challenges (Faria 2014: 3).

An important step in the efforts to consolidate more coherent and coordinated conflict responses came with the joint communication of the Commission and the high representative for foreign affairs and security policy (HRVP) in 2013 (EC and HRVP 2013). Building on the spirit of structural integration espoused by the Treaty of Lisbon, the European Commission and the HRVP further developed coordination by introducing the EU's 'comprehensive approach to conflict and crisis' (CA) in 2013. The joint character of the communication serves to illustrate the common understanding of the CA and the desire to jointly apply the CA.

The communication identifies two core elements of a CA: the coordination of EU instruments and resources, on the one hand, and the role of both EU-level actors and member states, on the other. What's more, it notes that "[c]omprehensiveness refers not only to the joined-up deployment of EU instruments and resources, but also to the shared responsibility of EU-level actors and Member States" (ibid.: 3). Four principles underpin a CA: the connection between security and development; the importance of context-specificity over blueprints and one-size-fits-all solutions; the need for collective political will and engagement; and the respect for competence allocation between the respective institutions and services of the EU and its member states.

While seen as a welcome step to further develop the EU's comprehensive approach – especially because it offers conceptual clarifications and a common understanding of the CA (Tercovich and Koops 2013) – the joint communication also sparked criticism. Overall, while it listed commitments and recommended a number of tangible actions, critics argued that the document did not, in fact, provide EU actors with the systems, mechanisms or means to put it into practice (Faria 2014: 9; Wilton Park 2014). Indeed, it does not set out very concrete and tangible structures and processes regarding who the Union should work with as well as when, where and how (Hauck and Sherriff 2013).

Moreover, a number of gaps were detected in the joint communication. While previous EU documents put a major stress on conflict prevention, the principal focus in 2013 – given the fallout of the Arab uprisings of 2011 – was on conflict situations and crisis management, raising the question of how the CA dealt with prevention (Faria 2014: 8). What's more, the issue of trade preferences, which can play an important role in overcoming instability and crisis, is excluded from the text, as are the roles of local structures, processes and government actors in conflict-affected countries (Hauck and Sherriff 2013). Another element missing from the joint communication were the relations with key international partners in the field (e.g. the UN, NATO, the African Union and the OSCE) despite the fact that a specific invitation to build on these partnerships was included in the Council conclusions on conflict prevention from 2011 (Council of the European Union 2011).

Eventually, the Council (i.e. the member states) endorsed the joint communication in its conclusions on the EU's comprehensive approach of May 2014 (Council of the European Union 2014) and through the adoption of subsequent action plans in 2015 and 2016/2017 (Council of the European Union 2015, 2016). Rather than presenting something new, the goal of the action plans was to focus on practical examples for CA implementation and feasible actions that the EU could implement rather than forging a shared understanding of CA in the EU (Faleg 2018: 38).

Nonetheless, the CA was quickly superseded by the EU's 'integrated approach to external conflict and crisis' (IA) in 2016. Stemming from the shortcomings of the CA, the European Global Strategy (EUGS) (EEAS 2016) sought to move forward the comprehensive approach by (re)introducing the concept of an 'integrated approach'. In fact, an IA numbers among the five priorities that the EU sets forward for its external action, together with the security of the Union, state and societal resilience, cooperative regional orders and global governance.

According to the EUGS, the integrated approach has the following four characteristics. It is:

- multi-phased, in that it enables the EU to act "at all stages of the conflict cycle" and to "invest in prevention, resolution and stabilisation, and avoid premature disengagement when a new crisis erupts elsewhere" (ibid.: 9–10).
- multi-dimensional, as it says that it is essential to use "all available policies and instruments aimed at conflict prevention, management and resolution", bringing together diplomatic engagement, CSDP missions and operations, development cooperation and humanitarian assistance (ibid.: 28).
- multi-level, as it acts to address the complexity of conflicts "at the local, national, regional and global levels" (ibid.: 29).
- multi-lateral, as it engages "all those players present in a conflict and necessary for its resolution", and it enables the EU to "partner more systematically on the ground with regional and international organisations, bilateral donors and civil society" and to build sustainable peace "through comprehensive agreements rooted in broad, deep and durable regional and international partnerships" (ibid.: 29).

The scope and actions of the IA have been defined in a Political and Security Committee (PSC) working document on external conflicts and crises of the EEAS and the European Commission released in 2017 (EEAS and EC 2017a). Since the action plans for implementing the CA were viewed as being too rigid, the 2017 working document outlined that the CA "established a process based on action plans and progress reports [...that...] has been valuable in establishing lessons learned on how the EU could most usefully work in a coherent way" (ibid.: 4). However, it adds that "this process made the system somewhat rigid by the nature of the process and by focusing in advance on a limited number of priorities." As a consequence, under the IA, it has been decided to focus on substance rather than process. The 2017 PSC working document also provides an overview of the results the EU envisions to achieve by implementing the IA, as outlined according to the particular phase of the conflict cycle (ranging from prevention to crisis response to stabilisation). In addition, the Council's 2018 conclusions regarding an IA to external conflicts and crises (Council of the European Union 2018) called for more concrete and significant progress in this realm. The conclusions welcomed that a report on the implementation of the IA is included as part of the yearly report on the implementation of the EUGS.

In general, compared to the CA, the IA does not add anything that was not already on the EU's security agenda, and it is mostly compatible with what was laid out in the European Consensus on Development agreed in 2005 (EC 2006) in terms of responding to conflict. However, it does reaffirm the relevance of the CA and states that its scope needs to be "expanded further" by adopting a new cross-sectoral focus on multi-phase and multi-level aspects (Tardy 2017: 2). The extended scope of the IA can be understood in two ways: First, it can be seen as more ambitious, more political and longer-term than the CA. And, second, it can be seen as more operational, i.e. as a means to operationalise the CA. Indeed, the IA has brought about some institutional changes to help operationalise the concept, such as the creation of the PRISM (Prevention of Conflict, Rule of Law/Security Sector Reform, Integrated Approach, Stabilisation and Mediation) division within the EEAS.

3 | Who are the main actors involved in cooperating in a WGA?

Implementing Europe's ambitious integrated approach (IA) to conflicts and crises poses challenges, which include securing sufficient buy-in from all EU actors and the problem of competition among institutions and mandates (Tardy 2017). This section investigates the key actors that drive the IA concept and assesses the ways in which intra- and inter-service as well as international coordination have been institutionalised.

When it comes to implementing the IA at an intra-service EU level, there is one key body that coordinates the EU's integrated approach within the EEAS: the Directorate Integrated Approach for Security and Peace (Dir. ISP). Established in March 2019, this new directorate has become the main coordination hub for EU conflict-cycle responses (Debuysere and Blockmans 2019a). Nestled under the Managing Directorate for CSDP and Crisis Response, Dir. ISP encompasses the old unit for Prevention of Conflicts, Rule of Law/SSR, Integrated Approach, Stabilisation and Mediation (PRISM), which was regrouped with other CSDP parts of the house. Thus, the new directorate is responsible for, inter alia, concepts, knowledge management and training; conflict prevention and mediation; and international strategic planning for CSDP and stabilisation.

A wave of institutional reform that started on 1 March 2019 led to the creation of Dir. ISP. The reforms were partly driven by the recent increase in human resources devoted to defence policies and instruments (in particular, the Permanent Structured Cooperation, or PESCO), which created a need to revise and extend the existing Crisis Management and Planning Directorate (CMPD). Other motivations underpinning the reform process have been to better embed the EU's integrated approach in the institutional structure of the EEAS as well as to facilitate and improve the EU's ability to address global instability and fragility in an integrated way by deploying all its relevant policies, players and tools in a holistic and well-coordinated manner.

It is not the first time, however, that institutional change has sought to smooth the way for the implementation of an IA. Already in January 2017, the EEAS's Peacebuilding, Conflict Prevention and Mediation unit was upgraded to the status of a division reporting directly to the deputy secretary-general (DSG) for the CSDP and crisis response. This division, called PRISM, became the focal point for EU responses to the conflict cycle, including prevention and resolution. Among other things, PRISM coordinated a working group of like-minded souls within the EEAS and the Commission – the so-called 'guardians of the integrated approach' – whose ultimate aim was to enhance operational capacity by adopting an IA to external conflicts and crises.

However, due to its slightly odd position in the EEAS organisational chart, the need was felt to place PRISM in a full-blown directorate with its own managing and deputy managing directors. The result was the Dir. ISP. Itself a pillar responsible for crisis response and planning, Dir. ISP simultaneously operates with a 'policy pillar' and a 'conduct pillar'. While the policy pillar (Security and Defence Policy, or SECDEFPOL) brings together all policies relating to security and defence (e.g. PESCO, the Coordinated Annual Review on Defence (CARD), and cybersecurity), the conduct pillar combines the operational headquarters of both civilian (Civilian Planning and Conduct Capability, or CPCC) and military (Military Planning and Conduct Capability, or MPCC) CSDP missions.

Incorporating a revamped PRISM unit into a full-fledged directorate should clarify and strengthen the chain of command in implementing the EU's integrated approach. In principle, its director and managing director will now be in a position to engage directly with counterparts at their level in the hierarchy. Indeed, the introduction of the new post of managing director means that it will no longer be necessary to turn to an over-solicited DSG to engage in intra-service deconfliction. For example, Dir. ISP hosts crisis meetings that bring together all relevant EEAS divisions and Commission DGs (ECHO, DEVCO, NEAR) involved in crisis management. More than before, the geographical desks play a prominent role in these meetings, which are chaired by the DSG for CSDP or his (or her) representative.

In addition to improving its managerial strength, formalising and upgrading the former PRISM division will also foster better integration and coordination within the EEAS. By absorbing the former Crisis Management and Planning Directorate (CMPD), which is tasked with the political-strategic planning of CSDP missions, Dir. ISP now looks at the crisis cycle in its entirety. In principle, merging PRISM with CSDP planning into a single directorate should facilitate the operational implementation of an integrated approach.

However, the fact that the directorate has been called 'Integrated Approach for Security and Peace' – with 'security' preceding 'peace' rather than the other way around, as is common in the international context – raises questions about where the unit's focus lies. The staff balance also tilts towards security, with over a third of all the directorate's personnel operating in strategic planning for CSDP and stabilisation. While, on paper, the (staff) capacity for prevention and mediation has improved compared to PRISM, it is clear that political will on the part of the member states will be needed to prioritise this aspect of the EU's crisis response.

However, this is exactly where the shoe pinches for Dir. ISP. Rather than merging the operational level with the political level, the new directorate only merges the operational side. The reforms did not further integrate the work of the geographical divisions and of the EEAS' DSG for political affairs. While Dir. ISP may trigger integrated action at the bureaucratic level, it will not necessarily do so at the political level. For a service that was expected to be the embodiment of inter-institutional cooperation, it is paradoxical to have developed thick bureaucratic walls within its own organisation.

Moreover, the member states are largely absent from the new directorate's activities even though the Political and Security Committee is permanently chaired by someone in-house and despite the efforts of Dir. ISP to convene meetings of an informal network of corresponding structures, which exist in some ministries of foreign affairs.

To be truly effective from an IA perspective, the latest wave of institutional reforms should have been more informed by, and geared towards, the DSG for political affairs. In this regard, lessons can be learned from the recent UN reforms, which tried to do just that: The former Department of Peacekeeping Operations (DPKO, now the Department for Peace Operations, or DPO) was integrated with the former Department of Political Affairs (DPA, now the Department for Political and Peacebuilding Affairs, or DPPA). This was done at both the assistant-DSG and geographical levels in headquarters and in-country through newly empowered resident coordinators.

By failing to realise the integration of the new structures for CSDP and crisis response into the geographical managing directorates of the EEAS, mainly due to limitations posed by the Treaties, Dir. ISP cannot be seen as a silver bullet for a 'whole-of-Europe' approach to external conflicts and crises. That said, the new directorate is an important step in efforts to improve the EU's bureaucratic capacity to coordinate its IA.

When it comes to implementing the IA at an inter-service EU level, there are some formal bodies that facilitate coordination among the various EU institutions – principally among the European Commission, the Council and the EEAS – in tackling external conflict and crisis.

The crisis meetings previously organised by PRISM are now convened by the new Dir. ISP on a 'need to act' basis (interview EEAS, May 2019). The goal of these meetings is to bring together all relevant EEAS and Commission services and actors – including EEAS crisis response/management structures, geographical divisions, the EU Military Committee and relevant European Commission DGs (ECHO, DEVCO, NEAR) – to ensure an adequate and timely crisis response. The crisis meetings are intended to establish a clear division of labour among the different services and to provide political and/or strategic guidance in the management of a given crisis (interview EEAS, May 2019).

The Commissioner's Group on External Action (CGEA) was reactivated by then-President Jean-Claude Juncker and represents one of the most important institutional initiatives in EU foreign policymaking since the merger of the position of the high representative for CFSP with that of vice-president of the Commission (to form the HRVP) and the creation of the EEAS (Blockmans and Russack 2015). The CGEA, chaired by the HRVP, brings together the commissioners for European Neighbourhood Policy and Enlargement Negotiations, International Cooperation and Development, Humanitarian Aid and Crisis Management, and Trade. Commissioners who do not belong to this pre-defined cluster of four, but who nevertheless have an interest in the items on the CGEA's agenda, are also invited.

Depending on the topic on the agenda, the Foreign Affairs Council (FAC) convenes member states' ministers of foreign affairs, defence, development or trade. The FAC is chaired by the HRVP and also attended by responsible members of the Commission (Keukeleire and Delreux 2014: 66). However, rather than by the FAC, most decisions are taken by the Committee of Permanent Representatives (COREPER II) or the Political and Security Council (PSC). While the former deals with EU external action (e.g. development cooperation and trade policy) and internal policies with an external dimension, the latter deals with CFSP/CSDP policies. The PSC, which is composed of one ambassador per member state as well as a representative of the Commission, of the EU Military Committee (EUMC) and of the Committee for Civilian Aspects for Crisis Management (CIVCOM), is in fact the logical counterpart in the Council of the CGEA. As the central body for preparatory work for the FAC, it convenes at least once a week in addition to exercising the political control and strategic direction of civilian and military CSDP operations (ibid.: 69–70).

Both in the Commission (SG Inter-institutional and external relations) and the EEAS (SG AFFGEN Inter-institutional relations, policy coordination and public diplomacy), there are also specific units that facilitate intra- and inter-service coordination. These units also facilitate an IA by setting up platforms and guidelines to cooperate (interview EEAS policy coordination unit, April 2019). In times of crisis, the heads of division operate in a rather informal but swift manner, including via a pre-established WhatsApp group (interview EEAS, April 2019).

The role of the European Parliament (EP) in EU foreign policy in general and crisis response in particular is quite limited. In the CFSP/CSDP framework, the EP has only a consultative role, and the Treaty on the European Union (Art. 36) says that the HRVP "shall regularly consult the European Parliament on the main aspects and basic choices" of the CFSP and CSDP, and that the EP "may address questions or make recommendations to the Council or the High Representative." When it comes to EU external action (outside CFSP/CSDP) and internal policies with an external dimension, the EP has two major instruments to influence EU foreign policy (Keukeleire and Delreux 2014). On the one hand, there is the consent procedure, which gives the EP a veto power over the ratification of international agreements. On the other hand, the EP has important budgetary powers, which it can indirectly use as leverage over EU foreign policy.

One 'crisis response' area in which the EP does play a role is mediation activities. What originally started as an informal consultation by Commissioner Johannes Hahn with certain MEPs in North Macedonia (or the FYROM, as it was then called) has gradually developed into a Mediation and Dialogue Unit (one pillar within the Directorate for Democracy Support at DG EXPO) in the European Parliament. In terms of conflict prevention and mediation, this unit regularly cooperates with DG NEAR, DG DEVCO, the EEAS and the EU delegation on the ground.

Regarding coordination at the international level, one can note that UN-EU cooperation has seen worse days, as both multilateral actors aim to preserve the importance of multilateralism in today's multipolar world (interview UNLOPS, May 2019). While the EU's CSDP missions and the UN's peacekeeping operations were somehow in competition a decade ago, the urgency of the threat posed to a multi-lateral, rules-based order – in combination with the important steering role played by HRVP Federica Mogherini and the UN Liaison Office representing the DPA and DPKO in Brussels – has greatly fostered EU-UN cooperation and coordination in the past five years.

EU-NATO relations have traditionally been described in lethargic terms due to longstanding political blockages (Duke 2008; Smith 2011). Nevertheless, bound by a shared commitment to universal values of freedom, democracy and the rule of law, NATO and the EU have not only strategic goals, but also global security challenges in common. The new security environment has driven the EU to assume a bigger role in security and defence, and has forced EU-NATO relations to evolve into a more practical strategic partnership. This has been prompted by the facts that their security is interconnected and that neither organisation has the full range of tools needed to address the new security challenges on its own.

Only limited progress has been made in developing synergies between the OSCE and the EU, which alone comprises already half of the membership of the OSCE (Jorgensen 2008). The contributions of the EU family make up over 70 percent of the OSCE's budget, not to mention the extensive financial support the EU gives to specific operations, such as the Special Monitoring Mission in Ukraine. Furthermore, there are many examples of cooperation between the OSCE and the EU, such as in electoral observation missions or in addressing protracted conflicts, such as the Transdniestrian settlement process. At the same time, there are areas in which this cooperation could be improved. For instance, conflict mediation in Bosnia-Herzegovina and elsewhere in the Balkan region would lend itself to more extensive EU-OSCE cooperation and a pooling of expertise.

The EU regularly cooperates with the International Network on Conflict and Fragility (INCAF), a subsidiary body of the OECD's Development Assistance Committee (DAC), which brings together DAC members and key multilateral agencies working in fragile and conflict-affected contexts (interview DG DEVCO, April 2019). Among the other international organisations with which the EU cooperates closely is the Council of Europe, whose Venice Commission plays a very valuable (and, in many respects, unique) role in buttressing the rule of law in Europe's wider neighbourhood. Furthermore, while civil society organisations play an important role in conflict theatres, their role at the headquarters level is generally limited to providing inputs in consultations for the development and review of policies.

4 | How does the EU operationalise a WGA?

Regarding operationalisation of its WGA, the EU's current external financing instruments, as established under the 2014–2020 multi-annual financial framework (MFF), have struggled to provide enough coherence and flexibility in responding to today's quickly shifting contexts. In the face of mounting instability in the neighbourhood (and beyond) and a sharp increase in refugee flows and migration, the key finding of a mid-term self-assessment by the Commission was the need for "more strategic and overarching programming" and "coherent interactions at operational level in the renewed international context" (EC 2017b: 2). The need for flexibility and the problem of silo approaches similarly figure in a 'Coherence Report' from external evaluators (EC 2017a) and the European Parliament's implementation assessment (EPRS 2018).

In an effort to address these recommendations, the Commission has come up with a new and bold proposal for future spending on issues relating to the neighbourhood, development and international cooperation (EC 2018a). By merging the 11 existing instruments (cf. Debuysere and Blockmans 2019b: Table 2) into one financial instrument, the so-called Neighbourhood, Development and International Cooperation Instrument (NDICI) put forward in the Commission's proposal seeks to increase simplification, coherence, responsiveness and strategic direction in EU external action.

The proposed NDICI consists of four components (EC 2018a). First, the geographic pillar, which takes up the biggest chunk of the NDICI budget (76%), ring-fences money for dialogue and cooperation with third countries in, for example, the neighbourhood and sub-Saharan Africa. The thematic pillar (8% of the budget) includes programmes for human rights, civil society organisations, and stability and peace. While the rapid response pillar (5%) aims at effectively responding to situations of crisis and instability, the additional emergency cushion (11%) is a flexible budget to account for emerging challenges and priorities.

An underexposed angle in the existing body of commentary on the NDICI is how the proposed instrument relates to the EU's commitment to an 'integrated approach to conflict and crisis' (EEAS 2016: 9). Pooled funding and joint financial instruments can be seen as a way to facilitate the implementation of this kind of integrated approach.

While the preamble of the Commission proposal (EC 2018a) outlines a commitment to the five priorities enshrined in the Global Strategy, the proposal does not mention the integrated approach explicitly. References are made, however, to "a more geographically and thematically comprehensive approach" by tackling policies in a "transregional, multi-sectoral and global way" with a goal of breaking down silos (EC 2018a: 9–10). But in what ways does the NDICI regulation actually live up to facilitating a multi-dimensional, -level, -lateral and -phased approach to conflict and crisis?

According to the Global Strategy, the integrated approach is multi-dimensional in that it draws on "all available policies and instruments aimed at conflict prevention, management and resolution" (ibid.: 28), and in that it brings together diplomatic engagement, CSDP missions and operations, development cooperation and humanitarian assistance.

Merging financial assistance for neighbourhood, development and international cooperation agendas under the NDICI should facilitate the financial implementation of a multi-dimensional approach to crises. However, one wonders how 'integrated' the NDICI actually is given that the budgets for, say, the 'neighbourhood' (under its geographic pillar) or 'stability and peace' (under its thematic pillar) remain ring-fenced.

Moreover, the NDICI proposal does not cover all dimensions of EU external action spending. For one, CSDP operations and military capacity-building for CFSP objectives cannot be included under the EU budget (and, hence, under the NDICI) due to limitations enshrined in the EU Treaty. Similarly, humanitarian aid resides outside the NDICI's scope in compliance with the humanitarian principles of neutrality, impartiality and independence. Sufficient coordination among the NDICI, the ECHO budget (including the EU's Emergency Aid Reserve), and different types of security funding will therefore be key.

In fact, four different security-related instruments and funds are currently on the table for the 2021–2027 period: the NDICI, the CFSP budget, the European Peace Facility and the European Defence Fund.

While the NDICI and the CFSP budget mainly seek to finance soft security needs, the proposed European Peace Facility (HRVP 2018) caters to CSDP operations with military and defence objectives and the European Defence Fund (EC 2018b) aims to encourage the development and operationalisation of joint defence capabilities among member states (Blockmans 2018). The envisaged split between the NDICI and other funds will continue to hamper the type of 'civ-mil' coordination that a truly integrated, nimble and effective approach to external conflict and crisis requires.

According to the Global Strategy, the integrated approach is multi-level in that it acts to address the complexity of conflicts "at the local, national, regional and global levels" (EEAS 2016: 29).

The NDICI proposal seeks to improve coherence between geographic and thematic interventions by transferring most (global) thematic actions into (country- or region-based) geographic programmes. Despite the intention to shrink thematic programming, clarifications will be needed about how coherence will be achieved between peace and security interventions financed under bilateral and regional envelopes, on the one hand, and those facilitated by the Stability and Peace thematic programme, on the other.

Moreover, while it makes sense to invest more in geographic programmes, given that these are closer to home (neighbourhood and Africa) and tailor-made, such an approach raises concerns about support for local-level actors. Since geographic programming and implementation take place via bilateral or regional cooperation, national governments and public authorities will have to endorse the decentralisation of allocations to, for example, authorities, councils or civil society organisations at the local level. In countries mired in conflict, repression and authoritarianism, this approach may prevent some local-level actors from having guaranteed access to EU support under the geographic pillar.

According to the Global Strategy, the integrated approach is multilateral in that it engages all players "present in a conflict and necessary for its resolution" and aims to partner "more systematically on the ground with regional and international organisations, bilateral donors and civil society" to achieve sustainable peace "through comprehensive agreements rooted in broad, deep and durable regional and international partnerships" (EEAS 2016: 29).

Generally speaking, the NDICI regulation outlines that programming should take place in cooperation with partner countries or regions, and preferably through joint programming with EU member states. Joint programming with other donors and consultation with representatives of civil society and local authorities shall take place "where relevant" (EC 2018a: 33). More specifically, when drawing up programming documents with partner countries and regions afflicted by conflict and crisis, the proposal (ibid.: 34) stipulates that "due account shall be taken of the special needs and circumstances of the countries or regions concerned", and that "special emphasis shall be placed on stepping up coordination amongst all relevant actors to help the transition from an emergency situation to the development phase."

The proposal remains vague, however, as to with whom and how financial coordination will be consolidated in conflict zones. For example, there is no explicit mention of joint programming or co-financing with the UN even though the latter is the EU's core strategic partner in the field of conflict prevention and peacebuilding (Debuysere and Blockmans 2019a).

Vagueness about "effective multilateralism" also predominates at an inter- and intra-institutional EU level. A truly integrated approach to conflict and crisis will require increased coordination both within the Commission (e.g. in the Commissioners' Group on External Action) (Blockmans and Russack 2015), the Council (among all relevant working parties) and the Parliament (between the AFET and DEVE committees, in particular), as well as among these institutions. However, at one point in the process, attempts to move the management of external financing instruments (e.g. the NDICI) from different line DGs and the FPI service (co-located in the EEAS) to DG DEVCO were interpreted as signalling an intended concentration of power of the purse, which is anathema to the philosophy of multilateralism within the EU's own apparatus.

According to the Global Strategy, the integrated approach is multi-phased in that it allows the EU to act "at all stages of the conflict cycle, acting promptly on prevention, responding responsibly and decisively to crises, investing in stabilisation, and avoiding premature disengagement when a new crisis erupts" (EEAS 2016: 9–10).

Under its different pillars, the NDICI provides financial assistance for all phases of the conflict cycle. However, given that the NDICI is to be employed in a flexible manner in line with policy priorities, some phases of the conflict cycle risk being gradually overlooked in favour of quick responses to unforeseeable challenges and crises. As such, short-term foreign policy interests (e.g. stopping migration flows) may trump longer-term preventive approaches to conflict. Further clarification regarding the flexible short-, medium- and long-term deployment and impact of, in particular, the rapid response pillar and the emergency cushion is therefore imperative.

At the intersection of a multi-lateral and -phased approach to conflict and crisis lies a difficult balancing act of reconciling complex 'multi-lateral' coordination with the need for responsive crisis intervention. While the rapid response pillar and the emergency cushion do not require time-consuming programming, clarification is needed on how swift coordination among key EU players (e.g. DG DEVCO, DG NEAR and the EU delegations) and non-EU players (e.g. the UN, NATO and the OSCE) will take place under these two envelopes in order to avoid increasing delays in responding appropriately and decisively to crisis situations.

In short, looking at it from the angle of an integrated approach to conflict and crisis, there lies a paradox at the heart of the current NDICI proposal. On the one hand, by streamlining all instruments into a single flexible instrument, there is a risk that certain conflict dimensions, levels or phases will outweigh others, such as if there is political pressure to serve the EU's direct internal and external interests. As such, a joint instrument risks undermining a truly holistic approach.

On the other hand, however, an integrated financial approach would likewise be undermined if the solution to this problem is to install excessive ring-fencing within the NDICI, thereby nullifying the philosophy of integration in the process. A difficult balance between merging instruments and preserving comprehensive action needs to be struck if the NDICI is to facilitate a genuine, rather than a merely cosmetic, integrated approach to conflict and crisis. Indeed, simplification is the hardest thing to do.

Yet despite the fact that the NDICI embodies the rationale of an integrated approach, the instrument may well be pulled apart by the future European Development Fund and the European Neighbourhood Instrument owing to a political decision late in the process. If so, this would indicate that, despite commitments and logic, more specialist interests sometimes run counter (and powerfully so) to achieving integrated action.

Furthermore, there are a number of other instruments and procedures that seek to facilitate an IA. For example, the 'Concepts, Knowledge Management and Training' division of the new Dir. ISP (ISP.1) seeks to boost a process of lessons learned. What is new about this procedure is that it will try to look at the EU's overall performance in a conflict zone. Rather than learning lessons about a certain aspect of EU intervention – as currently conducted by, e.g., DG DEVCO for development and the FPI service for financial instruments in external action – Dir. ISP.1 hopes to set up lessons learned processes in an integrated manner (interview EEAS, May 2019).

If it succeeds, this form of knowledge management will help to set up feedback loops, as the lessons learned will be used to impact the planning and training activities of Dir. ISP itself. However, it remains to be seen whether ISP.1 will manage to implement this kind of more integrated lessons learned procedure about the EU's overall performance. The fact is that ISP.1 lacks sufficient staff to execute this process properly, and that conducting these types of assessments may also not be appreciated across the board, as they are likely to identify structural failures (interview EEAS, May 2019).

For the next legislature, the EU is seeking to step up its own 'joint programming' in development cooperation, which means the joint planning, analysis and response efforts (in short, a joint strategy) by all relevant EU partners. While still under negotiation, development programming in the next MFF is supposed to happen in an even more integrated manner involving DG DEVCO, DG ECHO, the EEAS and the member states (interview DG DEVCO, April 2019). Indeed, there is an increased focus on joint programming with the EU member states in the Commission proposal on a new jumbo instrument for external action (EC 2018a; cf. supra).

Important for a successful IA is to enhance information- and analysis-sharing among the various actors involved in crisis response in order to facilitate the implementation of a joint conflict response. The first implementation report of the IA, which has since been issued on an annual basis, outlines that the EU institutions are improving shared conflict analysis with member states and other stakeholders (EEAS 2017). The work being done by Dir. ISP to foster a shared understanding and analysis of a given conflict is particularly appreciated by various Commission DGs (interview DG ECHO, May 2019). They believe that different actors can provide different perspectives on a conflict or crisis with, for example, DG DEVCO (which often operates in the capital) and DG ECHO (which also operates outside the capital) providing complementary analysis.

Furthermore, human resources (HR) do not necessarily facilitate or reflect the importance of an IA to external conflicts and crises. In fact, a widespread sentiment within the institutions is that in order to write policy at the EU level, one needs to work together by default. In this sense, an IA is inevitable and an HR policy is not the core driver behind cooperation or coordination among services (interview EEAS, April 2019). Nonetheless, some interviewees have identified HR as one realm in which there is major scope for improvement in the belief that fostering incentives could enhance the services' performance in working in an integrated manner.

Political leadership is also key when trying to implement an IA. There has been massive improvement in inter-institutional coordination in the last six years. One key factor behind this has been the leadership shown by Commission President Juncker and HRVP Mogherini (Interview EC SecGen, May 2019). In contrast to their respective predecessors, Jose Manuel Barroso and Catherine Ashton, who were reluctant to work in an integrated manner, Juncker and Mogherini have facilitated and encouraged inter-institutional cooperation. In a similar vein, one expects HRVP Josep Borrell and European Council President Charles Michel to cooperate better than their predecessors. After all, heads of state or government play an important role in foreign affairs, especially when acting in crisis mode in the European Council. Since the staff of the European Council's president is spread too thinly, it requires the preparatory support of the EEAS.

Furthermore, leadership at bureaucratic levels can also facilitate an IA. For one thing, having heads of units and DGs rotate among different services and institutions can help to foster better inter- and intra-service cooperation. For example, when DG DEVCO got a new DG who had previously worked at the EEAS, he managed to push for more and better cooperation with the EEAS (Interview DG DEVCO, April 2019). Similarly, effective rotation between the EEAS and its stakeholders – especially the member states – will be key to a better functioning of the EEAS as well as the success of the IA.

5 | Conclusions

Conceptually, over the past decade, the EU has been elaborating and deepening its WGA to external crises and conflicts. By gradually developing an integrated approach based on the security-development nexus (2003) into a 'comprehensive approach' (CA) (in 2013) and a more holistic 'integrated approach' (IA) (in 2016), the scope of the EU's so-called 'whole-of-governance approach' (WGA) has ambitiously expanded. While designing this approach, the EU has learned from and exchanged with other multilateral actors (the UN, NATO, the OSCE, the OECD-DAC and civil society), which in turn has led to a gradual conceptual convergence of all these actors' headquarters-level approaches to dealing with external conflicts and crises.

Today, the EU's IA aims to address all conflict dimensions – ranging from security challenges to development concerns to economic grievances – during all phases of a conflict, from prevention to post-conflict rehabilitation. To effectively implement such an approach, the EU wishes to coordinate and cooperate with all relevant actors at the local, national, regional and global levels.

Indeed, the EU's IA is system-wide in that it builds on various EU policies and instruments, including humanitarian aid, political dialogue, sanctions, CSDP, development cooperation, macro-financial assistance and trade (EEAS 2019). While the EU's core interests in terms of external conflict management lie in its extended neighbourhood, the IA is applied much more broadly and spans the entire globe, including when tackling conflicts in the Sahel (especially in Mali and Niger), the Horn of Africa (mainly Somalia), South-East Asia (notably Myanmar) and Latin America (Venezuela).

In order to operationalise its ambitious WGA policy, several platforms and mechanisms have been put in place to enable actors to interact and coordinate. The key player and facilitator of the EU's IA is the EEAS' new Directorate Integrated Approach for Security and Peace (Dir. ISP), which was founded in March 2019 to regroup the former division for the Prevention of Conflicts, Rule of Law/Security Sector Reform, Integrated Approach, Stabilisation and Mediation (PRISM) and the security/defence policy, planning and conduct parts of the house. In addition to conflict and crisis coordination by Dir. ISP, there are numerous inter-service platforms (e.g. crisis meetings and the Commissioners Group on External Action) and multilateral platforms that facilitate a joint crisis response of the HRVP/EEAS, the Commission's DGs, the Political Security Committee and other international actors. However, despite playing an interesting political role in the realm of conflict mediation, the European Parliament is generally not involved in inter-service coordination.

The latter is emblematic of one core challenge that hampers the establishment of a truly effective IA at the EU level: the remaining gaps between the political and operational dimensions in responding to external conflicts and crises. For instance, while the divisions of the EEAS with a conduct function in civ-mil security and defence cooperation have been merged into Dir. ISP, the geographical directorates under the DSG for political affairs remain largely detached and member states are not fully integrated into their activities. As a result, although the Dir. ISP may trigger integrated action at the bureaucratic level, it will not necessarily do so at the political and operational levels.

At a more technical-operational level, one key innovation that may enhance the implementation of an IA to crisis response is the NDICI, the jumbo financial instrument that has been proposed by the Commission for the next MFF. However, the intention to merge finances for development, international cooperation and the neighbourhood also lays bare one key paradox: While the NDICI has the ability to facilitate coordinated financial action, there is also a risk that it will actually undermine comprehensive action, as some conflict dimensions, levels or phases may outweigh others within the same instrument under political pressure of serving the EU's direct and immediate interests.

While it still remains to be seen whether the merging of financial instruments will be a success factor for an IA at the EU level, the importance of political leadership in encouraging cooperation and coordination unquestionably is. The cooperation of the HRVP with both the Commission president and the president of the European Council cannot be underestimated in this regard. Moreover, investing in human resources is important to facilitate an IA – and personalities matter. While specialised staff has been hired in Dir. ISP to operationalise an IA, more could be done to create the right incentives for people to work together within and across EU services and institutions.

6 | Reference list

Blockmans, Steven (2018). "The EU's modular approach to defence integration: An inclusive, ambitious and legally binding PESCO?" *Common Market Law Review* (55) 6: 1785–1826.

Blockmans, Steven, and Sophia Russack (2015). The Commissioners' Group on External Action – Key political facilitator. Centre for European Policy Studies. CEPS Special Report No. 125. 17 December 2015.

Council of the European Union (2003). *A Secure Europe in a Better World: European Security Strategy.* Brussels. 8 December 2003. http://data.consilium.europa.eu/doc/document/ST-15895-2003-IN IT/en/pdf.

Council of the European Union (2011). Council conclusion on conflict prevention. 3101st Foreign Affairs Council meeting. Luxembourg. 20 June 2011. www.consilium.europa.eu/uedocs/cms_data/docs/ pressdata/EN/foraff/122911.pdf.

Council of the European Union (2014). Council conclusions on the EU's comprehensive approach. Foreign Affairs Council meeting. Brussels. 12 May 2014. www.consilium.europa.eu/media/28344/ 142552.pdf.

Council of the European Union (2015). Taking forward the EU's Comprehensive Approach to external conflict and crises – Action Plan 2015. Joint Staff Working Document. Brussels. 14 April 2015. https://ec.europa.eu/europeaid/sites/devco/files/joint_swd_-_tak ing_forward_the_eus_comprehensive_approach_to_external_co nflict_and_crises_-_action_plan_2015.pdf.

Council of the European Union (2016). Taking forward the EU's Comprehensive Approach to external conflicts and crises – Action Plan 2016/17. Joint Staff Working Document. Brussels. 19 July 2016. https://ec.europa.eu/europeaid/sites/devco/files/joint_swd_-_tak ing_forward_the_eus_comprehensive_approach_to_external_co nflicts_and_crises_-_action_plan_2016-2017.pdf.

Council of the European Union (2018). Council Conclusions on the Integrated Approach to External Conflicts and Crises. 22 January 2018. https://ec.europa.eu/europeaid/sites/devco/files/2018-01-cnl _conclusions_on_ia.pdf.

Debuysere, Loes, and Steven Blockmans (2019a). "Crisis responders: Comparing policy approaches of the EU, UN, NATO and OSCE with experiences in the field." *European Foreign Affairs Review* (24) 3: 243–264.

Debuysere, Loes, and Steven Blockmans (2019b). *Europe's Coherence Gap in External Crisis and Conflict Management. The EU's integrated approach: Between political rhetoric and institutional practice.* Guetersloh: Bertelsmann Stiftung.

Duke, Simon (2008). "The Future of EU-NATO Relations: A Case of Mutual Irrelevance through Competition?" *Journal of European Integration* 30 (1): 27–43.

EC (European Commission) (2001). Communication from the Commission on Conflict Prevention. 11 April 2001. COM(2001) 211. http://eeas.europa.eu/archives/docs/cfsp/crisis_management/docs/com2001_211_en.pdf.

EC (2006). The European Consensus on Development. June 2006. https://ec.europa.eu/europeaid/sites/devco/files/publication-the-european-consensus-on-development-200606_en.pdf.

EC (2017a). Coherence Report – Insights from the External Evaluation of the External Financing Instruments. July 2017. https://ec.europa.eu/europeaid/sites/devco/files/coherence-report-main-report-170717_en_0.pdf.

EC (2017b). Report from the Commission to the European Parliament and the Council. Mid-term review report of the External Financing Instruments. European Commission. 15 December 2017. https://eur-lex.europa.eu/legal-content/EN/TXT/PDF/?uri=CELEX:52017DC0720&from=EN.

EC (2018a). Proposal for a Regulation of the European Parliament and of the Council establishing the Neighbourhood, Development and International Cooperation Instrument. 14 June 2018. https://ec.europa.eu/commission/sites/beta-political/files/budget-may2018-neighbourhood-development-international-regulation_en.pdf.

EC (2018b). Proposal for a Regulation of the European Parliament and of the Council establishing the European Defence Fund. Brussels. 13 June 2018. COM(2018) 476 final. https://ec.europa.eu/commission/sites/beta-political/files/budget-may2018-eu-defence-fund-regulation_en.pdf.

EC and HRVP (European Commission and High Representative of the European Union for Foreign Affairs and Security Policy) (2013). Joint Communication to the European Parliament and the Council. The EU's comprehensive approach to external conflicts and crises. 11 December 2013. https://publications.europa.eu/en/publication-detail/-/publication/31aeff51-6312-11e3-ab0f-01aa75ed71a1.

EEAS (European External Action Service) (2016). Shared Vision, Common Action: A Stronger Europe. A Global Strategy for the European Union's Foreign and Security Policy. June 2016. https://eeas.europa.eu/sites/eeas/files/eugs_review_web_0.pdf.

EEAS (2017). From shared vision to common action: Implementing the EU global strategy – Year 1. June 2017. https://eeas.europa.eu/sites/eeas/files/full_brochure_year_1_0.pdf.

EEAS (2019). EU Integrated Approaches to External Conflicts and Crises. PowerPoint presentation delivered by Melis Alguadis (EEAS-ISP1) at the EUNPACK conference in Brussels on 18 March 2019.

EEAS and EC (European External Action Service and European Commission) (2017a). The EU Integrated Approach to external conflicts and crises – EEAS-Commission services Issues Paper for PSC. EEAS working document. EEAS/COM(2017) 8 June 2017. Not available online due to limited distribution.

EPRS (European Parliamentary Research Service) (2018). EU external financing instruments and the post-2020 architecture. European Implementation Assessment. February 2018. https://publications.europa.eu/en/publication-detail/-/publication/160d5f8c-2216-11e8-ac73-01aa75ed71a1.

Faleg, Giovanni (2018). "The EU: from comprehensive to integrated approach." *Global Affairs* (4) 2–3: 171–183.

Faria, Fernanda (2014). What EU Comprehensive Approach? Challenges for the EU action plan and beyond. European Centre for Development Policy Management. Briefing Note No. 71. October 2014.

Hauck, Volker, and Andrew Sherriff (2013). "Important Progress, but Real EU Comprehensiveness Is Still Ahead of Us." European Centre for Development Policy Management. December 2013. https://ecdpm.org/talking-points/important-progress-real-eu-comprehensiveness-still-ahead-us/.

HRVP (High Representative of the European Union for Foreign Affairs and Security Policy) (2018). Proposal of the High Representative of the Union for Foreign Affairs and Security Policy, with the support of the Commission, to the Council for a Council Decision establishing a European Peace Facility. HR(2018) 94. http://data.consilium.europa.eu/doc/document/ST-9736-2018-INIT/en/pdf.

Jorgensen, Knud E. (ed.) (2008). *The EU and International Organisations*. London: Routledge.

Keukeleire, Stephan, and Tom Delreux (2014). *The Foreign Policy of the European Union (2nd ed.)*. Red Globe Press.

Smith, Simon J. (2011). "EU-NATO Cooperation: A Case of Institutional Fatigue?" *European Security* (20) 2: 243–264.

Tardy, Thierry (2017). The EU: from comprehensive vision to integrated action. European Union Institute for Security Studies. February 2017.

Tercovich, Giulia, and Joachim A. Koops (2013). Assessing the EU's Joint Communication on the Comprehensive Approach: Implications for EU Crisis Response and Conflict Prevention. Global Governance Institute. Briefing Paper.

Wilton Park (2014). EU programmes and action in fragile and conflict states: next steps for the comprehensive approach. Conference report. 18–20 February 2014. www.wiltonpark.org.uk/wp-content/uploads/WP1318-Report.pdf.

Austria

Christian Strohal, Ursula Werther-Pietsch, Markus Gauster
and Hans Lampalzer

1 | Introduction

Austria has a long-standing tradition of contributing to international peacekeeping, diplomatic engagement, civilian crisis management, humanitarian aid and development cooperation. The Austrian whole-of-government approach (WGA) model has been particularly inspired by some 60 years of participating in peacekeeping operations, efforts aimed at promoting effective multilateralism, and the principle of international solidarity. By being an actively involved honest broker and by deepening a holistic approach over the years, Austria has developed a special understanding of joint action in external engagement as well as a collaborative spirit and readiness to mediate. Additional orientation has been provided via Austria's active membership in international organisations, especially the OSCE, NATO's Partnership for Peace (PfP) programme, and the UN (one of whose headquarters is based in Vienna). Furthermore, Austria's membership in the EU has been particularly crucial in many regards and has certainly contributed to intensifying its focus on both political priorities and operational collaboration. In addition, Austria has been seeking to actively contribute to the development of the EU's policies and operational capacities.

Altogether, ensuring an effective multilateralism is one of the priorities of Austria's foreign and security policies; this, by its very nature, fosters coherence among Austrian stakeholders. Given the current threats emerging from the erosion of the global rules-based order, this has never been truer than today. For these reasons, Austria plays an active role in different multilateral fora and has formal coordination/cooperation procedures in place at all levels at the UN, the OSCE, the NATO-PfP and the OECD's Development Assistance Committee (OECD-DAC).

Thematic frameworks of current relevance to Austria's external engagement are the UN's 2030 Agenda for Sustainable Development; UN Security Council resolutions; the EU Global Strategy (EUGS), its implementation and EU CSDP decisions; the NATO-PfP agenda; and the European Consensus on Development. This multilateral approach is also inspired by the recognition of the steadily increasing interconnectedness of external and internal security. For example, Austria's 2013 security strategy states (BKA 2013: 4): "Comprehensive security policy means that external and internal aspects of security are inextricably interlinked, as are civil and military aspects."

Over the years, crisis response has been shaped primarily by events in Austria's geographic neighbourhood, such as political upheavals in Hungary in 1956 and in Czechoslovakia in 1968, the wars in the former Yugoslavia in the 1990s, and the so-called refugee or migration crisis of 2015. Security concerns regarding Czech and Slovak nuclear plants close to Austria's borders are another constant concern.

At the international level, one part of acting upon this recognition of interconnectedness between internal and external security has been the emphasis on complex operations against the backdrop of comprehensive policy programmes. A WGA has been a consequence. At the national level, a WGA is de facto built into all government decisions, as they are taken collectively, usually in the weekly cabinet (Council of Minister) meetings. In addition, a number of other legal and institutional provisions ensure that Austria's constitutional environment is respected, including its federal nature and its status of neutrality.

A WGA is also increasingly and explicitly being adopted in governmental programmes. The 2013 Austrian Security Strategy (ibid.) constitutes the cornerstone of Austria's overarching comprehensive approach, which is officially called the Comprehensive Security Provision (Umfassende Sicherheitsvorsorge). It postulates that modern security policy and efforts to respond to external conflicts and crises have become a cross-cutting issue that stands on an equal footing with other policy fields, and that "[s]ecurity decisions at both national and international level must be based on a comprehensive assessment of the situation by all of the stakeholders and a common understanding of the situation derived from this information" (ibid.: 10). On this basis, there is a growing understanding that policy coherence and existing interfaces need to be based on a comprehensive and integrated approach, allowing for active participation and implementation in a spirit of solidarity.

Government activities are based on an agreed governmental programme. These provide an overarching framework for the concrete division of competences as laid down in a specific law (i.e. the Federal Ministries Act (National Council 1986)) and the government's concrete work. A comprehensive approach to crises at the local and international levels has been increasingly reflected in government programmes.

Overall, a whole-of-government and, indeed, a whole-of-nation approach have emerged over the years in Austria's political priorities, and their implementation has been inspired and facilitated by active participation in international multilateral fora and through EU membership. While representing a good balance between administrative professionalism and political pragmatism, this approach would still benefit from being made more systematic (as is discussed in greater detail below).

2 | What policies have been developed to further policy coherence?

The Austrian Security Strategy (BKA 2013) promotes the implementation of WGA structures, including through different sectoral strategies. This concept basically systematises the interaction of various policy fields and stakeholders in addition to including a 'division of labour' among governmental and non-governmental actors. In contrast, Austria's Comprehensive Security Provision has only been implemented in parts to date.

A core document is the Strategic Guideline on Security and Development of October 2011 (BMEIA and BMLV 2011), which provided for an explicit WGA: "The Austrian contribution to security and development is a task for the whole of government. The joint goals can only be achieved through a coordinated, complementary and coherent [3C] approach by all actors (whole-of-government approach – WoGA).

Resources in security and development must be allocated in the most concerted way" (ibid.: 5). This approach has evolved over several stages, especially in light of the experiences of Austria's engagement in South-East Europe – in particular with NATO-led missions in Kosovo (KFOR) – and Afghanistan (ISAF and RSM) as well as with the EU-led training mission in the Central African Republic (EUTM RCA). Beginning in 2014 and continuing to this day, ministries and (increasingly) civil society have been regularly involved in a work-stream steered by the Federal Chancellery, i.e. the elaboration of the Foreign Deployment Concept (Auslandseinsatzkonzept) in the fields of planning for early warning, crisis prevention and management, peacebuilding and post-conflict reconstruction as well as handling its underlying legal issues.

While the sectoral strategy for defence policy of 2014 (BMLV 2014) and the Military Strategic Concept 2017 (BMLV 2017) stipulate that Austria's armed forces have to contribute to the implementation of the Comprehensive Security Provision within the framework of the Aus-trian Security Strategy, the 2017 sectoral strategy for foreign policy continues to be in draft form. Nevertheless, the draft document does reflect and inspire current foreign policy priorities and, like the poli-cies for internal security and defence, the foreign policy doctrine details international challenges as well as national priorities and responses. Prevention and management of crises and conflicts is one of the underlying priorities.

Complementary to the Austrian Security Strategy (BKA 2013) and the Strategic Guideline on Security and Development (BMEIA and BMLV 2011), the three-year programme on Austrian development pol-icy 2019–2021 (3YP) (BMEIA 2019a) engages in the humanitarian-development-peacebuilding nexus as well as in dialogue, mediation and conflict transformation in different regions, especially in South-East Europe, the Eastern Neighbourhood and sub-Saharan Africa. A conceptual priority is civilian and military capacity-building. The pro-gramme calls for all Austrian actors to engage in joint efforts to achieve human security through viable local capacities and institu-tions on the ground. Active civil society engagement is appreciated as a major contribution.

As they represent decisions taken by Austria's federal cabinet, the three documents mentioned in the paragraph above are binding on all government actors. For the time being, these three strategies provide the basis for additional non-binding guidelines for implementation. NGOs are consulted in the elaboration of strategies and may associate themselves on a voluntary basis as part of a so-called whole-of-nation approach.

Summing up, Austria's WGA framework for responding to external conflicts and crises is a mixed approach that combines formal and informal elements within the overall concept of the Comprehensive Security Provision. However, implementation guidelines remain informal, and there continue to be certain discrepancies regarding resource allocation and the sharing of competencies and responsibilities among the stakeholders involved.

In terms of international reference frameworks, as already mentioned, Austria bases its global engagement in international peacekeeping and peace-support operations, development cooperation, humanitarian action and disaster relief on the following major international frameworks: the UN's 2030 Agenda for Sustainable Development; UN Security Council resolutions; the 2016 EU Global Strategy for the foreign and security policy (EUGS), its implementation and EU CSDP decisions; the NATO-Partnership for Peace (PfP) agenda; and the political priorities developed in the framework of the OSCE and the European Consensus on Development (as reflected in the 3YP).

Austria particularly focuses on EU policies that establish a mutually reinforcing relationship, and it was actively involved in drafting the EUGS. In fact, even before the EUGS was adopted in 2016, Austria's security strategy (BKA 2013: 12) had clearly stipulated that "[t]he EU, as a comprehensive community of peace, security and solidarity, provides the central framework of action of Austria's security policy", and that "Austria will be involved in every dimension of EU security policy".

As part of further shaping the EU's role as a credible and reliable security provider, the EUGS has generally fostered increased collaboration among various stakeholders in Austria at the national level with a view to follow up on the concrete commitments of the EU's member states laid down in the EUGS, as the following examples demonstrate:

First, the EUGS promotes the EU's integrated approach, resilience and external action, among other priorities, while stressing the importance of complying with international humanitarian law. As the

Federal Ministry of Europe, Integration and Foreign Affairs (BMEIA) states on its website (BMEIA 2019b): "The protection of civilians and the commitment to upholding international humanitarian law are longstanding Austrian foreign policy priorities."

Second, geographical priorities of the EUGS (e.g. Africa) have had a clear impact on Austria's engagement. Austria's focus on Africa has been strengthened, and the use of military as well as civilian assets – from the foreign ministry and the Austrian Development Agency (ADA) – has been promoted. Consequently, Austria's increasing engagement in Mali (MINUSMA, EUTM Mali) and in Western Africa is generally in line with the EUGS. There is also Austrian support for ECOWAS in the fields of humanitarian support training and SSR. Indeed, Austria's current engagement in Mali can be viewed as a test case for Austria to strengthen a coherent WGA to external engagement.

Third, the EUGS has been setting the framework for the further evolution of internal coordination, cooperation and collaboration in two regards. On the one hand, with regard to increased European integration, the Austrian government adopted in 2017 the report on Austria's participation in the Permanent Structured Cooperation (PESCO), including the participation in four projects and the National Implementation Plan 2017 (Council of Ministers 2017). On the other hand, based on Council Decision (CFSP) 2018/1797 of 19 November 2018 (Council of the European Union 2018), Austria decided to increase its commitment by engaging in two additional projects and taking the lead in one project. What's more, in addition to implementation of the EUGS, in consultation with five other ministries, the BMEIA prepared a national report to the Council of Ministers on Austria's contribution to the Civilian Common Security and Defence Policy (CSDP) compact (BMEIA 2018).

Fourth, Austria has actively contributed to and taken a proactive stance towards discussions of the EU's Capacity Building in Support of Security and Development (CBSD) initiative, its Instrument for Peace and Stability, and its African Peace Facility.

Finally, Austria's presidency of the Council of the EU in the second half of 2018 saw successes related to stimulating coherent action at various levels. The first involves the establishment of the Civilian CSDP Compact, which fosters the EU's capacity to deploy civilian crisis-management missions. The second is related to the fact that the

EUGS's objective of "strengthening of peace and ensuring the security of the EU and its citizens" increasingly blurs the boundary between internal and external security. For this reason, during its presidency, Austria called for flexible and preventive measures to protect the EU's external borders and to address irregular migration.

3 | Who are the main actors involved in cooperating in a WGA?

At the federal level, Austria's WGA has both horizontal and vertical aspects. For example, horizontal inter-ministerial coordination normally involves a wide range of actors, including the Federal Chancellery and several ministries. While the lead ministries are the foreign (BMEIA), defence (BMLV) and interior (BMI) ministries, other ministries involved include the Ministry of Labour, Social Affairs, Health and Consumer Protection (BMASGK); the Ministry of Education, Science and Research (BMBWF); the Ministry of Digital and Economic Affairs (BMDW); the Ministry of Constitutional Affairs, Reforms, Deregulation and Justice (BMVRDJ); the Ministry of Sustainability and Tourism (BMNT); the Ministry of Transport, Innovation and Technology (BMVIT); and the Ministry of Finance (BMF). Vertically, there is cooperation with organisations such as the Austrian Economic Chamber (WKO), the Austrian Development Agency (ADA), the parliament, the federal states (Laender) and civil society organisations (discussed in more detail below). The National Security Council (with the involvement of parliamentary parties) and several more specialised coordination mechanisms at different levels ensure both strategic and day-to-day coordination.

Austria's WGA efforts also involve NGOs, the private sector and research/academic institutions. For example, the Vienna-based Global Responsibility Platform for Development and Humanitarian Aid serves as an umbrella organisation for 35 NGOs with humanitarian and development expertise and mandates, represents civil society in coordination mechanisms, and contributes to the mutual exchange of information with the ministries. NGOs receive 10 to 15 percent of Austria's Foreign Disaster Fund, which is administered by the BMEIA and has an annual budget of EUR 15 million. Furthermore, the Austrian Development Agency disposes of a separate NGO budget line, the BMEIA and the Austrian Red Cross organise regular seminars on the dissemination of international humanitarian law in cooperation with the universities of Graz and Linz, and the Austrian Red Cross has provided CIMIC trainings and training for police officers on the mandate of the Red Cross and Red Crescent and the work of the International Committee of the Red Cross (ICRC). Regarding the private sector, companies young and old are increasingly active, are filling funding gaps on the basis of multilateral commitments (e.g. SDGs), and are getting more and more involved in coordination mechanisms. In terms of research and academia, there are several specialised institutes that contribute to the public debate surrounding security and defence policies, including the Austrian Institute for European and Security Policy (AIES), the Austrian Institute for International Affairs (OIIP), the Austrian Study Centre for Peace and Conflict Resolution (ASPR), the National Defence Academy (LVAk) and the Diplomatic Academy of Vienna. In addition, these institutions are regularly commissioned by various ministries to undertake related research work.

Before moving on to discuss other relevant players, a geographical focus is necessary: Austria's WGA efforts currently focus on South-East Europe (SEE), the MENA region, the Near and Middle East, and North and sub-Saharan Africa. Of these, given its geographic proximity, political instability, elements of radicalisation, and migration flows, the SEE region is of crucial importance to Austria's security interests and can be defined as being of 'strategic' importance to Austria. The high number of Austrian troops deployed there – over 350 in Bosnia and over 460 in Kosovo (BMLV n.d.) – together with substantial financial and political support, shows the country's strong commitment to this region. Austria complements its military engagement by deploying a contingent of almost 180 soldiers to UNIFIL in Lebanon (ibid.). In Western Africa, Austria's civil and military engagement is increasing on the basis of a WGA (in particular with EUTM Mali). However, as stipulated in the 2011 Strategic Guideline on Security and Development (BMEIA and BMLV 2011), joint actions are to be given priority over unilateral projects. This principle of concentrating human resources, capabilities and assets has also been introduced at the strategic level, such as with the 3YP (BMEIA 2019a).

In terms of government stakeholders currently engaged abroad, Austria's armed forces have been contributing to international peacekeeping efforts since 1960, deploying altogether more than 100,000 Austrian troops and civilians in more than 50 missions abroad. Also, there are currently around 30 members of the interior ministry (BMI) deployed abroad in advisory positions and civilian missions of the OSCE, EU and UN with a focus on the SEE region, Eastern Europe and Central Asia (e.g. the OSCE mission in North Macedonia, SMM Ukraine, EUMM Georgia and the OSCE mission in Tajikistan). Overall, current civilian and military deployment can be summarised as follows: Total: 1,110 EU (military), 376 EU (civilian), 13 NATO, 493 OSCE, 27 UN. Furthermore, the Austrian Development Agency focuses on least-developed countries (LDCs), partner countries in the SEE region, and (with a global view) countries in fragile contexts.

In this framework, the scope of Austria's WGA can be described as 'system-wide' in South-East Europe (including trade and economic incentives) and in the Eastern Neighbourhood, and as 'medium' in West Africa as well as in other African countries and regions, such as where the efforts of various Austrian stakeholders (e.g. the Austrian Economic Chamber, the Austrian Development Agency, defence attaches and civil society organisations) are concentrated or where training programmes are in place, such as in Addis Ababa, Ethiopia, or Accra, Ghana, home to the Kofi Annan International Peacekeeping Training Centre (KAIPTC).

4 | How does your country operationalise a WGA?

In terms of administrative structures and processes, the formal WGA-level coordination/cooperation at the top level is ensured in Austria by the weekly sessions of the federal cabinet – officially known as the Council of Ministers – and, more specifically on security matters, by the National Security Council (NSC). This central advisory body to the government in matters of foreign, security and defence policy is composed of ministers, members of parliament, and designated liaison officers.

In all ministries, intra-ministerial coordination mechanisms exist to discuss WGA-relevant topics, including external conflicts and crises. Inter-ministerial working groups serve as platforms for information exchange as well as the preparation and negotiation of strategies regarding countries, regions or specific topics. Specific coordination units and structures are in place within and among relevant ministries (especially the BMEIA, the Federal Chancellery, the BMI and the

BMLV) to prepare coordinated positions and instructions for discussions of crisis and conflict situations in the relevant council.

Regarding crisis management, the formal format of the National Crisis and Disaster Management (SKKM) panel includes representatives from all federal ministries, all federal provinces, and the rescue and fire services (BMI n.d.). Meetings of this body, which is housed within the BMI, are convened in the event of major incidents or trainings. Based on the Ministerial Council Decision of 20 January 2004 (BMI 2004), the National Crisis and Disaster Management (SKKM) framework had been reorganised and put under the guidance of the BMI's director-general for public security. Supplementing the WGA is the 'SKKM Penta++', an informal gathering of the SKKM panel that brings together senior civil servants from the BMI, the BMEIA, the BMLV, the Federal Chancellery, the Vice Chancellery, the Cabinet Office of the head of state, and one of the federal provinces. This group meets regularly (at least once a month) to be briefed on and to discuss related matters, including (potential) external conflicts and crises. Furthermore, procedures related to responding to cyber-crises are regulated by Austria's Network and Information System Security Act (NISG) (National Council 2018). The tasks within the coordination structures are shared between the Federal Chancellery and the BMI and supported by two (inter-ministerial) coordination committees: IKDOK (Inner Circle of the Operational Coordination Structure) and OpKoord (Operational Coordination Structure) (BKA, BMI, BMLV and BMEIA 2019).

In more horizontal terms, there is extensive formal and informal coordination and cooperation between executive and legislative powers. For example, regular coordination takes place in parliamentary committees (e.g. the Foreign Policy Committee or the Defence Committee). Austrian contributions to international crisis management and peace missions require formal approval by the Main Committee of parliament. Parliamentarians are also regularly involved in annual 3YP preparations, which has led to some criticism regarding the separation of powers.

According to the Austrian Development Act (EZA-G) (National Council 2019) and the updated 2012 Austrian Mission Statement of all stakeholders as an integral part of the 3YP (BMEIA 2019a: 24–25), as well as in line with the Vienna 3C Appeal (ADC 2010), consultation processes are run throughout the year and include NGOs and other

Austrian civil society actors. In this regard, since 2011, a 3C conference has been organised annually on WGA-related topics at both the policy and operational levels.

5 | Conclusions

Austria's strategic culture concerning international engagement is evolving towards a more coordinated and coherent approach. However, overall, it continues to be fragmented to a certain degree owing to the various mechanisms of coordination at different levels as well as budgetary regulations. In addition, Austria's WGA still seems to be inspired to a considerable degree by informal gatherings and personal leadership.

Austria's Federal Ministries Act (National Council 1986), which sets out the administrative architecture of the ministries, does not explicitly propel inter-ministerial cooperation in a WGA sense, as it is designed to delineate competencies between the various ministries (i.e. to build boundaries rather than bridges). The only body with the power to coordinate all relevant governmental players is the federal chancellor (via the 'Kompetenz-Kompetenz' of the Federal Chancellery). This setup legally puts a constraint on the implementation of the full spectrum of WGA. However, policy-wise, Austria's Comprehensive Security Provision (discussed above) represents a layer of the WGA at the strategic level.

There is a mix of instruments in Austria to support the implementation of its WGA. This includes institutional arrangements (e.g. the Foreign Disaster Relief Fund (AFDRF) managed by the BMEIA, the Austrian Platform of Development and Humanitarian Aid, and evaluations of guidelines and programmes) and ad hoc mechanisms (e.g. pooled funding for Austria's civil-military engagement in Mali). However, a certain weakness lies in the fact that there is no overarching strategic platform, stabilisation fund or task force. Pooled funding has been met with political resistance and, due to budget-law constraints, a compromise at the inter-ministerial level has yet to be achieved. The humanitarian angle of external engagement (e.g. the AFDRF, for which the federal cabinet makes decisions) reflects an existing imbalance between short-term political decision-making needed to respond to crises and a needs-based human-security approach stressing prevention tools. A more coherent and strategic approach regarding a transparent, foreseeable and sustainable allocation of financial means would minimise the risk of political instrumentalisation as well as enhance the financial predictability for implementing partners.

As far as the concrete functioning of a WGA-oriented setup is concerned, work on a practical basis can be assessed positively despite constitutional gaps and a certain disconnect that persists between the working and political levels. Moreover, in practice, a compulsory implementation of a WGA is hampered by a certain degree of reluctance, which has prevented full political backing. But since it is a relatively young working method, and one that often depends on engagement by individuals ('champions'), a WGA would need constant political backing.

International debate contributes to sustaining joint efforts to establish a WGA (e.g. the EUGS, but also the SDGs, the UNDP and World Bank policies). Inter-departmental coordination and the effectiveness and quality of institutional arrangements varies and is predominantly driven by individual leadership as well as the significance of the respective policy for Austria. Furthermore, departments in different ministries with a key role in implementing a WGA are often understaffed, and personnel-training efforts are often undertaken on an ad hoc basis. Indeed, more human resources should be dedicated to a WGA, as more staff could administer more programmes, thereby creating a leverage effect for certain prioritised areas. There is a strong willingness among experts and staff at the working level across the line ministries to implement a WGA, but the necessary political leadership at the strategic level has yet to live up to its full potential.

In conclusion, regarding Austria's WGA-like approach, the current state of play can be summarised as follows: First, without any doubt, the spirit of a WGA is shared by Austrian stakeholders (especially in the administration) as well as at the level of experts and NGOs. However, a systematic WGA is limited to a certain degree by the existing legal framework (e.g. division of competencies among ministries and the deployment of personnel) as well as by budgetary legislation (i.e. the 'budget sovereignty' of the ministries involved). Second, coherence issues under the umbrella of a WGA can and should be improved through a number of measures (e.g. comprehensive political guidance, prioritisation of a WGA at the political level, specialisation of personnel, inter-ministerial trainings and pooled funding) and by having a more consistent institutional framework. Third, enhanced political backing of a WGA could contribute to a more proactive management as well as to higher and more sustained funding to address conflicts and crises. Fourth, prioritisation based on joint assessments and analyses of all stakeholders in given contexts could be improved to substantially promote coherent action. Fifth, strategic communication would be a prerequisite for the successful implementation of a WGA. And, lastly, the establishment of WGA focal points drawing on, for example, expertise from respective country teams in the lead ministries would certainly improve the preparation of joint action, and this work should be interlinked with the NSC and/or the federal cabinet.

Altogether, one can expect that Austria will continue its interactions at the EU level related to further strengthening WGA and comprehensive cooperation and thereby benefit, in turn, from an enhanced WGA at the national level.

6 | Reference list

ADC (Austrian Development Cooperation) (2010). Wiener 3C Appell: Koordiniert, komplementar und koharent agieren in fragilen Situationen. www.entwicklung.at/fileadmin/user_upload/Dokumente/Publikationen/Downloads_Themen_DivBerichte/Friedensfoerder ung_und_Konfliktpraevention/Wiener_3C_Appell_04.pdf.

BKA (Federal Chancellery of Austria) (2013). Austrian Security Strategy: Security in a New Decade – Shaping Security. Vienna: BKA. www.bundesheer.at/pdf_pool/publikationen/sicherheitsstrategie _engl.pdf.

BKA, BMI, BMLV and BMEIA (Federal Chancellery, Federal Ministry of the Interior, Federal Ministry of Defence, and Federal Ministry of Europe, Integration and Foreign Affairs) (2019). Report: Cyber Security 2019. www.bundeskanzleramt.gv.at/dam/jcr:0a5d5734-a53f-4a60-9e64-70092b554c09/EN-Cybersicherheit_Bericht_2019.pdf.

BMEIA (Federal Ministry for Europe, Integration and Foreign Affairs) (2018). EU-Pakt fuer die zivile GSVP (Civilian CSDP Compact); oesterreichisches Engagement; Bericht. GZ. BMEIA-EU.2.13.47 /0024-III.3/2018. www.bundeskanzleramt.gv.at/dam/jcr:b6e88b17 -5222-457c-910c-fac3c6685a70/36_10_mrv.pdf.

BMEIA (2019a). Working together. For our world: Three-Year Programme on Austrian Development Policy 2019–2021. www.ent wicklung.at/fileadmin/user_upload/Dokumente/Publikationen/3 _JP/Englisch/3JP_2019-2021_EN.pdf.

BMEIA (2019b). Protection of Civilians. www.bmeia.gv.at/en/europe-an-foreign-policy/austria-and-the-united-nations/protection-of-civ ilians/.

BMEIA and BMLV (Federal Ministry for Europe, Integration and Foreign Affairs and Federal Ministry of Defence) (2011). Strategic Guideline on Security and Development in Austrian development policy: Strategic Guideline. www.entwicklung.at/fileadmin/user_ upload/Dokumente/Publikationen/Strategien/Englisch/EN_Guid eline_Security_and_Development.pdf.

BMI (Federal Ministry of the Interior) (n.d.). Civil Protection in Austria: National Crisis and Disaster Management. www.bmi.gv.at/ 204_english/skkm/start.aspx.

BMI (2004). Ministerial Council Decision of 20 January 2004: Neuorganisation des Staatlichen Krisen- und Katastrophenschutzmanagements sowie der internationalen Katastrophenhilfe (SKKM). www.bmi.gv.at/204_english/skkm/files/001_Ministerratsbeschlu ss.pdf.

BMLV (Federal Ministry of Defence) (n.d.). Overview: Foreign Deployments of the Austrian Armed Forces. www.bundesheer.at/eng-lish/introle/introle.shtml (Accessed on 19 October 2019).

BMLV (2014). Teilstrategie Verteidigungspolitik 2014. www.bundes heer.at/download_archiv/pdfs/teilstrategie_verteidigungspolitik. pdf.

BMLV (2017). Militaerstrategisches Konzept 2017. www.bundesheer. at/pdf_pool/publikationen/msk2017.pdf.

BMLV (2019). "Sicher. Und morgen? – Sicherheitspolitische Vorschau 2019." www.bundesheer.at/pdf_pool/publikationen/sipol_jvs2019. pdf.

Council of Ministers (2017). Beschlussprotokoll des 1. Ministerrates vom 19. Dezember 2017 (Point 76). www.bundeskanzleramt.gv.at/bundeskanzleramt/die-bundesregierung/ministerratsprotokolle/ministerratsprotokolle-der-xxvi-regierungsperiode-2017-2018/beschlussprotokoll-des-01-ministerrates-vom-19-dezember-2017.html.

Council of the European Union (2018). Council Decision (CFSP) 2018/1979 of 19 November 2018 amending and updating Decision (CFSP) 2018/340 establishing the list of projects to be developed under PESCO. https://eur-lex.europa.eu/legal-content/EN/TXT/PDF/?uri=CELEX:32018D1797&from=EN.

National Council (1986). Federal Ministries Act of 1986. www.ris.bka.gv.at/Dokumente/Erv/ERV_1986_76/ERV_1986_76.pdf.

National Council (2018). Network and Information System Safety Act 2018. www.parlament.gv.at/PAKT/VHG/XXVI/I/I_00369/fname_722293.pdf.

National Council (2019). Austrian Development Act (EZA-G). www.ris.bka.gv.at/GeltendeFassung.wxe?Abfrage=Bundesnormen&Gesetzesnummer=20001847.

Belgium

Alain Spoiden

1 | Introduction

Today's world has become increasingly complex, and challenges can be political, military, social, environmental, economic or security-related. In facing such a situation, governments are more and more obliged to develop means to make their foreign policies more efficient. Belgium is a complex institutional country in which political responsibilities are spread across the federal, regional and community levels. Furthermore, as elsewhere, the Belgian political system is one of coalition governments in which the governing parties very often have their own political agendas.

For decades, the Belgian government has been confronted with external conflicts and crises. Belgium's ministries of Foreign Affairs and Defence as well as the Development Cooperation Directorate of the former regularly cooperate as part of a so-called '3D' (defence-development-diplomacy) approach. Since the Ministry of Justice (law) and the Ministry of the Interior (order) are sometimes also involved, a so-called '3DLO' concept has been elaborated.

These federal bodies have traditionally worked together well despite sometimes have conflicting national agendas. However, there was an acknowledgement that there was a need for aligning policy options and instruments spread across the different levels of government. At present, Belgium is formulating a so-called 'Comprehensive Approach' that takes inspiration from a number of instruments embodying a whole-of-government approach (WGA) (as discussed in greater detail below). In 2017, Belgium's Ministry of Foreign Affairs initiated a Strategy Note on a Comprehensive Approach, which determines a framework agreed at the inter-ministerial (or inter-departmental) level with the aim of "jointly identifying, where possible, over-arching priorities and increasing the coherence and effectiveness of [Belgian] foreign policy" (Kingdom of Belgium 2017: 2). The note also stresses that the strategy is meant to be "a framework and methodology for foreign policy in the broadest sense" as well as "a working method and not an end in itself" (ibid.) It was approved by the Council of Minister on 20 July 2017.

2 | What policies have been developed to further policy coherence?

The Strategy Note discussed above is binding for the federal government and contains general guidelines for implementation. In contrast, governments at the regional and community levels are not obliged to step in, though they may do so if they wish. A comprehensive approach can be applied in any region, country or sub-national area. However, the most probable regions where Belgium can be involved are the African Great Lakes region (Burundi, the Democratic Republic of the Congo, and Rwanda), sub-Saharan Africa and the Middle East. Its scope of implementation is system-wide, covering military interventions, situations where defence and diplomacy are the key elements, situations in which humanitarian issues are the key elements, and situations in which the full range of actors is needed to help fragile states to recover: defence, diplomacy, development cooperation, law and order, economic and trade incentives. Although the Comprehensive Approach concept can be implemented in any possible field of action, it mainly favours the 3D (diplomacy-development-defence) dimension.

The European Union Global Strategy on Foreign and Security Policy has been one of the major sources of inspiration to help Belgium formulate its Comprehensive Approach. Other WGA-oriented instruments that enjoyed Belgium support and helped to inspire Belgium's Comprehensive Approach were the EU's (amended) Instrument Contributing to Stability and Peace (IcSP), the European Commission's Joint Communication on Security Reform, and the EU Emergency Trust Fund for Africa. Belgium had urged the European Union to adopt a comprehensive approach when it comes to its external actions. Indeed, as one of the founding members of the European Union, Belgium has always been committed to being a reliable partner and to strengthening the EU's external-action capabilities. It sees the European Union Global Strategy on Foreign and Security Policy as being hugely important in the context of the internal-external nexus. Belgian diplomats and military officials, acting in the various arenas of the European Union (e.g. the Political and Security Committee, the European Union Military Committee and the Political-Military Group) have been very active in supporting the development of the European Union's Global Strategy. However, it should be noted that, in the last decade, Belgium did not launch any special comprehensive approach initiative within the EU framework.

Belgium is also a solid member of the United Nations (UN), the North Atlantic Treaty Organization (NATO), the Organization for Security and Co-operation in Europe (OSCE), and the Organisation for Economic Co-operation and Development (OECD). Coordination and cooperation with these international institutions take place through the Belgian permanent representations to them. Belgium is also a solid member of the Peacebuilding Commission of the United Nations, and it believes that the UN's 2030 Agenda for Sustainable Development represents a comprehensive framework within which any national comprehensive approach should evolve and develop. Furthermore, Belgium sees the United Nations' focus on preventive diplomacy, crisis management and the defence of human rights as extremely important based on the belief that these matters are better addressed in a coordinated and comprehensive manner.

As one of the founding members of NATO, Belgium also plays an important role in supporting crisis-management bodies. Belgium considers it correct for NATO to deploy its military forces at the conflict stage, and that this takes place within a larger strategic and diplomatic framework in which civil comprehensive-approach actors play a major role in a post-military phase. It should also be noted that Belgian efforts have led to a significant evolution of the OECD's Development Assistance Committee (OECD-DAC). ODA criteria were clarified and extended, such as ones related to passing on the costs of certain military expenditures, deploying military personnel or military equipment in certain international-development contexts, and providing humanitarian aid.

As regards Belgium's Comprehensive Approach, it is crucial for a task force to assess the opportunities offered by the OECD guidelines in this area. With regard to the support that Belgian foreign policy has provided to international WGA policies, remarkable work has been done by Belgian diplomats, who have been constantly involved in developing and influencing the WGA policies of the UN, NATO, the OECD-DAC and the OSCE. At present, as a non-permanent member of the United Nations Security Council (2018–2020), Belgium will continue to "make an effort to reinforce the central role of the United Nations to promote peace and security in the world" (Kingdom of Belgium n.d.).

At the federal government level, the Strategy Note stipulates that each department (as the ministries are called) always take foreign policy as an explicit starting point and articulate its own role and contribution to it. Under the auspices of the Ministry of Foreign Affairs, weekly meetings are held with the prime minister and representatives from all relevant ministries (defence, development cooperation, etc). In foreign locations in which Belgium has specific interests, the ambassador meets regularly with his or her attachés (political, economic and commercial, defence, development) and consular section. The Interdepartmental Commission on Policy Coherence for Development (ICPCD) seeks to focus on security, migration, climate and trade. At the Ministry of Foreign Affairs, intra-departmental coordination meetings involving the relevant directorates are held to achieve maximum coherence of policies related to external conflicts and crises as well as to trade and development cooperation. Within the Ministry of Defence, formal coordination take place on a daily basis under the lead of the chief of defence. Within other departments, informal coordination mechanisms do exist, but only on a case-by-case basis.

At the federal parliamentary level, when needed, the Senate Commission for External Affairs and the Chamber of Representatives Commission for Defence can work together as a joint commission. A special commission dealing with the follow-up of foreign missions meets regularly. As regards coordination between the executive and parliament, it is important to highlight the fact that the minister of foreign affairs is obliged to meet with the Senate Commission for External Affairs on a regular basis, and that the minister of defence is obliged to meet with the Chamber of Representatives Commission for Defence on the same basis.

Belgium's Ministry of Development Cooperation meets its objectives through various partnerships. Civil society actors (e.g. NGOs and universities) are privileged partners in these efforts. In Belgium's view, the EU's Common Foreign and Security Policy (CFSP) must serve to foster internal cohesion within the European Union and as an influential multiplier on the international stage. In the areas of peace and security, the ministry's objectives are realised through concrete actions related to conflict prevention, crisis management, peacebuilding and peace-enforcing. According to the Strategy Note, Belgian's eventual Comprehensive Approach will need to "connect with" the European Union External Action Service's Prevention of Conflict, Rule of Law/Security-Sector Reform, Integrated Approach, Stabilisation and Mediation (EEAS-PRISM) directorate, a new part of the EU's diplomatic structure (Kingdom of Belgium 2017: 11; see pp. 23–24, which discuss how PRISM was integrated into the new Directorate ISP in March 2019). What's more, the Comprehensive Approach should "be inspired by/absorbed into EU positions and strategies, with a view to policy coherence" (ibid.).

3 | Who are the main actors involved in cooperating in a WGA?

Once adopted, Belgium's Comprehensive Approach will be steered and monitored by three entities: a diplomatic mission relevant for the chosen region or issue, a steering group, and a task force. The role of the diplomatic mission will be to establish a consultation platform with the Belgian authorities in the country to serve two functions. First, it will aim to identify and optimise the upstream flow of available information from the field and to thereby participate in the early warning system. Second, it will serve to aid the downstream flow of information to the field for implementation and monitoring.

At the political-strategic level, the steering group – chaired by a representative of the Foreign Affairs Direction Committee and attended by representatives of the federal departments – will manage the Comprehensive Approach. In doing so, it will be responsible for orienting Comprehensive Approach activities and prioritising themes and countries as well as for periodically reviewing and adapting the Comprehensive Approach. Other participating departments will also provide input. For example, the Military Intelligence Service of the Ministry of Defence will supply relevant strategic and operational intelligence to the steering group.

Once the goals of a specific Comprehensive Approach effort have been defined by the steering group, a dedicated Comprehensive Approach task force will be set up on an ad hoc basis. This task force will be chaired by the director of the Geographical Directorate (DGB) of the Ministry of Foreign Affairs or by another director with expertise in the particular issue at hand. However, if the country or theme concerns a partner country in development-cooperation efforts, the task force will be co-chaired by the director of the DGB and the director of the Directorate-general for Development Co-operation and Humanitarian Aid (DGD). Co-chairmanship may also be used when the country or issue involved plays a major role for another department (e.g. defence). The task force is responsible for implementing the Comprehensive Approach. It will be supplied with tactical intelligence and information from the Military Intelligence Service or the relevant officials in the field, and it will report to the steering group.

The system just described will be a flexible and pragmatic way to balance the potentially diverging interests of various participants. Indeed, creating a dedicated task force is the best way to cope with diverse cooperation levels, which may gradually become more integrated. In addition to promoting better information exchange, they can also determine whether synergies with external actors (e.g. the EU, the UN, NATO, the OSCE or regional organisations) are possible. Moreover, they can play a key role in developing common analyses and exploring ways to foster dialogue with partners with a shared agenda. The task force will also be able to work on joint planning, financing, implementation, monitoring and evaluation of joint projects and programmes.

At the Ministry of Foreign Affairs, the Directorate-general Coordination and European Affairs (DGE) is responsible for preparing, defining, representing, managing and following Belgium's European policy. The DGE and the Directorate-general for Multilateral Affairs and Globalisation (DGM) are both responsible for following the EU's external policy in its entirety. At the European level, the DGE is in contact with foreign partners. At the national level, it liaises with the technical departments; the French-, Dutch- and German-speaking communities; and the Flemish, Walloon and Brussels-Capital regions. Furthermore, it helps to shape public opinions about the country's EU policies, including, of course, those involving external actions.

Furthermore, the DGE plays a key role in facilitating policy coherence within the European Union framework. The EU External Relations Directorate of the DGM follows the European Union's external relations, while its Security Policy Directorate is responsible for managing, promoting, developing and coordinating European security and defence policy. It is also in charge of international security in the boarder sense and, in this role, participates in all aspects of the decision-making process within international organisations, such as NATO and the OSCE. On the other hand, the United Nations Directorate is responsible for promoting and developing global international cooperation within the framework of the United Nations. This organisation of the Ministry of Foreign Affairs already existed before the Strategy Note on a Comprehensive Approach was formulated. As past experiences shaped this structure, its efficiency and quality may be considered fully optimised.

Belgian military advisers are present at the level of the permanent representations to the UN, NATO, the EU and the OSCE. Moreover, a diplomat seconded to the Ministry of Defence may represent the department at the level of the steering group together with the chief of staff. Under the chief of staff, the Belgian Armed Forces General Staff has an assistant chief of staff (ACOS) responsible for strategic issues, an ACOS responsible for operations, and an ACOS responsible for intelligence. The three departments are those that could be involved in a Comprehensive Approach. The Strategy Note also contains a series of rather generic guidelines for the other federal departments.

4 | How does your country operationalise a WGA?

In terms of administrative structures and policies in place to operationalise Belgium's eventual Comprehensive Approach, no specific human resources policy exists yet to support its implementation except for some positions on the steering group discussed above. It would be highly advisable for human resources officials in each department concerned to designate in advance competent and available personnel to be ready to join potential task forces. As human resources are very limited and expensive, the departments will probably not provide the needed number or quality of personnel. Information or intelligence produced by assets of the Ministry of Defence (military intelligence) or the Ministry of Foreign Affairs (diplomatic missions) are already shared among the departments that are supposed to be most intimately involved in a comprehensive approach. But this is not necessarily the case with information that is generated within other departments.

In terms of early warning, there is no joint integrated cell at the governmental level that could provide any strategic resources to collect, analyse and exploit strategic information. Of course, creating such a cell would pose an issue of subordination, unless it were attached to the Prime Minister's Office. A second issue would be convincing (or even forcing) departments with relevant personnel to second them to the cell, as they could lose scarce personnel resources in the process.

However, the most important item contributing to WGA operationalisation is the budget. The Strategy Note does not foresee any joint integrated budget if a comprehensive approach is about to be operationalised, and the needed budget will apparently be provided by the participating departments themselves. This would clearly oblige federal departments (and possibly even departments at the regional or community levels) to put aside a certain budget line in their annual budget to cope with any potential operationalisation of a comprehensive approach. As in most countries, budgetary resources are scarce in Belgium, and the temptation to use them for core business activities within each department is very high. Indeed, it is precisely here that one can see what one of the most problematic issues will be, and only time will tell whether the federal government decides to provide a common budget to a specific comprehensive approach after the first experience of operationalising the concept. In any case, efforts should be made to use a joint integrated budget to support a comprehensive approach, as this will be key for avoiding any confrontations with departments that refuse to cooperate in WGA undertakings due to a lack of budgetary resources.

In terms of strategic communication, the Strategy Note highlights the importance of internal and external communication for gaining sufficient consensus among departments and for fostering the desired level of motivation. The plan is to let the communication services within each department coordinate with its counterparts in other departments. If task forces involve several departments, the steering group will play the role of clearinghouse for press material with the help of the press and communication department of the Ministry of Foreign Affairs.

Regarding the development of a joint lessons learned process, the Strategy Note provides no clear guidance, so it would presumably be the responsibility of the steering group. Of course, a joint lessons learned process can be pre-defined, but it will only be exercised once initial experiences have been made. The effectiveness and quality of the leadership will mainly depend on the political will to designate the right people within the steering group and task force(s).

Another important enabler could be the development of a new working culture that differs from the traditional siloed one. Apart from the usual cooperation between the ministries of Defence and Foreign Affairs, which has been established and reinforced by jointly participating in many missions and operations, the other departments have developed a few coordinating processes especially dedicated to fostering a comprehensive approach to conflicts and crises. For example, since 2006, Belgium's Royal High Institute for Defence and the Royal Institute for International Relations (AKA the Egmont Institute) have been organising an annual course on security and defence issues that brings together, inter alia, senior Belgian personnel from the ministries of Defence, Foreign Affairs, the Interior and Migration, the police and customs forces, the defence industry and NGOs active in development- or security-related matters. In addition to up-to-date and necessary knowledge on security and defence issues, this course also provides a forum for exchanging ideas on these fields and thereby creates an interesting network and common culture.

5 | Conclusions

It is, of course, very difficult to assess whether Belgian's future Comprehensive Approach concept will be successful or not. This will only be possible after the Comprehensive Approach has been operationalised and lessons learned have been identified. Nevertheless, we can identify four main factors that might aid in its success. First, the fact that there already is a document approved by the federal government sends a strong and clear message to various government bodies in Belgium as well as to the outside world – namely, that Belgium has decided that a comprehensive approach to conflicts and crises is the best way to proceed. Second, there is an obvious multiplying factor resulting from the cooperation between the ministries of Foreign Affairs and Defence. Indeed, these two traditional participants already have a long history of working together in addition to personnel of a very high quality and with much experience in collaborating with others. What's more, although both departments will surely play major roles in Comprehensive Approach processes, the leading role will always played – and rightly so – by the Ministry of Foreign Affairs. Third, the fact that Belgium supported the Integrated Approach developed by the European Union contributes to better global coherence with activities of not only the European Union External Action Service, but also with those of the UN, NATO, the OSCE, the OECD and regional organisations. Fourth, the structures set in place to steer (steering group) and monitor (task force) the WGA process are light, flexible and pragmatic.

However, as discussed in more detail above, some aspects of the concept could unfortunately prevent it from achieving its full potential. First, the lack of a joint integrated budget and a well-defined joint human resources policy will likely cause some difficulties when it comes to operationalising the Comprehensive Approach. Second, if Belgium has to implement two operations at the same time, it could result in added complications. Third, operationalising the Comprehensive Approach could be made harder owning to the 'constitutional lasagne', so to speak, of the country, as its three levels of government – federal, regional and communal – will not have the same coalition governments and will most likely prioritise their own needs, which could make them reluctant to participate in joint efforts. But, as always, we will simply have to wait and see.

6 | Reference list

Kingdom of Belgium Foreign Affairs, Foreign Trade and Development Cooperation (n.d.). In the UN system. https://diplomatie.belgium.be/en/policy/international_institutions/in_the_un_system.

Kingdom of Belgium Foreign Affairs, Foreign Trade and Development Cooperation (2017). "Comprehensive approach-Strategy Note." https://diplomatie.belgium.be/sites/default/files/downloads/comprehensive_approach_en.pdf.

Bulgaria

Antoinette Primatarova

1 | Introduction

A whole-of-government approach (WGA) is not common in Bulgaria as a concept even at the level of rhetoric. 'Vseobkhvaten metod', the concept most common at the level of rhetoric, can be considered the proper translation of the English term 'comprehensive approach' (CA). In very broad terms, it implies the need for a complex, holistic and coordinated approach to problems and tasks in an increasingly complex environment.

In Bulgaria, well-established inter-ministerial councils facilitate addressing the multiple dimensions of the issues on the government's agenda. With regard to security issues, CA in the Bulgarian context implies awareness of the multi-level complexity of challenges that need to be addressed not only at the local and national levels, but also at the regional and global ones. Multilateral cooperation within the framework of NATO and the EU is considered crucial for addressing the multi-level complexity of security challenges. With regard to external conflicts and crises, CA has been adopted at the level of rhetoric, but it has not resulted in the introduction of new institutional practices in either the legal or administrative fields. Instead, decision-making related to and the organisation of Bulgaria's involvement in external conflicts and crises are the result of an ad hoc, pragmatic approach.

If CA to external conflicts and crises is defined as a so-called 3D issue (i.e. one involving the coordination of diplomatic, defence and development instruments), the Bulgarian preference for the ad hoc approach rather than for any institutionalisation of a multi-dimensional CA is to be understood against the background of the complex transition from being part of the Soviet sphere of influence – as a member of the Warsaw Pact and the Council for Mutual Economic Assistance (COMECON) – to membership in NATO (2004) and then the EU (2007).

With regard to the development D, it matters that Bulgaria's involvement with the 'third world' during the Cold War was linked to the ideological aspiration to convert 'fraternal' parties and countries to communism. Bulgaria's ideologically motivated support for loss-making projects during this period can hardly be viewed as useful know-how for 'development policy'. On the eve of the fall of communism, the accumulated debt of 24 developing countries to Bulgaria amounted to USD 2.79 billion, with Algeria, Iraq and Libya being the major recipient countries (Vachkov and Ivanov 2008). Owing to its high level of indebtedness and economic mismanagement at the start of the transition, Bulgaria itself had to rely on development and humanitarian aid beginning in 1990 and lasting until its EU accession in 2007. Consequently, despite Bulgaria's stated commitment to EU development policy, its levels of development and humanitarian aid are low, and any enthusiasm for adopting a legal and institutional framework for development policy has been waning since 2016 (Fileva, Valkanova and Buchkov 2018).

With regard to the diplomacy D, Bulgaria's difficult economic transition is a major factor for understanding why the country did not have a capacity for active diplomatic involvement in issues that were not of immediate national concern. Furthermore, in its 15 years of NATO membership and 12 years of EU membership, Bulgaria has not been an active shaper of peace and security policies. This inaction can be seen in the results of the European Foreign Policy Scorecard, a project conducted by the European Council on Foreign Relations (ECFR 2010/11–2016) between 2010 and 2016 to provide a systematic annual assessment of the EU's and its individual member states' performance in dealing with the rest of the world. Depending upon their performance, member states were assigned 'leader', 'slacker' or 'supporter' status. Bulgaria got mostly the neutral "supporter" status, but it did occasionally fall into the 'slacker' category. Indeed, except for its active involvement with the Western Balkans during Bulgaria's recent presidency of the Council of the EU (in the first half of 2018), Bulgaria cannot pretend to assume a leadership role with regard to the EU's CFSP and CSDP anytime soon.

Last but not least, with regard to the defence D, it is important to consider that defence reforms started late in Bulgaria and are still ongoing. Prior to 1989, Bulgaria was an appendix to the Soviet Union in military and defence terms. In 1968, the country was involved in the Warsaw Pact invasion of Czechoslovakia. Throughout the Cold War, Bulgaria had to cover 6 percent of the military and logistic expenses of the Warsaw Pact, and it actually spent 12 percent of its GDP on Soviet military equipment (compared to the 2 percent that it has yet to achieve to meet its commitment to NATO).

Whereas membership in the EU was accepted as a national priority early on (in 1990), political consensus on Bulgaria's security policy only emerged slowly. Until 1998, Bulgaria's political elite remained deeply divided over the nature of national security and the aspiration to join NATO. However, that same year saw the formulation of the National Security Concept (NSC), which stipulated integration into the EU and NATO as being among the country's foreign policy priorities. What's more, it was the first document of its kind to treat national security as being affected in a comprehensive way by global economic, political, scientific and environmental processes as well as by regional developments.

The NSC of 1998 facilitated a CA to Bulgaria's preparation for EU and NATO membership. On its basis, Bulgaria made fast progress in establishing the operational and institutional infrastructure needed for EU and NATO accession in the form of various inter-institutional councils and working groups. They were good enough to allow Bulgaria to comply in a reactive way to the blueprints of the EU and NATO and to thereby join NATO in 2004 and the EU in 2007. However, they were not designed to facilitate proactive policymaking either in general or more specifically with regard to Bulgaria's stance towards external conflicts and crises.

On the eve of Bulgaria's accession to NATO, the scholar Blagovest Tashev criticised the slow emergence of fresh strategic thinking in Bulgaria and pessimistically predicted (Tashev 2004: 15): "If no change in strategic thinking is to take place, Bulgaria will then assume a relatively low profile in the Alliance, doing only the minimum required as a member and frequently refusing to take a firm stand on issues which do not appear to concern the narrowly defined national interest." A decade later, in a critical assessment of the post-Cold War defence reforms in Bulgaria, the scholar Georgi Tzvetkov also identified "a critical need for a strategic vision and governance in defence" (Tzvetkov 2014: 77).

In sum, owing to its complex economic and political transitions as well as its quite recent memberships in NATO and the EU (not to mention its still-pending negotiations related to OECD membership), Bulgaria does not aspire to assume a leadership role with regard to the management of external conflicts and crises. This lack of aspiration, in turn, most likely explains the country's lack of eagerness to consider any kind of institutionalisation of a CA to external conflicts and crises.

2 | What policies have been developed to further policy coherence?

As a result of the slow evolvement of strategical thinking, Bulgaria's National Security Concept of 1998 was not replaced until the adoption of a National Security Strategy in 2011 (National Assembly of Bulgaria 2011) after two failed attempts, in 2005 and 2008. Although the 2011 NSS did not explicitly refer to a CA, its mention of various related concepts (e.g. inter-institutional coordination, effectiveness and synergies) can be interpreted as implicit references to a CA. The 2011 NSS was elaborated with 2020 as a horizon, but it was already updated in 2018 (the horizon being respectively shifted to 2025) (National Assembly of Bulgaria 2018). A review planned for 2019 might result in either a new update or in a new document.

The updated 2018 NSS (ibid.) makes several references to the EU Global Strategy (EUGS) of 2016. Although it mentions a comprehensive approach (CA) on three occasions, it does so without providing any specific definition, thereby allowing for different interpretations. The CA mentioned in point 158 of the NSS comes the closest to the CA concept as used in the EUGS. Diplomatic, political, communication, economic, financial, intelligence and legal instruments are mentioned as being complementary to military instruments in a CA in order to achieve the goals of defence policy. CA is also mentioned once in the seven paragraphs of the NSS's new chapter on 'crisis management'. One should note, however, that CA in the framework of the crisis-management security policy does not have a special focus on external crisis management. Rather, the focus is on the multi-phased, -lateral and -level aspects of crisis management as well as on the use of instruments and resources at all possible levels: local, regional, national and international. In the concluding point (204) of the 2018 NSS, there is a statement that the updated strategy builds upon "a comprehensive approach to security", but this creates the impression of having resulted from a 'copy-and-paste' operation.

Thus, CA has no doubt influenced the general approach to crisis management as one out of a total of 11 sectorial security policies in the 2018 NSS. These are: financial and economic security, transport security, communication security, social security, energy security, environmental security, justice and home affairs security, foreign policy security, defence security, cybersecurity and crisis management security. The section on foreign policy (points 144–156) makes reference to the countries from the Western Balkans (point 150), to the Black Sea region (151), to the Middle East (152) and to Afghanistan (153). Reference to the same regions or countries is already made in the descriptive chapter on the external security environment (III.1). Instability in these regions, which (with the exception of Afghanistan) are geographically close to Bulgaria, is the evident reason behind Bulgaria's interest in navigating the internal-external security nexus.

The assessment of the external security environment in the 2018 NSS covers important thematic priorities, such as geopolitical and military balance, terrorism, human trafficking, violent extremism, asymmetric threats, radical Islam, migration, energy security and cybersecurity. The 2018 NSS also refers to Bulgaria's commitments as a member of NATO and the EU, but it does not go into details regarding the possible fields of action.

At present, Bulgarian support for international peace and security is provided in line with the 2015 Programme for the Development of the Defence Capabilities of the Bulgarian Armed Forces 2020. According to the document (Council of Ministers 2015: 5): "The Armed Forces maintain state of readiness for participation in multinational allied and coalition crisis response operations. In terms of size, they contribute to prolonged operations with concurrent rotation of one reinforced battalion (Battle Group) or [a] greater number [of] smaller units and assets from the military Services exclusively within the resource equivalent to the level of ambition (on the average, about 1,000 troops). The Navy participates with declared forces within the resource equivalent to one frigate for a period up to 6 months per year. The Air Force participates with transport aviation without rotation for a period [of] up to 6 months per year with the necessary personnel. The needed logistics and other elements for participation in operations are also ensured."

According to Ministry of Foreign Affairs (MFA) data from April 2019, 334 Bulgarians are deployed in NATO missions (157 in the Resolute Support Mission in Afghanistan and 153 in the Operation Sea Guardian mission in the Mediterranean) and 55 in OSCE missions (44 in the Special Monitoring Mission to Ukraine). What's more, 72 Bulgarians are currently participating in 12 of the 17 CSDP missions. A review of Europe's civilian capacities published a decade ago (Korski and Gowan 2009) divided EU member states into four categories: professionals, strivers, agnostics and indifferents. With only 46 civilians deployed at that time, Bulgaria was put in the 'indifferents' category. Although larger, the current deployment of Bulgarians in CSDP missions can hardly foster expectations that Bulgaria could qualify for a higher category anytime soon.

With regard to development policy, 2011 was a turning point for Bulgaria, as it marked the first time that development policy was formally classified as being part of the country's foreign policy (Council of Ministers 2011). With regard to the financial implications, Bulgaria had committed itself to achieving the level of 0.33 percent of GDP for development policy by 2015. However, owing to the international financial and economic crises, this target date was pushed back to 2030. Only a small part (3.41% in 2015) of Bulgarian development aid is spent on a bilateral basis, but there is no direct or indirect link to external conflicts and crises. Bulgaria's response to the 2015/2016 refugee crisis led to a temporary spike in bilateral development and humanitarian aid (18.03%) because of ad hoc aid provided to the Middle East.

3 | Who are the main actors involved in cooperating in a WGA?

With regard to dealing with external crises and conflicts, the main actors that cooperate in Bulgaria are the Ministry of Foreign Affairs, the Ministry of Defence, and the Ministry of Interior.

Parliament can play an important role with regard to Bulgaria's positioning on external conflicts and crises. Article 84 (11) of the constitution stipulates that parliament must give its consent to any deployment of Bulgarian military forces abroad. The proposal for the deployment is prepared by the government.

The parliament also adopts the annual state budget proposed by the government. Budget lines linked to humanitarian aid, development policy and Bulgaria's participation in NATO and CSDP missions are not issues that trigger extensive debate.

The parliament or individual parliamentary committees have the right to put questions to ministers and to invite representatives of the executive to attend hearings on any issues of interest, including external conflicts and crises. One format for debate on politically controversial foreign policy issues can be the Consultative Council for National Security (CCNS), which is chaired by the president of Bulgaria. The CCNS includes representatives of the political groups in parliament; the speaker of the parliament; the prime minister; the ministers of foreign affairs, defence, the interior and finance; the chairman of the state security agency; and the chief of the general staff of the Bulgarian Army (President of the Republic of Bulgaria 2012). Depending on the issue under discussion, other government or political parties may be invited to either the regular (quarterly) or extraordinary meetings (ibid.).

With regard to crises in the last 10 years, the CCNS had a meeting in March 2014 in the immediate wake of Russia's annexation of Crimea. Although there was agreement that the sanctions which would eventually be imposed on Russia would also have negative impacts on Bulgaria, this did not prevent the government from supporting the sanctions. However, at present, the incumbent president and the incumbent government are quite often at odds on several foreign policy issues, especially when Russia is involved in a direct or indirect way. Most recently, the president also criticised the government for its support for Juan Guaidó as the de facto head of state of Venezuela.

Bulgaria has opted not to operationalise its involvement with external conflicts and crises under the 2016 EUGS. However, this does not mean that ad hoc decisions are not taken in a coordinated manner.

There are two inter-ministerial councils that can be used for coordination on issues related to external conflicts and crises. First, there is the Inter-ministerial Security Council (ISC) chaired by the prime minister, which was introduced by a decree of the Council of Ministers in 1998. Second, there is the Inter-ministerial Council on Bulgaria's Participation in NATO and the EU's CSDP (IC NATO/CSDP), which was introduced by a degree of the Council of Ministers in 2005. The latter council is jointly chaired by the minister of foreign affairs and the minister of defence. Furthermore, the Consultative Council for National Security (CCNS) (discussed above) is another body that can be used to facilitate the elaboration of national positions on external conflicts and crises. All three of these bodies have much broader tasks than external conflicts and crises, but they can be used in an ad hoc way for this purpose.

If necessary, the Situational Centre attached to the Security Council at the Council of Ministers and its secretariat also have the potential to fulfil coordinating tasks in a CA manner. This was the case, for example, at the peak of the refugee crisis of 2015, which mainly affected the Western Balkans but also impacted Bulgaria.

Moreover, discussion about external conflicts and crises involve the intelligence and counter-intelligence services in different formats and can be linked to the international exchange of intelligence information.

With regard to development policy, one should mention the UN and Development Aid Cooperation unit within the MFA, which serves as the secretariat of an inter-institutional International Development Aid Cooperation Council chaired by the minister of foreign affairs. The council's members also include the deputy ministers of foreign affairs, finance, economy, education and interior. Unfortunately, a draft law from 2016 on international development got stuck in the pipeline. With provisions for establishing a special agency for development aid and for facilitating the financing of NGOs to enable them to participate in big international development projects, it had the potential to become an operational enabler of better coordination with regard to development aid. However, given the scarcity of resources, the medium-term development programmes operate with a limited geographic (Western Balkans and Black Sea region) and thematic (democratic and economic transition) scope.

Political disagreement as well as public opinion can be powerful disablers for involvement in external conflicts and crises, especially in regions that are perceived as not being linked to narrow national interests and not presenting any threat to Bulgarian nationals or interests. Cases in which there was political polarisation and negative public opinions regarding Bulgarian involvement in foreign conflicts have included the UNTAC mission in Cambodia between 1992 and 1993 as well as the Multi-National-Force – Iraq between 2003 and 2005 (see Slatinski 2005 and Cantir 2011).

A good example (though not a recent one and thus not linked to the 2016 EUGS) of a successful application of a CA to an external crisis is Bulgaria's involvement in the 1999 Kosovo refugee crisis. Instead of taking refugees from Kosovo on a quota basis, as proposed by the US, the Bulgarian government decided to assist in the management of Radusa, one of the four refugee camps on Macedonian territory, as well as to provide aid to the other camps. A Bulgarian-run crisis centre operated around the clock coordinating both information and assistance in terms of food, shelter, clothing, medication and transport supply. In addition, the centre included a hospital as well as operations to transport patients to Bulgaria for treatment. The crisis centre was so successful, in fact, that some thought was given to maintaining it as a permanent coordinating structure. However, worries that this might trigger public anxiety about a permanent Bulgarian involvement in the crisis led to a decision not to keep the centre in operation.

Regarding the nexus of internal and external security policies, one should not neglect to mention that Bulgaria's decisive involvement in the 1999 Kosovo refugee crisis primarily resulted from concerns about Bulgaria's internal security. More recently, this nexus also played an important role in Bulgaria's decision to support a CA to the 2015/16 refugee crisis and to the migration dossier in general. In this case, however, a CA should be interpreted as a common European solution to border control and migration rather than as a matter of coordination at the national level.

Last but not least, it deserves to be mentioned that, since 2013, Sofia has hosted NATO's Centre of Excellence for Crisis Management and Disaster Response (CMDR COE), for which Bulgaria is a 'framework nation' and Poland and Greece are 'sponsoring nations'. The centre's activities are based on a shared understanding of the importance of cross-cutting matters within a framework of a comprehensive approach to peace and security. With its strong education and training branch, the centre organises events under the auspices of the European Security and Defence College (ESDC). Since the centre trains and educates leaders and specialists from NATO member and partner countries, this COE can be considered an important asset in Bulgaria for the promotion of strategic thinking and the adoption of a comprehensive approach to peace and security.

5 | Conclusions

Bulgaria has opted not to operationalise or institutionalise a WGA to external conflicts and crises at the national level. What's more, to presuppose that the eventual institutionalisation of a WGA would increase the level of Bulgarian involvement and effectiveness in responding to such events would be highly speculative.

However, Bulgaria does explicitly support the 2016 EUGS, and general references to it are part of both public and internal documents of various ministries and the government. The 2018 National Security Strategy (National Assembly of Bulgaria 2018) concludes with a statement that it builds upon "a comprehensive approach to security", but it does not include any explicit definition of comprehensive approach. In the Bulgarian context, a 'comprehensive approach' implies awareness of the multi-level complexity of challenges that need to be addressed not only at the local and national levels, but also at the regional and global ones. This understanding explains the importance that Bulgaria attaches to multilateral cooperation within the framework of NATO, the EU and other multilateral organisations and operations.

With regard to development policy, bilateral aid is only a small part of Bulgaria's rather low level of overall contributions, with the lion's share being channelled through the relevant multilateral body or bodies. Similarly, coordination at the EU, NATO, OSCE and UN levels is essential for the effectiveness of the missions in which Bulgaria participates in fulfilling its membership obligations. This might explain why Bulgarian tends to view the need for a WGA to external conflicts and crises as an issue to be addressed at the European and international levels rather than at the national one.

References to external conflicts and crises in Bulgarian political debates and policy documents are always related to the nexus of internal and external security. Political consensus and a supportive public opinion are important preconditions for Bulgarian involvement in external conflicts and crises.

6 | Reference list

Cantir, Christian A. (2011). "Leaving the War in Iraq or 'Staying the Course': Why Did Bulgaria Withdraw and Romania Stay?" In *Issues in EU and US Foreign Policy*, edited by Muenewer Cebeci. Plymouth: Lexington Books: 179–201.

Council of Ministers (2011). Decree No. 234 of the Council of Ministers of 01.08.2011 on the policy of the Republic of Bulgaria regarding its participation in international development cooperation (English excerpts). www.mfa.bg/upload/37952/22%20Annex%201. doc.

Council of Ministers (2015). Programme for the Development of the Defence Capabilities of the Bulgarian Armed Forces 2020. www. mod.bg/en/doc/cooperation/20181009_DefCapab_Program_EN. pdf.

ECRF (European Council on Foreign Relations) (2010/11–2016). European Foreign Policy Scorecard. www.ecfr.eu/scorecard.

Fileva, Petranka, Anna Valkanova and Petar Buchkov (2018). *Development Policy: From development aid towards global development partnership. Bulgarian Platform for International Development*. Sofia: Ciela. https://gcap.global/wp-content/uploads/2018/07/BPID-Polit ica-za-razvitie-INTERNET-fileva.pdf.

Korski, Daniel, and Richard Gowan (2009). *Can the EU Rebuild Failing States? A Review of Europe's Civilian Capacities*. London: European Council on Foreign Relations. www.ecfr.eu/page/-/ECFR18_-_ Can_the_EU_rebuild_failing_States_-_a_Review_of_Europes_C ivilian_Capacities.pdf.

National Assembly of Bulgaria (2011). National Security Strategy of the Republic of Bulgaria. Approved on 25 February 2011. www.bbn.gov.pl/ftp/dok/07/BGR_National_Security_Strategy_Republic_Bulgaria_2011.pdf.

National Assembly of Bulgaria (2018). Updated National Security Strategy of the Republic of Bulgaria. Approved on 14 March 2018. www.mod.bg/bg/doc/strategicheski/20180330_Aktualizirana_SN SRB_2018.pdf.

President of the Republic of Bulgaria (2012). Consultative Council for National Security. www.president.bg/cat70/82/Consultative-Council-for-National-Security.html&lang=en.

Slatinski, Nikolay (2005). "Reporting for Duty: The Legacy of the Blue Helmets in Cambodia (1992–1993)." In *Managing Political Crises in Bulgaria: Pragmatism and Procrastination,* edited by Kjell Engelbrekt and Markus Foerberg. Stockholm: Crisis Management Europe Program: 75–97.

Tashev, Blagovest (2004). "In Search of Security: Bulgaria's Security Policy in Transition." *Papeles del este* 8: 1–20. https://pdfs.semanticscholar.org/5ce3/7ef41ad7b9a6b242f0fe8f05a61f86e7c628.pdf.

Tzvetkov, Georgi (2014). "Defence Policy and Reforms in Bulgaria since the End of the Cold War: A Critical Analysis." Partnership for Peace Consortium of Defense Academies and Security Studies Institutes. *Connections* (13) 2 (Spring): 65–78. https://pdfs.semanticscholar.org/1f8e/888e79a88c0dfaea23ff9bfc90dfb2d1dc8a.pdf?_ga=2.37660064.1802827859.1570375339-1605863491.1570375339.

Vachkov, Daniel, and Martin Ivanov (2008). *Bulgaria's External Debt 1944–1989: The Bankruptcy of the Communist Economy.* Sofia: Ciela.

Croatia

Tonci Prodan

1 | Introduction

Croatia has had a systematic and complete whole-of-government approach (WGA) since 2017, when the current National Security Strategy (Republic of Croatia 2017) was issued and the Act on National Security System (Croatian Parliament 2017) was enacted. This kind of approach is fully in line with Croatia's constitution and includes cooperation between the executive, legislative and judicial branches. What's more, unlike those of many other EU countries, Croatia's WGA explicitly includes crisis management and emergency responses at the levels of NATO and/or the European Union in its strategic and legal documents.

There are several specific characteristics of Croatia's WGA, of which the following are the most important. The first involves the country's relative youth. As a young democracy and small country, it took Croatia some time to firmly establish a number of governmental mechanisms, including those related to security, which Croatia views holistically as encompassing both the internal and external dimensions. The best (and the integrated) approach to doing so involved producing strategic documents that followed pre-existing European strategies, directives and best practices.

A second factor that contributed to Croatia's adoption of a holistic WGA has been the degree of (in)security in the surrounding region of South-East Europe. Tragic war circumstances and the war's convulsions played a major role in the ultimate breakup of the former Yugoslavia and the creation of new independent states since the mid-1990s, a time when this area was one of the key crisis regions in the world. In that period, Croatia faced a grave threat from the so-called 'Greater-Serbian Aggression' (AKA the 'Homeland War'), suffered a large number of human casualties and widespread destruction, and even had to contend with the possibility of no longer existing. To this day, the war and the post-conflict state-building that followed have continued to exert a significant influence on the regional security of Croatia. For example, political objectives have become particularly radicalised at the moment, as the leadership of the Republika Srpska has sharpened its secessionist rhetoric and is flirting with the possibility of a referendum on the secession of the Republika Srpska from Bosnia-Herzegovina (BiH), leaving the Croats with the prospects of life in a rump state in which Bosniaks would make up an absolute majority of the population and ethnic Croats would be a national minority. The Croatian Democratic Union (HDZ), the main centre-right party in Croatia and holder of the most seats in its parliament, supported the idea of a 'third entity', i.e. a reorganisation of BiH into a confederation of three ethnic states or at least into a federation of three or more ethnic units/territories (Kasapovic 2016: 181).

The third important factor contributing to Croatia's adoption of this kind of holistic WGA lies in the threat of modern terrorism, especially the international one, which is made even more palpable due to Croatia's geographical location near troubled countries and on one of the main routes used by organised criminal groups. As noted in the National Security Strategy (Republic of Croatia 2017), several hundred people in the region of South-East Europe joined terrorist organisations active in conflicts in Syria and Iraq and then returned to their home countries, where other individuals have also been indirectly radicalised through terrorist propaganda. Indeed, the Republic of Croatia views modern, extremist-led terrorism – which does not respect national borders or limits on the scale of destruction – as one of the greatest security threats in general, both today and in the foreseeable future, and calls for comprehensive, harmonised national and international responses to it. Furthermore, it is very important to add that, as noted in the National Security Strategy (ibid.: 8), the Croatian neighbourhood "is showing trends of strengthening of intolerance, radicalism and extremism, especially of Islamic radicalism."

2 | What policies have been developed to further policy coherence?

The WGA that is used in Croatia is explicitly outlined in official state documents at the national level: the National Security Strategy (Republic of Croatia 2017) and the Act on National Security System (Croatian Parliament 2017), which firmly and formally establishes the framework for coordination and cooperation among the various ministries of the Croatian government at the national level. The purpose of the act was to put in place a national security system that could effectively respond to modern-day threats and risks. Among other things, the act regulates the coordinated actions of the national security bodies related to crisis management and emergency responses at the levels of NATO and the EU as well as those of the homeland security system, which will be discussed in more detail below.

For example, regarding counterterrorism efforts, the first document (Republic of Croatia 2017: 12) states that: "Countering terrorism will be implemented by [an] integrated approach and interdepartmental cooperation through measures of prevention, suppression, protection, prosecution and strengthening of international cooperation." Given the country's location on an external EU border and requirements for joining the Schengen Area, the strategy (ibid.) notes that Croatia "will continue to develop its Integrated Border Management capacities." Regarding domestic security, the strategy (ibid.: 14) states that the homeland security system "will comprise coordinated operation, the use of capability and potential of all components of national security, beginning from public security, defence, civil protection system, security-intelligence system, diplomacy and economy, and other bodies and institutions in the Republic of Croatia."

Croatia's homeland security system complies with and is connected to related EU frameworks. Indeed, the Act on National Security System (Croatian Parliament 2017) explicitly states that the Coordination of the Homeland Security System (CHSS) (a body discussed in more detail below) is responsible for giving supervising state bodies recommendations on how to harmonise national procedures and regulations with the crisis procedures of NATO and/or the EU.

Croatia also strongly supports the European Union Global Strategy for foreign and security policy, and it fully supports (and upholds) the WGA strategies of the UN, NATO, the OECD-DAC and the OSCE.

Indeed, these WGA strategies have strongly influenced the formation of Croatia's own WGA approach. What's more, Croatia is actively involved in the field in implementing mutual WGAs. For example, as part of the UN, Croatia is present in India/Pakistan, the Western Sahara and Lebanon, and it holds a two-year membership on the United Nations Human Rights Council. As part of NATO, Croatia is supporting missions in Afghanistan and Kosovo (KFOR) in addition to participating in the NATO EFP (Enhanced Forward Presence) military posture. Croatia is also part of the Adriatic Trilateral together with Albania and Montenegro, and it continues to support FRONTEX operations in Bulgaria, Greece, Italy and North Macedonia. For example, a FRONTEX airplane for conducting surveillance along the EU-BiH border is stationed in the Croatian coastal city of Zadar.

3 | Who are the main actors involved in cooperating in a WGA?

Croatia's WGA is executed by a well-defined and robust leadership body, which includes the deputy prime minister (who simultaneously serves as the minister of defence) and a number of state secretaries from the more important ministries. At the intra-ministerial level, WGA-related coordination takes place in both formal and informal ways. Formal cooperation is firmly established and formalised within separate committees that are significant for supporting WGA, which hold weekly or monthly meetings. Informal cooperation, on the other hand, takes place on an almost daily basis.

On the legislative level, there is formal WGA coordination within Croatia's parliament. Formal cooperation is firmly established and formalised within various parliamentary committees that are important for the WGA (e.g. the Defence Committee, the Legislation Committee, the Foreign Affairs Committee, and the Domestic Policy and National Security Committee), all of which hold regular meetings. When it comes to coordination between the executive and legislative branches, Croatia's government informs its parliament once a year about the actions that have been taken in pursuing a WGA towards external crises.

There are also a number of other efforts aimed at coordination and cooperation within and among various bodies. For example, the Ministry of Interior cooperates with the Jesuit Refugee Service. Furthermore, Croatia formally cooperates with PESCO, the Schengen Information System (SIS), the European Defence Agency (EDA), the UN, NATO, the OECD-DAC and the OSCE, although the precise constellation of governmental bodies involved in these efforts changes depending on the particulars of the collaborative effort. For example, the parliament's European Affairs Committee formally cooperates with the UN, the EU, the OSCE and NATO. A recent example of such cooperation involved horizontal cooperation within the Ministry of Defence followed the next day by vertical cooperation in a meeting chaired by the prime minister.

Another example of cooperation relates to Croatia's efforts to boost its integrated border-management capacities, as discussed above, although this cooperation comes more in the form of financial assistance to Croatia from the European level. For example, in response to increased migration pressure, Croatia has had to reinforce the parts of its border making up part of the EU's external border with additional police officers. In addition, Croatia's Ministry of the Interior requested and subsequently received almost EUR 6.8 million in additional financial support from the European Commission. These funds have been used for a number of enhancements, such as a stationary surveillance system for the borders with BiH and Montenegro, stationary day-night long-range cameras, and seven surveillance drones (Croatian Government 2019).

There are also a number of smaller cooperations. For example, as part of the EU's Common Foreign and Security Policy (CFSP), Croatia is supporting missions along the Somalian coast (piracy), in the Mediterranean Sea (migrants), and in Ukraine as part of the EU's advisory mission there (EUAM). As part of the European Asylum Support Office (EASO), Croatia's Ministry of the Interior is also providing migration-related support to EU member states, including Cyprus, Greece and Italy. Croatia's government has an agreement with the Council of Ministers of Bosnia-Herzegovina on European partnership. What's more, at Croatia's urging, the EU has paid more attention to fostering political reforms in BiH, especially when it comes to electoral law.

Croatia has made significant institutional reforms that underscore the country's commitment to pursuing a WGA on the national level. For example, significant changes were made to how multiple governmental organisations operate, and a new state infrastructure was formed to respond to crises. This infrastructure, which is provided with sufficient human resources, is made up of the homeland security system (HSS), the National Security Council (NSC), and the body known as the Coordination of the Homeland Security System (CHSS).

The HSS aims to "provide an integral methodology and systematic monitoring of the risks for national security and establishment of the priorities in procedures" as well as to provide "coordinated preparation and implementation of regulations that will determine the measures and procedures of the security protection of importance for national security, particularly the protection of critical infrastructures" (Republic of Croatia 2017: 14). The HSS consists of: central bodies responsible for defence activities, domestic and foreign affairs, civil protection, finances, the administration of justice, security and intelligence; public and private companies (especially those involved in the private-protection sector); civil society organisations; other central bodies of the state administration that are crucial for defence or protection-and-rescue operations (e.g. the Croatian Firefighting Association, the Croatian Red Cross or the Croatian Mountaineering Association); and skilled private individuals who can help the HSS with tasks related to risk management or in crisis situations that could potentially impact national security. When the issue involves homeland security, governments at the local and regional levels can also be engaged.

The National Security Council (NSC) is the central body of the HSS. The National Security Strategy (ibid.: 14–15) notes that the NSC has several tasks. First, it takes into consideration "the risks and issues from the scope of work of the government bodies related to national security." Second, it enacts "guidelines, decisions and conclusions on the manners of protection and realisation of the national interests and strategic goals." And, third, it is also supposed to "regularly review reports on the state of risks and threats to national security and other strategic and planning documents and give recommendations to competent governmental bodies for the purpose of harmonisation [of] the development of capabilities and operation."

Lastly, the Coordination of the Homeland Security System (CHSS) was formed to coordinate the operation of the HSS; to see that the decisions, conclusions and guidelines of the NSC are implemented; and to "launch and coordinate development of the National Security Strategy or update the existing strategic documents" (ibid.: 14). To list some of its tasks in more detail, the CHSS is responsible for: supervising security threats and risk reports created by other government bodies as well as coordinating the creation of national security risk assessments; supervising the application of strategic and planning documents that have an influence on the HSS as well as giving recommendations to the relevant government bodies about capabilities development; supervising crisis-response capabilities and coordinating the development of relevant plans among various homeland security bodies; organising and participating in crisis-response exercises planned at the national government level; and providing recommendations to pertinent governmental bodies on how to align the risk-response procedures of Croatia with those of other organisations, such as NATO and the EU. Lastly, pursuant to Article 13 of the Act on National Security System, the CHSS must keep Croatia's president, prime minister and speaker of the parliament informed about the results of its meetings in addition to submitting an annual report on the system's activities. Although this has not yet happened in practice, the CHSS is authorised to recommend that the government declare an emergency and establish a crisis-management headquarters.

This CHSS is comprised of: the deputy prime minister of Croatia, who is in charge of national security, as a president of the CHSS; the president's national security adviser; several federal ministers (including those from the ministries of Defence, Foreign and European Affairs, Finance, the Interior, Justice, Health, Croatian Veterans' Affairs, and Sea, Transport and Infrastructure; the head of the General Staff of the Croatian Armed Forces; the general director of the police; the general director of the firefighters; the general director of the Office of the National Security Council; the general director of the Security-Intelligence Agency; and the general director of the National Information Security Authority.

5 | Conclusions

The Republic of Croatia has almost completely implemented a WGA that is fully in line with the country's constitution and includes cooperation among executive, legislative and judicial authorities. The national WGA was patterned after the EU framework and shares aspects in common with several other WGAs, including those of the UN, NATO and the OSCE. As a result, the national WGA enjoys effective and high-quality institutional arrangements.

Croatia has had a WGA since 2017, when the current National Security Strategy (Republic of Croatia 2017) was adopted and the Act on National Security System was passed (Croatian Parliament 2017). There are integrated processes for initiating, programming and implementing the WGA on the national level. Furthermore, funds for enforcing the implementation of the WGA (in the form of the homeland security system) are provided by the government budget pursuant to Art. 18 of the Act on National Security System (ibid.). If the funds are not sufficient, it is possible to redistribute some funds within the government budget after officially notifying the parliament.

Furthermore, Coordination for the Homeland Security System (CHSS), the body in charge of coordinating the activities of the homeland security system and seeing that the decisions of the National Security Council are implemented, has a composition that itself reflects a horizontal WGA, as it includes the heads of several ministries and other organisations involved in responding to crises. What's more, it serves a vertical WGA function in its role as a communications channel between members of the executive and legislative branches, including the president, the prime minister and the speaker of the parliament.

6 | Reference list

Croatian Government (2019). Implementation Report: National Security Strategies of the Republic of Croatia. https://vlada.gov.hr/UserDocsImages//2016/Sjednice/2019/138%20sjednica%20VRH//138%20-%203.pdf.

Croatian Parliament (2017). Act on National Security System. 27 October 2017. Narodne novine 108(2017).

Kasapovic, Mirjana (2016). "Lijphart and Horowitz in Bosnia and Herzegovina: Institutional Design for Conflict Resolution or Conflict Reproduction?" *Politicka misao: Croatian Political Science Review* (53) 4: 174–190.

Republic of Croatia (2017). National Security Strategy. www.soa.hr/files/file/National-Security-Strategy-2017.pdf.

Cyprus

James Ker-Lindsay

1 | Introduction

For many years, Cyprus' attention was exclusively focused on the so-called 'Cyprus Problem' that arose from the inter-ethnic tensions on the island in the 1960s and the division of the island in 1974. Even to this day, the main scope of cross-government planning has concentrated on the possibility of a crisis with Turkey. However, following Cyprus' accession to the EU in 2004, the Cypriot government started to change its focus as senior figures realised that Cyprus needed to become more outward-looking so as to avoid being seen as a 'single-issue' member state. The big transformation occurred in 2006, when an outbreak of fighting in Lebanon led to a massive influx of refugees into Cyprus (see, e.g., Zeno 2007). It was at that moment that both Cyprus and the European Union understood the significance of Cyprus' location on the doorstep of the Middle East and North Africa. Since then, considerable efforts have been made in Cyprus to plan for future crises of this kind using a whole-of-government approach (WGA). Indeed, crisis management has now emerged as a central plank of the island's foreign and security policy. At the same time, in 2014, the European Union explicitly acknowledged Cyprus' important role in assisting EU crisis-management efforts in the Eastern Mediterranean, when then-President of the European Commission Jean-Claude Juncker appointed Christos Stylianiades, a Cypriot, to be European Commissioner for Humanitarian Aid and Crisis Management.

2 | What policies have been developed to further policy coherence?

It is clear that Cyprus takes conflict management incredibly seriously. Indeed, crisis management had emerged as one of the prime goals of the country's foreign policy. To this extent, a whole range of initiatives have been undertaken to strengthen its crisis management using a WGA. Although led by certain key ministries – the Ministry of Foreign Affairs, the Ministry of Defence, and the Ministry of the Interior – it is certainly the case that the ambition extends across the whole government. Given the importance of energy as another pillar of Cypriot foreign policy (following the recent discovery of significant energy resources in the Eastern Mediterranean), it is likely that the Minister for Energy, Commerce and Industry will be involved in related issues.

In 2013, a basic national plan named 'Zenon' was unveiled that set out the scope of Cyprus' crisis-management strategy and the way that the government would coordinate its activities. Under the plan, 22 types of major crises were identified. Since then, the institutions and procedures have improved considerably. The emergence of a number of other crises has also helped to refine and enhance the mechanisms for cooperation across the government. Another important development was the establishment of a Joint Rescue Coordination Center (JRCC) in Larnaca. This was explicitly set up to organise the search-and-rescue system of the Republic of Cyprus "in order to be able to find and rescue in the least possible time people whose [lives] are threatened as a result of an air or naval accident" (JRCC 2019) in its maritime area of responsibility and jurisdiction in the Eastern Mediterranean. As such, it serves as a coordination centre for humanitarian operations in response to natural or other disasters.

Since then, the development of crisis-management policies and procedures has continued at a fast pace. Indeed, it is often noted that it is difficult to keep up with the pace of change, and that the situation changes enormously from one response to the next as the Cypriot government further develops and enhances its capabilities.

3 | Who are the main actors involved in cooperating in a WGA?

The main actors in the development of WGA policies have been the Ministry of Foreign Affairs, the Ministry of Defence, and the Ministry of the Interior. At the core of these activities is the Ministry of Foreign Affairs, which houses the Crisis Management Department (Ministry of Foreign Affairs 2017). This organisation acts as the hub for cross-governmental activities related to managing external crises. Formally speaking, the Republic of Cyprus is a presidential executive somewhat like the United States. Ultimate authority therefore rests with the president of the republic in his capacity as head of the Council of Ministers. In practice, however, the actual authority for managing a crisis tends to depend on the specific nature of the crisis. For example, in many cases, it is the foreign minister who takes responsibility for managing such crises. Nevertheless, it seems as though the other relevant ministers or the president would be able to step in and take the lead depending on the circumstances.

In addition to the three key ministries that are most closely involved in crisis management at present, other state actors are obviously key to the implementation of Cyprus' WGA. Officially, Cyprus has 11 ministries. Other key ministries are likely to include: the Ministry of Health; the Ministry of Energy, Commerce and Industry; the Ministry of Transport, Communications and Works, which has oversight over airports and ports on the island; the Ministry of Agriculture, Natural Resources and the Environment; and the Ministry of Justice and Public Order. For example, the Ministry of Transport, Communications and Works is given direct responsibility for coordinating the following three plans: 'Aristeas', which deals with an interruption to communications and information networks; 'Nikias', which deals with a terrorist attack on civil aircraft in flight; and 'Pindaros', which deals with a shutdown of the main air- and seaports (cf. Liassides 2016 for a brief overview of Cyprus' emergency plans). In addition, other key branches of the state are likely to be involved, including the country's Central Intelligence Service (KYP). Although the parliament is not understood to have a direct role in immediate crisis management, it does play a part in the longer-term development of crisis-management capabilities.

In addition to the internal dimensions, it has been interesting to see how these crisis-management efforts have also shaped the country's external relations. As noted, crisis management has become a central theme in Cypriot foreign policy. Cyprus works closely with its EU partners on developing its crisis-management capabilities, and has actively sought expertise- and knowledge-sharing opportunities. However, such capabilities have also become a key part of its wider regional relations with its neighbours, most notably Egypt, Israel, Jordan and Lebanon. As part of a wider strategy of defence diplomacy, Cyprus has used crisis management as a way to strengthen its ties to these countries by engaging with them in crisis-management activities and exercises. This has been particularly beneficial, as it allows for foreign and defence cooperation to be enhanced in a way that is not deemed to be threatening or confrontational by other actors in the region, including by countries that Cyprus is working with but that do not necessarily have good relations with one another. This underlines once again just how central crisis management has become to Cyprus.

4 | How does your country operationalise a WGA?

When it comes to Cyprus' WGA-related efforts, the most transformation has occurred in the area of administrative structures and processes related to realising the country's ambitions to become a centre of regional crisis management in the Eastern Mediterranean. Indeed, the Cypriot government has established the necessary policies, bodies and processes to operationalise its WGA to crisis management. For example, much work has been done to upgrade the performance of the Crisis Management Department discussed above and to ensure that it operates effectively. And 'Zenon', the basic national crisis-management plan, has been developed and complemented by a range of ministry-level 'specific national plans' outlining how the country should respond to a range of difference crisis scenarios, including attacks on energy infrastructure, health crises, terrorist attacks and a regional crisis triggering a large influx of refugees. The key one in terms of an external crises is 'Estia', the programme that aims to help authorities cope with an influx of third-country nationals fleeing from political crisis, military conflict or natural disaster.

However, it is less clear just how effective these policies have been in real terms across the entire government. While there is ample evidence to suggest that crises primarily involving the Ministry of

Foreign Affairs and/or the Ministry of Defence (e.g. a hijacking incident) can be managed very well, it is perhaps less clear how effectively other ministries could respond to threats that fall directly within their purview. While there may be a theoretical need to ensure that they are properly involved in managing such crises, it seems that it is only when the full details of the situation are known that the actual need for such cooperation becomes entirely clear. For example, the emergence of Ebola in West Africa as well as the realisation that students from that region were studying at universities in the North seemed to spur the Ministry of Health to consider how it would respond if a major outbreak of the disease occurred on the island. In addition, the Cypriot government now stages crisis-management exercises, often in conjunction with other regional countries and EU partners. In this sense, the country's overall preparedness to manage crises has improved dramatically over recent years. Furthermore, having started with little expertise in the subject, there is clearly a desire to learn from other countries.

5 | Conclusions

The past decade has seen a huge transformation in Cypriot foreign policy. At one time, the entire emphasis of the country's foreign-policy and security establishment was on the so-called Cyprus Problem and ways to manage tensions with Turkey. However, since joining the European Union in 2004, Cyprus has sought to broaden in foreign policy. The emergence of a crisis in the Middle East in 2006 that triggered a large influx of refugees from Lebanon into Cyprus showed just how important Cyprus could be as a base for international humanitarian operations in the Eastern Mediterranean. Driven by its wish to play a more useful role in the European Union and its desire to form better relations with its regional partners, and given its strategic location at the far end of the Eastern Mediterranean, external crisis management has emerged as a central plank of the government's foreign policy strategy. This important role has also been explicitly recognised by the European Union. The 2014 appointment of Christos Stylianides as the EU Commissioner for Humanitarian Aid and Crisis Management was a clear acknowledgment of the valuable role that Cyprus plays regarding these issues. As a result, crisis management has become a key element of the foreign and security policy of the Republic of Cyprus.

In terms of the broader elements of the policy, it is clear that Cyprus sees its activities as being intimately connected to its membership in the European Union. It has worked closely with the EU and individual EU member states to establish and enhance its crisis-management capabilities. Likewise, crisis management has emerged as a key dimension of the country's relationship with other regional states. As Cyprus looks to extend its ties to Egypt, Israel, Jordan and Lebanon – largely as a result of its desire to build a stronger presence in the region in terms of energy-related issues – it has viewed crisis management as a key element of its efforts to establish non-contentious military and security cooperation with these neighbours.

More broadly, however, it is less clear how Cyprus' efforts tie in with those of other organisations. While it would seem that it enjoys good cooperation with the Organization for Security and Co-operation in Europe (OSCE), cooperation with NATO is constrained, if not entirely off-limits, due to the still-unresolved Cyprus Problem and Turkey's objections to having any formal or informal engagement with Cyprus. Another interesting constraint is the degree to which Cypriot activities tend to have been narrowly focused on its region. Although Cyprus does participate in EU Common Security and Defence Policy (CSDP) missions, it is clear that it sees its advantage as lying in the fact that it is an EU outpost on the doorstep on the Middle East and North Africa. In fact, Cyprus has shown little willingness to engage more widely, although this may simply be a recognition of its limited capabilities as a small country.

In any case, it is clear that crisis management is now a central feature of Cyprus' foreign and security policy. As a result, in addition to creating the necessary basic documents defining its crisis-management strategy, including a range of detailed scenarios, the Cypriot government has also taken considerable steps to realise this in an integrated, whole-of-government manner. Starting with the Ministry of Foreign Affairs, the Ministry of Defence, and the Ministry of the Interior, which have been central to developing crisis-management capabilities on the island, there is evidence to suggest that the process now closely involves other relevant ministries. However, it is unclear just how integrated they are in real terms. While some observers have praised the way in which Cyprus seems to be prepared to manage major crises, other have expressed scepticism about whether various ministries would really be able to deliver in the event of a major incident.

6 | Reference list

JRCC (Cyprus Joint Rescue Coordination Center) (2019). Mission. www.mod.gov.cy/mod/cjrcc.nsf/cjrcc01_en/cjrcc01_en?OpenDocument.

Liassides, Panayiotis (2016). "Cyprus Emergency Plans and Practices." Paper presented at the PACES Scenario Workshop, Heraklion, 19 April 2016. www.paces-project.eu/images/content/ScenarioWorkshop/Presentations/8_Cyprus_Contigency_Plans_and_Practices_P_Liassides.pdf.

Ministry of Foreign Affairs (2014). "Implementation of the 'Estia' Plan exercise in the framework of the 'Argonaftis 2014' multinational exercise." 16 May 2014. www.mfa.gov.cy/mfa/mfa2016.nsf/All/2BEF4325B1F1A05CC2257FA000459830?OpenDocument.

Ministry of Foreign Affairs (2017). Crisis Management Department of the Ministry of Foreign Affairs. www.oikade.gov.cy/mfa/OIKADE/register.nsf/page02_en/page02_en?opendocument.

Zeno, Ambassador Alexandros N. (2007). "The Cyprus Experience in the Crisis of Lebanon." Speech delivered the Permanent Secretary of the Ministry of Foreign Affairs of the Republic of Cyprus. Vienna, 26 September 2007. www.mfa.gov.cy/mfa/mfa2016.nsf/All/CD7F67AED44E5EBAC2257FA0004588E1?OpenDocument.

Czech Republic

Vit Dostal

1 | Introduction

The foreign policy of the Czech Republic has not introduced a whole-of-government approach (WGA) as a general framework for coping with external conflicts and crises. In fact, official and working foreign policy documents do not even mention one. Officials working in the field of foreign policy planning and security policy who were interviewed for this report said they are aware of the term (or of the terms 'comprehensive approach' and/or 'integrated approach'), and point out that Czech foreign policy coordination mechanisms are indeed designed to fulfil the principle functions of a WGA. A de facto WGA has been introduced in a few cases for which a specific strategy or implementation plan was elaborated. These cases include Afghanistan, Iraq, the Sahel and Syria. The main motivation for introducing a specific strategy has been the need (or desire) of the involved domestic institutional actors to request additional budgetary resources.

From a broader perspective, three things should be noted. First, standard foreign policy coordination in the Czech Republic already involves some mechanisms of a WGA. Second, there are some parallels with a WGA in the country's crisis-management system. And, third, the Czech provincial and reconstruction team that was in Logar, Afghanistan, from 2008 to 2013 as well as recent initiatives related to Iraq, Syria and the Sahel could be perceived as embodying a type of WGA, although there is no mention of this term or a 'comprehensive/integrated approach' in the related documentation.

The constitutional and administrative framework related to foreign policy coordination makes it possible to apply WGA policies to external conflicts and crises. For example, the constitution stipulates that the government has executive power, which also includes responsibly for foreign policy. The key government authority dealing with foreign policy issues is the Ministry of Foreign Affairs (MFA). However, some instruments for successful WGA efforts are located within other ministries, such as the Ministry of Defence (MoD) and the Ministry of Interior (MoI), which also play a key role in crisis management, as well as the Ministry of Industry and Trade. While foreign policy coordination is performed on the governmental level, coordination of EU affairs is done through the Committee for the European Union and the (similarly named) Committee for the European Union on the Working Level.

Thus, in the Czech constitutional system, the MFA plays the leading role when it comes to foreign engagement. All information on conflict prevention, security, stabilisation, conflict settlement and reconstruction is pooled within the MFA, which usually proposes any subsequent action. In case of a very serious crisis, the government may launch crisis-management efforts, as defined in the act on crisis management (Crisis Management Act 2000). These procedures are well planned and often tested, and they would mobilise a huge amount of human, material and financial resources. Nevertheless, any engagement with a crisis situation would be reactive and expected to be short-term.

2 | What policies have been developed to further policy coherence?

The Czech Republic has recently made efforts related to responding to external conflicts and crises. For example, a Czech provincial reconstruction team (PRT) served for five years (2008–2013) in Logar, a province in central-eastern Afghanistan, and specific strategies for Iraq and Syria have recently been elaborated. However, the most important related act has been a new initiative regarding the Sahel, which was about to be approved by the government at the time of writing. The initiative, which follows the country's strategy for the region adopted in 2018 (Committee for the European Union 2018), integrates various individual projects that were previously introduced, adds new ones, and is supposed to be provided with special funding.

Despite these actions, strategies and initiatives, Czech policy documents currently make no references to a WGA. Nevertheless, the country's systems for crisis management and foreign policy coordination do include some aspects of a WGA. Below, both systems will be described in more detail and their respective quality will be assessed. After that, the Sahel initiative will be further discussed.

Czech crisis management is conducted according to Act No. 240/2000 (Crisis Management Act 2000). The act stipulates that the government may form a Central Crisis Staff (CCS) as "its own working body for solving crisis situations". The CCS brings together key ministries and other institutions needed to successfully cope with a crisis. If the crisis involves a military threat, the Ministry of Defence presides over the CCS. For all other crises, the Ministry of Interior is responsible for coordinating CCS efforts. The CCS may also deal with an external threat, which leads to a well-coordinated approach to responding to international conflicts and crises.

Crisis-management efforts may only be invoked if there is a direct threat to the state or if there is a military situation that significantly impacts the security interests of the Czech Republic. These security interests are described and ranked in the country's 2015 security strategy (MFA 2015), where they are categorised as 'vital interests', 'strategic interests' or 'other important interests'.

The comprehensive list covers nearly all security-related interests, from safeguarding the Czech Republic's sovereignty to protecting the environment, which in turn gives the government a free hand to invoke its crisis-management procedures as it sees fit. However, one can hardly imagine that the government would launch such procedures for a conflict or crisis that is in a faraway place or has little impact on the Czech Republic. That said, this may still happen if an allied (NATO and/or EU) country is in danger or when major exercises (e.g. NATO's annual CMX crisis-management exercise) are conducted.

As mentioned above, the Czech crisis-management system is unique in terms of the number of domestic actors involved. However, there are no preventive or follow-up mechanisms in place that would permit one to call its activities 'integrated'. Instead, engagement with crisis situations is reactive, and crisis-management mechanisms are expected to be a short-term. For example, since no set mechanism exists for transitioning from responding to a major crisis to investing in stabilisation efforts, follow-up activities may suffer from departmentalism and a lack of coordination (MoI Interview 2019). In fact, the Czech stance holds that preventive and follow-up policies should be introduced through standard foreign and European policy coordination.

Act No. 2/1969 (Czech National Council 1969) designates the MFA as "the central state authority for the area of foreign policy". As such, the ministry is in charge of preparing foreign policy concepts as well as coordinating humanitarian aid and external economic relations. It also manages the Czech Republic's relations with other countries, international organisations and integration groupings in addition to coordinating all bilateral and multilateral cooperation. Thus, the MFA is responsible for monitoring the situation in conflict regions while instrumentalising embassies or information from international organisations. Furthermore, the MFA manages the country's development assistance, humanitarian aid and transition-promotion programme, which is a financial instrument for fostering democracy. When it comes to external economic relations, the MFA shares responsibilities with the Ministry of Industry and Trade. The MFA's key partner in security issues is the MoD, which is also responsible for Czech international military engagement. Last but not least, the importance of the MoI has risen as the issue of managing international migration has climbed to the top of the political agenda. The MoI also plays a key role in the country's participation in civilian missions. Although there has been a constant clash for competences (mainly with the Ministry of Industry and Trade) and the recent emergence of new actors (e.g. the MoI), the MFA is still the only institution with the capacity to comprehensively follow the developments in conflict regions and propose new actions.

The main authority for foreign policy coordination is the government, and an inter-ministerial comment procedure is in place to facilitate the coherence of its activities. Each ministry may suggest amendments to legislative and non-legislative acts, but the ultimate decision of the government must be followed by all ministries. There is also the National Security Council (NSC) and its committees, which serve as auxiliary authorities and contribute to better policy coherence. The NSC may prepare draft measures for the government aimed at safeguarding the Czech Republic's security.

On the working level, EU-related dossiers are discussed in an inter-ministerial working group and at the Committee for the European

Union on the Working Level. Final positions are approved (often just formally) by the Committee for the European Union, which is chaired by the prime minister and de facto mirrors the composition of the government.

Lastly, the initiative related to the Sahel represents what might be called the Czech Republic's first WGA-like policy. The initiative is being introduced as a follow-up in response to a changing international environment, and it also reflects changes in the country's foreign policy interests. This ad hoc application of a WGA brings together a limited number of actors, including the MFA, MoD and MoI. It aims at achieving coherence among and integration of various activities – both those already being conducted in the Sahel region and those planned for the future. Moreover, launching a new, comprehensive programme should result in the allocation of additional financial sources. Indeed, this desire for more funding was openly expressed in an interview with an MFA official while discussing the motivation behind launching the new programme (MFA Interview 2019a).

The prime minister has directly tasked several ministries with preparing such a programme. His motivations are probably twofold – domestic and international. For example, the government has made tackling migration (to the EU) one of its priorities. Since the Sahel is viewed as one of the main sources of illegal migrants to Europe, the government wants to contribute to migration-management efforts in that region. Second, the Czech Republic is one of the EU member states opposed to the reform of the common European asylum system as long as it includes a relocation mechanism with binding quotas. Along with other countries, the Czech Republic is in favour of so-called 'flexible' or 'effective' solidarity, which means that countries unwilling to accept asylum seekers should be active in other areas of migration management. Enhanced Czech involvement in the Sahel could be perceived as an example of an activity that aligns with the 'effective solidarity' logic.

3 | Who are the main actors involved in cooperating in a WGA?

The actors involved in WGA-like activities in the Czech Republic vary depending upon the nature of the issue demanding their attention. For example, in the case of foreign policy coordination, the main source of information on the conflict regions is the respective territorial department. The department collects information from the embassies, international organisations, other ministries, civil administration actors and NGOs.

If action is required, it may occur in two kinds of situations. First, if a conflict or crisis is about to be discussed in an international organisation (e.g. the EU, NATO, the OSCE or the UN), a national position is prepared (or, more often, merely updated). The position is drafted by the department and is discussed in the ministerial collegium comprising the minister and all deputy ministers, and then it is forwarded to the inter-ministerial level.

On the other hand, if the issue is security-related, it is usually also discussed on the National Security Council or its Committee on Coordination of Foreign and Security Policy. This committee is chaired by the deputy minister of foreign affairs and comprises the deputy ministers from various ministries, the directors of the intelligence services, and directors of other institutions. While it has 20 members, the National Security Council chaired by the prime minister has only nine members: the minister of the interior (serving as deputy chairman) as well as the ministers of defence, foreign affairs, finance, industry and trade, transport, health and agriculture. The president may also attend NSC meetings.

If the issue is one that will be discussed in the Council of the EU or the European Council, it is part of the European policy coordination mechanism. In this case, the draft position is first debated in the inter-ministerial working group, which brings together all relevant ministries represented (usually on the level of department directors). Second, the issue is discussed on the Committee for the European Union on the Working Level, which is presided over by the state secretary for European affairs and includes deputy ministers responsible for the EU agenda. The final national position is adopted on the Committee for the European Union, which is chaired by the prime minister and mirrors the composition of the government.

Any ministry may also suggest its own activity, such as delivering special humanitarian aid or development assistance. Since these cases usually have budgetary implications, they must be discussed on the governmental level. The government has to adopt a decision that tasks individual ministries and usually dedicates extra financial resources for the initiative.

If a crisis-management effort is launched, the Central Crisis Staff (CCS) is formed. The CCS has 16 members, comprising representatives of several ministries and other authorities (e.g. the General Staff, the fire rescue service and the police). All institutions involved in the crisis-management effort have clear instructions to be followed depending on the specific type of crisis situation.

The Czech Republic's specific initiative regarding the Sahel has brought together three ministries: those of Foreign Affairs, Defence and the Interior. The MFA serves as the de facto coordinator, as the standard mechanism for foreign policy coordination is applied in this case. Moreover, it is responsible for humanitarian aid and development assistance, and it was also tasked with opening a new embassy in the region. The MoD is part of the initiative because Czech troops have participated in the EU Training Mission in Mali (EUTM Mali) and the United Nations Multidimensional Integrated Stabilization Mission in Mali (UN MINUSMA). The MoI provides civilian experts and has incorporated the region into the national Medical Humanitarian Programme (MEDEVAC). Coordination is done on the level of department directors and is generally less formal. The drafting of a new initiative, which is supposed to follow on the strategy adopted in 2018, has been done in a small team comprising MFA, MoD and MoI officials. However, since they were tasked with preparing a new initiative by the prime minister and since there are budgetary implications, the new strategy has to be formally adopted by the government and the respective governmental decision must be issued.

4 | How does your country operationalise a WGA?

In both general and specific cases (e.g. the Sahel initiative), the Czech WGA is operationalised through standard processes of foreign or European policy coordination.

The MFA is responsible for foreign policy coordination. In this case, the respective territorial department plays the role of a key operational enabler, as it collects all relevant information on the crisis region. If an international organisation has asked for Czech engagement, the department is the first actor to voice an opinion on it. It may also informally contact other relevant actors, such as other ministries or NGOs. Then, the Czech position is debated at the MFA's collegium, where the minister of foreign affairs voices his or her support or opposition to it.

If the issue needs to be discussed with any other ministries, additional coordination is necessary. The EU-related dossiers would need to be discussed in the inter-ministerial working group and the Committee for the European Union on the Working Level, and then adopted or rejected by the Committee for the European Union.

If it is not necessity to follow the European policy coordination procedure, a standard inter-ministerial comment procedure is followed. In this case, the MFA sends a proposal to the comment procedure, receives replies and then deals with any criticisms of the proposed position. In this phase, settling objections can be less formal on the bureaucratic level and involve high-ranking officials, in which case it may become more political in nature.

Unless absolutely necessary, the MFA usually tries to avoid using comprehensive coordination mechanisms. However, it is obliged to do so when the European coordination mechanism is involved. This happens quite often, in fact, as conflict regions are usually discussed at meetings of the European Council and, of course, of the EU's Foreign Affairs Council.

However, the MFA is motivated to put the issues on the governmental level if its initiative related to the conflict or crisis requires additional budgetary resources. In these cases, the Ministry of Finance is usually the main disabler since it is rarely willing to release additional funds, and the prime minister assumes the role of the enabler. This has also been the case when it comes to the Sahel initiative. And since the prime minister has his own political motivations (as discussed above regarding migration and asylum) for the initiative to be launched and for the WGA to be applied, it is likely that extra funding will be provided.

5 | Conclusions

Although a WGA to external conflicts and crises is not explicitly mentioned in Czech foreign policy documents, it is implemented in practice. Interviewed officials from the MFA have stated that there are WGAs to countries like Ukraine or those in the Western Balkans region, but that there is no specific, detailed 'umbrella' strategy under which all initiatives could be placed. Moreover, they also stated that they do not see a need to change this approach, as this de facto WGA works well under standard foreign policy coordination mechanisms. When asked about potentially launching more robust WGA mechanisms, the MFA officials interviewed for this report voiced worries about a possible over-bureaucratisation of policy coordination and did not see added value in it in any case (MFA Interview 2019a, 2019b).

There are special mechanisms for crisis settlement within the Czech crisis-management system. These procedures are well developed and regularly tested during both national and international exercises. However, in reality, crisis-management efforts would only be launched were there to be a larger international conflict with significant implications for the security of the Czech Republic.

Nevertheless, one can identify some cases of WGA implementation in a narrower sense. The first such initiative was the Czech provincial reconstruction team that served in the Logar province of Afghanistan from 2008 to 2013 as part of the NATO-led ISAF mission. This is generally viewed as having been a significant achievement (MFA Interview 2019b). The main factors contributing to its success were political determination and the non-conflictual relations between the actors on the ground, which were the MFA and MoD.

Another WGA-like initiative is the relatively new Czech engagement in the Sahel region. It is not possible to evaluate the initiative at this point, as it only started in 2018 and because the application of a WGA in this case is still a quite new phenomenon. However, it is clear that political interests and the personal priorities of the prime minister were key motivations for launching it.

6 | Reference list

Committee for the European Union (2018). Resolution of the Committee on the EU of 18 April 2018 No. 13 on the Strategy of the Czech Republic in Support of the Stabilisation and Development of the Sahel Countries 2018–2021. www.vlada.cz/assets/ppov/veu/usneseni/usneseni_veu_458.pdf (in Czech only).

Crisis Management Act (2000). Act. No. 240/2000. www.hzscr.cz/hasicien/file/crisis-management-act-n-240-2000-coll-pdf.aspx.

Czech National Council (1969). Act of the Czech National Council on the Establishment of Ministries and Other Central State Administration Bodies of the Czech Socialist Republic. Act. No. 2/1969 Coll. www.zakonyprolidi.cz/cs/1969-2 (in Czech only).

MFA (Ministry of Foreign Affairs) (2015). Security Strategy of the Czech Republic 2015. www.army.cz/images/id_8001_9000/8503/Security_Strategy_2015.pdf.

MFA Interview (2019a). Interview with a high ranking official at the Ministry of Foreign Affairs.

MFA Interview (2019b). Interview with an official from the Foreign Policy Planning Department of the Ministry of Foreign Affairs.

MoI Interview (2019). Interview with an official working in crisis management at the Ministry of Interior.

Denmark

Peter Viggo Jakobsen

1 | Introduction

Denmark's comprehensive whole-of-government approach (WGA) concept was introduced in 2004 as part of the 2005–2009 Defence Agreement in order to improve cooperation between Danish humanitarian organisations and the Danish military and to thereby enhance the effectiveness and visibility of all related efforts. The concept was launched in response to various problems encountered in Iraq, where the civil-military cooperation (CIMIC) model established during NATO's KFOR operation in Kosovo proved unworkable due to the non-permissive environment, which made it impossible to get civilian experts and organisations to support the work of the Danish military contingent. After similar problems were encountered in Afghanistan, Denmark decided to formulate WGA strategies to help shape its efforts there. The lessons learned in Iraq and Afghanistan – in addition to inspiration from the United Kingdom, with whom Denmark cooperated closely in the field in both countries – resulted in the establishment of a WGA institutional framework in 2010.

This framework is composed of an inter-ministerial steering committee, an inter-ministerial secretariat and a Peace and Stabilisation Fund (PSF) for financing stabilisation activities in fragile countries. Since then, Denmark's WGA has been strengthened by a general WGA strategy (Ministry of Foreign Affairs, Ministry of Defence and Ministry of Justice 2013) as well as by a number of regional strategies and programmes, WGA programming guidelines, annual reports and increased funds (Jakobsen 2014). The Defence Agreement covering the 2018–2023 period will almost double the annual contribution to the PSF coming from the Ministry of Defence, from DKK 84 million in 2018 to DKK 150 million in 2023. These amounts highlight the principal shortcoming of Denmark's WGA, namely, that the funds earmarked for WGA in the PSF (2018: DKK 477.1 million) constitute a very small fraction of the total amounts spent on defence (2018: DKK 22.496 billion) and development (2018: DKK 15.878 billion). This said, the WGA principles and the ideas behind the PSF are being embraced more broadly and are having more and more influence on the stabilisation activities funded by the defence and development budgets.

2 | What policies have been developed to further policy coherence?

Since 2010, all Danish policies related to prevention, stabilisation and development have been explicitly formulated as WGA strategies. This applies to general stabilisation strategies, stabilisation strategies at the regional and country levels, foreign policy white papers, and the government's foreign and security policy strategy, which has been published annually since 2017. Since the WGA is also guiding Denmark's strategy for development cooperation and humanitarian action, one can say that it goes beyond the relatively small programmes financed by the PSF. In doing so, the WGA is beginning to exert an influence on all Danish efforts at the nexus of security and development.

WGA mainstreaming is beginning to become evident, and a WGA mindset, so to speak, is becoming more widespread in the ministries of Foreign Affairs and Defence. Furthermore, it is noteworthy how the PSF has become a frame of reference for all related Danish strategy documents. This centrality is also reflected in the current guidelines for the PSF (Ministry of Foreign Affairs and Ministry of Defence 2018). They point out that the PSF is an integral part of Denmark's Foreign and Security Policy Strategy 2017–2018, that its significance was reconfirmed in the current 2018–2023 Defence Agreement, and that it makes an important contribution to Denmark's strategy for development cooperation and humanitarian action (Ministry of Foreign Affairs 2017a).

In addition, 11 principles have been formulated to guide the implementation of Denmark's WGA, including the projects funded by the PSF as well as the Danish stabilisation efforts funded by the defence and development budgets. Quoting verbatim from the guidelines (Ministry of Foreign Affairs and Ministry of Defence 2018: 5–7), these 11 principles are: (1) Whole of Government: Continues to constitute the underlying basis of the Fund and places it in an intersection between security, development and foreign policy, where efforts can be financed with both ODA and non-ODA funds and integrate with other Danish efforts in the areas of development, foreign affairs and defence. The Fund's efforts can also support the coherence between internal and external security. (2) Regional focus: Takes advantage of the fact that the Fund is not country-specific since the conflicts the Fund focuses on usually have 'spill-over' effects in the surrounding countries, which means, among other things, that the Fund can also operate where Denmark has no actual development programmes and will in most contexts cover several priority countries. (3) Danish interests: The Peace and Stabilisation Fund (PSF) shall focus on efforts that are of particular importance to Danish interests, such as efforts to help prevent irregular migration flows and violent extremism as well as to contribute to stabilise regions in close proximity [to] Denmark. It is also possible to respond to Danish business interests with actions in relation to, for example, maritime security. (4) Partnerships and alliances: The PSF's efforts ought, where feasible and relevant, to be implemented in partnerships and/or alliances with other relevant countries or international and regional actors, where 'like-minded' interests with Denmark exist, or where Denmark has an interest in strengthening the relationship. (5) Danish influence: The PSF efforts shall focus on Danish comparative advantages in regards to what Denmark can contribute to and with, and where Danish contributions can make a clear difference and add value. (6) Achievement of results: The PSF efforts often take place in complex and difficult contexts. Therefore, a realistic level of ambition is necessary regarding the results that the individual engagements and the overall programmes can achieve, also recognising that results generally require long-term perspectives and timelines. (7) Innovation and flexibility: Means that programmes are designed to ensure [that] efforts can be adjusted continuously and remain agile with a fast response capacity. At the same time, there is a willingness to test new methods, approaches and relevant thematic areas. (8) Risk tolerance: Means that the Fund, more so than other efforts, can support particularly risk-prone peace and stabilisation efforts of developmental or political nature. It will be important to consider how administrative challenges can be handled when implementing programmes in risk-prone contexts. (9) Emphasis on a programmatic approach that provides a long-term and predictable framework, where this is appropriate for achieving results with long-term effects and allowing for solid theories of change, but also recognising the need for flexibility within the timeframe. (10) Administrative resource base: Experience indicates that the presence of a Danish representation or embassy in or near the area of effort, or the deployment of advisors to anchor the administration of the PSF engagements, strengthens the implementation and monitoring and helps to support the overall Danish influence. Moreover, this helps to secure the necessary resources in regard to security needs. (11) Complementarity with other Danish efforts, which includes the avoidance of duplication and overlap.

These 11 principles are accompanied by six thematic priorities (again quoted here verbatim): (1) Directly stabilising efforts, which respond quickly to needs for safety and security, access to basic services, build-up of local resilience and reconstruction efforts in, for example, liberated areas in conflict-affected areas. (2) Preventing or countering violent extremism (P/CVE) with focus on, e.g., disengagement, preventive efforts, capacity-development of intelligence services and financial intelligence units, and other efforts that aim to counter terror-financing as well as promote human-rights compliant counter-terrorism efforts. (3) Conflict prevention and conflict resolution, including capacity- and institution-building as well as political dialogue, reconciliation and potential transitional justice, including securing judicial evidence. (4) Security- and justice-sector efforts, focusing on developing the capacity of national and regional security forces, and their democratic oversight, who can partake in ensuring national security, international or regional operations/missions, as well as relevant areas of the justice sector, including Responsibility to Protect (R2P) (where possible), as well as focusing on 'disarmament, demobilisation and reintegration efforts' (DDR). (5) Countering transnational, organised crime and illegitimate financial flows, including networks that support irregular migration and human trafficking, which contributes to, among others, countering or preventing destabilisation of fragile regions. (6) Strengthening maritime security, e.g. through countering piracy and maritime crime by focusing on capacity-building-relevant authorities and information-collection and

-sharing. In addition, focus on harmonisation of relevant laws, rules and strategies that deal with the countering and prosecution of regional maritime crime.

Finally, it is stressed in the guidelines that Denmark applies a "human rights-based approach", and that it has zero tolerance for corruption. On the positive side, these principles and priorities allow for a lot of flexibility and agility, which enables Denmark to respond pragmatically to crises and requests from international partners. At the same time, one has to ask if there is anything Denmark cannot fund using these principles, and whether there is any prioritisation in Denmark's WGA. One also wonders how Denmark copes with the dilemmas that arise during efforts to stabilise fragile states. In any case, it is certainly hard to think of a programme or an activity that meets all the Danish principles at the same time.

3 | Who are the main actors involved in cooperating in a WGA?

At the strategic level, the main actors cooperating in a WGA-like fashion are the ministries involved in the WGA Steering Committee: the Ministry of Foreign Affairs, the Ministry of Defence, the Ministry of Justice, and the Prime Minister's Office. The Ministry of Foreign Affairs and the Ministry of Defence are the most important of these four actors. They provide the funds for the Peace and Stabilisation Fund (PSF), chair the meetings in the steering committee, provide the personnel supporting the steering committee, and manage the projects funded by the PSF in addition to providing most of the personnel deployed in the field. Furthermore, they translate the political guidance provided in the multi-party defence agreements, agreements on development assistance and humanitarian assistance, and the annual foreign and security policy strategies published by the Danish government into specific programmes and objectives that can be funded by the PSF. These programmes and objectives, in turn, form the basis for the plans developed by the relevant offices in the ministries of Defence, Foreign Affairs and Justice, which task their organisations and agencies to formulate programmes and projects and to provide the personnel contributions required for the PSF-funded activities.

The Defence Command, the Home Guard, the Danish National Police and the Stabilisation Office in the Ministry of Foreign Affairs are the principal actors responsible for finding the required personnel. In addition to providing personnel and implementing projects, they are also tasked with coming up with ideas for new ones that can be funded by the PSF. Besides military personnel, the PSF also finances the deployment of Danish police and police instructors to international missions led by the EU or other organisations. The civilian personnel provided through the Peace and Stabilisation Response (PSR) roster is also part of the WGA framework. The PSR is a Danish stand-by roster comprising approximately 490 civilian experts with a wide range of skills relevant to international missions in support of peace and stability in fragile and conflict-affected regions as well as to observing democratic elections in fragile democracies (Ministry of Foreign Affairs 2017b).

The major Danish humanitarian and development NGOs are also part of the WGA system, as they play a key role in implementing PSF-funded projects and activities. Institutionalised cooperation between the Ministry of Foreign Affairs and the NGOs takes place within the Humanitarian Contact Group (HCG). The HCG is a forum for exchanging information regarding ongoing and upcoming humanitarian, preventive and follow-up efforts. When a disaster strikes, the group helps to ensure that there is an effective and coordinated humanitarian response.

Thus, together, the WGA institutions form what might be called a formal chain of collaboration and coordination stretching from the political/strategic level through the operational level to the tactical level. The political ambitions expressed by politicians are translated into programmes and plans, which in turn are translated into specific contributions of funds and personnel at the tactical level. Most contributions are provided in support of activities undertaken by international partners, NGOs, international organisations (notably the EU, NATO and the UN), the Nordic states (Finland, Norway and Sweden), and the countries in the Stabilization Leaders Forum (Australia, Canada, France, Germany, the Netherlands, the United Kingdom and the United States).

4 | How does your country operationalise a WGA?

The programmes and activities funded by the Peace and Stabilisation Fund (PSF) constitute the core of Denmark's WGA activities. They are planned, funded, implemented and monitored in accordance with a detailed set of WGA guidelines. The overall objective of the PSF-funded stabilisation efforts is to counter the threats from migration and terrorism, both of which must be tackled with a long-term perspective and through a broad spectrum of efforts that make use of the full range of foreign, security, defence and development policy tools. These instruments are employed to prevent conflicts in fragile countries and regions as well as to stabilise areas that have already been affected by conflict. In 2018, the PSF funded peace and stabilisation activities in Afghanistan, Georgia, the Horn of Africa, Iraq, Pakistan, the Sahel, Syria and Ukraine. Furthermore, additional activities focused on a number of thematic priority areas, such as anti-radicalisation and the prevention of terrorism in the Middle East, maritime security in the Gulf of Guinea, and the UN's capacity for conducting stabilisation and peacekeeping activities. Finally, the PSF allocates resources to sudden crises.

The regional programmes are carried out in cooperation with the EU, NATO, the UN and a variety of strategic partners, such as France, the Nordic countries, the United Kingdom and the United States. The regional stabilisation programme for Syria and Iraq, which was launched in 2016, is carried out within the framework of the US-led coalition against the Islamic State group also known as Daesh. In Iraq, support for mine removal and basic services have contributed to making it possible for displaced persons to return to newly liberated areas in Iraq. In Syria, the programme has focused on supporting the police, the civil emergency services and service providers in opposition-controlled areas as well as on promoting inclusive political dialogue. In the wake of the liberation of Raqqa, the programme was also able to support the removal of hazards involving explosives.

The stabilisation programme for the Horn of Africa focuses geographically on Ethiopia, Kenya and Somalia. One of its overarching goals is to strengthen regional peacekeeping capacity, and Denmark supported a major field training exercise for the Eastern African Standby Force (EASF) in 2017. Moreover, that same year, Denmark contributed once again to the Somalia Stability Fund, which strengthened its strategic focus by, for example, adopting a new approach to ensuring the inclusion of women. The combined programme for Afghanistan and Pakistan provides support to developing and operating the Afghan police forces, support functions for the Afghan army, and training to Afghan officers. For example, the Afghan police were supported through the Law and Order Trust Fund for Afghanistan via delegated cooperation with the EU. Through the regional peace and stabilisation programme for the Sahel, Denmark has supported the EMP school of peacekeeping in Bamako by, for example, deploying training instructors from the Danish Home Guard. It is also supporting the establishment and build-up of the G5 Sahel Joint Force, a regional force with forces from Burkina Faso, Chad, Mali, Mauritania and Niger that is supposed to contribute to the stabilisation of the Sahel region. Denmark also contributes to strengthening democratic control over the use of force, such as by conducting courses for parliamentarians. The programme is carried out in cooperation with France.

The PSF also runs a programme aimed at preventing and countering violent extremism in the Middle East. The focus of the programme, which involves initiatives in Iraq, Jordan and Lebanon, is on strengthening the capacity of states bordering territories controlled by the Islamic State to prevent and combat terrorism. By strengthening the capacity of local authorities to check recruitment for and the financing of terrorism, Denmark has contributed to limiting the spread of violent extremism in the region.

Since 2015, the PSF has provided support to the Gulf of Guinea Interregional Network (GoGIN), an EU-led programme that aims to foster maritime security in the Gulf of Guinea. Denmark has set priorities within the regional maritime coordination centres and provides support to the countries' judicial system, such as to prosecute pirates. Denmark has also deployed a maritime adviser from the Danish military to Nigeria who is tasked with identifying activities that can strengthen local and regional capacities to effectively tackle challenges related to maritime piracy and robbery in the Gulf of Guinea. In addition, Denmark's Frogman Corps has engaged in capacity-building of partner units from Nigeria and Cameroon with the aim of training and conducting exercising with these units to improve practical skills, such as sanitation, vessel-boarding and securing evidence at sea.

In Ukraine, the PSF has supported the development of the country's defence capabilities. For example, Denmark's armed forces contributed to the training of Ukrainian soldiers and instructors by seconding a language officer to Operation Unifier, the Canadian training mission in Ukraine, in addition to seconding an adviser to NATO's liaison office in Ukraine, which has contributed to developing civilian skills in the defence and security sectors, such as ones related to implementing reforms (The Prime Minister's Office, Ministry of Foreign Affairs, Ministry of Defence and Ministry of Justice 2018, 2019).

5 | Conclusions

Denmark has successfully established its own distinct WGA. It is centred on the Peace and Stabilisation Fund (PSF), which is jointly funded by the Ministry of Foreign Affairs (development budget) and the Ministry of Defence (defence budget). The funds are jointly managed by an inter-ministerial steering committee composed of senior officials from the Ministry of Foreign Affairs, the Ministry of Defence, the Ministry of Justice, and the Prime Minister's Office. The PSF combines a programmatic regional long-term perspective with a mechanism enabling it to provide funds quickly for sudden emergencies. Its work is guided by a set of detailed guidelines ensuring that the funds are spent on activities at the nexus of security and development. Projects involving personnel contributions are generally provided by Danish state agencies and NGOs in close coordination and cooperation with international partners, notably the Nordic states, the members of the Stabilization Leaders Forum, the EU, NATO and the UN. Denmark's WGA framework ensures a high degree of national policy coherence and coordination, which minimises duplication at both the national and international levels. Although the PSF only constitutes a small fraction of the total funds that Denmark spends on prevention, stabilisation and development, it has become a point of reference for all Danish strategy documents and white papers, and it is constantly touted as a Danish priority and success story in official communications and documents. As a result, the WGA has begun to influence how Denmark uses non-PSF funds for defence, stabilisation and development purposes, and a WGA mindset, so to speak, has spread throughout the involved ministries and state agencies from the strategic to the tactical levels.

Since its creation in 2010, the PSF – with its associated institutions, procedures and guidelines – has changed how Denmark engages in diplomatic, defence and development efforts, and it has successfully mainstreamed a WGA in Denmark's state institutions. Judged from the available evaluations of PSF-related activities, Denmark's WGA also appears to have made its stabilisation activities more effective. The international evaluation of the PSF carried out in 2014 was generally positive (Ministry of Foreign Affairs 2014), and the assessments that have been carried out to date by Danish researchers have also been positive. Their primary criticisms have been that the definition of stabilisation is too vague, that the funds available to the PSF are too small, and that stabilisation remains a relatively low priority within the Ministry of Foreign Affairs and the Ministry of Defence (Jacobsen and Engen 2017; Larsen and Nissen 2018). To this, one can add that it is impossible to meet all the Peace and Stability Fund guidelines at the same time, and that they actually give officials a free hand to do whatever they feel like.

6 | Reference list

Jacobsen, Katja Lindskov, and Torben Toftgaard Engen (2017). *Stabilisering – fra intention til indsats: Prioriteringen af forsvarets bidrag til internationale stabiliseringsindsatser.* Copenhagen: University of Copenhagen Center for Military Studies. https://static-curis.ku.dk/portal/files/188269471/CMS_Rapport_2017_Stabilisering_fra_intention_til_indsats.pdf.

Jakobsen, Peter Viggo (2014). "Danish lessons learned: The comprehensive/integrated approach after Iraq and Afghanistan." *Contemporary Conflicts* (2) 1 (February 2014). www.fak.dk/en/news/magazine/Pages/DanishlessonslearnedThecomprehensiveintegratedapproachafterIraqandAfghanistan.aspx.

Larsen, Jessica, and Christine Nissen (2018). How to consolidate the Danish comprehensive approach: The Peace and Stabilisation Fund as 'the good example'? DIIS Comment. 25 October 2018. www.diis.dk/en/research/how-to-consolidate-the-danish-comprehensive-approach.

Ministry of Foreign Affairs (2014). Evaluation of the Danish Peace and Stabilisation Fund. Copenhagen. www.netpublikationer.dk/um/1 4_eval_danish_peace_stabilisation_fund/index.html.

Ministry of Foreign Affairs (2017a). Peace and Stabilisation Response 2017. Copenhagen. http://um.dk/~/media/UM/English-site/Docu ments/Danida/About-Danida/Danida%20transparency/Documen ts/U%2037/2017/PSR.pdf?la=en.

Ministry of Foreign Affairs (2017b). The World 2030: Denmark's strategy for development cooperation and humanitarian action. Copenhagen. http://fnnewyork.um.dk/~/media/fnnewyork/UNGA70/De nmarks%20strategy%20for%20development%20cooperation%20 and%20humanitarian%20action.pdf?la=en.

Ministry of Foreign Affairs and Ministry of Defence (2018). Guidelines: The Peace and Stabilisation Fund. Copenhagen. http://amg. um.dk/~/media/amg/Documents/Tools/Guidelines%20for%20t he%20Peace%20and%20Stabilisation%20Fund/Bilag%205%20G uidelines%20for%20the%20Peace%20and%20Stabilisation%20F unddocx.pdf?la=en.

Ministry of Foreign Affairs, Ministry of Defence and Ministry of Justice (2013). Denmark's Integrated Stabilisation Engagement in Fragile and Conflict-Affected Areas of the World. Copenhagen. http://um.dk/en/~/media/UM/Danish-site/Documents/Danida/N yheder_Danida/2013/Stabiliseringspolitik_UK_web.pdf.

The Prime Minister's Office, Ministry of Foreign Affairs, Ministry of Defence and Ministry of Justice (2018). Denmark's Integrated Peace and Stabilisation Engagements 2017. Copenhagen. http:// um.dk/~/media/UM/Danish-site/Documents/Udenrigspolitik/A nnual%20report%202017.pdf?la=da.

The Prime Minister's Office, Ministry of Foreign Affairs, Ministry of Defence and Ministry of Justice (2019). Denmark's Integrated Peace and Stabilisation Engagements 2018. Copenhagen. http:// um.dk/~/media/UM/Danish-site/Documents/Udenrigspolitik/Fr ed-sikkerhed-og-retsorden/FSF%20rsrapport%202018%20eng.pdf.

Estonia

Maili Vilson and Kristi Raik

1 | Introduction

In the case of Estonia, the presence of a whole-of-government approach (WGA) is difficult to discern. WGA has not been formulated
as the explicit policy response to external crises. On the one hand,
certain elements of a WGA (e.g. policy coordination between different
national actors and coherence between different levels of policymaking) are clearly present. On the other, the extent to which this is a
deliberate policy decision and not simply one born of situational
necessity is unclear.

There are at least two structural explanations for this situation.
First, the implicit presence of WGA principles in Estonian policymaking can be explained by Estonia's overall integration into Western policy structures over the past 20 years. The most impactful has been its
accession to the European Union with the adoption of the EU acquis,
which resulted in significant 'downloading' of EU policies to the domestic (member state) level. Joining the EU required significant efforts from Estonian policymakers, such as expanding or developing
expertise in various policy fields. This affected the institutional structures, existing policy networks and policymaking practices. It also influenced Estonia's method of formulating its foreign policies and enabled Estonia to benefit from the EU's policymaking networks and
structures. In short, horizontal structural changes and policy align-
ment already started taking place at that time.

Similar, although much less extensive tendencies could also be observed when it came to other international organisations (NATO, the
UN, the OSCE and, later, the OECD). Indeed, gradually increasing

Estonia's contribution to the settlement of external conflicts and crises has been one of the implications of joining these organisations, and this contribution has been developed by and large in accordance with the expectations of Estonia's partners and allies in the framework of the EU, NATO and other institutions.

The second structural explanation for this situation is related to the need to realistically assess Estonian policymaking against the backdrop of its resources. As a relatively small country, Estonia has had to balance active participation in international organisations and limited resources within a small government structure. While this requires effective governance and clear policy preferences, it also means that Estonia has directed its capabilities at select policy priorities and that, in doing so, few people have often had to carry out several tasks. As a result, responses to external crises may vary depending on both policy priorities and available resources.

While a WGA is not explicitly present in the Estonian policymaking framework, there is a clear tendency towards more engagement between various national actors as well as active participation in various international organisations, especially in the recently altered European security environment. In any case, WGA-based thinking is clearly more discernible and elaborate in addressing national security and defence than in the area of external crisis management.

2 | What policies have been developed to further policy coherence?

While there are no explicitly formulated WGA policies in Estonia, this should not be understood as indicating that the principle is altogether absent from its policymaking. What's more, there are non-explicitly formulated policies. First, there are references to a 'comprehensive' approach in Estonian foreign policy strategy documents as well as to a 'broad concept of security' in defence development plans. These highlight engagement across various policy domains and require cooperation among multiple governmental institutions and agencies. For example, the National Development Plan for Foreign Policy 2030 (MFA 2019) defines the further strengthening of cooperation and coordination among relevant institutions as a priority.

Very broadly, these mentions pertain to the national policy preferences of Estonia when it comes to policies on protecting Estonian national interests at home and policies towards third countries (see discussion on post-2013 Ukraine below). However, the downside of comprehensive approaches is that they tend to require a significant amount of resources in both financial and organisational terms.

Second, external actors influence Estonian foreign policy through shared policy positions. Above all, the EU, NATO and the UN play key roles in framing Estonia's foreign and security policies. For example, clear references to shared values and principles, decisions taken at the EU level, and NATO summit commitments are often incorporated into Estonian policy positions.

In the area of crisis management, Estonia emphasises the need to complement military operations with civil contributions and development aid. Relative to its small size, Estonia has been an active and significant contributor to missions of the UN, NATO and the EU. In the field of development and humanitarian aid, the UN and the Organisation for Economic Co-operation and Development's Development Assistance Committee (OECD-DAC) provide a rationale and basis for Estonia's bilateral activities, such as identifying countries for humanitarian aid, coordinating aid donation and harmonising national reporting with that of the OECD-DAC.

Third, principles similar to that of a WGA are pursued through clearly established national priorities that are then projected to the international level. A good example of this is Estonia's profile in the world as an expert in e-governance and cybersecurity. Identifying specific fields of expertise that cut across various policy domains helps to ground coordination efforts among different institutions aimed at joint foreign policy goals. Estonia's activity in the field of digital society and cybersecurity encompasses legal, political, technological and military fields while requiring the engagement of various actors from the public and private sectors as well as civil society.

An important overarching goal is to ensure the application of international law in cyberspace. More specifically, for example, the cybersecurity domain is relevant when sharing expertise in the case of electronic voting, protecting citizens' personal data, or storing state secrets in the case of an attack. Establishing such special expertise (and a reputation for it) obviously requires a lot of effort, which needs to be backed up by resources.

Finally, more specifically in the EU framework, Estonia's experience of holding the EU presidency for the first time ever in the second half of 2017 provided important impetus to the country to enhance coordination both at the national level and with EU institutions and member states regarding EU policies. Preparedness for external crises and readiness to engage and coordinate among various actors and policy areas was one aspect of this work.

3 | Who are the main actors involved in cooperating in a WGA?

Policy coordination and cooperation in terms of a WGA is largely informal in Estonia, with the exception of obvious formal cooperation and reporting taking place between the executive and legislative branches. However, the practices of cooperation have developed over a long period of time and have become sufficiently established.

In formal terms, cooperation and coordination take place between the legislative (parliament) and executive (government, ministries) branches. Members of the government are accountable to the MPs and subject to hearings during parliamentary plenary meetings. Parliamentary committee meetings regularly feature representatives from ministries and, if necessary, from other governmental bodies. The Chancellery of the Parliament provides policy and research support to the committees and parliamentary groups (factions) and, when necessary, can organise ad hoc meetings and inquiries for the MPs.

The main actors involved in WGA-like policy framework in Estonia are at the ministerial level. The national contact point or leading institution in the case of most external conflicts or crises is the Ministry of Foreign Affairs (MFA). In terms of formulating policies, foreign policy and diplomacy is led by the MFA in cooperation with the Government Office, both of which have specific regional or thematic policy departments that work in close cooperation. The MFA also emphasises cooperation with the parliament, the ministries, the Office of the President, civil society organisations and academic institutions. The Government Office is the main governmental body tasked with coordinating Estonia's policies in the EU.

Depending on the nature and the extent of the crisis at hand, other ministries and agencies can be involved in responses to external conflicts or crises on a case-by-case basis. Rather than being anchored in specific policy documents, this principle is often an informal practice developed over a longer period of time. For example, in security matters, the involvement of the Ministry of Defence is crucial, and representatives from other bodies (e.g. the Estonian Foreign Intelligence Service or the Defence Forces) may be invited. In the case of humanitarian crises or natural disasters, the Ministry of the Interior, the Police and Border Guard Board, the Estonian Rescue Board, the Ministry of Finance, or the Ministry of the Environment may also be involved.

The best-documented examples of multi-level engagement of various actors in Estonia can be observed in the field of development and humanitarian aid. While the MFA acts as the focal point of national development policy, the policy itself is drafted and executed by the MFA in cooperation with several actors. Most development aid is distributed through projects funded by the MFA and implemented in third countries by its partners. These can include other Estonian ministries, various public-sector institutions, institutions of higher education, Estonian and local NGOs, private companies and international organisations. The humanitarian aid is usually channelled through international organisations, such as various UN agencies (e.g. the UN Refugee Agency, UNICEF, UN OCHA, the UN World Food programme), the World Health Organization (WHO) or the International Committee of the Red Cross.

4 | How does your country operationalise a WGA?

In terms of structures, the main points of coordinating responses to external crises and conflicts are in the Government Office and include, among others, the EU Secretariat, the National Security and Defence Coordination Unit, and national ministries. While the processes of coordination can be both formal and informal, there are certain policies and policy cases in which a WGA can be seen in practice, notably development aid and Estonia's policy towards Ukraine since 2013.

One of the most advanced and well-documented coordination fields is development aid. Estonia has defined a list of priority partner countries for bilateral development aid (specifically, these are Afghanistan, Belarus, Georgia, Moldova and Ukraine) with the justification that these are "countries to which Estonia can offer added value based on its own experiences" (MFA n.d.: 5).

It should be noted that Estonia's selection of priority partners in the field of development aid strongly reflects national security concerns. A focus on Eastern Europe aligns well with one of Estonia's bilateral foreign policy priorities: the Eastern Partnership. Additionally, Estonia's contributions in Afghanistan (in the fields of both security and development) have been an important way to enhance relations with key allies (e.g. the US, the UK and other NATO partners).

More generally, the documents emphasise flexibility both in development aid and crisis response, which can also be observed in everyday policy decisions (e.g. humanitarian aid to refugees in Jordan, Lebanon, Turkey). In setting up, managing and assessing the development aid framework and related activities, even though the MFA takes the lead, it also involves a wide range of partners in the execution stage. Depending on the specific activity and aid target, cooperation partners may include various ministries, other public-sector institutions (e.g. the justice sector or institutions of higher education), private companies and NGOs.

An example of the application of a comprehensive foreign policy approach would be Estonia's policy towards Ukraine since 2013. The events in Ukraine constitute a clear-cut case of an external crisis that had both domestic and foreign policy repercussions for Estonia. The annexation of Crimea by Russia and the war in Eastern Ukraine triggered a severe security crisis for Europe with significant security-related impacts on Estonia and the Baltic Sea region, as well.

Estonian foreign policy decisions were consequently focused on two main objectives at the international level: diminishing the effects of the crisis on Estonia and supporting Ukraine. To achieve these aims, Estonia employed a strategy of active engagement both in bilateral relations (e.g. in transatlantic relations) as well as through supranational and inter-governmental cooperation (e.g. with the EU, NATO, the UN and others). Bilaterally, Estonia's support to Ukraine in all its various forms tripled in 2014 (compared to 2013). This support entailed humanitarian aid, civilian missions and aid through international organisations, and it reached EUR 1.2 million (or 10% of Estonia's annual budget for humanitarian and development aid) beginning in 2015, and Estonia's annual support to Ukraine has ranged between EUR 2.2 million and EUR 2.7 million (or over 20% of the budget).

The palette of Estonian activities has been extensive and included support for democratisation, the provision of digital solutions, corrupting-fighting efforts, and assistance to educational and media organisations. Among the implementors have been various governmental bodies and ministries, local and Estonian NGOs, and international organisations. Domestically, extensive policy coordination has developed among various security institutions with respect to building up the military and enhancing civil-military relations, internal security and strategic communication.

5 | Conclusions

The Estonian case suggests that being small in size is both a curse and a blessing when it comes to developing a national WGA. On the positive side, people working in different institutions in a small state inevitably know each other and interact more than their counterparts in larger countries. Inter-personal ties and the relatively small size of various state organisations contribute to flexible, ad hoc cooperation and the ability to take decisions and mobilise resources quickly, if need be.

On the other hand, a more explicit and elaborate development of a WGA would require additional resources and put an extra strain on institutions that are already operating under a rather heavy workload. Estonia's response to the Ukraine crisis that broke out in 2013 serves as an example of a rather successful WGA-type approach, including a quick and comprehensive mobilisation of resources and the involvement of a wide range of actors, both domestic and external.

Estonia's related activities have truly been broad-ranging, encompassing major efforts to enhance different aspects of national security and resilience, on the one hand, and support to Ukraine in a number of fields, including e-government, the fight against corruption, and supporting education and media organisations, on the other. National security concerns have been the main underlying motivator for these activities, with Ukraine being an obvious example of possible far-ranging implications of an external conflict for Estonia's national security.

A comprehensive approach is particularly visible – and regarded as vital – in the area of national defence, where a broad concept of security has become increasingly important in recent years – again, partly due to the crisis in Ukraine. For a small state with a somewhat precarious geopolitical location, national security and defence are inevitably top priorities. As the nature of threats has become more wide-ranging and complex due to technological developments and a high level of global interconnectedness, involving a wide range of actors and issue areas in national security planning has become a necessity. Although focused on national security, this experience is also relevant for Estonia's engagement in external crises and conflicts, irrespective of the presence of a clear national security interest.

To conclude, it is worth noting that Estonia will become, for the first time ever, a rotating member of the UN Security Council (UNSC) in the 2020–2021 period. Cybersecurity and conflict prevention will be among Estonia's priorities in the UNSC, together with a broad emphasis on the importance of international law for peace and security. Again, for a small state with limited resources, the campaign for the UNSC seat was already a major effort that forced the country to strengthen the global dimension of its foreign policy. Participation in the UNSC can be expected to contribute significantly to the further development of a comprehensive approach to international security and external crises in Estonia.

6 | Reference list

MFA (Estonian Ministry of Foreign Affairs) (n.d.). *The Strategy for Estonian Development Cooperation and Humanitarian Aid 2016–2020*. Tallinn: MFA. https://vm.ee/sites/default/files/content-editors/development-cooperation/2016_2020_arengukava_eng_kodulehele_0.pdf.

MFA (2019). *Eesti valispoliitika arengukava 2030* [National Development Plan for Foreign Policy 2030]. Tallinn: MFA. www.valitsus.ee/sites/default/files/content-editors/arengukavad/valispoliitika_arengukava_koostamise_ettepanek_kodulehele.pdf.

Finland

Juha Jokela

1 | Introduction

Finland has introduced whole-of-government approaches (WGAs) in responding to external conflicts and crises, most notably in the field of crisis management and under the rubric of a comprehensive approach. Mutual coordination and complementarity of military and civilian crisis management, as well as development policy and humanitarian aid, have formed a key narrative and a policy objective for consecutive Finnish governments. Given the objectives of the EU's foreign, security and defence policies, the scope of the comprehensive approach has been steadily broadening in Finland to also include peace-mediation and broader economic relations.

Finland has an extensive track record of participating in United Nations peacekeeping operations since 1956. As an EU member state since 1995, developing and contributing to the EU's crisis-management efforts have constituted an important feature of Finnish foreign and security policy. Finland has also participated in NATO's crisis-management operations in Afghanistan, Bosnia-Herzegovina, and Kosovo. However, as Finland does not belong to NATO or any other military alliances, contributing to international operations has been framed in terms of Finland's aspiration to emerge as a security provider rather than a security consumer. In any case, participating in international operations has also been viewed as contributing to Finland's national security and defence.

Finland's success in introducing WGA into its foreign and security policies also owes something to its specific national characteristics. On the one hand, the country's limited resources have made it eager to strive for efficacy and impact – i.e. to hit above its weight, so to speak – in its engagement in international operations, and the comprehensive approach has been understood as being beneficial in this regard. It has also opened up new possibilities for different types of contributions by EU member states in the Union's responses to external crises and conflicts.

On the other hand, the relatively small size of Finland's governmental administration has porous bureaucratic and cross-sectoral administrative boundaries. Relatedly, actors in Finland's security sector have a long tradition of collaborating with the government on issues related to comprehensive security thinking in national security doctrines. In the postwar era, the aim has been to bring together all the resources of Finnish society, both civilian and military, in defence of the country in different crisis scenarios.

2 | What policies have been developed to further policy coherence?

Strategic programmes of consecutive Finnish governments, as well as documents related to their implementation, largely set the overall scene for the WGA in the country's central governmental administration, including ministries and agencies. These documents often refer to a comprehensive approach in various forms and policy fields as being a guiding principle of the government's policy planning and decision-making. In this context, the recommendations of the OECD and examples of general administration reforms in close reference group countries (e.g. Sweden) are often noted. While the general administrative landscape for a WGA is seen as being very good in Finland, the role of strong and autonomous ministries is often mentioned as creating some institutional hurdles to cross-sectoral and horizontal collaboration (OECD 2015).

In terms of external conflicts and crises, Finland's WGA policies have been most clearly evident in the field of crisis management under the rubric of a comprehensive approach. Relatedly, it features high in development policy in terms of policy-coherence objectives. In these contexts, direct links have been made to humanitarian aid and human rights policies as well as to those for sustainable development. Broader economic relations (i.e. trade) are also increasingly connected to Finland's aspiration to foster peace and stability via its foreign policy and the EU's external relations.

The comprehensive approach seems to constitute a relatively coherent narrative that runs through key policy documents and impacts the planning and making of policies related to Finland's responses to external conflicts and crises. Importantly, the scope of its comprehensive approach has been enlarging from civil-military cooperation towards a more general aspiration to work with a 'WGA mindset'.

Regarding crisis management, a strategy on comprehensive crisis management was adopted in 2009 (Ministry for Foreign Affairs of Finland 2009) and, five years later, the government revised its strategy on civilian crisis management. The latter states (Prime Minister's Office of Finland 2014: 10): "Finland aims to develop the effectiveness of crisis management, impact assessments and its capacities to participate in crisis management in a comprehensive manner which takes into account Finland's fortes." In addition, Finland underlines the "need for cooperation and coordination between different instruments, such as civilian and military crisis management, mediation, development cooperation, humanitarian assistance, diplomacy, and economic relations and sanctions" (ibid.).

Pursuing a comprehensive approach has also been underlined by the recently appointed government of Antti Rinne. Its programme states that "Finland will implement and promote a comprehensive approach to crisis management" (Programme of Prime Minister Antti Rinne's Government 2019). Furthermore, it argues that the main objective in crisis management will be to enhance security and stability in conflict areas and "to boost the competence and capacity of countries affected by conflict" (ibid.). The programme also suggests that achieving tangible results in protracted conflicts requires "good coordination between peacebuilding, humanitarian assistance and development cooperation", and that the government aims to enhance this "through more flexible funding of humanitarian assistance and development cooperation and by enabling multiannual funding arrangements" (ibid.).

A WGA is also evident in the recent government documents on sustainable development goals and Finland's development policy. For example, one description of Finland's development policy states (Ministry of Foreign Affairs of Finland n.d.): "Many other government ministries also have a role in development policy, because developing countries are affected by many decisions made at national, EU and international level in other fields, e.g. safety and security, trade, agriculture, environment and migration policies. Coherence between the various policy sectors is a key principle in development policy."

It is broadly accepted that the EU has had a significant impact on Finnish aspirations to advance a comprehensive approach to external conflicts and crises. Yet Finland's role in promoting the comprehensive approach at the EU level is equally often noted in Helsinki. For example, the government report on Finnish foreign and security policy (Prime Minister's Office of Finland 2016: 20) states that the EU "must continue to further develop its common preparedness and arrangements for closer defence cooperation", and that the "foundation for this includes the arrangements created for the implementation of the Common Security and Defence Policy as well as the capacity of the Union to comprehensively combine different policy sectors and instruments" (ibid.). The government has also reconfirmed Finland's aspiration to participate in the EU's Common Security and Defence Policy (CSDP) in crisis management, and it states that it is placing "progressively more emphasis [...] on conflict prevention and pre-emptive action." The document also notes that "[t]he coherence of the EU's external policies is improved by, among other things, taking into account the connection of the CFSP to the requirements for sustainable development and the implementation of the [UN's] 2030 Agenda", and that the "internal and external action of the EU must better complement each other" (ibid.: 21).

While peace-mediation, humanitarian aid, human rights policies and post-conflict reconstruction are understood to be closely connected to crisis-management operations, the emphasis on preventative action is an interesting development. Fostering stability and preventing conflicts (along with poverty reduction) are also increasingly being viewed as key aims in development policy as well as in broader economic relations and diplomacy, and they have also been directly linked to the management of migration to the EU.

Against this background, Finland appears to share the EU's aspiration to highlight multi-phased, -dimensional, -level and -lateral responses to external conflicts and crises.

3 | Who are the main actors involved in cooperating in a WGA?

In terms of crisis management, Finland's comprehensive approach has constituted a narrative and a policy objective, which has led to a need to clarify mechanisms of decision-making and coordination. The key actors here are the Ministry for Foreign Affairs (MFA), the Ministry of Defence (MoD), the Ministry of the Interior, the Ministry of Justice, the Ministry of Finance, and the Defence Forces. As the president of the republic and the prime minister are key actors at the highest level of decision-making, their offices are included in the co-ordination. Coordination takes place at various levels in both formal and informal formats. The relatively small size of the general administration, personal links, efficacy and impact requirements, budgetary constraints, and a long tradition of cross-sectoral collaboration in matters related to national security and defence have been seen to constitute a relatively fertile environment for WGA approaches to develop in Finland.

Given the broadening scope of the Finnish comprehensive approach to external conflicts and crises, intra-ministry collaboration has also been highlighted. The MFA, for instance, is responsible for, inter alia, foreign and security policy, development policy and external economic relations, all of which are key policy fields of Finland's comprehensive approach.

In general, the functioning logic (and governance structures) of the ministries are increasingly geared towards internal coordination and cooperation among departments and units. This does not mean that there are not any of the kinds of significant 'silos' or 'bureaucratic power struggles' that tend to negatively impact collaboration and joint policy planning. Yet there seems to be a clear understanding that having swift, effective responses to external crises and conflicts requires a joint effort both within and among ministries and agencies. Moreover, there is a willingness to work around difficulties related to institutional boundaries within and among ministries when rapid responses are needed in different crisis scenarios. Indeed, there is more and more discussion of efficacy and impact, which also underlines coordination and cooperation within and among ministries (also in terms of budgetary restrictions).

In terms of the broader context of the Finnish political system, the role of the parliament in promoting a comprehensive approach is interesting. Furthermore, the role and inclusion of civil society actors should be noted.

To discuss the parliament first, one can note that it has played an active role in Finnish foreign and security policy debates in the post-Cold War context. In the 1990s and 2000s, Finland's participation in EU- and NATO-led crisis-management operations sparked a lively political debate related to changes to legislation on crisis management (Raunio 2018). The parliament's Foreign Affairs Committee has been very active in the policy discussion on comprehensive crisis management, and debates on Finland's engagement have spilled over into the plenary sessions, as well.

One can say that the civilian component of crisis-management – and its emphasis on pursuing a comprehensive approach – have constituted an important part of these debates and contributed to consensus-building among political parties. What's more, civilian crisis management and the comprehensive approach have also opened up new possibilities for Finland to engage in international operations by other-than-military means.

Against this background, it is noteworthy that the 2009 strategy on comprehensive crisis management (Ministry of Foreign Affairs of Finland 2009) was initiated by the parliament, and that its implementation has been scrutinised by it. Besides legislative powers, parliament also holds the budgetary powers, which further highlights its role.

Turning to civil society actors, the 2009 crisis management strategy also calls for their active involvement in the comprehensive approach. Collaboration with these actors largely takes place within formal collaboration platforms. For example, the Advisory Board on Civilian Crisis Management within the Ministry of the Interior acts as a forum for debate among different administrative branches and civil society, and it aims to contribute to the development of domestic capacity-building (Prime Minister's Office 2014).

Another relevant body for civil society engagement is the government-appointed Development Policy Committee, which has a mandate to monitor and evaluate Finland's development policy. Its members include representatives of parliamentary parties, advocacy organisations, NGOs and universities. A comprehensive approach and policy coherence are constant themes in the committee's meetings. The same holds true for the 20- to 40-member strong Human Rights

Delegation appointed by the national Human Rights Centre, which operates under the parliament as the national human rights institution.

Regarding peace-mediation efforts, the work of the Crisis Management Initiative (CMI) should be mentioned. It is an independent Finnish organisation that works to prevent and resolve violent conflicts through informal dialogue and mediation. Martti Ahtisaari, a Nobel Peace Prize laureate and former president of Finland, founded the CMI in 2000. Several other major national NGOs, such as the Finnish Red Cross and Finn Church Aid, are also seen as being important partners for the successful planning and implementation of the country's comprehensive approach.

4 | How does your country operationalise a WGA?

Formal and institutional cooperation that assumes a WGA-like approach is most pronounced in the field of crisis management. However, it is also increasingly evident in development policy, and its link to broader economic relations is often highlighted.

Parliament's propositions to the government to address shortcomings in the planning, coordination and monitoring of Finland's comprehensive crisis-management in 2008 were addressed in the comprehensive crisis management strategy of 2009 (Ministry for Foreign Affairs of Finland 2009). Its implementation led to the formation of a strategic coordination group for comprehensive crisis management. The group includes representatives from the MFA, the MoD, the Office of the President of the Republic, the Prime Minister's Office, the Ministry of the Interior, the Ministry of Justice, and the Ministry of Finance.

While the establishment of the coordination group has been valuable in many respects, particularly with regard to information-sharing at the higher levels of the ministries and agencies, its role in advancing coordination has been deemed as being somewhat limited (National Audit Office of Finland 2013). Relatedly, even if (as noted above) the official narrative has changed from one of 'aspirations towards' to the 'actual implementation of' the comprehensive approach, the structural and institutional changes enabling its genuine operationalisation are still lacking despite the stated commitment to this approach (Suonio 2018).

Other interesting institutional innovations in Finland relate to crisis-management expertise, recruitment and training. For example, the Crisis Management Centre Finland was established in 2007 to be "a governmental institution and a centre of expertise in civilian crisis management" (CMC Finland 2019a). Its main duties are training, recruiting and equipping Finnish experts for international missions as well as conducting relevant research and development work. It also acts as the national head office for all seconded Finnish civilian crisis-management professionals.

Furthermore, the Finnish Defence Forces International Centre (FINCENT), founded in 1969, is "a nationally and internationally recognised forerunner, expert and active participant in crisis-management education and training" (FINCENT n.d.). It organises military crisis-management training for command and expert personnel in crisis-management operations led by the UN, NATO, the African Union and the EU, and it has been granted several international quality certificates.

Together, these agencies established the Finnish Centre of Expertise in Comprehensive Crisis Management in 2008, which was joined in 2018 by the Finnish Police University College. The centre "aims at developing common and joint training in crisis management as well as promoting overall understanding of comprehensive crisis management" (CMC Finland 2019b).

Furthermore, a task force set up by the Ministry of the Interior has recently suggested a transition towards a comprehensive operational logic by setting up a new cross-sectoral, comprehensive crisis-management centre into which the current CMC Finland would be merged. The new centre would implement Finland's comprehensive crisis management. Special attention is supposed to be devoted to collaboration between civilian and military crisis-management bodies as well as to peace-mediation, development policy and humanitarian aid. It is, however, an open question whether this proposal will be acted upon.

When zooming out from crisis management to the broader context of responding to external crises and conflicts, informal mechanisms as well as political steering from the top of the government are often underlined. In addition to formal mechanisms of coordination, informal and ad hoc WGA coordination also takes place on various administrative levels within and among the ministries. This is often highlighted in terms a 'common' and 'everyday' practice of addressing external conflicts and crises. The particular membership makeup of these various groups depends on the type of crises and the envisaged response(s) needed.

In terms of general administration and policymaking, the Prime Minister's Office has overall responsibility for making WGA happen, so to speak. It also manages many inter-administrative projects and bodies. Importantly, the WGA is part of the mandate of officials in the Prime Minister's Office. For example, they are tasked with ensuring that the WGA has been taken into account before policy proposals reach the political level (i.e. that of government decision-making). This also applies to Finland's responses to external conflicts and crises. Detected shortcomings in policy planning usually result in requests for further coordination activities within and among ministries. The general working method of the government, based on various permanent ministerial configurations, is also seen as being helpful for the WGA and is credited with providing political leadership and steering for it.

This assessment of Finland's WGA has been rather positive. However, that is not meant to imply that there would not be some difficulties and needs for further enhancement of the WGA to external conflicts and crises. While the civilian and military crisis-management components seem to be operating under clear WGA structures, the next steps – including development, humanitarian aid and human rights policies as well as economic relations – are still somewhat of a work in progress. Bureaucratic power struggles among and within ministries continue to create some obstacles for the WGA. Even if a move towards joint funding and programming instruments has featured in recent discussions on the operationalisation of comprehensive crisis management, the current system based on clarification of responsibilities and allocation of resources in different ministries seems to continue to be firmly in place.

5 | Conclusions

In terms of external conflicts and crises, Finland has successfully implemented a WGA, most notably in the field of crisis management. This has been done under the rubric of a comprehensive approach to crisis management. While the roots of this approach are clearly to be found in civil-military collaboration, it has been expanding to also encompass other policy sectors, most notably development policy, humanitarian aid, peace-mediation and human rights policy. Recently, Finland's external economic relations and diplomacy generally seem to reflect Finland's aspirations to promote peace and stability in the EU's neighbourhoods and beyond.

Against this backdrop, the comprehensive approach constitutes a highly relevant narrative and policy objective shaping Finland's responses to external conflicts and crises. Yet the operationalisation of the WGA still faces some challenges in terms of planning, making and implementing related policies. Granted, the decision-making, coordination structures and financing mechanisms have been largely clarified over the past decade. Nevertheless, this has not led to any major institutional transformations that would enable collaboration and coordination through joint objective-setting and programming. At present, to what extent this would be needed is a somewhat open and under-examined question in Finland.

This analysis suggests that there are some major external and internal enablers of the WGA in Finland's responses to external conflicts and crises. First, Finland's aspiration to emerge as a security provider in the European and international contexts has highlighted its active participation in EU-, NATO- and UN-led crisis-management efforts. Accordingly, Finland has become a strong supporter of the comprehensive approach in regional and international fora. It has also aimed to contribute to developing a comprehensive approach in the EU, such as by providing expertise on the implementation of this approach. Second, Finland's emphasis on a comprehensive approach has opened up possibilities for it to also engage in international operations through civilian means, which has been an important part of the consensus-building on foreign and security policies among the country's political parties. Third, the relatively small size of the general administration, personal links, efficacy and impact requirements, as well as a long tradition of cross-sectoral collaboration in national security and defence have fostered a relatively conducive environment for WGA approaches to develop in.

Finally, there is evidence that Finland's comprehensive approach has spilled over from crisis management to the broader context of foreign and security policy. The EU's aspiration to utilise all the tools available to it in a coherent manner in order to promote peace and stability as well as to address conflicts and crises is very much a shared objective in Helsinki. This means that while innovations on the EU level shape national developments within Finland, the latter also often feed back to the EU level and other relevant actors through expertise and a commitment to further developing comprehensive approaches in general.

6 | Reference list

CMC Finland (Crisis Management Centre Finland) (2019a). Homepage. www.cmcfinland.fi/en/cmc-finland/.

CMC Finland (2019b). The Finnish Centre of Expertise in Comprehensive Crisis Management. www.cmcfinland.fi/en/cmc-finland/the-finnish-centre-of-ex

pertise-in-comprehensive-crisis-management/.

FINCENT (Finnish Defence Forces International Centre) (n.d.). Homepage. https://puolustusvoimat.fi/en/web/fincent/frontpage.

Ministry of Foreign Affairs of Finland (n.d.). Goals and principles of Finland's development policy. https://finlandabroad.fi/web/afg/finland-s-development-policy-and-development-cooperation.

Ministry of Foreign Affairs of Finland (2009). Finland's Comprehensive Crisis Management Strategy. www.cmcfinland.fi/wp-content/uploads/2017/02/41979_Finland_s_Comprehensive_Crisis_Mangement-1.pdf.

National Audit Office of Finland [Valtiontalouden tarkastusvirasto] (2013). Tuloksellisuustarkastuskertomus: Sotilaallinen kriisinhallinta. Valtiontalouden tarkastusviraston tarkastuskertomus 9, 2013.

OECD (Organisation for Economic Co-operation and Development) (2015). Public Governance Reviews: Estonia and Finland. Fostering Strategic Capacity across Governments and Digital Services across Borders. www.oecd.org/gov/oecd-public-governance-reviews-estonia-and-finland-9789264229334-en.htm.

Prime Minister's Office of Finland (2014). Finland's National Strategy for Civilian Crisis Management. Helsinki: Prime Minister's Office Publications 10, 2014. http://julkaisut.valtioneuvosto.fi/bitstream/handle/10024/79664/J1014_National%20Strategy%20for%20Civilian%20Crisis%20Management.pdf?sequence=1&isAllowed=y.

Prime Minister's Office of Finland (2016). Government Report on Finnish Foreign and Security Policy. Helsinki: Prime Minister's Office Publications 9, 2016. https://um.fi/documents/35732/48132/government_report_on_finnish_foreign_and_security_policy/0d34912c-d2aa-4f96-3e83-42e74d499ea6?t=1525861463131.

Programme of Prime Minister Antti Rinne's Government (2019). Inclusive and competent Finland – a socially, economically and ecologically sustainable society. 6 June 2019. Helsinki: Publications of the Finnish Government 25, 2019.

Raunio, Tapio (2018). "Parliament as an arena for politicisation: The Finnish Eduskunta and crisis management operations." *The British Journal of Politics and International Relations* (20) 1, 2018: 158–174. https://trepo.tuni.fi/handle/10024/102987.

Suonio, Aaro (2018). "Kriisinhallinnan kehittamisen haasteet." In *Yhdessa enemman – Kriisien hallintaa kokonaisvaltaisesti,* edited by Roope Siirtola and Anne Palm. Helsinki: Wider Security Network: 65–68.

France

Francois Gaulme

1 | Introduction

France's traditional way of coordinating the bureaucratic implementation of government policy has been through the Prime Minister's Office (Secrétariat général du Gouvernement), which has a staff of 100. However, since the last decade, France has adopted a whole-of-government approach (WGA) that is generally referred to as the 'approche intégrée'. Indeed, the French civil service does not use the term 'whole-of-government approach', its acronym or even the official French translation from the Organisation for Economic Co-operation and Development's Development Assistance Committee (OCDE-DAC): 'Approche a l'échelle de l'ensemble de l'administration'.

At the moment, the French 'approche intégrée' is still strictly limited to defining and implementing the national strategy for responding to external conflicts and crises in an integrated way under the banner of the so-called '3 D's' (diplomacy, defence, development). The 3D system is still strictly limited to security, development and diplomacy (i.e. peacemaking). Granted, the AFD, France's development agency, did list "support for the private sector in vulnerable contexts" as part of its WGA strategy for the 2017–2021 period (AFD 2018: 24), and when commenting specifically on the Sahel situation, President Emmanuel Macron referred to a link between climate change and armed conflicts. However, such issues are generally beyond the scope of the 'approche intégrée' system. Ministries, such those in charge of trade or environment issues, are not brought into an 'approche intégrée' process unless this is explicitly requested by the president or the 3D ministries. In this case, they would send one or two specialised agents/experts to high-level meetings at the Elysée Palace or elsewhere, whose involvement would be kept to a necessary minimum and would not be placed on a formalised and/or permanent basis.

Macron is the first French president to have ever explicitly referred to the 3D formula, which he did in speeches delivered to the Annual French Ambassadors' Conference in 2017 and 2018. Under the highly presidential and centralised system of the France's Fifth Republic, such formal speeches are an overarching statement for developing any further governmental action in a strategic field.

For France, adopting a WGA strategy to responding to crises and conflicts in developing countries was the consequence of the decision to join the international coalition in Afghanistan following the 11 September 2001 attacks on New York and Washington, DC. From the start, its involvement had a military (troop deployments in the field) and a civilian (development projects) aspect, with the latter projects being viewed as supporting further military action in the medium to long terms. Both were part of what was acknowledged in the West at the time as an 'end-state strategy' that would supposedly lead not only to a military victory as a final stage, but also (and as a final stage) to a permanent state of 'sustainable peace' featuring economic and social development under a fair, inclusive and democratic system of governance.

Emerging WGA concepts were discussed among the coalition's member states in military circles (in particular, within and around the NATO network) and among official development assistance (ODA) institutions, whether bilateral (national) or multilateral (international). The conceptual debate focused on the OECD-DAC's semi-formal efforts with specialised subsidiary bodies on conflicts and, under American and British pressure, on 'fragile states' after the invasion of Iraq in 2003. Although it was not a member (and was very critical) of this new coalition, France did opt to send representatives to the forum on fragile states held in London in January 2005, which was jointly organised by the OECD and the World Bank. French development experts – originally from the AFD and subsequently also from what was then the Ministry of Foreign Affairs and International Development – participated in an international process that led to the "10 principles for good international engagement in fragile states" that were defined by consensus and formally adopted (at the ministerial level) by the OECD-DAC members in April 2007 (OECD 2007).

The fifth of the above-mentioned principles ("Recognise the links between political, security and development objectives") led France to adopt additional WGA strategies at the national level. However, the government body directly responsible for ODA got this process off to a somewhat tentative and slow-moving start. For example, the OECD-DAC reference document of 2006 titled "Whole of Government Approaches in Fragile States" (OECD 2006) had no noticeable impact on governmental processes in France at the time. Nevertheless, in 2006, France's Ministry of Defence did ask the AFD to become a civilian element of a series of NATO-style civilian-military crisis-containment simulation exercises, such as ones involving scenarios in Afghanistan and West Africa. Then, in 2008, the establishment of the Crisis and Conflict Unit (CCC) inside the AFD's Strategy Directorate signalled that the French government had made a significant – and lasting – shift to a new conflict-sensitive approach to the country's ODA.

The word 'lasting' was stressed above because this was not France's first tentative experience with a WGA. During the 1990s, the British 'New Labour' government instituted a new policy for dealing with the kinds of civil wars in West African countries (Liberia, Sierra Leone, Guinea) that were spilling over into neighbouring countries. As part of this policy, a new 'Conflict Pool' was set up in 2001 to serve as a fund for conflict-prevention and peacebuilding projects around the world, with its budget being shared by the Department for International Development, the Foreign and Commonwealth Office, and the Ministry of Defence. This innovation supplied a new and creative international WGA model to other Western nations. Applying such a model to a French structured response to African conflicts was contemplated once by the development assistance section of the Ministry of Foreign Affairs and the AFD, but the project was ultimately short-lived. This was due not only to the usual administrative turf battles, but also – and mostly – to a tradition in place since the beginning of the Fifth Republic of coordinating any whole-of-government policies at the very top of the state system – i.e. at the level of the presidency.

In the end, the crucial political event that led to the adoption of a formal, geographically centred WGA system in France was the fight against terrorism in the Sahel and, specifically, the country's direct military intervention in the region in Operation Serval (January 2013 to July 2014) and Operation Barkhane (July 2014 to present). This integrated approach, or 'approche intégrée' in France's bureaucratic terminology, marked the first time that France had ever dealt with a sub-regional African problem in such a way. It was both strategically and operationally top-down in that it was strictly and personally defined and controlled by the president with the assistance of various government sections on an ad hoc basis.

2 | What policies have been developed to further policy coherence?

In its 2018 Development Co-operation Peer Review for France, the OECD-DAC noted some progress in ODA policy coherence for France since the previous review from five years earlier (OECD 2018: 30–32). In their report, the DAC reviewers, or 'examiners', (including the Netherlands and Luxembourg) also emphasised (ibid.: 31) that there is "great awareness of international developments within ministries", and cited two examples to demonstrate this: (1) the signing in June 2016 of the framework agreement between the Ministry of Defence and the AFD, and (2) the International Migration and Development Plan 2018–2022 (DGM/MEAE 2018). The report describes the latter as "the culmination of an interministerial effort involving close co-operation with local governments and civil society".

However, the DAC's positive assessment was also delivered with a clear and final caveat (ibid.), saying that "France needs to ensure that it does not subordinate development aid to issues related to security, domestic policy or regulation of migratory flows". Thus, when it comes to ODA, the DAC continues to prioritise the fighting-against-poverty dimension, even when taking 'security' issues and outcomes into account.

At the same time, on the military-security and armed-forces side, as was noted in a recent report of the UN's secretary-general on the Sahel (UN 2019: 4): "In January [2019], the Joint Force, the European Union, MINUSMA, Operation Barkhane and Malian armed forces created the Coordinating Body for Mali, which is convened on a monthly basis and serves as a framework to enhance information-sharing and coordination among the various military and security forces present in Mali."

If we except such external commitments, France's WGA policy remains strictly defined on a domestic basis by a couple of not-so-binding framework papers and, more importantly, is disseminated via formal bureaucratic instructions from the presidency throughout the whole governmental system. During our survey in preparation for this report, interviewees stressed the important of the 'independence' of French policy vis-à-vis UN policy in Mali, for instance. As to the European Global Strategy, with its very limited operational character, it seems to have had no direct influence on France's WGA.

At present, France's WGA strategy is being defined by official documents from the Ministry for Europe and Foreign Affairs (MEAE) and the AFD, but political decisions will only be taken on the presidential level. Similarly, coordinated implementation will be controlled via a series of top-down arrangements that include daily follow-up by the president with the support of his staff (i.e. diplomatic advisers and the 'chef d'etat-major particulier', the military chief of staff to the French president) and with regular inter-governmental meetings formally taking place at the Elysée Palace.

The main official document on WGA related to crisis-containment is the 2018 report titled 'Prevention, Resilience and Sustainable Peace (2018–2022): A Comprehensive Approach to the Fragilization of States and Societies' (DGM/MEAE 2018). One should note, however, that this report has a deliberately vague status as a 'strategy report' rather than being the simple 'strategy' one would expect, which means it is not a fully binding policy document. In fact, on the the report's back cover, it specifically acknowledges that "France's new strategy on responding to situations of fragility" was the document issued by the (prime minister-chaired) Interministerial Committee for International Cooperation and Development (CICID) on 8 February 2018, which was the first time the committee met after President Macron's election.

Since then, the president's verbal references to a 3D approach have had more policy-binding power within the French civil service and the military than administrative communications documents, such as the 'strategy report' discussed above, which are mostly aimed at the limited part of the governmental system in charge of ODA.

3 | Who are the main actors involved in cooperating in a WGA?

At present, the French actors involved in WGA are almost exclusively concerned with situations in Africa. However, this has not always been the case. For example, in 2009, a four-member 'Afpak Unit' ('Cellule Afpak') was created in Paris within the Asia Directorate of what was then called the Ministry of Foreign and European Affairs. The unit was tasked with overseeing daily coordination among French diplomatic, military and civilian-assistance actors in Afghanistan and Pakistan. During the international '3 C' Conference on improving results in fragile and conflict situations held in Geneva in March 2009, France formally presented this unit as a novel and efficient example of implementing a WGA policy in a context – in this case Afghanistan – in which France did not agree with the coalition's policies of using provisional reconstruction teams (PRTs) to coordinate military and civilian actions in the field.

However, since 2012 and the presidency of Francois Hollande, France's geo-strategic priorities have pivoted back from Asia and the Middle East towards Africa, especially due to the surging crises in the Sahel and the Central African Republic (CAR).

During Hollande's presidential term, inter-departmental meetings were held at the presidency every Thursday to discuss the implementation of the WGA in Africa. These formal meetings (i.e. they had an agenda and minutes were taken) were jointly chaired by the diplomatic cell (Africa section) and the deputy military chief of staff to the president. Joining them were about 25 to 30 specialised higher civil servants (i.e. at the level of a director or ministerial cabinet adviser), including representatives of the parastatal AFD and the military intelligence. The agenda for each weekly meeting included three to four items. These mostly concerned the Sahel, the CAR and other matters requiring urgent attention, but they also touched on more structural matters related to African crises. According to a former presidential aide, the political aim was to keep a tight and closed loop for decision-making. While those attending the meetings would discuss at length issues related to timing and the level of military and civilian engagement, the president alone – as the person formally in charge of foreign policy at the top – took every final decision.

Meanwhile, on a lower and more technical level, one could at the time (and might still be able to) observe in the Ministry of Defence a concentration of the strategic and operational WGA activities related to both civilian-military collaboration and strictly military efforts under the leadership of the general chief of staff (CEMA). This official also has overall responsibility for strategic conceptualisation and testing, but these tasks are managed in practice by the major-general in charge of the 'Centre interarmées de concepts, de doctrines et d'expérimentations' (CICDE), a military establishment that has traditionally focused on developing and testing concepts for activities on the national or multinational levels while taking an operational prospective. In fact, this unit played a major role in developing and disseminating the 'approche intégrée' and 'end-state strategies' to the French civil service and AFD.

On the development-assistance side, one would also notice a similar separation. More general WGA conceptualisation is handled by the Democratic Governance Mission of the MEAE. And more operational-level coordination among the implementation projects run by the AFD is overseen by its Africa Directorate, which itself is supported by the in-house advisory work of the Crises and Conflict Unit (CCC).

A major change occurred at the top level of France's WGA system when Emmanuel Macron became president in May 2017. According to higher French civil servants in Paris, Macron's administration took a more 'pragmatic' approach to the country's priorities in Africa than the Hollande administration had, focusing mostly but not exclusively on the Sahel region and the immediate and growing security and immigration threats to France that has emerged since 2013.

As part of the change, the formal weekly WGA meetings on Africa of the Hollande era were replaced with on-the-spot meetings at the Elysée Palace organised by the Africa/Indian Ocean Directorate (DAOI) of the MEAE and attended by a limited but varying number of participants drawn from the administration. The meetings were and continue to be focused on the more than 4,000 French troops deployed to the entire region as parts of Operation Serval and its successor, Operation Barkhane. The missions are under a US mandate and are supported by the 'G5 Sahel' ('G5 S'). This new regional grouping, created in 2016 on Mauritania's initiative, is made up of forces from Burkina Faso, Chad, Mali and Niger, and it has both development and military objectives. The 'G5 S' surge and the deteriorating military situation in Mali and Burkina Faso led to new coordination and a more hands-on role for French diplomats under the new president's strict personal control.

On 4 September 2017, with the president's blessing, Minister of Europe and Foreign Affairs Jean-Yves Le Drian appointed Jean-Marc Châtaigner, a career diplomat who had previously specialised on development and fragile-state issues, to be France's ambassador/special envoy to the Sahel for a two-year period. Directly under the minister's supervision, Châtaigner's main task was to pilot the coordination of French military and civilian action in the region, especially in connection with the 'G5 S' and the Sahel Alliance. This alliance of international donors was launched in July 2017 to enhance stability and global development in the region by financing and coordinating projects. Its members include the African Development Bank, the United Nations Development Programme (UNDP), the EU and eight of its member states.

This Sahel 'special envoy' system was confirmed in September 2019 when Christophe Bigot, the outgoing ambassador to Senegal, replaced Châtaigner at the end of his mandate. What's more, at the G7 summit held in Biarritz in August 2019, France announced that the 'G5 S' civilian-military cooperation and coordination would be extended to the coastal West African countries of Ghana, Ivory Coast and Senegal.

Under a rather complex administrative system, the Sahel special envoy – with the support of a full-time assistant, a junior desk officer from the MEAE's Africa Directorate – manages the first among a set of two coordination task forces. This first task force is a regrouping of military (Ministry of Defence), development (AFD, Alliance Sahel) and stabilisation (the MEAE's Crisis and Conflict Unit) actors with social and economic-development objectives. The second task force, controlled at the MEAE's West Africa Sub-directorate level and not by the special envoy, focuses on Mali and deals with more sensitive politico-military affairs strictly between diplomats and the military.

The two converging task forces meet every three months to review their objectives. Depending on the specific matter under consideration at the time, they may reassign – on a temporary basis and as required – specialised agents from any ministerial department and the AFD and then report the agents' finding to the upper political level (i.e. the presidency and the cabinet). The task forces are also in charge of jointly implementing the Sahel Survey ('Revue Sahel'), a roughly 10-page document produced annually on an inter-ministerial basis and then discussed and revised at the higher level of the permanent council of defence and security (CDSN) specifically for Mali that Francois Hollande created in the Elysée Palace after the January 2013 military intervention in Mali.

According to French diplomatic sources in Paris, four main 'pillars' are considered by the joint Sahel task forces: politico-military, development, inter-departmental communication and criminal trafficking. The Sahel task forces, outcomes have included joint regional mapping, joint analysis of the 3D activities, and a shared review of the different paces of implementation of diplomatic, military and humanitarian agents as well as longer-term development actors. At the field level, the joint task forces have tried to improve the working environment in the less secure zones for the humanitarian and development actors. In the 'G5 S' countries, the actions of the development task force have been placed under the authority of the French heads of diplomatic missions. Exchanges of personnel have also been facilitated. For example, since September 2018, an AFD adviser has been assisting the major-general in charge of Operation Barkhane on development issues.

At the moment, France does not have any WGA arrangements like those for the Sahel either for the CAR or other conflicts in Central Africa or the rest of the world. With the exception of possibly broadening the 'G5 S' coordination area in West Africa, the French government will probably not give serious consideration to putting in place a more global WGA policy in the foreseeable future.

4 | How does your country operationalise a WGA?

Inherited from the Bourbon kings, perfected during the military- and emperor-centred Napoleonic system of power, and never drastically reformed since then, France's modern and strictly pyramidal formal administrative structure is still capable of smoothly implementing any kind of coordinated action directed from the highest political level under a regulated process, whatever the specific aim or subject may be.

Though limited in its scope, France's WGA policy for the Sahel is a good example of such a system's present successes as well as its limitations. The latter especially results from the lack of policymaking dialogue between the executive and parliament as well as from the difficulty of properly dealing with the predominantly informal nature of African politics, economies and societies.

According to statements by members of the 'special envoy' task force for the Sahel interviewed during the preliminary survey for this report, the actual efficiency and framing of the Sahel WGA policy reflected lessons learned from previous French WGA experiments in the Balkans (Kosovo) and Afghanistan during the two last decades. The approach, they argued, was more flexible and less bureaucratic than before in its integrated inter-departmental structures. For example, each ministerial department and the AFD were given free rein to define their own actions and needs within the broader framework of the two coordinated task forces.

To an external observer of the French system as it is operating in mid-2019, enablers of a WGA policy are to be found in two places. First, they are at the very top level of the French political system, where the presidency's influence has been strengthening under Emmanuel Macron's bold, dedicated and personalised leadership. Second, in terms of a more inclusive top-to-bottom approach, they are found among the military, whose members are generally keen to be supported by civilian development programmes in efforts to bring lasting stability to the Sahel region. On the AFC side, as a unit that has specialised on conflicts and crises since 2008, the CCC is also a structural enabler for WGA and one that is becoming increasingly important for providing topical support to operational programmes and projects.

On the other hand, disablers of a WGA are to be almost randomly located all along the cross-departmental spectrum. For example, there are many civil servants working in silos and in a very traditionally bureaucratic way who sometimes – and particularly during recent years – have been reluctant to be forced to 'mingle' with military affairs.

According to my own experience, another obstacle to implementing a WGA can be found among development practitioners at the lower and middle levels. A rather common feeling among them, either in the field or at the headquarters, is that they already have to take into account too many diligence processes when implementing ODA projects, and that they would definitely be overburdened if new WGA-related responsibilities would be added to their existing workload.

A deeper, though less visible problem is a vague but widespread desire to return to silos, so to speak – that is, to abandon coordinated strategies and go back to the traditional system of having independent ministerial departments and agencies. Indeed, this desire for less uniformity can be detected in some slight differences in vocabulary used in various strategic documents. For example, it is 'strategy report' for 2018 (DGM/MEAE 2018), the MEAE's Directorate-general for Global Affairs preferred to use the political term 'fragilité' (fragility). On the other hand, in its strategy-framing document for the same year (AFD 2018), the AFD opted for the more economic term 'vulnerabilité' (vulnerability).

An additional and quite structural obstacle to fully operationalising a WGA in France is the lack of parliamentary and/or civil society involvement in actually conceptualising and implementing such an approach. This has been particularly emphasised by an official working paper commissioned by the prime minister and submitted in August 2018 by Hervé Berville, a young development practitioner of African origin who is a member of parliament from President Macron's party (Berville 2018). Well covered by the media, military operations in the Sahel have become an object of both national pride and suspicion as well as a common topic of heated public discussion in France. However, as Berville pointed out, ODA does not enjoy widespread popular support, it is still very technical and uncoordinated, and it is not sufficiently monitored or evaluated. Furthermore, a distinctive feature of the critiques and recommendations in Berville's report focus on European rather than strictly French solutions. For example, in the third of his 36 'propositions', Berville calls for the establishment of a new European commissioner in charge of the "Europe-Africa partnership".

The Berville Report was briefly mentioned and praised by President Macron in the speech he delivered to French ambassadors at the Elysée Palace on 27 August 2018. A new law on development assistance is on the (very packed) 2019 agenda of the parliament, and there is growing pressure to review immigration and ODA policies on both the national and EU levels. However, it is unlikely that any new WGA structures will emerge in France in the near future.

5 | Conclusions

Since the turn of the 21st century, France has certainly made progress in terms of developing its WGA strategy for mitigating crises and conflict situations in less developed countries, mostly in the former

French colonial territories of West Africa now referred to as the Sahel. Still, the government's current WGA system is incomplete, loosely implemented and concentrated at the top, and it has a shallow conceptual and procedural grounding within the various departmental structures.

Given these circumstances, the external observer is led to question the hypothesis that a WGA which is regulated in a manner that is more formalised and thus more independent of the respective actors will be more likely to give rise to synergies and reduce or avoid any friction losses. However, France's experiences with its national 'approche intégrée' version of a WGA seems to argue against this hypothesis. Indeed, the country has been able to smoothly implement responses to crises and conflicts using a policy that is exclusively managed from the top by a highly restricted group of political decision-makers rather than through a cross-governmental consensus among middle-rank civils servants and military officers who are supposed to produce a regulated WGA restricted to the '3 D's' (diplomacy, defence, development) and supported by procedural documents with binding stipulations regarding actions.

Regarding France's rationale for adopting its 'approche intégrée,' it would seem that the aim is more geared towards making the decision-making process as tight and streamlined as possible for the president, who is head of both the civilian state and the army, than towards institutionalising a formal set of administrative practices. In support of this argument, one can point to the non-compulsory nature of the 2018 CICDE WGA handbook of practical regulations for military officers in the theatre of war as well as its quite limited influence outside defence circles. One can also detect in places a strong reluctance to accept the technocratic jargon associated with the debate around WGAs. For example, one senior diplomat interviewed for this report stressed that he was proud to play his part in a traditional and broadly defined 'approche intégrée', but that he would strongly reject any WGA instructions in the form of what he compared to "novlangue", the French translation of 'newspeak', the term George Orwell used in his 1949 novel Nineteen Eighty-Four for what the Cambridge Dictionary defines as a "language used by politicians and government officials that is intentionally difficult to understand and does not mean what it seems to mean and is therefore likely to confuse or deceive people."

Such a non-bureaucratic and politically dominated option is particularly visible in France's WGA practice in several contrasting features of the whole system. This first and most striking one is that, since the process of forming permanent WGA structures was started in the last decade, they have been limited to the Ministry of Defence (with its CICDE) and the AFD (with its CCC), both of which are small units and no more than in-house thinktanks. Tellingly, the Ministry of Foreign Affairs has never considered establishing an analogous body.

One should note that a group of civil servants and military officials did give thought to the possibility of introducing 3D 'conflict pools' like those of the British (discussed above). Nevertheless, despite increasing external security threats, nothing concrete has come of this in the political or administrative contexts of France under the last four presidents. Under President Macron, the one and only effective and wider-ranging WGA arrangement has been the joint Sahel task forces, a temporary and strictly ad hoc arrangement, as was the more informal Africa network under Hollande's presidency.

Another indication that France's WGA structure is not fully mature is the fact that there continues to be a strong separation between the country's diplomatic/military sphere and the development-assistance sector, as their various agents have unequal access to classified intelligence and/or scripted 'diplomatic notes' (NDIs).

A persistent and dominant feature is that France's WGA strategy tends to be presented as being fundamentally more pragmatic than conceptual both at home (by its actors and the political and administrative classes in Paris) and abroad. The persistent of this attitude regardless of the party in power (in addition to budgetary restrictions) might explain the disconnect between developing a WGA strategy and actually implementing it. For example, although a large set of goals have been clearly identified (especially for the Sahel and West Africa), the human resources specifically allocated to coordinating the implementation of these goals along the whole process have been extremely limited. In fact, as mentioned above, there are only 20 to 30 people permanently tasked with WGA-related issues in all the ministerial departments and the AFD. What's more, the presidential diplomatic team, which is in charge of ensuring the coherence of upper-level decision-making together with the military advisers in the president's 'maison militaire', is notoriously understaffed.

Finally, another limit to an effective WGA in France is the fact that parliament is kept out of the decision-making loop. This major feature of the Firth Republic's system is a legacy of the 'monarque républicain' style of governance of General De Gaulle. Such an attitude persists to this day. As one interviewee pointed out when discussing the specific issue of (the lack of) cooperation or coordination with parliament: "This is not our culture."

6 | Reference list

AFD (Agence francaise de devéloppement) (2018). *Strategy –Vulnerabilities to Crises and Resilience 2017–2021*. Paris: AFD. www.afd.fr/ sites/afd/files/2019-04-04-34-15/strategy-vulnerabilities-to-crises-resilience-afd-2017-2021.pdf.

Berville, Hervé (2018). *Un monde commun, un avenir pour chacun. Rapport sur la modernisation de la politique partenariale de développement et de solidarité internationale*. Paris: Assemblée nationale. www.ladocumentationfrancaise.fr/var/storage/rapports-publics/18 4000579.pdf.

CICDE (Centre interarmées de concepts, de doctrines et d'expérimentations) (2018). La contribution des armees à l'approche globale dans la prévention et la gestion de crise extérieure. Doctrine interarmées DIA-3.4 AG(2018). No. 124/ARM/CICDE/NP du 7. Paris: Ministère des Armées. www.cicde.defense.gouv.fr/images/docum entation/DIA/20181207_NP_DIA-3.4_AG-2018-VF-signee.pdf.

DGM/MEAE (Directorate-General for Global Affairs, Culture, Education and International Development/French Ministry for Europe and Foreign Affairs) (2018). *Prevention, Resilience and Sustainable Peace (2018–2022): A Comprehensive Approach to the Fragilization of States and Societies*. Paris: MEAE. www.diplomatie.gouv.fr/IMG/ pdf/meae_strategie_fragilites_en_bat_web_cle497968-1.pdf.

OECD (Organisation for Economic Co-operation and Development) (2006). *Whole of Government Approaches in Fragile States*. Paris: OECD. www.oecd.org/dac/conflict-fragility-resilience/docs/378262 56.pdf.

OECD (2007). *Principles for Good International Engagement in Fragile States & Situations*. Paris: OECD. www.oecd.org/dac/conflict-frag ility-resilience/docs/38368714.pdf.

OECD (2018). *OECD Development Co-operation Peer Reviews: France.* Paris: OCDE. www.oecd.org/publications/oecd-development-co-operation-peer-reviews-france-2018-9789264302679-en.htm.

UN (United Nations) (2019). Joint Force of the Group of Five for the Sahel. Report of the Secretary-General. 6 May 2019. New York: UN Security Council. https://reliefweb.int/sites/reliefweb.int/files/resources/S_2019_371_E.pdf.

Germany

Stefani Weiss

1 | Introduction

Germany did not begin addressing the issue of policy coherence in its responses to external crises and conflict management until the late 1990s. Thus, the government was rather late to jump on a train that had already started a long journey within the UN, EU or OECD-DAC frameworks and that had resulted in advanced concepts in the UK and the Netherlands (Weiss, Spanger and van Meurs 2010). Thereafter, Germany's 'networked approach', as it is now called, evolved in two phases, each reacting to profound changes in the security environment. In the beginning, the agenda was driven by the many secessionist and civil wars that followed in the wake of the Cold War and, in particular, the threat of international terrorism so vividly embodied by 9/11. Then, in the mid-2010s, the rise of the Islamic State and the wars in Syria and Iraq, in particular, drew fresh attention to this issue. The ensuing so-called migration crisis, which prompted Germany to take in roughly 1 million refugees in 2015, made conditions in Africa the focus of political and public attention in addition to putting the government under massive pressure to limit the flow of refugees and migrants.

Germany's almost unconditional supra- and multilateral orientation has also had a strong influence on the country's coherence agenda and its priorities. For the Federal Ministry of Defence (BMVg), the strategy developments within NATO – which adopted its own 'Comprehensive Approach' in 1999 to justify out-of-area operations to manage crises and conflicts – were essential. For its part, the Federal Ministry for Economic Cooperation and Development (BMZ) closely followed the related discussions within the United Nations Development Programme (UNDP) and the OECD's Development Co-operation Directorate (OECD-DAC). The latter's work on fragile states and its recommendations on the 'humanitarian-development-peace nexus', to which Germany contributed, were of particular importance. On the other hand, the conceptual thinking of Germany's Federal Foreign Office (AA) was guided by the security and peace strategies adopted in the EU, OSCE and UN, which Germany, as a member of these organisations, has undertaken to implement.

Germany has adopted a rather instrumentalist approach to joining multilateral efforts to respond to conflicts and crises. The reasons for this can be found in two casually related factors: a mindset forged by historical events and concrete constitutional limitations that this mindset gave rise to in the immediate postwar years.

Regarding the first factor, Germany has been described as a "post-heroic society" that rejects military values and, ultimately, heroism (Muenkler 2015). Indeed, the pledge 'Never again war, never again Auschwitz' is deeply engrained in the collective consciousness and severely limits the use of force other than in territorial self-defence (Weiss 2016). Such sentiments have made Germany's federal government feel obliged to comply with the 'do no harm' principle. The first fundamental policy shift (or watershed moment) in the German postwar doctrine only came about with the first deployment of German troops outside of NATO, during the Kosovo War in the late 1990s. Externally, embracing a strategy of policy coherence was viewed as useful for showing Germany's international partners that it was willing to take on more responsibilities. And, domestically, the strong emphasis that this approach laid on peacebuilding and the civilian side of conflict management made it easier to frame to a public reluctant to see its soldiers back in action abroad.

Turning to the second factor, one can say that the shadow of history does not only manifests itself in German society's widespread rejection of everything military. At the instigation of the Allied occupying powers, the German constitution (or Basic Law) contains a multitude of checks and balances whose impact reaches all the way to embrace attempts to pursue a networked approach. In order to prevent any renewed concentration of power – and, thus, the possibility of its abuse – the departmental principle (Ressortprinzip) gives federal ministers a very large degree of autonomy. No chancellor can command his or her ministers to do anything, and the chancellor's authority to issue directives does not change this fundamentally.

What's more, Germany's system of proportional representation legally reinforces this legislative effort to prevent any concentration of power by making it practically impossible to gain an absolute majority while at the same time granting small and medium-sized parties a right to participate in politics (provided they surpass a relatively low hurdle). As a result, postwar Germany has always been governed by coalitions of parties rather than any single party. However, as another result, the ministries of foreign affairs (AA), development (BMZ) and defence (BMVg), which are the most important bodies for a networked approach, have never been in the hands of a single party, which in turn creates a political environment that effectively promotes rivalry rather than cooperation. Furthermore, the distribution of ministries along party lines during coalition-forming negotiations is also the reason why the chancellor's authority to issue directives is a blunt sword. In fact, once drawn, the result is almost inevitably the collapse of the governing coalition.

2 | What policies have been developed to further policy coherence?

Strictly speaking, Germany's coherence agenda and its government's efforts to maintain and improve its capacities to respond to external crises and conflicts has developed as an elaborate method rather than a distinct policy or group of policies. Before diving into the documents that explicitly formulate this method, one should note that Germany's overall approach is based on the supposition that the country will only keep pace with the increasingly complex and multidimensional security challenges and threats if two prerequisites are met: First, supra- and multinational cooperation must be intensified. And, second, a security policy structure must be developed at the national level that goes beyond the traditional (and traditionally separate) foreign, development and defence policy portfolios by integrating all the relevant policies.

In specific terms, the history of Germany's networked approach begins with a one-pager in 2000. In that year, the governing coalition formed by the Social Democrats and the Green Party, which had taken on (federal) government responsibility for the first time, adopted the Comprehensive Concept of the Federal Government on Civilian Crisis Prevention, Conflict Resolution and Post-Conflict Peace-Building (Federal Government of Germany 2000), which laid foundations for Germany's approach that are still valid today. Based on a broad understanding of security that encompassed political, economic, ecological and social aspects, it committed Germany to the concept of "human security" (ibid.: 84).

It then took another four years before this approach was fleshed out even more with the Action Plan: Civilian Crisis Prevention, Conflict Resolution and Post-Conflict Peace-Building (Federal Government of Germany 2004). The political goal of this plan was to strengthen the preventive orientation of Germany's contributions to peace, security and development with a view to reducing the risks of crisis-prone developments and to thereby minimising the need to engage in military interventions – which was of paramount importance to Germany for the reasons discussed above. This was to be achieved in two ways: by establishing cross-departmental structures involving all ministries and by using their respective tools in a more harmonised way. The resulting policy approach encompasses conflict management before the outbreak of violence, crisis management and post-conflict rehabilitation (i.e. state-building). Notably, peace enforcement was not dealt with explicitly. Furthermore, the action plan calls also calls for improving strategies, structures and capabilities, particularly in response to inter-state conflicts, state disintegration and fragility, asymmetric wars with non-state actors, and terrorism. With a typically German kind of thoroughness, the paper formulated 163 different actions to develop the approach.

The subsequent development of Germany's approach is consistently marked by a grappling with the question of how the country can reconcile its values-based peace orientation with the security policy requirements that have come to the fore. In the years that followed the 2004 action plan, the BMZ issued a series of strategy papers that elaborated on the nexus between peace, development and security in addition to highlighting the need to address the structural causes of conflict in the broadest sense. What's more, guidelines and methods for conflict-sensitive development cooperation geared to local social, societal and economic conditions were adopted.

The preliminary conclusion of this first phase was reached with the publication of the White Paper 2006 on German Security Policy and the Future of the Bundeswehr (BMVg 2006), which should not be confused with a national security strategy. Section 1.4 of the paper, titled 'Networked Security', essentially repeats the points of the 2004 action plan, thereby underlining its importance for guiding Germany's coherence policy.

The second phase of establishing the political and administrative framework for Germany's policy-coherence ambitions starts in 2016 with the publication of the White Paper on German Security Policy and the Future of the Bundeswehr (Federal Government of Germany 2016). The following year saw the publication of the German government's 15th development policy report (BMZ 2017) and, more importantly, the Guidelines on Preventing Crises, Resolving Conflicts, Building Peace (Federal Government of Germany 2017), which replaced the action plan from 2004.

The new white paper (Federal Government of Germany 2016) includes a careful analysis of the security environment and identifies a broad spectrum of challenges and risks. The fact that most of them are non-military in nature and cannot be dealt with by force underlined the need to implement a coherence agenda, and the government renewed its pledge to further develop networked action and to optimise its implementation. To do so, the paper highlights four fields of action: strengthening the political working and decision-making structures of the federal government on the central issues of German foreign and security policy; expanding the government's abilities to analyse and evaluate by networking situation centres; intensifying the exchange of personnel among ministries; and promoting the joint training of governmental and non-governmental actors for action in the entire crisis cycle.

The guidelines (Federal Government of Germany 2017) flesh out the areas of action identified in the 2016 white paper, particularly regarding the issues of joint analysis as well as strategic and operative planning. They are meant to provide additional guidance to the government in its efforts to promote peace while focusing on how best to implement the concrete policy objectives set out in the UN's Agenda 2030. In particular, the guidelines spell out specific measures to promote economic development, employment and social security in Africa as well as in the host countries of refugees. In addition, the

German government pledges to provide NATO and EU missions with capabilities across the entire spectrum – a commitment that the BMVg was presumably allowed to insert into the text – and to support the further development of the CSDP.

Like its predecessor, the 2004 action plan, the 2017 guidelines primarily focus on civilian fields of action and instruments for conflict prevention and post-conflict management, such as peace mediation, security-sector reform, strengthening the rule of law, and support for reconciliation. To this end, three inter-ministerial working groups were established to draft sectoral strategies and to lay the conceptual foundations to be shared by all ministries. After completing their tasks, these three working groups published three strategy papers in autumn 2019 titled Interministerial Strategy to Support Security Sector Reform (SSR) in the Context of Crisis Prevention, Conflict Resolution and Peacebuilding (Federal Government of Germany 2019a), Strategy of the Federal Government for promoting the rule of law in the fields of crisis prevention, conflict resolution and peacebuilding (Federal Government of Germany 2019b), and Interministerial Strategy to Support 'Dealing with the Past and Reconciliation (Transitional Justice)' in the Context of Preventing Crisis, Resolving Conflicts and Building Peace (Federal Government of Germany 2019c).

The guidelines also aimed to more closely dovetail instruments for early warning, to improve knowledge management (particularly in the field of fragile statehood), and to introduce systematic monitoring and evaluation processes. Furthermore, it undertook to draw up practical guidelines for principles of action (e.g. the 'do no harm' principle) to ensure that international quality standards are applied in all ministries. Work on the practical guidelines was also completed in summer 2019, and was published in the autumn as Operations Manual: Interministerial Approach to Preventing Crises, Resolving Conflicts and Building Peace (Federal Government of Germany 2019d).

With the 2017 guidelines, the government once again set out a large number (60) of specific and far-reaching commitments. This is admittedly fewer than the 163 commitments in the 2004 action plan. However, it is now easier to verify whether the government is complying with its obligations, as the commitments are separately listed in a special annex rather than being scattered throughout the document. Given that the guidelines are fairly new, their testing still lies ahead.

The first implementation review is expected after four years and should be presented by the government in 2021.

3 | Who are the main actors involved in cooperating in a WGA?

In the many documents that have underpinned Germany's approach and have helped to continue developing it, there is not a single, standardised nomenclature regarding the unified approach under discussion. Instead, and even though all of them officially come from a single source (i.e. the federal government), the documents bear the signature of the specific ministry (or sometimes ministries) they originated in. The range of terms used have included, among others, the modifiers "cross-departmental" and "networked" and the noun "whole-of-government approach" (WGA). For example, the 2017 guidelines (Federal Government of Germany 2017), which is the most recent related document, introduces "inter-ministerial" for national-level coordination whereas the multilateral dimension is captured under the heading "international partnerships". Last but not least, in the coalition agreement of the current 'grand coalition' government (Federal Government of Germany 2018: 20), the concept is summarised under "comprehensive and networked approach", which makes this phrase seem to be the term that all ministries and the ruling parties (CDU, CSU and SPD) have been able to agree upon.

This phenomenon of having too many cooks in the nomenclature kitchen, so to speak, hints at just how coherent (or incoherent) a coherence policy might get in Germany. The decentralised federal administration grants ministries a high degree of autonomy in terms of management, policymaking and implementation. In this system of diffuse leadership, even the Chancellery is only the primus inter pares. In other words, despite being the most important body for coordination, its steering powers are weak in terms of execution. However, whenever responsibilities for policies are shared and relate to cross-cutting issues, decision-making relies exclusively on cooperation and negotiation regarding which procedural rules of the federal government will apply. To make this process run more smoothly, there are two inter-departmental coordination mechanisms. The first mechanism is somewhat negative, as it enshrines what is commonly known as turf battling. In this case, policies are developed in one ministry, then successively checked and amended by other ministries, and then adopted (or not) in the federal cabinet. The second, which is more ambitious as well as used to a certain extent in the realm of crisis and conflict management, is positive in that it involves jointly drafting policies in specially established inter-departmental formations.

Despite the lack of consistence terminology discussed above, it is nevertheless evident that all German federal ministries that have traditionally been involved with external affairs have embraced the coherence agenda and are actively participating in further developing the approach. Federal ministries dealing with justice, education, the environment, health, social and cultural issues, migration, economic matters, food, gender and trade policies are also included, as the related documents underline through many cross-sectoral references. In fact, all ministries have been invited to join the Interministerial Steering Group for Civilian Crisis Prevention, which has been the central coordination structure of the networked approach since it was launched by the action plan of 2004 (Federal Government of Germany 2004).

The AA plays a prominent role in the triad of the traditional external actors. All crisis- and conflict-related issues as well as related cooperation with other ministries are centred in the AA. The Directorate-General for Humanitarian Assistance, Crisis Prevention, Stabilisation and Post-Conflict Reconstruction, created in March 2015 after a review of German foreign policy, is in charge of these tasks. This so-called Directorate-General S (D-G S) has 150 diplomats and a considerably increased annual budget of EUR 3 billion at its disposal (which also includes humanitarian aid). Unlike before, the AA now has an outright operative role within the new coherence policy framework in that it designs and implements its own projects. These projects focus on front-loaded stabilisation measures lasting a maximum of one year, which allows for an immediate and likewise more political reaction. The operational role now assumed by the AA serves two purposes at once: In addition to being able to take early action before a crisis manifests itself, it aims to prove to its international partners that Germany is meeting their demands to take on more responsibility. What's more, the AA has established the offices of special representative for crisis prevention and one for humanitarian aid within the D-G S to enhance the public visibility of its policies.

When it comes to international commitments and coordination with the EU, the picture is not quite so simple. For obvious reasons, the AA's European Directorate-General is in charge of overseeing and coordinating all EU-related policies. It has a special unit for foreign and security policy and crisis prevention (which, of course, raises the question of how this unit relates to the new D-G S unit for crisis prevention). Then there is the Political Directorate-General 2, whose EUCOR unit is tasked with coordinating CFSP and CSDP policies as well as interactions with three Brussels-based organisations: the European Union's Political and Security Committee (PSC), the European Commission's Directorate-General for External Relations (RELEX), and the Foreign Affairs Council (FAC) of the Council of the European Union. Contrary to what one would expect, responsibility for all matters related to the EU's integrated approach to external crises and conflict management is bundled in this political directorate-general rather than in the DG-S.

Among the AA's actors is the Centre for International Peace Operations (ZIF), which is the ministry's implementing organisation for recruiting, training, preparing, deploying and supporting civilian experts for peace operations, such as observing elections, mediation and democracy promotion. At present, the non-profit company has a pool of over 1,000 experts.

The civilian orientation of German crisis responses has long given the Federal Ministry for Economic Cooperation and Development (BMZ) a key role in managing peacebuilding and human-security efforts. It has done so by taking a long-term, structural approach and by developing tailor-made budget lines and a sophisticated administrational structure, such as its own crisis early warning system. Since 1999, it has maintained its own pool of experts, the Civil Peace Service (ZFD). Together with the GIZ, Germany's society for international cooperation, it also commands a long-established technical implementing organisation, whose over 20,000 members are active in 120 countries worldwide. Without question, the BMZ has the greatest experience and resources available to design and implement projects aimed at combating poverty, building social and economic infrastructure, or promoting human rights, democracy and the rule of law. Furthermore, the BMZ recently overhauled its structures and created a whole new directorate-general, called 'Marshall Plan with Africa: Displacement and Migration', in the belief that conflict prevention is best served by fighting the root causes of conflict and migration. This directorate-general also houses the division (223: Peace and Security, Disaster Risk Management) responsible for all aspects of networked security policy, which represents the BMZ on the Interministerial Steering Group for Civilian Crisis Prevention (discussed above).

The primacy of the German approach's civilian orientation to crisis and conflict management has (as expected) had the opposite effect on the Federal Ministry of Defence (BMVg), which has been rather sidelined. Nevertheless, its contributions to Germany's prevention approach have increased over the years in the area of security-sector reform (SSR) and post-conflict reconstruction, most recently with the just published strategy on these issues (Federal Government of Germany 2019b). In fact, owing to its roughly three decades of deployments on multilateral missions abroad, the BMVg is perhaps the ministry that requires the least convincing regarding the usefulness of a coherence approach. In terms of soldiers deployed and mission duration, the provincial reconstruction teams (PRTs) in Afghanistan stand out. However, these were under the command of civilian organisations rather than the armed forces (the Bundeswehr).

The white papers of both 2006 (BMVg 2006) and 2016 (Federal Government of Germany 2016) place the Bundeswehr unconditionally within the larger context of an increasingly networked security architecture in which military instruments take a back seat to civilian ones. Of note is the fact that the 2016 white paper talks more about the need for civil-military coordination than does the 2017 development report (BMZ 2017). Furthermore, with the Centre for Civil-Military Cooperation of the Bundeswehr in Nienburg, Lower Saxony, the BMVg has created its own competence centre for civil-military cooperation in missions abroad. The centre supports a wide range of similar initiatives on both the multinational and civil society levels. An example of the former is its annual hosting of NATO's biggest CIMIC exercise ('Joint Cooperation'), and an example of the latter is the centre's recent engagement in the 'Common Effort Community' network.

In the course of implementing the networked approach, the BMVg has also changed its ministerial setup. In Political Department 1, which deals with security and defence policy as well as the management of all directorate-generals of the BMVg, a separate unit (Pol I 5) has been created for networking security measures and interacting with academia and civil society. In addition, two units have been set up in Political Department 2, which focuses on strategy development, operations and arms control. The Pol II 1 unit deals explicitly with the basics of networked security policy and represents the BMVg in the Interministerial Steering Group for Civilian Crisis Prevention. The second unit (Pol II 5) deals with the Enable and Enhance Initiative (discussed in greater detail below).

Let us now turn from horizontal inter-ministerial cooperation to vertical coordination involving Germany's lower house of parliament (the Bundestag) and civil society. Germany's constitution gives the Bundestag a strong position in foreign and security policy. For example, without a mandate from the Bundestag, the Bundeswehr cannot take part in missions abroad. Politically, however, this position is rather weak, as the public and the media (the direction of causality can be debated) have tended to show little interest in foreign and security policy issues. Indeed, it must be stressed that political careers in Germany are made (and broken) in the realm of domestic politics. In any case, since 2010, parliamentary monitoring and control of Germany's coherence agenda has been exercised by the Subcommittee on Civilian Crisis Prevention, Conflict Management and Integrated Action. Perhaps due to its small size, the subcommittee seems to have developed a working relationship that transcends mere party allegiance. For example, in its hearings, it has presented a very united front to members of the executive branch and, in doing so, it has also indirectly contributed to fostering more inter-ministerial coordination in preparation for such hearings.

Turning to civil society, for historical reasons, the peace movement has been particularly strong in Germany. Its political roots lie in the environmental Green Party and the far-left Left Party, but also in the centre-left Social Democratic Party (SPD). Strictly speaking, one should speak of distinct development and peace movements. However, since the objectives of both movements overlap for the most part in terms of advocating a purely values-based peace policy and rejecting force as an acceptable means in conflict transformation, one can speak of a single 'peace community' organised into two major platforms: the umbrella organisation of development and humanitarian aid NGOs in Germany (VENRO) and the German Platform for Peaceful Conflict Management. Furthermore, the churches play a particularly prominent role in the developmental organisations. Indeed, their influence on the framing of Germany's coherence approach has been

– and will continue to be – both far-reaching and profound, and the 'rebranding' of the German approach from 'networked security' to a more neutral and peace-friendly 'networked approach' can primarily be attributed to their lobbying. In addition, there are a number of thinktanks with close ties to the 'peace community'. Their research likewise focuses on the peaceful resolution of conflicts and arms control. What's more, there is not a (visible) 'strategic community', such as the one used to characterise Anglo-Saxon discourses on peace and security.

4 | How does your country operationalise a WGA?

As already mentioned, the autonomy that the German constitution confers on the federal ministries unquestionably has an impact on how they work together. Rather than replacing established practices, the networked approach as well as the new structures and procedures that it has created merely complement them. Indeed, they are intended to intensify the exchange of information and to facilitate collaboration and coordination. However, they do not create joint offices, joint training or new joint decision-making procedures that would influence established ministerial prerogatives. This is explicitly highlighted in the introduction of the Operations Manual (Federal Government of Germany 2019d), where we read that the agreed-upon practises and procedures do not invalidate either the departmental principle (Ressortprinzip) or the long-established guidelines under which the BMZ (BMZ 2008) operates in development cooperation. In particular, it says (Federal Government of Germany 2019d: 4): "The principle of ministries, as enshrined in the Basic Law, remains intact. In other words, each federal minister self-sufficiently directs and is accountable for his or her own area of operations." Thus, the greater part of Germany's crisis- and conflict-management policies will continue to be formulated and implemented outside the newly created structures. This concerns day-to-day work as well as dealing with the issue at the highest political level.

The institutional building block of Germany's coherence approach is the Interministerial Steering Group for Civilian Crisis Prevention (Ressortkreis), which was formed in 2004 and is open to all ministries. Also under the new guidelines, this steering group continues to be the working body at the ministerial level of heads of units for information exchange and coordination on all relevant crisis-prevention and conflict-management issues. However, the steering group does not have any operational powers, as the relevant ministries retain their authority to decide on and support the development of respective crisis-prevention capacities within the framework of their respective jurisdictions. Thus, day-to-day business is carried out not within the steering group, but rather by units in the ministries responsible for individual crisis countries or regions, which are usually chaired by the responsible country department or the regional representative of the AA. In addition, the body forms the interface to the roughly 20-person Advisory Board for Civilian Crisis Prevention, which is composed of representatives drawn from civil society, academia and the business community.

In 2012, with the adoption of the first-ever inter-ministerial guidelines 'for a coherent policy of the Federal Government towards fragile states' (AA, BMVg and BMZ 2012), special task forces were set up among the AA, the BMVg and the BMZ. Meetings of these task forces are convened and chaired by the responsible regional commissioner/ envoy of the AA rather than by the recently established D-G S. This is done in coordination with counterparts from the BMVg, the BMZ or other relevant ministries in individual cases. The task forces perform context analyses and coordinate policies for Iraq/Syria/Anti-IS, Libya, Yemen, Somalia, Mali, the Sahel and the Lake Chad region while remaining in close contact with the diplomatic missions on the ground. For Afghanistan and Pakistan, such inter-ministerial working groups already existed beforehand. Rather than having set meeting dates, they convene when doing so is deemed appropriate.

A new body, introduced with the 2017 guidelines (Federal Government of Germany 2017), were the inter-ministerial working groups tasked with developing joint strategies for promoting the rule of law, supporting security-sector reform and dealing with the past/reconciliation. Their respective strategy reports were published in autumn 2019 (Federal Government of Germany 2019a-c). One of the results of this strategy-development process is that the three previous sectoral strategy working groups are to be merged into a cross-strategy working group, which is to begin its work in the course of 2019. It is not yet known whether further inter-ministerial strategy groups are planned to deal with other relevant topics in the field of crisis prevention, conflict management and peacebuilding.

According to the Operations Manual (Federal Government of Germany 2019d: 6), early warning and crisis detection shall be taken care of in a newly established special inter-ministerial 'Horizon Scanning' working group that shall be able to draw on all analytical capacities, including those of the Federal Intelligence Service (BND). Likewise, in the future, departmental analyses are to be regularly shared with other departments and, where this exchange does not lead to a sufficiently shared evaluation of the situation, joint analyses are to be commissioned.

In addition to the above-mentioned formations and on the next-higher ministerial level, the guidelines (Federal Government of Germany 2017) establish the 'Preventing Crises, Resolving Conflicts, Building Peace' inter-ministerial coordinating group, which is composed of the heads of the relevant directorate-generals in the various ministries and is tasked with dealing with the results and recommendations of the Horizon Scanning working group as well as with other outstanding issues that the Interministerial Steering Group for Civilian Crisis Prevention or the task forces and strategy groups could not reach agreement on. The body meets on a quarterly basis as well as when required. In this case, the chair rotates between the Federal Chancellery, the BMVg, the BMZ and the Federal Ministry of the Interior, Building and Home Affairs (BMI).

Outside the framework defined by the guidelines, at the highest level of inter-ministerial coordination, the state secretaries and the head of the Federal Chancellery's Directorate-General 2 (Foreign, Security and Development Policy) meet in various formats to deal with crisis-management issues. One of these formats is the so-called weekly security policy jour fixe, which brings together representatives of the Chancellery with the state secretaries of the AA, the BMI and the BMVg. Another such jour fixe deals with foreign and development policy issues and brings together representatives of the Chancellery, the AA, the BMVg and the BMZ. Additional formats include the Round Table of State Secretaries on Afghanistan and Mali (with representatives from the Chancellery, the Federal Ministry of Finance, the BMI, the AA, the BMVg, the Federal Ministry of Economic Affairs and Energy, the BMZ and the Foreign Intelligence Service) and the

Inter-ministerial Steering Group on Africa at the level of state secretaries and heads of the directorate-generals.

Above all stands the federal cabinet, which has overall responsibility for overseeing coherence policies. The cabinet's Federal Security Council (Bundessicherheitsrat) coordinates the government's security and defence policies and is responsible for approving arms exports. Although its meetings are secret, all publicly visible indications are that the council's efforts are predominantly geared towards arms-export controls rather than coordinating German foreign and security policy. A separate cabinet formation, such as the one recently established for climate protection, does not yet exist for the area of crisis and conflict management.

Furthermore, as explicitly highlighted in the guidelines (Federal Government of Germany 2017) and the sectoral strategy reports (Federal Government of Germany 2019a-c), there are the diplomatic missions abroad, which reportedly play an important role in assessing situations as well as in planning and implementing measures. German embassies have long been staffed with personnel from other ministries. What's more, as the conception of security becomes broader and more cross-cutting, the number of such staff members is growing and the ministries are increasing their involvement in the activities listed above.

Turning now to the issue of culture and training, one can say that the experience which government staff have gained while on assignments abroad has undoubtedly boosted their eagerness and ability to cooperate at home. The exchange of civil servants between ministries also contributes to the latter, as was called for in the 2006 white paper (BMVg 2006) and again underlined in the Operations Manual (Federal Government of Germany 2019d). However, to date, the number of liaison officers exchanged between ministries each year has remained in the single digits.

In the field of training and deploying civilian, police and military personnel, no uniform training schedule or inter-ministerial facilities exist. However, the respective academies of the AA and BMVg appear to have included the networked approach in their curricula, and their future role is highlighted in the Operations Manual as well as by the three sectoral strategy reports (Federal Government of Germany 2019a-d), which echo the need to establish good practices and promote inter-ministerial learning by including the topics of SSR, rule of law and transitional justice in ministry-specific and inter-ministerial training measures. In addition, the AA has added mediation courses to its attaché training, which are provided by the Centre for International Peace Operations (ZIF).

Regarding advanced training, the Federal Academy for Security Policy (BAKS), in particular, offers courses designed to meet these requirements. However, these courses are not compulsory. Together with the BMZ, the BMVg and the BMI, the AA organises an annual seminar for junior staff entitled 'Joint Action in Fragile Contexts'. Training in the field of civil-military cooperation and mission preparation is especially provided by BMVg institutions, such as the aforementioned Centre for Civil-Military Cooperation of the Bundeswehr in Nienburg and the German Armed Forces United Nations Training Centre in Hammelburg, Bavaria, where a two-week course on post-crisis preparation was held for the first time in 2019.

In terms of procedures and budgets, the 2012 inter-ministerial guidelines on fragile states (AA, BMVg and BMZ 2012) set out the first rules of procedure applying to the working level. As a follow-up, the 2017 guidelines (Federal Government of Germany 2017) obliged the government to issue an inter-ministerial practical guide, which was published in autumn 2019 as the Operational Manual (Federal Government of Germany 2019d). The latter stipulates that better coordination is mainly to be achieved in the areas of early warning, policy planning and steering, and monitoring and evaluation. What's more, the procedure for developing future strategies (e.g. via scenario workshops and retreats) was also further elaborated, and decision criteria for dealing with other potential crisis countries and regions were adopted. Nevertheless, all the many procedural improvements for inter-ministerial cooperation set forth in the Operations Manual – whether concerning analysis and needs assessment, joint strategy development, planning, exchange with partner institutions and international organisations, mutual information-sharing and participation in departmental planning, financial contributions to international funds and facilities, or cooperation in government negotiations and international conferences – are still dependent on the discretion and (voluntary) willingness of the respective ministries.

Although under discussion for quite some time and repeatedly demanded by the parliamentary Subcommittee on Civilian Crisis Prevention, Conflict Management and Integrated Action, the Operations

Manual did not introduce a common or pooled budget for crisis and conflict management. The only exception relates to the Enhance and Enable Initiative, whose measures are almost exclusively dedicated to SSR as well as jointly financed and administered by the AA and the BMVg on the basis of a framework agreement concluded in 2015 (BMVg and AA 2019). Nevertheless, the pressure to better harmonise instruments and to pool funding is growing. For example, the first-ever spending review of the Federal Ministry of Finance conducted on the policy area 'Humanitarian aid and transitional aid including the interfaces crisis prevention, crisis response, stabilisation and development cooperation' (BMF 2018) has revealed the many duplications and overlaps between measures implemented by the AA and the BMZ. This inefficient use of budget funds prompted these two ministries to develop a concept for joint analysis and coordinated planning. Whether additional spending reviews will lead to better coordination in other fields is anybody's guess. For now, however, the Operations Manual (Federal Government of Germany 2019d) at least suggests a systematic recording of measures in countries in which several ministries are active. Such a database already exists for Afghanistan. In addition, in accordance with Chapter 5.1 of the Federal Government's Joint Rules of Procedure of the Federal Ministries (GGO) (BMI 2011), it is now envisaged that, in the case of payments to international organisations, the ministry responsible for the organisation in question will involve the other contributing ministries in the preliminary stages.

Furthermore, when it comes to implementation reports and scrutiny, the guidelines (Federal Government of Germany 2017) have established a review process that could serve as a lessons learned process and help to improve policy coherence. This offers parliament and civil society a chance to measure the government by its words and deeds. The parliamentary Subcommittee on Civilian Crisis Prevention, Conflict Management and Integrated Action has already stated that it sees monitoring the implementation of the Operations Manual as one of its primary tasks in the current legislative term. The first implementation report is expected in 2021, and a fundamental overhaul is due four years later. Regarding parliamentary scrutiny, the Free Democratic Party (FDP) launched a governmental inquiry in February 2019 titled 'Strengthening networked action in foreign, security and development' (Deutscher Bundestag 2019). With over

160 questions, the inquiry will force Germany's government to take a position on its performance regarding the entire networked approach. The government's response is expected in late autumn 2019.

5 | Conclusions

For all those who envision tight leadership and clear decision-making structures as key factors behind successful political coherence, the conditions prevailing in Germany must seem like a nightmare. For one thing, there are multiple players and the chancellor, despite being the primus inter pares, must convince rather than command his or her team. On top of that, political processes are protracted, are based on consensus, and end in compromises that often (though not always) do less to achieve the stated goals than to satisfy party and power preferences or even personal vanities.

In the absence of an outright national foreign and security strategy that would establish a fundamental and goal-oriented framework for action, Germany's networked approach still seems to be more about establishing 'an equal footing' or 'a level playing field' among relevant ministries. A case in point is the fact that there are three key documents in the field of crisis and conflict management in external affairs, each of which seems to highlight the specific responsibilities and ambitions of one of the three key players: the foreign (AA), defence (BMVg) or economic cooperation and development (BMZ) ministries.

During the drafting phase of the guidelines on preventing crises, revolving conflicts and building peace (Federal Government of Germany 2017), it became apparent just how much the three leading ministries were still demarcating and asserting their competences and decision-making sovereignty in relation to each other while struggling for recognition and leadership in the process. The BMZ, in particular, but also the BMVg contested the AA's tight grip on coordination among the three bodies. Indeed, both the BMZ and the BMVg saw their contribution to international crisis management as being just as relevant as that of the AA given that the BMZ was implementing the majority of projects on the ground and the BMVg was guaranteeing a secure environment for such efforts. Even the title of the guidelines was long contested. In fact, to ultimately break the logjam, it was made longer so that every ministry could find itself represented, and the word "civil" was deleted so as not to implicitly indicate the absence of the military arm. After all, seeing that the term 'networked security' had already been dropped in favour of the more civilian-sounding 'networked approach', inserting 'civil' would have constituted the second affront to the BMVg.

Despite the ever-growing consensus in Germany that a well-functioning networked approach to crisis and conflict is required, it has yet to be seen to what degree the inter-ministerial coordination bodies – whether reinforced or newly established by the 2017 guidelines – will ultimately succeed in meeting their goals. However, doubts about this success are raised by the fact that the actual day-to-day operational work related to managing external crises and conflicts is primarily carried out outside the newly established framework. Furthermore, the guidelines cannot obscure the fact that their focus is predominately on the civilian side of crisis and conflict management and does not cover the entire conflict cycle. This is in line with Germany's previous involvements in EU-, UN- and NATO-led missions. With the exceptions of the Kosovo and Afghanistan missions, Germany's contributions have predominantly been humanitarian or limited to advisory or support roles, such as monitoring, transport, training or surveillance via air or ship. In all these cases, fewer than 100 civil or military staff were seconded.

These days, however, Germany's engagement is particularly focused on supporting reforms in the military- and civil-security sectors, as is shown by the support it is providing to the ongoing EUTM missions in Mali and Somalia and to the EUAM Ukraine. It can be assumed that Germany will maintain this level of commitment, particularly in the Sahel region, and is prepared to be similarly engaged in the Middle East, as well, should the course be set for ending the wars in Syria or Yemen. What would come as a real surprise (and would constitute a genuine paradigm shift) is if Germany were to take on the risks associated with leadership within the EU, NATO or the UN as well as to engage in peace-enforcing missions. As long as this is not the case, it must be said that Germany is failing to live up to the ambitions it set forth in the 2006 and 2016 white papers on security policy as well as underlined in many official speeches. Instead, the non-holistic nature of its approach shows once again how much the Nazi past still affects today's policymaking. Indeed, despite all the new rhetoric to the contrary, Germany has so far failed to answer the question – and back it up with deeds – of what it means to assume more responsibility in an increasingly crisis-ridden world. Accordingly, the frustration among its partners – not only in the EU and NATO, but also in the UN – is unlikely to vanish anytime soon.

6 | Reference list

AA, BMVg and BMZ (Federal Foreign Office, Federal Ministry of Defence, and Federal Ministry for Economic Cooperation and Development) (2012). Fuer eine koharente Politik der Bundesregierung gegenueber fragilen Staaten – Ressortuebergreifende Leitlinien. www.bmz.de/de/zentrales_downloadarchiv/Presse/leitlinien_fragile_staaten.pdf.

BMF (Federal Ministry of Finance) (2018). Abschlussbericht. Spending Review (Zyklus 2017/2018) zum Politikbereich "Humanitare Hilfe und Uebergangshilfe einschliesslich der Schnittstellen Krisenprae-vention, Krisenreaktion, Stabilisierung und Entwicklungszusammenarbeit." Preliminary notification of the Chairman of the Budget Committee of the German Bundestag, Peter Boehringer, by the Federal Ministry of Finance.

BMI (Federal Ministry of the Interior, Building and Community) (2011). Joint Rules of Procedure of the Federal Ministries (GGO). www.bmi.bund.de/SharedDocs/downloads/EN/themen/moderne-verwaltung/ggo_en.pdf?__blob=publicationFile&v=1.

BMVg (Federal Ministry of Defence) (2006). White Paper 2006 on German Security Policy and the Future of the Bundeswehr. http://responsibilitytoprotect.org/Germany_White_Paper_2006.pdf.

BMVg and AA (Federal Ministry of Defence and Federal Foreign Office) (2019). Die Ertuechtigungsinitiative der Bundesregierung. www.bmvg.de/resource/blob/61338/cd9d85538033514c96f03665fd52e98d/b-02-03-ertuechtigungsinitiative-data.pdf.

BMZ (Federal Ministry for Economic Cooperation and Development) (2008). Guidelines for bilateral Financial and Technical Cooperation with cooperation partners of German development cooperation. www.bmz.de/en/zentrales_downloadarchiv/wege_und_akteure/190221_Guidelines_Financial_and_Technical_Cooperation.pdf.

BMZ (2017). Development as a Future-oriented Peace Policy: The German Government's 15th Development Policy Report. www.bmz.de/en/publications/type_of_publication/information_flyer/information_brochures/Materialie305_development_policy.pdf.

Deutscher Bundestag (2019). Grosse Anfrage der Bundestagsabgeordneten und der Fraktion der FDP. Vernetztes Handeln in der Aussen-, Sicherheits- und Entwicklungspolitik starken. Drucksache 19/8058. 19. Wahlperiode. 27.02.2019. Berlin. http://dipbt.bundestag.de/doc/btd/19/080/1908058.pdf.

Federal Government of Germany (2000). Comprehensive Concept of the Federal Government on Crisis Prevention, Conflict Resolution and Post-Conflict Peace-Building. www.konfliktbearbeitung.net/downloads/file711.pdf (Annex 5).

Federal Government of Germany (2004). Action Plan: Civilian Crisis Prevention, Conflict Resolution and Post-Conflict Peace-Building. www.konfliktbearbeitung.net/downloads/file711.pdf.

Federal Government of Germany (2016). White Paper on German Security Policy and the Future of the Bundeswehr. www.bundeswehr.de/resource/resource/MzEzNTM4MmUzMzMyMmUzMTM1MzMyZTM2MzIzMDMwMzAzMDMwMzAzMDY5NzE3MzM1Njc2NDYyMzMyMDIwMjAyMDIw/2016%20White%20Paper.pdf.

Federal Government of Germany (2017). Guidelines on Preventing Crises, Resolving Conflicts, Building Peace. www.auswaertiges-amt.de/blob/1214246/057f794cd3593763ea556897972574fd/preventing-crises-data.pdf.

Federal Government of Germany (2018). A New Awakening for Europe. A New Dynamic for Germany. A New Solidarity for Our Country: Coalition Agreement between CDU, CSU and SPD. 19th Parliamentary Term. (Unofficial translation of abstracts by the Konrad Adenauer Stiftung). www.kas.de/c/document_library/get_file?uuid=bd41f012-1a71-9129-8170-8189a1d06757&groupId=284153.

Federal Government of Germany (2019a). Interministerial Strategy to Support Security Sector Reform (SSR) in the Context of Crisis Prevention, Conflict Resolution and Peacebuilding. www.auswaertiges-amt.de/blob/2248208/44c6eebba11f48b74243f2434535943d/190917-sicherheitssektorreform-data.pdf.

Federal Government of Germany (2019b). Strategy of the Federal Government for promoting the rule of law in the fields of crisis prevention, conflict resolution and peacebuilding. www.auswaertiges-amt.de/blob/2248210/65a178ff3ed0b537fd08e92b24a2bd7d/190917-rechtsstaatsfoerderung-data.pdf.

Federal Government of Germany (2019c). Interministerial Strategy to Support "Dealing with the Past and Reconciliation (Transitional Justice)" in the Context of Preventing Crisis, Resolving Conflicts and Building Peace. www.auswaertiges-amt.de/blob/2248206/633d49372b71cb6fafd36c1f064c102c/190917-vergangenheitsarbeit-und-versoehnung-data.pdf.

Federal Government of Germany (2019d). Operations Manual: Interministerial Approach to Preventing Crises, Resolving Conflicts and Building Peace. www.bmz.de/en/zentrales_downloadarchiv/themen_und_schwerpunkte/frieden/Praxisleitfaden_EN.PDF.

Muenkler, Herfried (2015). *Kriegssplitter: Die Evolution der Gewalt im 20. und 21. Jahrhundert.* Berlin: Rowohlt.

Puglierin, Jana (2016). Germany's Enable and Enhance Initiative: What is it about? Security Policy Working Paper, No.1/2016. Berlin: Federal Academy for Security Policy. www.auswaertiges-amt.de/blob/285472/0c7879dac682e82c0aed36a98f9d7e93/ertuechtigungsinitiative-bkas-data.pdf.

Weiss, Stefani (2016). "Germany's Security Policy: From Territorial Defense to Defending the Liberal World Order?" In *Newpolitik. German Policy. Translated.*, edited by the Bertelsmann Foundation. Washington, D.C.: Bertelsmann Foundation. www.bertelsmann-stiftung.de/en/publications/publication/did/newpolitik/.

Weiss, Stefani, Hans-Joachim Spanger and Wim van Meurs (eds.) (2010). *Diplomacy, Development and Defense: A Paradigm for Policy Coherence. A Comparative Analysis of International Strategies.* Guetersloh: Verlag Bertelsmann Stiftung. www.bertelsmann-stiftung.de/de/publikationen/publikation/did/diplomacy-development-and-defense-a-paradigm-for-policy-coherence/.

Greece

Giorgos Triantafyllou

1 | Introduction

The global political, economic and security environment is increasingly characterised by complexity and instability, demanding joint efforts to address highly interrelated problems. To that end, the development of a whole-of-government approach (WGA) aims to provide a formula for the effective coordination of actors, both at the national and international levels, in order to maximise the effectiveness of policies and to ensure their coherence when pursuing common objectives.

However, in many countries – including Greece – the concept of WGA has long been an overlooked priority, and it is only recently that they have started taking the steps needed to adopt a WGA in their national policies. For many years, Greece has been characterised by deep-seated departmentalism, with various ministries being responsible for the development and implementation of policies in their respective field. The rigid structures of public institutions have nurtured the perception that different problems should be addressed independently by the responsible ministry or other national authority, while coordination of actors has been very limited and has usually only taken place on an ad hoc basis.

Nevertheless, over the last decade, Greece has had to face two unexpected crises that would challenge this perception, highlighting the need for both horizontal and vertical cooperation aimed at finding common solutions. Indeed, the country's economic breakdown, coupled with an unprecedented influx of refugees, presented a set of problems that no ministry was able to deal with on its own. At the same time, leading international organisations (e.g. the UN, NATO and the OECD) were increasingly making explicit references to a WGA as a useful framework for policy development. Thus, over the last decade, Greece has started to take small, yet obvious steps towards the introduction of the WGA concept at the national level. At present, although there is still a long way to go before Greece will be implementing a WGA on all its internal and external policies, the country offers some tangible evidence that, in certain policy areas, a WGA has begun to underpin both policy development and the operational coordination of the actors involved. The policy areas that provide the most significant indications of a WGA are sustainable development and Greece's participation in CSDP missions and PESCO projects.

2 | What policies have been developed to further policy coherence?

Greece does not have any explicitly formulated WGA policies regarding the management of external crises and conflicts. However, certain evidence exists that either implicitly or explicitly indicates that the county is moving towards the formulation of WGA policies. The best example of such a WGA policy under development stems from Greece's adoption of the 2030 Agenda for Sustainable Development and its 17 Sustainable Development Goals (SDGs), as defines by the UN in 2015. Indeed, in July 2018, the General Secretariat of the Government published a document titled Voluntary National Review on the Implementation of the 2030 Agenda for Sustainable Development (VNR) (General Secretariat of the Government 2018: 15), presenting a detailed account of the progress made over the previous two years toward successfully accomplishing the SDGs at the national level. More precisely, the VNR aimed to: (1) present the institutional mechanism put in place in Greece that ensures the collective political ownership and commitment to accomplish successfully the SDGs and to foster a whole-of-government approach; (2) highlight the national policy and legal framework that incorporates the SDGs, focusing on the eight national priorities for the SDGs; (3) showcase the role played by key stakeholders in the implementation of the SDGs through the adoption of a whole-of-society approach; (4) provide some keys means of implementation that ensure the comprehensive and integrated achievement of the SDGs at all governance levels (national, regional, local); and (5) present the main steps to be taken with regard to the follow-up and review process of the 2030 Agenda and the SDGs.

The VNR builds on Greece's National Strategy for Sustainable Development (NSSD) of 2002 (Ministry for the Environment, Physical Planning and Public Works 2002), which was developed following the adoption of the European Strategy for Sustainable Development in 2001, and which provided the basis for the development of Greece's National Strategy for Sustainable and Just Development 2030 (NSSJD) (Ministry of Economy and Development 2019), drawing from the SDGs of 2015. Unlike the NSSD, the NSSJD presented a truly strategic approach in which sustainable development issues are anchored at the highest political level. Thus, through the VNR, Greece is pursuing policy coherence both horizontally across policy sectors (e.g. economic, industrial, agricultural, tourism-related and cultural) and vertically at all levels of governance (national, regional and local).

Highlighting the premise that the successful implementation of the SDGs goes beyond the responsibilities of the central government, the VNR notes that Greece has adopted a "whole-of-society approach" that pays particular attention to ensuring strong stakeholder engagement at all stages (stock-taking, policy design and implementation) as well as to raising awareness at all levels. Most importantly, however, the VNR indicates that the key for successfully implementing the SDGs at the national level will be setting up a robust, long-term institutional mechanism that follows a WGA. This explicit reference to a WGA is the first – and, to date, the only – clear evidence of a WGA concept related to a specific policy in Greece.

Although they do not include an explicit reference to the WGA concept per se, elements of a WGA can also be detected in two other policies. The first relates to Greece's provision of development and humanitarian aid to developing countries as defined by Law 2731/1999 (Government Gazette 1999). This law established the Directorate General of International Development Cooperation (Hellenic Aid) in the Ministry of Foreign Affairs as the competent national authority. While shaping and coordinating Greek development policy, the DG is responsible for (Ministry of Foreign Affairs 2018): (1) coordinating all relevant allocations out of the development budget; (2) submitting proposals on the national development strategy to the Inter-Ministerial Committee for the Organisation and Coordination of International Economic Relations; (3) coordinating, implementing, promoting and monitoring humanitarian and development projects and activities to the benefit of developing countries; (4) representing the country in matters of international development at the relevant international fora and organisations (e.g. the EU, the OECD-DAC and the UN); (5) evaluating the humanitarian/development project proposals submitted thereto by NGOs and other institutions, and monitoring their implementation; (6) collaborating closely with competent authorities of the public and private sector, aiming at the effective administration of national development funds, the complementarity of projects and activities, and the coherence of national policies; (7) compiling statistical data on bilateral and multilateral official development assistance and preparing annual reports for Greece's parliament and the OECD-DAC; (8) proposing development policies in the context of the New European Consensus on Development; and (9) focusing on important development frameworks and submitting the relevant findings and recommendations to the minister for foreign affairs. To successfully perform this wide array of tasks, Hellenic Aid must continuously and closely interact and coordinate with many different national and international actors, which in turn results in what can be viewed as an indirect adherence to the WGA concept.

The second policy relates to the recently reinforced attempts to strengthen Greece's defence industry by participating in the EU's Permanent Structured Cooperation (PESCO). At the European level, the WGA in this area was explicitly championed by the EU Global Strategy of 2016, which has been strongly supported by Greece. According to the General Directorate of National Defence Policy and International Relations (GDNDPIR) of the Greek Ministry of National Defence (MoD), Greece has welcomed PESCO as a unique opportunity to increase the capabilities of its security forces through the country's participation in multilateral projects related to technology, research and development. However, the clearest indication that Greece is moving towards adopting a WGA in this policy area is the emphasis that the MoD has placed on the establishment of a national framework for the "compulsory" participation of small and medium-sized enterprises in Greece's defence industry in the PESCO projects in which Greece is involved (Ministry of Defence 2018). At present, together with France, Germany and Italy, Greece is among the EU member states most actively participating in such projects. While it is leading five PECSO projects, it is participating in an additional nine projects. As Greece moves towards adopting a WGA, the MoD aims to engage with all enterprises in the Greek defence industry – both public and private – to create economies of scale, halt the brain drain of Greek scientists, and strengthen the capacity-building of the Greek security forces.

3 | Who are the main actors involved in cooperating in a WGA?

As already mentioned, Greece has no explicitly formulated WGA policies on external crises and conflicts. However, the country actively participates in many EU CSDP, NATO and UN missions (e.g. EUFOR Althea, EULEX Kosovo, EUAM Ukraine, EUMM Georgia, EUTM Mali, EUNAVFOR Atalanta, EUNAVFOR MED Sophia, UNIFIL, KFOR, RSM Afghanistan and Operation Active Endeavour), providing both military and civilian personnel, depending on the mission's nature.

At the national level, the main actors responsible for Greece's participation in international missions are the government, the Ministry of Foreign Affairs (MFA), and the Ministry of National Defence (MoD). Elements of a WGA can be found in the cooperation between the MFA and MoD at two different levels: first, at the ministerial level, through the direct communication of the responsible ministers; and, second, at the directorate-general level, between the General Directorate of National Defence Policy and International Relations (GDND-PIR) of the MoD and the various competent directorates of the MFA, depending on the international mission's framework (e.g. the EU, the UN or NATO). Moreover, regarding the participation of Greece in non-military CSDP missions, a WGA-like coordination is in place between the MFA, the MoD and the Ministry for Citizen Protection. Indeed, the inter-ministerial decision 1027/4/26d of 2010 between the three ministries stipulates that, in close coordination with the MFA and the MoD, the Ministry for Citizen Protection is responsible for selecting police personnel for civilian CSDP missions, when necessary (Government Gazette 2010). Other actors at the national level cooperate in a WGA-like manner, albeit not in relation to external conflicts and crises.

In the policy area of migration, Presidential Decree 123 of 2016 established the Ministry of Migration Policy (MMP) to address the ongoing migration crisis (Government Gazette 2016). Creating the MMP, whose responsibilities had previously been part of the mandate of the Ministry of Interior, was prompted by the realisation that coordinating the wide array of actors involved in the management of migrant populations in Greece demanded a dedicated authority that would assume full responsibility. Indeed, following a WGA on migration policy, the MMP is responsible for coordination among ministries (horizontal coordination) as well as coordination with regional and local authorities, international and national NGOs, and all other civil society actors (vertical coordination). Following the national elections of July 2019, the MMP became an integral part of the Ministry for Citizen Protection (Government Gazette 2019a). Although the government claimed that this would ensure more direct coordination between the relevant agencies dealing with migration, the opposition has criticised this decision as an attempt to treat migration primarily as a security concern.

Regarding sustainable development, a policy area on which Greece has recently been placing particular emphasis, the General Secretariat of the Government is the main actor for the WGA-like coordination of all actors involved. In the relevant inter-ministerial committee, all the ministries of the government are represented by their dedicated focal points at the level of directorate or directorate general. The WGA of the committee's work is reinforced by the participation of other actors, such as the Hellenic Statistical Authority (ELSTAT) and the office of the deputy prime minister of Greece. Moreover, also in the area of development, the Directorate General of International Development Cooperation (Hellenic Aid) is the responsible agency for coordinating the efforts of national and international actors to provide humanitarian and development support overseas.

Finally, on the policy area of migration management, there are ongoing initiatives that indicate the application of a WGA at the local level, both horizontally (between municipalities) and vertically (between municipalities and civil society organisations that provide services to refugees). The most illustrative example of a WGA at the municipal level is the Athens Coordination Centre for Migrant and Refugee Issues (ACCMR), an organisation created by the City of Athens to map the different actors that provide support to migrants and refugees as well as to effectively coordinate their activities.

4 | How does your country operationalise a WGA?

Although they are not explicitly related to external conflicts and crises, there are various structures in place in Greece that bring together various authorities and actors and facilitate their cooperation and coordination in a WGA-like manner. The most well-known of those structures, the Government Council for Foreign Affairs and Defence (KYSEA), is the supreme decision-making body on issues of foreign policy and national defence in Greece, and its decisions are binding for all participating agencies. It was first established in 1986 and although its composition has changed many times, at the time of writing (July 2019) it comprised: the prime minister (serving as chairman); the minister of foreign affairs; the minister for citizen protection; the minister for national defence; the minister for shipping and island policy; and the chief of staff of the Hellenic National Defence General Staff (Government Gazette 2019b). In practice, the activities and utility of KYSEA have attracted a lot of criticism. For example, contrary to its stated mandate, the council most often limits itself to issues related to promoting or discharging high-ranking military staff rather than making decisions on the full range of policy fields it is responsible for.

Another structure that draws from the principles of a WGA is the National Council for Foreign Policy (NCFP). According to Law 3132/2003, which set the framework for the NCFP's establishment, the NCFP comprises: the minister of foreign affairs (serving as chairman); the chairman of the Standing Committee on National Defence and Foreign Affairs of the Hellenic Parliament; the secretary general of the MFA; the head of the Centre for Analysis and Planning (CAP) of the MFA; two representatives of every political party holding seats in the parliament; and an equal number of foreign policy experts (Government Gazette 2003). The council was first established in 2003 and, unlike the KYSEA, it is responsible for providing guidance and advisory opinions to the Greek government for the strategic framing of the country's foreign policy. The NCFP has also been criticised over time for its failure to act as a genuine advisory body, with the most frequent critique being that it has become merely a channel for the government to inform opposition political parties about its foreign policy decisions.

The General Secretarial for Civil Protection (GSCP) is yet another institutional structure that implements a WGA as it pursues its mission "to design, plan, organise and coordinate actions regarding risk assessment, prevention, preparedness, information and response to natural, technological or other disasters or emergencies, to coordinate rehabilitation operations, to monitor the above actions and to inform the public on these issues" (GSCP 2019). More precisely, the Civil Protection Operations Centre (CPOC), as part of the GSCP, applies a WGA in managing crises and coordinating the personnel of various agencies (e.g. the Armed Forces, the Hellenic Police, the Hellenic Coast Guard, the Hellenic Fire Service and specialised medical staff). Additionally, the GSCP has direct ties to the European Response Coordination Centre (ERCC), which operates in the framework of the European Union Civil Protection Mechanism (EUCPM). If a public authority (whether of Greece, of another country or of an international organisation) calls on Greece to provide assistance, the CPOC applies the procedures for the sending and receiving of international assistance. In doing so, it cooperates with the International Relations, Volunteerism-Training and Publications Directorate of the GSCP in accordance with instructions of the Secretary General for Civil Protection.

In April 2019, Greece's MFA presented a draft bill on the "modernisation of foreign policy" (Ministry of Foreign Affairs 2019), which, among other things, provided the framework for the establishment of a National Security Council (NSC). Doing so represented a long-anticipated step towards the creation of an administrative structure to assume primary responsibility for national security. Although it did not make any explicit reference to a WGA, the draft bill made clear that the NSC would follow a WGA in pursuing its responsibility for "the development of an integrated and functional system of security and crisis management". According to the draft, the NSC would consist of: the prime minister (serving as chairman); the deputy prime minister; the minister of foreign affairs; the minister for citizen protection; the chief of the Hellenic National Defence General Staff; the chairman of the Standing Committee on National Defence and Foreign Affairs of the Hellenic Parliament; the director of the National Intelligence

Service; the secretary general of the MFA; an official from the Head Diplomatic Office of the prime minister's political office; and the national security adviser (serving as the principal rapporteur). The NSC would be an advisory structure to the prime minister responsible for the continuous coordination of all actors involved in national security affairs.

Following the national elections of July 2019, the newly elected prime minister appointed a national security adviser for the first time ever. The opposition criticised this decision as being too hasty given that there were still no final provisions for the establishment, composition and authorities of the NSC. Nevertheless, in August 2019, the Greek government introduced Law 4622/19 on the organisation, function and transparency of the government, the government bodies and the central state administration (Government Gazette 2019c). This law is essentially a blueprint for the restructuring and reorganisation of government institutions and various other administrative bodies. Despite lacking any explicit references to a WGA, the law introduced a top-down, centralised WGA, placing emphasis on the continuous interaction of all competent agencies for the successful implementation of government policies, including those related to foreign affairs and security.

5 | Conclusions

To sum up, elements of Greece's implementation of a WGA in relation to external crises and conflicts are evident in the country's participation in CSDP missions and PESCO projects. Yet, as already mentioned, it was not until 2018 that a formal national document, the Voluntary National Review on the Implementation of the 2030 Agenda for Sustainable Development (VNR) (General Secretariat of the Government 2018), made an explicit reference to the adoption of a WGA in efforts to successfully accomplish the SDGs at the national level. Unquestionably, this is a rather significant indication that the WGA concept is no longer an alien idea in Greece, and that it is likely that similar references will be made at some future point regarding different policy areas. Nevertheless, the country is still quite far from implementing a comprehensive WGA that encompasses all policy areas, including those related to external crises and conflicts.

Indeed, for the most of part, policy coherence in Greece depends not on the existence of a formally articulated WGA strategy, but rather on the degree of cooperation and coordination among actors engaged with the given policies. Law 4622/19 (Government Gazette 2019c) (discussed above) was definitely a step towards introducing elements of a WGA at the central-government level, yet a clearly articulated WGA framework is still missing.

Drawing from the information presented above, it can be argued that the factors underpinning the success of a WGA in Greece are: (1) the level at which a WGA is initiated, with evidence indicating that policy coherence is more effective when initiated above the ministerial level; (2) the number of actors involved in the WGA framework, which is something that differentiates WGA from more narrow coordination frameworks; (3) the nature of the coordinating actors, as rather than being narrowed to inter-ministerial cooperation, a comprehensive WGA framework should also incorporate actors from regional and local administrations, the private sector and civil society; and (4) the existence of a well-developed WGA framework at the international level. Although these factors would not guarantee a WGA at the national level, they may offer valuable guidance for those wishing to develop and implement a WGA in Greece.

Taking into consideration these factors, the policy area in which Greece seems to be closer to an effective implementation of a WGA model is sustainable development. In addition to providing secretarial support to the relevant inter-ministerial committee, the General Secretariat of the Government coordinates with a wide array of actors in this area in order to develop policies aligned with the WGA framework set out by the UN.

6 | Reference list

General Secretariat of the Government – Office of Coordination, Institutional, International & European Affairs (2018). Voluntary National Review on the Implementation of the 2030 Agenda for Sustainable Development. Athens. https://sustainabledevelopment.un.org/content/documents/19378Greece_VNR_Greece_2018_pdf_FINAL_140618.pdf.

Government Gazette (1999). Issue A 138/05-07-1999. Athens.

Government Gazette (2003). Issue A 84/11-04-2003. Athens.

Government Gazette (2010). Issue B 845/16-06-2010. Athens.

Government Gazette (2016). Issue A 208/04-11-2016. Athens.

Government Gazette (2019a). Issue A 119/08-07-2019. Athens.

Government Gazette (2019b). Issue A 124/18-07-2019. Athens.

Government Gazette (2019c). Issue A 133/18-07-2019. Athens.

GSCP (General Secretariat for Civil Protection) (n.d.). Objective and mission of the GSCP – Civil Protection Operations Centre. www. civilprotection.gr/en/civil-protection-operations-centre.

Ministry of Defence (2018). General Directorate of National Defence Policy and International Relations (GDNDPIR). Greece and the Permanent Structured Cooperation (PESCO). Athens. www.gdpe ads.mod.mil.gr/index.php/en/.

Ministry of Economy and Development (2019). National Strategy for Sustainable and Just Development 2030. Athens.

Ministry of Foreign Affairs (2018). Hellenic Aid. Athens. https://hell enicaid.mfa.gr/en/.

Ministry of Foreign Affairs (2019). Draft bill on the Modernisation of Foreign Policy. Athens.

Ministry for the Environment, Physical Planning and Public Works (2002). National Strategy for Sustainable Development. Athens.

Hungary

Gyorgy Tatar

1 | Introduction

Preventing and managing fragile and crisis situations, rendering assistance to societies in post-conflict situations, and emerging security challenges require the international community to pool resources and pursue comprehensive and coordinated approaches. This is especially the case for the member states of the European Union, which is a global actor on the international stage and possesses a huge set of instruments for these purposes.

After the change of regime in 1990, Hungary reorganised its administration and adjusted it to new values, conditions and requirements. One of the first steps was the introduction of new reporting lines corresponding to the values, rules and regulations of a parliamentary democracy as well as the establishment of the Conference of State Secretaries for Administrations, whose members represent the ministries and create an effective framework for a whole-of-government approach (WGA).

Hungary joined NATO in 1999 and the European Union in 2004. These new memberships prompted the state to introduce further measures and mechanisms for ensuring coherence and consistency in its decision-making system. It was vital to establish governmental bodies and coordination mechanisms which ensure that agreed and coordinated positions are represented. This applies to both the development and implementation of policies, including those related to external relations and participation in efforts to respond to fragile and crisis situations worldwide. The tasks involved with holding the EU presidency in 2011 presented Hungary with additional challenges and forced its government to pay specific attention to a coherent governmental approach.

The report below aims to take stock of the measures and efforts of Hungarian governments in recent decades to develop an intra-governmental decision-making system (in other words, a WGA) in order to ensure more coherence and consistency in cases of external crisis situations.

2 | What policies have been developed to further policy coherence?

The Foreign Policy Strategy of Hungary adopted in 2011 (MFA 2011) serves as a fundamental document providing guidance for foreign policy activities, including responses to crises, in both geographical and horizontal terms. However, it does not contain any explicit reference to a WGA.

The National Security Strategy (NSS) (MFA 2012: Art. 43) adopted in 2012 points to the requirement of "a comprehensive, whole of government approach" to comprehensively manage the threats mentioned in the strategy, and it tasks all government institutions "to continuously evaluate in their own area of responsibility the elements of national and international security and exposure to threats, and to take steps necessary to manage and avert them." What's more, it specifically states the need to apply a WGA ("government-wide coordination") in the field of international cooperation. The ensuing articles of the strategy tackle the issues of cooperation in the fields of civil-military cooperation, development and multilateral collaboration. At the same time, however, the document does not provide any guidance for establishing specific structures and mechanisms dedicated to the type of WGA it calls for. Nevertheless, a number of specific strategies based on the NSS have been prepared in some ministries (e.g. the Ministry of Defence), and these have further strengthened the coordinated governmental approach.

At present, the most significant legal document that ensures coherence and coordination in addition to setting up structures and mechanisms for intra-governmental cooperation is Governmental Resolution 1144/2010 (VII.7.) on the "operation of the government". The document designates the Conference of State Secretaries for

Administration as the highest governmental structure. The conference convenes once a week to prepare documents in a coherent and coordinated manner for the government's decision-making process, and it also sets on its agenda the issues related to foreign affairs, including governmental responses to crises and conflicts. In this context, proposals are mainly submitted by the Ministry of Foreign Affairs and Trade (MFAT). As a general rule, the MFAT reaches agreements about the proposals with the Ministry of Defence and the Ministry of Interior as well as with other relevant ministries prior to the submission of documents.

A similarly important decision-making channel aimed at ensuring a coherent governmental approach is established by Governmental Resolution 1007/2004 (II.12.) on "harmonization of the participation of the government in the decision-making activities of the European Union" and its updated versions, 1169/2010 (VII.18.) and 1742/2014 (XII.15.). These documents set up structures, rules and mechanisms for a WGA to all EU policies, including the Common Security and Defence Policy (CSDP).

Governmental Resolution 152/2014, which stipulates that the minister of the Prime Minister's Office is responsible for coordinating and harmonising WGA activities, should be considered another legal tool reflecting the efforts of different parts of the government to act in concert.

Regarding legislation related to Hungary's WGA, Governmental Resolution 1682/2014 (XI.26.) established the Interdepartmental Committee for Coordination of International Development Cooperation, which plays a key role in coordinating governmental activities in the fields of development and humanitarian aid.

Turning briefly to structural changes aimed at facilitating a WGA, in 2014, the portfolio of the Ministry of Foreign Affairs was expanded to include international trade, energy and international investments. One of the aims of this change was to better concentrate governmental efforts and activities in the domain of external relations.

A regulation adopted on 3 July 2018 regarding the structure and operation of the Prime Minister's Office is the latest legal document to expand the domains of governmental coordination through the establishment of the State Secretariat for the Aid of Persecuted Christians and the Hungary Helps Program within the Prime Minister's Office (cf. Hungarian Government n.d.). The Hungary Helps Program is tasked with coordinating all of Hungary's bilateral humanitarian aid activities as well as with participating in the implementation of the Hungarian international development policies and multilateral humanitarian aid efforts when the MFAT is in the lead. Both structures enable the government to respond to some global security challenges (e.g. migration) in a coherent manner.

The International Development Cooperation Strategy and Strategic Concept for International Humanitarian Aid of Hungary for the 2014–2020 period (Hungarian Government 2013), which was adopted in 2013, constitutes a solid basis for Hungarian governmental and non-governmental structures to work together in a coordinated manner in the field of development and humanitarian aid. The MFAT bears primary responsibility for its implementation.

The Western Balkans, the eastern and southern neighbourhoods of Hungary, the post-Soviet states as well as the Middle East and North Africa are the regions where Hungary seeks to play a proactive role in contributing to regional stability, settling conflicts and supporting democratic processes. For obvious reasons, though to different degrees, the stability of these regions has impacts on the security of Hungary. The 2014–2020 development strategy (ibid.) also gives priority to the sub-Saharan region and some underdeveloped states in Asia. What's more, protecting the rights of Hungarian minorities in the neighbourhood plays a significant role when shaping relations with adjacent countries.

When it comes to regions farther away from Hungary, the country's key priorities are migration, the positions of local Christian communities, and the stabilisation of security situations in the theatre. These have been the main guiding principles of Hungary's positions when discussing the common EU stances in areas such as Egypt, Libya, Mali and the Sahel. For example, the Hungarian Red Cross and the Prime Minister's Office have cooperated in efforts to provide humanitarian aid in Iraq. Furthermore, since the Hungarian government views halting illegal migration flows and countering hybrid threats as external challenges of vital importance to the country's internal security, it pays specific attention to these risks.

The aforementioned criteria have also been the main guiding principles when it comes to Hungary's positions on elaborating common EU policies and activities as well as on Hungary's contributions to efforts to settle crisis situations. These have included the launch of

CSDP- or NATO-led missions, such as Operation Althea in Bosnia-Herzegovina, NATO's IFOR in Kosovo, the NATO-led mission in Afghanistan as well as the EUMM in Georgia. The MFAT usually assumes the leading position when it comes to coordination and cooperation with the concerned governmental bodies (e.g. the Ministry of Defence and the Ministry of Interior), and these effort have functioned smoothly to date.

Cooperation between the government and the National Assembly is regulated by Act XXXVI of 2012 (National Assembly 2012: Sections 62–68) and Act 10/2014 of the National Assembly (National Assembly 2014: Section 140). Government Resolution 1742/2014 (XII.15.) regulates cooperation between the government and the National Assembly, including when it comes to foreign and EU affairs. At present, Government Resolution 1742/2014 (XII.15.) regulates cooperation between the government and the National Assembly, which is the main body responsible for the supervision of governmental activities in EU affairs.

3 | Who are the main actors involved in cooperating in a WGA?

As a general rule, the Conference of State Secretaries for Administration within the Prime Minister's Office is the main body that coordinates and harmonises all activities at the governmental level.

Between 2004 and 2018, the Ministry of Foreign Affairs was responsible for coordinating EU affairs and policies. However, this responsibility was transferred to the minister of the Prime Minister's Office in 2018 by Government Resolution 94/2018 (V.22.).

Government Resolution 1007/2004 (II.12.) on the "harmonisation of the participation of the government in the decision-making activities of the European Union" establishes the Committee of EU Intradepartmental Coordination (CEIC) and its 52 working groups, which are the key structures for coordinating and harmonising the preparation and implementation of tasks emanating from EU membership. The CEIC is chaired by the state secretary of the Prime Minister's Office and overseen by the State Secretariat for European Policies and Coordination, which is also part of the Prime Minister's Office.

Each CEIC working group is led by a representative of the primarily concerned ministry and its staff. Additionally, each working group has permanent seats for representatives of the Prime Minister's Office, the Ministry of Justice, the Ministry of Finance, and the permanent representation to the EU in Brussels, which together ensure the horizontal coordination of governmental activities.

Working Group 24 is responsible for the common foreign, security and defence policies, and ensures that the idea of a WGA is translated into practice. It is led by a representative of the MFAT and includes representatives from the staff of the minister of the Prime Minister's Office, the Ministry of Justice, the Ministry of Interior, the Ministry of Defence, and the Ministry of Finance. On the other hand, Working Group 27 is in charge of development and humanitarian aid, and led by the Directorate-General for International Cooperation and Development in the MFAT. The two working groups closely cooperate to ensure coordination of the so-called '3D' (diplomacy, defence and development) activities. In addition to the working groups, the Interdepartmental Committee for Coordination of International Development Cooperation, comprising representatives of eight ministries, also ensures a coordinated governmental approach in the areas of development and humanitarian aid.

This integrated approach is supported by the fact that the minister of foreign affairs and trade is also responsible for policies related to foreign economic relations as well as for those involving energy, trade/investment, migration and EU visa issues in addition to overseeing the domestic intelligence agencies.

Within the MFAT, the Directorate-General for EU Common Foreign and Security Policy and Neighbourhood Policy is the key structure for coordinating and harmonising intra-ministerial and intra-governmental activities relating to EU external relations, including crises and conflicts. Within the DG, a senior diplomat at the rank of deputy director-general is responsible for the proper functioning of this coordination mechanism. The DG operates in close partnership with the Directorate-General for Security and Non-Proliferation Policy, which is in charge of NATO affairs as well as of coordinating cooperation related to the common defence policy within the MFAT and with other concerned ministries, including the Ministry of Defence and the Ministry of Interior. The WGA is also facilitated by the Directorate-General for European Affairs, which is the main contact point both within the ministry and between the ministry and the State Secretariat for European Policies and Coordination within the Prime Minister's Office when it comes to EU policies.

Furthermore, the coordinated approach is enabled by the fact that the deputy state secretary for security policy, who is the political director of the MFAT, and the deputy state secretary for responses to migration challenges (whose responsibilities also include governmental activities within the UN and other international organisations) are under the supervision of the state secretary for security policy.

The legislative branch also approaches these issues in a coordinated manner. In 2002, the National Assembly established the High Committee on the European Union, which held its first meeting on 19 September 2002. Its objective has been to ensure both a consensus on integration-related issues among political parties in the National Assembly as well as coordination between the government and the National Assembly at the highest level. The committee's meetings are chaired by the president of the National Assembly. It consists of the leaders of the parliamentary groups (fractions) and the presidents of the Committee on Foreign Affairs, the Committee on European Affairs, and the Committee on Justice. The prime minister and the minister of foreign affairs are permanent members of the meetings. The meetings are adjusted to the meetings of the European Council, where participants receive regular briefings on Hungary's positions.

The government of Hungary has developed close relationships with EU actors and institutions through its permanent representation to the European Union in Brussels, which is supervised by the minister of the Prime Minister's Office. Its staff mirrors the setup of the government, which enables it to contribute to any issue or policy.

Similarly, the staffs and coordination mechanisms of the Hungarian representations delegated to international organisations (e.g. the UN, NATO and the OSCE) are composed and regulated in such a way as to ensure a coordinated governmental approach.

In order to facilitate adoption of common EU decisions, the MFAT shares the positions of the Hungarian government with the embassies of the EU member states in Budapest as well as the European Commission representatives in Budapest prior to the meetings of the EU's Foreign Affairs Council and the European Council.

4 | How does your country operationalise a WGA?

As general rule, the Conference of State Secretaries for Administration is the main platform for preparing governmental decisions in Hungary and ensuring the coherence of governmental positions. ,

In the case of EU affairs, including external relations, governmental coordination takes place within the relevant working group of the Committee of EU Intradepartmental Cooperation (CEIC), which also meets once a week. In the MFAT, the structure responsible for coordination takes the lead in efforts to elaborate the ministry's positions, which are shared with and commented on by the representatives of the other ministries participating in the working group.

In the case of the monthly meetings of the EU's Foreign Affairs Council and the European Council, the usual preparatory procedure is complemented by two video conferences held during the week prior to the meetings. During these virtual conferences, the concerned departments of the MFAT in Budapest and the staff of the permanent representation in Brussels discuss and finalise Hungarian positions.

In the context of the EU Global Strategy and crisis management, the government of Hungary is particularly interested in enhancing the EU's defence capacities and avoiding any duplications in the activities of the EU and NATO. For this reason, Hungary supports the development of the Permanent Structured Cooperation (PESCO), the implementation of programmes within the European Defence Fund, and the development of the concept of European battlegroups. On the national level, Hungary is also making specific efforts to modernise its own military capabilities as part of the 'Zrinyi 2026' programme. In these areas, cooperation and coordination of positions between the MFAT and the Ministry of Defence are particularly strong.

The main direction of the governmental decision-making mechanism is bottom-up. Cooperation among ministries and other governmental agencies mainly takes place at the level of desk officers, whose common positions or debates over certain issues are submitted to the ministerial hierarchy for approval or settlement. The interactions of staffs are governed by protocols relating to intra-governmental and intra-ministerial affairs.

In cases that touch upon 'core national interests' (e.g. migration, rights of Hungarian minorities abroad, neighbourhood policies, Christians experiencing persecution, and sensitive human rights issues), decision-making shifts to a top-down direction. In such cases, the task of the administrations is to implement the political guidance received from the political leadership above.

In the case of the CEIC's Working Group 24 (discussed above), the top-down direction means that the coordinator for the CSDP in the MFAT, through the established hierarchy, receives clear political instructions from the Prime Minister's Office. In such cases, the tasks of the administrations and the duties of the coordinators in the ministries are limited to carrying out instructions and sharing information with relevant partners.

Lastly, a note on training. Members of the government's staff do not receive any specific training on WGA-related matters. Instead, their participation in the coordination mechanism is simply a matter of 'learning by doing'.

5 | Conclusions

There is no official document in Hungary that has the term 'whole-of-government approach' in its title. Nonetheless, there are several governmental decisions (particularly regarding EU affairs) aimed at fostering effective intra-departmental cooperation, information-sharing and decision-making, drawing lessons and accountability. The decision-making mechanism is multi-tiered, which enables the concerned governmental structures to act in concert and to harmonise any diverging views and positions. It also provides sufficient space for discussing and resolving conflicting positions.

The current practice of the Hungarian Government ensures coherence and consistency as well as an integrated, coordinated and holistic approach to decision-making regarding external relations. The national approach is in line with the political objectives, spirit and ambitions of the EU Global Strategy, particularly in the domain of common defence policy.

In practice, national and bilateral interests occasionally prevail over the principled common EU approach in Hungarian decision-making. In implementing the principle of human security, the Hungarian government gives priority to joint activities when the security of Christian communities is at risk.

The main objectives and direction of governmental decisions are to ensure the exercise of a 'central' political will. The modifications introduced in the governmental setup and decision-making mechanism in recent years have enhanced the lead role of the Prime Minister's Office, encouraged the centralisation of power, and ensured more space for the top-down approach even though the bottom-up approach continues to be the basic direction of decision-making.

Hungary's political leadership has justified the shifts by citing the dramatic changes in the international balance of power, a need for more effective representation of the interests of the whole Hungarian nation at both the global and European levels, and a need for better linkages between responses to external and internal threats.

While the top-down approach theoretically allows for subjective decision-making, a lack of impact studies and potential collateral damage, high-level interventions and 'political steering' have also helped to effectively cope with the usual disagreements within the system, to take swift decisions and to effectively address some global challenges, such as migration and the protection of 'core' national values.

The integration of foreign policy and relevant economic tools within the Ministry of Foreign Affairs and Trade has greatly contributed to the application of a WGA approach. However, there is a gap between the proactive conflict-preventive approach of the EU institutions and the basically reactive decision-making principles and mechanisms in Hungary. Sharing WGA-related best practices between the EU and national levels could prove useful for further developing Hungary's capabilities.

6 | Reference list

Hungarian Government (n.d.). State Secretariat for the Aid of Persecuted Christians and for the Hungary Helps Program. www.kormany.hu/en/prime-minister-s-office/state-secretariat-for-the-aid-of-persecuted-christians-and-for-the-hungary-helps-program.

Hungarian Government (2013). International Development Cooperation Strategy and Strategic Concept for International Humanitarian Aid of Hungary 2014–2020. https://nefe.kormany.hu/down-
load/3/93/c0000/International%20Development%20Cooperation
%20and%20Humanitarian%20Aid%20Strategy%20of%20Hung
ary-v%C3%A9gleges.pdf.

MFA (Ministry of Foreign Affairs of Hungary) (2011). Hungary's Foreign Policy after the Hungarian Presidency of the Council of the
European Union. https://eu.kormany.hu/admin/download/f/1b/30
000/foreign_policy_20111219.pdf.

MFA (2012). Hungary's National Security Strategy 2012. www.eda.eu
ropa.eu/docs/default-source/documents/hungary-national-security
-strategy-2012.pdf.

National Assembly (2012). Act XXXVI of 2012. www.parlament.hu/
documents/125505/138409/Act+XXXVI+of+2012+on+the+Nation
al+Assembly/b53726b7-12a8-4d93-acef-140feef44395.

National Assembly (2014). Act 10/2014 on certain provisions of the
Rules of Procedure. www.parlament.hu/documents/125505/1384
09/Resolution+on+certain+provisions+of+the+Rules+of+Procedur
e/968f2e08-f740-4241-a87b-28e6dc390407.

Ireland

Isaac Bennett and Ben Tonra

1 | Introduction

There are several likely explanations for why whole-of-government approaches (WGAs) to external security crises are underdeveloped in Ireland compared to other EU countries. The majority of these are practical and related to the nation's small geographical size and relatively small population. Both of these factors allow for the centralisation of government departments and agencies, and therefore make it possible to have all stakeholders in a particular external security crisis in the same room at the same time. Indeed, because of the 'everyone knows everyone else' factor that is unique to countries with smaller populations, the need for formal WGA structures has not been a priority. That is not to say that the WGA structures and protocols are nonexistent or that those that do exist are wholly deficient, but rather that they exist in a more ad hoc and informal manner without any strictly defined overarching policy or government documentation setting out how these structures may be operationalised.

The historical context is important for understanding why this informal WGA has been taken and is reflective of Ireland's long-established and active engagement in international security – most notably, an unbroken record of 60 years' service with UN peacekeeping missions. As a result of this historical context, Ireland has developed many informal and rapid-response mechanisms to gather key actors together in one room and to develop an effective plan for responding to external crises. Over time, this has evolved into what can be called a WGA to dealing with external security crises without being bogged down by unnecessary red tape and administrative log-jamming. Particularly in the field of responses to external security crises, our WGA may be ad hoc and informal on paper. But, in practice, the relevant agencies and departments are able to organise, mobilise and deploy in a rapid and orderly manner.

There are mechanisms and processes that go into effect without the need for formal recognition of their existence and function, which in turn enables the relevant actors and agencies to cooperate and coordinate without the restrictions that formalisation brings. Of course, such a setup creates significant trade-offs. In the first place, there is little to no parliamentary interactions or cross-party consultation on responses to external crises. Information requests for briefings and updates can be made and are dealt with through the relevant constitutional channels, but this is considered to be the exception rather than the norm. The second considerable trade-off is that without any formal documentation of how WGAs are dealt with and the ways and means to carry out a WGA to external security crises, there is a risk of knowledge loss over time.

2 | What policies have been developed to further policy coherence?

There are no formal WGA policies or strategies that explicitly state how Ireland is to come together to respond to an external security crisis. Instead, as noted above, there is a standing inter-departmental committee that deals with such crises on a case-by-case basis. This committee draws on participants from all sectors of government and ministerial departments as well as associated agencies, as needed. Consultations with civilian actors or NGOs that might have a stake in the region or crisis itself are also facilitated. Military commanders are key stakeholders and ones who have a role in this committee, whether they are reporting in person or via secure teleconference from the region experiencing the crisis. Various members of the myriad sections within the Department of Foreign Affairs and Trade, the Department of Justice and Equality, the Taoiseach (i.e. the prime minister's office), and the Department of Defence are gathered together in order to establish the exact context of the crisis and the best way to respond to it. Of course, these decisions are not made in a vacuum. Instead, consultation with EU member states and institutions is an important aspect of the committee's work, as it ensures that there is no duplication of efforts among these various bodies.

There are other reasons for this coordination and cooperation that are practical in nature. While Ireland is often willing to deploy its armed forces as part of international security operations, the fact that it does not have a full-spectrum military capacity means that it must rely on collective infrastructures provided by multilateral actors (e.g. the EU, the UN and NATO). In addition to coordinating with the EU, it may be necessary at times to contact and arrange cooperation with other external actors, such as those just cited or the African Union (AU). This may be for several reasons, such as: to facilitate passage across other nations' sovereign territory en route to the crisis region; to ensure that the mission does not conflict with any existing mission in the region; to facilitate a transfer of intelligence and information in a more efficient manner; or to establish basic protocols for troop inter-action, the provision of support, and deconflicting the airspace over the crisis theatre.

The WGA mechanism that Ireland employs during responses to external crises is not a formalised structure with directly supporting human resources (HR) and administration assets to call upon. How-ever, this does not limit its effectiveness in achieving efficient mission deployment and successful outcomes in responses to external crises. In fact, the argument can be made that this model of WGA is ideal for geographically small nations with smaller populations and central-ised governments. Sources within the ministries that were inter-viewed for this analysis discussed the utility of having all main stake-holders in the same room in person for ensuring clarification of roles and responsibilities as well as for dealing with any disputes or con-flicts that might arise due to having so many different actors involved in an operation. This conflict resolution and clarity generation does not merely come from formal 'roundtable' discussions, but also from informal conversations – or so-called 'water-cooler' moments – which allow for issues to be discussed and resolved on an inter-personal basis. Government documents analysed for this report refer to the im-portance of WGAs for future interaction within both the national and international security realms.

As has been noted throughout, Ireland uses an inter-departmental committee to coordinate within the administration and to respond to external crises and conflicts, but the documentation and strategies make no reference to this committee other than acknowledging the "current arrangements". It is possible, however, to identify a renewed commitment to a more robust defensive military posture in the most recent White Paper on Defence (Department of Defence 2015). Indeed, there are explicit commitments made regarding continued participation in the CSDP and a recognition of the importance of having national militaries possess "expeditionary potential" so they can better intervene and assist in conflicts and crises outside the borders of the EU (ibid.: 27). Rather than making any direct references to a WGA, these documents assume that the response mechanism (i.e. the Interdepartmental Committee for Peacekeeping) is the only vector through which developments or issues in the military sphere will be pursued. It is evidence nonetheless that the bureaucratic and military leadership is aware of the concept of a whole-of-government approach to military affairs.

3 | Who are the main actors involved in cooperating in a WGA?

The main departments and agencies involved in the whole-of-government approach to responding to external crises are primarily: Defence, Foreign Affairs and Trade, the Taoiseach, the Defence Forces, the Gardai (i.e. the police force) and Justice as well as any elements of these various sub-departments that might be needed (e.g. international security policy experts, members of the Conflict Resolution Unit, human rights experts, etc). While the overall scope of the WGA is broad – in the sense that it encompasses many different fields of expertise and gathers actors from politics, policy, economics, security, development and crisis response – the structure and form of Ireland's government and WGA allow for many, if not all, of these actors to be a direct part of the response under the auspices of the committee formed to respond to external security crises and conflicts.

Cooperation and coordination is visible across many levels of the WGA response mechanism, which leads to better communication not merely vertically, but also horizontally as facilitated by the Interdepartmental Committee on Peacekeeping. Indeed, one of the most important elements highlighted by interviewees was the ability to communicate and coordinate with colleagues on the same level as oneself across a variety of government agencies and organisations. This was said to improve efficiency, to lead to better relationships among all actors, and to be critical when it comes to making important decisions that impact both civilians in the crisis area and the security forces being deployed to assist them.

4 | How does your country operationalise a WGA?

As already noted, the key structure underpinning Ireland's WGA to international security crises is the sub-cabinet-level Interdepartmental Committee for Peacekeeping. Originally designed to manage Irish contributions to UN peacekeeping operations, the committee's remit has effectively been expanded in recent years to encompass all Irish multilateral engagement with international security operations across EU, UN and NATO platforms. This is supplemented by formal structures within particular government departments, such as the Conflict Resolution Unit (CRU) within the Department of Foreign Affairs and Trade, whose remit is to assess and direct policy towards areas of conflict management and to promote reconciliation strategies more broadly based on Ireland's national experience and its own peace process.

On the face of it, without a large, all-encompassing policy doctrine to support them, these limited structures lack institutional depth. Indeed, while Ireland's WGA to external crises and conflicts is not formalised into any strict legal mechanism or organisational response, its informal nature has served well to direct Ireland's engagement in international security operations. The character of that engagement has been praised for its high degree of communication and efficiency, and it has improved the ability of the state and its defence forces to react quickly to crises in regions external to the EU. Operationalisation of a WGA towards international security crises is therefore effectively directed by key policy players operating in concert within a clear national context developed over 60 years of continuous UN engagement. While 'success' in this context is difficult to determine, there is no doubt but that Irish engagement in peace-support operations has consistently enjoyed strong public support across all demographics and political parties, is deemed central and critical to the mission of the Defence Forces of Ireland, and is regularly showcased within Irish foreign policy as a key feature of the country's global engagement. Its relevance may further be judged by the fact that this is a key high-lighted policy within Ireland's 2021 campaign for a seat on the UN Security Council.

'Success' in terms of policy outcomes in third countries, of course, is more difficult to assess. Ireland's engagement in international security operations have ranged from the traditional 'blue hat' UN cease-fire-monitoring efforts to the most robust UN interventions using military forces. With the end of the Cold War, Ireland extended that UN engagement to wider international peace-support operations. First by joining NATO's Partnership for Peace in 1999 and then later through the EU's development of its Common Security and Defence Policy, Ireland adapted itself to much greater interoperability and engagement in a variety of command structures, such as the UN, NATO and the EU. Over the last 20 years, hundreds of Irish troops have served across thousands of individual deployments in international security operations in Europe (Kosovo), the Middle East (Iraq, Israel, Jordan, Kuwait, Lebanon and Syria), Africa (Central African Republic, Chad, Congo, Eritrea, Ethiopia, Ivory Coast, Liberia, Mali, Somalia and Uganda), and the Asia-Pacific region (Afghanistan and East Timor). While calculating the 'success' of Irish contributions to each of these operations is a complex undertaking, the fact that Ireland is subject to repeated and ongoing requests to contribute to such operations is at least some testament to its success as a small security provider.

In terms of management, the efficacy of Ireland's WGA is less a function of its institutional design than of the country's political commitment, bureaucratic culture and public administration. This is marked by a high level of informal communication, a lack of bureaucratic hierarchy, permeable institutional and agency borders, and the limited number of policy players. Together, this gives rise to a structure that is nimble, flexible and potentially creative in response to policy challenges. Policy disablers are largely the obverse of its enablers. The small size of the Irish policy network also means that it will have few resources, limited policy specialisation and a somewhat generalist approach to crises. Furthermore, the lack of institutionalisation and the small size of the supporting infrastructure can also give rise to policy capture by special interests and a disproportionate degree of influence from personalities and individual entrepreneurship. While these risks do exist, to date they have not given rise to significant policy failures or weaknesses.

5 | Conclusions

As noted, the success factors in Ireland's WGA are rooted in the nature, size and adaptability of its public administration, whose very light but well-focused institutional structure has been consistently engaged in peace-support and crisis-management operations since the late 1950s. It admittedly does suffer from the absence of an overall policy concept and the lack of administrative resources and policy specialisation. Nevertheless, Irish policymakers are also eager for the European Union to develop a stronger WGA infrastructure and policy orientation to which they can contribute their added value. To that end, they have championed improved EU-UN-AU coordination on both the policy and operational levels in addition to enthusiastically promoting the Civilian CSDP Compact as a means by which a broader 'security' remit can be brought to bear to prevent, manage and resolve international security crises. Due to a comparatively benign national security threat assessment, Irish policymakers can also prioritise international security engagement without also having to triangulate between national security or defence interests. This allows for a WGA that is rooted in addressing the centrality of third-country security needs rather than only seeing such needs through the prism of national security priorities. Indeed, Ireland's overall approach to WGAs may be of interest as an adaptable model for countries with similar geographic sizes and populations given its flexibility and ability to enable effective communication and problem-solving.

6 | Reference list

Department of Defence (2015). White Paper on Defence. Dublin. www.defence.ie/system/files/media/file-uploads/2018-06/wp2015 eng_1.pdf.
Interviews with sources within the government.

Italy

Luca Giansanti

1 | Introduction

Italy is likely to be peculiar among EU member states, as it has not formally adopted a whole-of-government approach (WGA) to external crises and conflicts. However, since the 1990s, it has increasingly felt the need to ensure coherence among different dimensions of its foreign and security policy in the framework of crisis-management initiatives, and it has pursued a WGA on a case-by-case basis without significantly upgrading or adapting the relevant administrative structures and coordination arrangements.

The absence of national-level documents explicitly outlining a WGA can be explained by the absence of a national security strategy and some peculiarities of Italy's political and institutional system, such as historical and political difficulties in dealing with the concept of 'national interest' and the ambiguity surrounding that concept. Despite some recent improvements, the prime minister (or, according to the constitution, the 'president of the Council of Ministers') remains a relatively weak figure from an institutional point of view compared to analogous positions in other major EU member states. There is weak national sentiment for historical reasons, and a track record of coalition governments with relatively short stays in power (despite some exceptions) does not facilitate the emergence of a sense of a shared purpose. What's more, as foreign policy has grown closely connected to domestic politics and its intricacies, it has been losing what has traditionally been its largely bipartisan nature.

As a consequence, there is no real tradition in Italy of cross-government joint analysis and strategies. Indeed, there is little institutionalised coordination within the government (and even less when relevant ministers belong to different parties in a coalition government). And there is a lack of institutional memory at the level of political leaders and of an institutionalised lessons learned process.

Since WGA is both a matter of national culture and a highly political concept that can be better defined and implemented when there is a broad consensus on a shared vision of crises and conflicts and of the country's role in responding to them, the above-mentioned details explain why a WGA has yet to find its place in official government documents. Nevertheless, the shortcomings of Italy's political and institutional systems have still not prevented the country from implementing an ad hoc WGA. What's more, with its own distinctive features, this WGA has been providing added value to both national and international initiatives.

In the last 20 years, the Ministry of Defence has been increasingly embracing the concept of employing a 'comprehensive' or 'integrated' approach. This has created greater space for WGA initiatives and – by joining forces with the foreign service, local governments (at the regional and municipal levels), and civil society – it has contributed to defining a special Italian 'species' of a WGA for dealing with external conflicts and crises.

Italy remains a committed supporter of the strategies adopted in multilateral fora, such as the EU Global Strategy, the UN Integrated Approach, NATO's CIMIC concept, the OECD's WGA and the OSCE's comprehensive approach to security. Furthermore, it also supports increased cooperation among international organisations (EU-UN, NATO-UN, EU-NATO, EU-UN-AU, etc) aimed at establishing a more comprehensive approach at the international level.

In fact, inputs for a gradual and case-by-case implementation of a WGA in Italy first came from NATO and then, more substantially, from the EU. Indeed, the EU played a key role in raising Italy's awareness about the WGA concept and in influencing and shaping its related activities. Even before the adoption of the joint communication by the European Commission and the High Representative of the Union for Foreign Affairs and Security Policy on the 'EU's comprehensive approach to external conflict and crises' in 2013 and of the EU Global Strategy (EUGS) in 2016, the EU's debates and documents on the comprehensive/integrated approach to external conflicts and crises had a clear influence on policies and behaviours at the national level.

On the other hand, the impacts of the strategies of other international organisations have been rather sectoral and limited in scope to date. For example, NATO's evolving doctrine on enhanced civil-military cooperation (CIMIC) initially had a positive impact on the Ministry of Defence's approach to such cooperation. However, the military-driven nature of the doctrine creates certain limitations, and it mainly plays a role in security-related efforts. For this reason, its potential for moving in the direction of a broader WGA strategy are limited.

2 | What policies have been developed to further policy coherence?

Elements of a WGA can be found in some Italian policy documents. For example, early EU debates on the comprehensive approach were the main influence behind the initiative taken by the ministries of Defence and Foreign Affairs to draft a joint paper in 2011 and 2012 defining a national multi-dimensional and multilateral approach to crises (Ministry of Foreign Affairs and Ministry of Defence 2012). This was an informal conceptual document that required follow-up at the government level, which did not take place.

Then, in 2014, a new law on development cooperation confirmed that "international cooperation for sustainable development, human rights and peace [...] is an integral and qualifying part of Italian foreign policy" (Italian Parliament 2014: Art. 1.1). Italy's development-cooperation efforts, it continued, will pursue, among other things, "preventing conflicts, supporting peace-building and reconciliation processes, as well as post-conflict stabilisation and the consolidation and reinforcement of democratic institutions" (ibid.: Art 1.2(c)).

Furthermore, the White Paper for International Security and Defence of July 2015 (Ministry of Defence 2015), which was endorsed by the government, acknowledges the role of the armed forces in the context of a comprehensive approach (SSR, capacity-/institution-building, stabilisation, reconstruction), the need for more active non-military participation in order to achieve a global approach to crisis management, the increasing need for better coordination and integration at the national system level, and the need to work closely with diplomatic personnel, personnel from other ministries, and representatives of international governmental and non-governmental organisations. Then, a law passed the following year (Italian Parliament 2016) concerning Italy's participation in international missions and operations confirmed a comprehensive approach to crises and conflicts by bringing together the participation of armed and police forces in missions and initiatives abroad with participation in humanitarian missions, CIMIC initiatives, development-cooperation initiatives and initiatives aimed at supporting peacebuilding and stabilisation.

However, the above-mentioned laws and documents neither provide for clear commitments nor contain guidelines for implementation or lessons learned processes. Thus, their actual contribution to the concrete implementation of a WGA is limited.

Policy coherence has been furthered mainly by the procedure aimed at approving and allocating for the coming year (but sometimes for a shorter period of time) the special budget needed to fund both military and civilian initiatives abroad. Since there has historically been little room within the regular defence budget for funding missions abroad, a special procedure was put in place, and the regular national budget now provides for a specific fund to finance international missions and initiatives. However, the allocation of this fund to different initiatives is dealt with via a separate, specific procedure.

Until 2016, this procedure provided for a decree with the force of law to be adopted by the government and then debated and enacted into law by the parliament within 60 days. Since 2017, however, the new provisions concerning Italy's participation in international missions and operations from the 2016 law mentioned above (Italian Parliament 2016) provide for a different process. According to this process, a detailed proposal concerning initiatives to be continued, adapted or newly launched during the coming year is adopted by the government, and then it is discussed (together with a detailed report to be presented by the government on the previous year's initiatives) and authorised by the parliament (by adopting resolutions that can provide for comments and amendments). Then, one or more decrees are drafted by the prime minister to allocate the authorised funding. And, lastly, the parliament has 20 days to provide its advice on such decrees before they can be formally adopted.

Whatever the procedure being followed, it has become usual practice to present parliament with a package covering various initiatives: military and police missions abroad; specific humanitarian and development-cooperation initiatives related to the crisis areas where those missions are deployed to or where conflicts are ongoing (N.B. The core of the funding for development cooperation and humanitarian assistance comes from the regular budget); and stabilisation, peacebuilding and other initiatives related to the same areas. This package, which bears general resemblances to a WGA to crises and conflicts, is meant to make the proposal of military/police missions more palatable to parliament by taking into account the concerns of the centre/ left political parties and their preference for civilian instead of military initiatives and, if necessary, for military initiatives that are limited in scope and duration.

In recent years, Italy has made progress towards a WGA approach to external crises and conflicts that focuses on countries where Italian military assets (including Carabinieri) are deployed under a national or multinational mandate and, in some cases, as the consequence of a long-term national commitment to a specific country (e.g. Afghanistan or Lebanon).

Italy's experience with implementing a WGA also includes its contribution to international responses to natural disasters, namely, the 2004 tsunami in South-East Asia and the 2010 earthquake in Haiti. These humanitarian crises provided an opportunity for Italy to transfer abroad the well-established coordination mechanism from the national level led by the Protezione Civile, Italy's national body for predicting, preventing and managing exceptional events. In particular, the WGA that characterised Italy's contribution to the international relief efforts in Haiti provided inspiration to then-EU High Representative for Foreign Affairs and Security Policy Catherine Ashton for her subsequent work on the comprehensive approach when establishing the EEAS.

Italy's WGA covers countries in its former colonies and in the broader southern neighbourhood, including Afghanistan, Iraq, Lebanon, Libya, Niger, the Palestinian territories and Somalia. The fields of action can vary from country to country, depending on their specificities. However, humanitarian aid, development cooperation, stabilisation, cultural heritage, training and providing support to civil society and to the most vulnerable (e.g. women, children, migrants, people with disabilities) are always part of Italy's WGA.

Among Italy's main thematic priorities, the following are worth mentioning: First, so-called stability policing (SP) is one of the distinctive features of Italy's contribution to the comprehensive approaches of the EU, NATO and the UN. The Carabinieri had a hand in developing the SP concept, and Italy has assumed a leading international role in developing its doctrine, in training and in actual deployments on the ground. This has also led to the establishment of structures and organisations based in the north-eastern Italian city of Vicenza: the Center of Excellence for Stability Police Units (CoESPU) for the UN and the African Union, the NATO Stability Policing Center of Excellence, and the European Gendarmerie Force (EGF/EUGEND-FOR).

A second joint priority is women, peace and security. For example, Article 1 of the 2016 law concerning Italy's participation in international missions and operations (Italian Parliament 2016) explicitly provides for initiatives aimed at implementing UN Security Council Resolution 1325 (and subsequent resolutions) as well as the national action plans on women, peace and security. Among the many initiatives, a Mediterranean Women Mediators Network was established in 2017.

A third priority is the protection of cultural heritage. In the belief that defending cultural heritage is key to fostering peace and sustainable development, Italy's WGA always includes initiatives – also in cooperation with the UN and UNESCO – aimed at protecting cultural heritage from terrorism and mass atrocities; supporting Italian archaeological, anthropological and ethnological missions abroad as well as local cultural institutions; and countering the illicit trafficking of cultural artefacts and recovering illegally exported artworks.

Lastly, training is also one of the main priorities of Italy's WGA. This embraces a number of different fields, including: police and military training; training of local workers (including transfer of technologies) in archaeology, restoration and historic conservation; and technical and legislative assistance in various fields (e.g. anti-corruption).

3 | Who are the main actors involved in cooperating in a WGA?

The main actors that cooperate in Italy's WGA-like activities are the Ministry of Foreign Affairs, the Ministry of Defence, the Prime Minister's Office, the Ministry of the Interior, and the intelligence services. A special role is played by the embassy/ambassador in the country concerned. Parliament has to be fully involved in any decision-making.

The core of Italy's WGA lies in a joint approach of the ministries of Foreign Affairs and Defence, and it also depends on the political and personal relationships between the two respective ministers. When in agreement, they can be the driving force behind most WGA initiatives, under the guidance and supervision of the prime minister. Both ministries have been directly involved in the debates in Brussels concerning the EU's comprehensive approach and the EU Global Strategy (EUGS), which has clearly had an influence on their approach to crises and conflicts.

At the government level, inter-ministerial coordination on external crisis management should in principle take place within two bodies established at the level of the Prime Minister's Office as part of the national organisation for crisis management created by decree in 2010 (Prime Minister's Office 2010): the Political and Strategic Committee (CoPS) and the Inter-ministerial Team for Situation and Planning (NISP). However, coordination can also take place within the Inter-ministerial Committee for the Security of the Republic (CISR) established by law in 2007 as part of a reform of the intelligence sector, as well as within the Supreme Council of Defence (CSD), a body set forth by Italy's constitution to debate and analyse issues concerning national security and defence.

In practice, however, decisions on external crises and conflicts (including those involving a WGA) are mainly taken by small groups of ministers meeting informally at the initiative of the prime minister. These meetings, which are chaired by the prime minister, bring together the relevant ministers (Foreign Affairs, Defence, the Interior, etc), the chief of defence (CHOD), and representatives of the intelligence agencies to deal with specific crisis situations. For example, in recent years, this was the case concerning Libya.

In addition, the Ministry of Foreign Affairs has an established practice of convening regular coordination meetings – both formal and informal – with other ministries. This happens regularly with the Ministry of Defence (at different levels), less regularly with the Ministry of the Interior, and informally with the intelligence agencies. These meetings provide for concrete coordination. Their usefulness, however, depends on their level (a higher/political level usually ensures a concrete follow-up), on the personal relationships between the respective ministers (such as whether they belong to the same political party), and on their relationships with the prime minister.

In principle, formal and informal coordination mechanisms within each ministry work smoothly. But their effectiveness in practice differs according to the administration concerned, as it also depends on the roles assumed by individual leading figures, even among civil servants. In this context, some peculiarities have to be taken into account. For example, coordination between the CHOD and the Defence General Staff, on the one hand, and the minister of defence and his/her cabinet, on the other, can require some efforts at times. And, within the Prime Minister's Office, coordination is not made easier by the differences in the bureaucratic backgrounds of the actors involved, the presence of both political appointees and permanent staff, and the presence of members of the various political parties in the governing coalition. Lastly, coordination in the Ministry of Foreign Affairs is more informal, as it involves a limited number of actors and is often based on personal contacts, emails and telephone calls.

4 | How does your country operationalise a WGA?

Because there are no national documents on an Italian WGA, there are also no guidelines, joint financial instruments, joint lessons learned processes, special units or inter-departmental structures of coordination related to the country's WGA. However, this has not prevented the establishment of some coordinating bodies that could provide for a potential 'WGA architecture'.

The provisions of the 2010 decree concerning the national organisation for crisis management (Prime Minister's Office 2010) have only been partially implemented so far, which could also be attributed to the fact that they were adopted by decree rather than by law. On the other hand, both the CoPS and the NISP could provide for the core of a national WGA architecture. But the CoPS has never convened and, even though it meets regularly, the NISP has mainly been dealing with the protection of critical infrastructures (responding to NATO and EU inputs), hybrid threats (in response to EU inputs), and EU-NATO exercises rather than with real-time political and security crises and conflicts. The secretariat of both the CoPS and NISP is provided for by the Office of the Military Adviser to the Prime Minister.

This could explain why their activities have so far been limited to a few sectoral issues, since it is very difficult to implement a WGA when military officials are in the lead.

There are two major problems with having small, informally meeting groups of ministers make decisions on external crises and conflicts. First, no formal records are available regarding their outcomes. And, second, the civil servants who are actually in charge of the issues being discussed at these meetings are only involved in preparing them to a limited degree.

A significant institutional change that could strengthen Italy's commitment to a WGA would be the establishment of a National Security Council within the Prime Minister's Office and the appointment of a national security adviser (who could potentially be the diplomatic adviser to the prime minister). Such a change should be discussed by parliament and provided for in a law, as this would ensure that the WGA will benefit from broad political and institutional support and be sustainable over time. For the time being, however, the implementation of political decisions related to a WGA is entrusted to individual ministries and follows their respective procedures.

A number of enablers have facilitated this process. For example, there is the fact that development cooperation has always been part of what was recently renamed the Ministry of Foreign Affairs and Development Cooperation as well as an integral part of Italy's foreign policy.

Second, there is the fact that the Carabinieri, who are one of the main features of Italy's WGA, are under the leadership of the Ministry of Defence when deployed abroad, whereas they (and other police forces) are coordinated by the Ministry of the Interior when operating within Italy.

The third enabler involves a bit of administrative reshuffling. In 2010, a few steps in the direction of ensuring better policy coherence were taken in the Ministry of Foreign Affairs. On the one hand, most of the WGA-relevant geographical desks were brought under the leadership of the political director. On the other hand, the CSFP/CSDP desk was shifted from the EU Department to the Political Affairs Department and upgraded to the level of a unit under the direct leadership of the political director. These moves have enabled increased coordination among the structures dealing with the EU, NATO, the UN and the OSCE and the geographical desks dealing with Italy's neighbourhood, and they have made it possible to have a single individual in a leadership position (i.e. the political director) interact with other ministries (primarily the Ministry of Defence). That said, one should note that this remains a tactical rather than a strategic change. Furthermore, despite these improvements, one thing is still missing: bodies to deal with stabilisation and peacebuilding issues while taking a horizontal approach. In theory, one unit could be established within the Foreign Ministry (Political Affairs) to deal with policy, and another unit could be set up in the Italian Agency for Development Cooperation for implementing concrete projects.

The fourth enabler is the process, involving both the government and parliament, through which Italian participation in international missions and operations is agreed and funded. This process, as well as the parliament's process of reviewing the previous year's initiatives, provides for a coherent and transparent overview of both military and civilian initiatives undertaken with regard to external crises and conflicts.

The procedure being followed in this context facilitates the design and implementation of a WGA, as a single decision-making process provides for the allocation of financial resources to different ministries and to both military and civilian initiatives.

However, the 2016 law concerning Italy's participation in international missions and operations (Italian Parliament 2016) was a missed opportunity in terms of a national WGA to external crises and conflicts. This piece of legislation originated from parliament and was only meant to better define its role in this field. As such, it mainly deals with the process and not the substance of the issue, nor does it contain explicit obligations or commitments in terms of a WGA.

As Italy does not have a formal strategic framework for ensuring a coordinated approach for all stakeholders involved in responding to crises and conflicts, there is also no strategic framework for its development-cooperation efforts (e.g. those of the newly established Italian Agency for Development Cooperation) that would ensure a cohesive approach to its initiatives, contribute to synergies with other actors, and facilitate a coordinated approach at the country level. This leads to a situation in which competing priorities are resolved in a pragmatic way: through trade-offs.

Furthermore, to this day, the Ministry of the Interior seems reluctant to be a full partner of the foreign and defence ministries in designing and implementing a national WGA. Since it was less involved in the relevant debates within the international fora, it is somewhat of a missing element in Italy's contributions to the WGA strategies of the EU, the UN, NATO and the OSCE. In this case, getting the Ministry of the Interior to become more involved would require more of a change of cultural mindset than new institutional arrangements.

Since the initiative and political input for a WGA often come from cooperation and coordination among individual ministers, a major 'disabler' in terms of WGA is when relevant ministers (foreign affairs, defence and the interior) belong to different political parties in the governing coalition and do not enjoy good personal and/or professional relationships.

5 | Conclusions

Italy's WGA tends to be pragmatic and based on a case-by-case approach with a limited conceptual basis. Despite some institutional weaknesses, it has been successful in ensuring greater policy coherence between different ministries and departments as well as in building mutual trust and confidence through the real-world cooperation of military and civilian personnel.

In terms of its success factors, one can say that dialogue and cooperation with and ownership by the local authorities (at all levels) play a central role. Another factor is the role de facto entrusted with the embassy/ambassador in the country concerned, which continues to be crucial when it comes to designing a vision for Italy's engagement and to bringing various national and local actors together.

Since the political and institutional system does not provide for clear and permanent leadership or guidance, the role of individual personalities (both members of the government and civil servants) matters more than formal coordination mechanisms in the decision-making process. When the right network of the right people has been in place, the guidance provided has been effective in enabling a WGA, despite the fact that a lot of follow-up work has remained to be done at the administrative and working levels.

Owing to the absence of national documents, guidelines and procedures, almost every initiative requires additional efforts to be designed and implemented as well as daily monitoring to ensure that coordination continues to be practiced by all actors involved. Once put in motion, the push for a WGA is usually sustained over time, even when there are subsequent changes in the political leadership.

Since the EU played a significant role in raising Italy's awareness about the WGA as well as in influencing and shaping Italy's WGA-related activities, Italy has high expectations of the EU and it has been consistently pushing for an EU WGA in Libya, on migration issues, and in the Horn of Africa. Regarding Libya and the migration issue, Italy has provided inputs and leadership to the relevant EU CSDP initiatives. What's more, via the so-called 'Global Compact for Migration', Italy has made a written contribution to a comprehensive and long-term strategy for EU external action on migration, which has influenced subsequent European Council conclusions and European Commission proposals in this field.

A WGA approach also characterises Italy's participation in the Global Coalition Against Daesh. Italy supported a multidimensional approach identified in the coalition's different lines of action (military progress, stabilisation, counter-financing, preventing the movement of foreign terrorist fighters, and countering propaganda) and the subsequent involvement of a multitude of actors at the national level. Italy is also among the top contributors to the Global Coalition in Iraq, supporting its efforts in all lines of action and developing a multi-dimensional strategy that integrates international and national engagement in order to maximise effectiveness and coherence.

6 | Reference list

Italian Parliament (2014). Law no. 125 of 11 August 2014. General law on international development cooperation. 14G00130. www.aics. gov.it/wp-content/uploads/2018/04/LEGGE_11_agosto_2014_n_1 25_ENGLISH.pdf.

Italian Parliament (2016). Law no. 145 of 21 July 2016. Disposizioni concernenti la partecipazione dell'Italia alle missioni internazionali. 16G00159. www.gazzettaufficiale.it/eli/id/2016/08/01/16G001 59/sg.

Ministry of Defence (2015). White Paper for International Security and Defence., Rome. www.difesa.it/Primo_Piano/Documents/20 15/07_Luglio/White%20book.pdf.

Ministry of Foreign Affairs and Ministry of Defence (2012). Approccio Nazionale Multi-Dimensionale alla gestione delle crisi. Joint conceptual paper (revised). Feb. 2012. www.difesa.it/SMD_/Staff/ Reparti/III/CID/Dottrina/Pagine/Approccio_Nazionale_Multi_D imensionale.aspx.

Prime Minister's Office (2010). Decreto del Presidente del Consiglio dei Ministri. Organizzazione nazionale per la gestione di crisi. 10A07594. 5 May 2010. www.gazzettaufficiale.it/eli/id/2010/06/17 /10A07594/sg.

Latvia

Maris Andzans

1 | Introduction

A whole-of-government approach (WGA) to dealing with external conflicts and crises has not been defined as a specific objective in Latvia. Though there accordingly is not any specifically defined WGA in place, and neither such nor similar terms are used in legislation and policy planning documents, it is implicitly but clearly present in policy planning and implementation. Engagement of all relevant institutions has been a common practice roughly since Latvia regained its independence in 1991 and commenced re-establishment of its diplomatic corps, armed forces and other institutions.

Latvia's current approach to dealing with external conflicts and crises is primarily determined by four factors: the size of its public administration (and the country itself), resources devoted to external engagements, level of political priority, and its membership in international organisations. Given the small size of Latvia, its relatively compact public administration, its limited resources devoted to external crises and conflicts, and the lack of consistent and meaningful political initiatives to foster a more active role, Latvia has compact crisis-management mechanisms and it has not hit above its weight in dealing with external crises and conflicts. This, however, does not impede its fairly good whole-of-government operation in practice.

As Latvia has been a member of both the European Union (EU) and the North Atlantic Treaty Organization (NATO) for over 15 years, its approach and engagement abroad primarily fits within the mechanisms, approaches and priorities of those two organisations.

2 | What policies have been developed to further policy coherence?

There is no single specific document defining Latvia's foreign policy, though various laws and policy planning documents unambiguously set the margins of Latvia's foreign policy. In particular, they underscore that its membership in the EU and NATO as well as its strategic partnership with the US are cornerstones of its foreign and defence policies, as outlined further below.

Short-term priorities of external relations are addressed in declarations of governments (cf. the current declaration: Cabinet of Ministers of Latvia 2019) and annual reports of the minister of foreign affairs (cf. the latest report: Minister of Foreign Affairs of Latvia 2018).

Less parsimony can be seen with long-term national security and state defence documents. The National Security Concept (Saeima 2015) takes a wide view of national security, covering various military and non-military issues; it serves as an umbrella document for internal and external security issues. Russia here stands out as the most notable adversary (it is mentioned 43 times in the strategy alone, up from five times in the previous edition from four years earlier (Saeima 2011)). The Concept underlines that membership in NATO and the EU are the cornerstones of Latvia's national security, while the role of the United Nations, the Organisation for Security and Co-operation in Europe (OSCE), and the Council of Europe are also noted with regard to international security issues. In terms of specific external regions, most attention in the Concept is devoted to the conflict in Ukraine, and the Middle East is also mentioned in the context of risks to Europe emanating from the region. In what can clearly be attributed to the whole-of-government approach, the document stresses that "[t]he spectrum of threats to the national security of Latvia exceeds the responsibility of the institutions of defence and interior system. [...] [T]he whole public administration has to be involved in identifying, preventing and overcoming threats to the national security." Furthermore, the Concept underlines the importance of having centralised management both in regard to policy and coordination, of having inter-institutional mechanisms that are constantly operational, and of having each institution manage issues falling under its respective responsibility (Saeima 2015). The State Defence Concept, which primarily focuses on military-security issues, largely stands in the same line with the National Security Concept in terms of inter-institutional cooperation and information exchange (Saeima 2016).

Latvia's development-cooperation (aid) policy, as outlined in the Development Cooperation Policy Guidelines for 2016–2020, focuses on fostering sustainable development, eradicating poverty, and promoting the rule of law and good governance. In Latvia's bilateral development cooperation, the priorities are the countries in the EU's Eastern Partnership (especially Georgia, Moldova and Ukraine) and in Central Asia (especially Kyrgyzstan, Tajikistan and Uzbekistan) along with places where Latvian soldiers or civilian experts are deployed. The development-cooperation policy is implemented by the Ministry of Foreign Affairs with the support of other institutions and NGOs (Cabinet of Ministers of Latvia 2016).

All three of the aforementioned documents exemplify an integral whole-of government approach. The first two are well supported at the political level, and most of the priorities are backed by adequate resources, especially those falling under the responsibility of military authorities (since 2018, Latvia's defence expenditures have amounted to 2 percent of GDP (Saeima 2017)). The same cannot be said about Latvia's development-cooperation policy, which, though clearly defined, has lacked both financial and political support. For example, in 2017, Latvia provided the lowest net official development assistance (ODA) as a percentage of gross national income among all EU member states (0.11%), which was the second-lowest figure in the EU in absolute terms (USD 31.92 million) (OECD 2018). Given this, it is difficult to characterise Latvia's development aid as a significant instrument in dealing with external crisis and conflicts.

The issue of funding can be viewed as a detrimental factor for a bolder and better-integrated whole-of-government approach and foreign policy in general. Funding for crisis-management issues is fragmented, with each of the institutions requesting and receiving funds for its own operational purposes. There is no dedicated funding for enhancing inter-institutional mechanisms for external affairs. There is also no clear and comprehensive human resources policy that would foster a whole-of-government approach. For example, there are no comprehensive training programmes for the government apparatus at the national level to foster inter-institutional cooperation (Official of the Ministry of Foreign Affairs of Latvia 2019; Official of the Ministry of Defence of Latvia 2019).

Finally, there are no explicit political initiatives to foster a smoother whole-of-government approach to external affairs. Granted, there is a clear understanding that no major issue concerning external crises and conflicts can be dealt with by one institution alone. But there has been no clear and consistent push to strengthen a multistakeholder approach that, among other things, would include targeted funding and a comprehensive role for civil society actors.

3 | Who are the main actors involved in cooperating in a WGA?

There is fairly well-established formal and informal coordination and cooperation in the framework of national security and state defence. Though it is difficult to pinpoint a distinct approach in regard to external crises and conflicts from (internal) national security and state defence, all relevant ministries and other institutions are covered by the respective regulations and mechanisms.

Most engaged in dealing with external crises and conflicts are the Ministry of Foreign Affairs, the Ministry of Defence, and the Ministry of Interior as well as their subordinate institutions, such as the National Armed Forces and the State Border Guard.

The Saeima, as the parliament is called, is in charge of the main strategic decisions regarding national security and state defence, including adopting laws and strategies related to national security and state defence, as well as approving deployments of Latvian troops abroad. Meanwhile, the Cabinet of Ministers is tasked with implementing the policies adopted by the Saeima and operational tasks, as well as deciding on deployments for international rescue and humanitarian operations (Saeima 2000).

The National Security Law tasks the Cabinet of Ministers with dealing with threats to the state, while each ministry is responsible for planning for and countering threats to the state in its respective field of responsibility (ibid.).

Among the national inter-institutional coordination mechanisms, two have to be underlined. First, the National Security Council, tasked with coordination of national security policy, consists of the president of Latvia, the chairperson of the parliament, the prime minister, chairpersons of two committees of the parliament, and the ministers of defence, foreign affairs and the interior. Second is the Crisis Management Council, which is tasked with operational-level coordination issues. It consists of the prime minister and the ministers of defence, foreign affairs, economics, finance, the interior, justice, health, transport and communications, environmental protection and regional development (ibid.).

Issues related to significant external crises and conflicts are dealt with by the National Security Council, whose work is usually not discussed in detail publicly. It is generally considered to be an effective coordination mechanism at the highest political level. The Crisis Management Council tends to be seen as a reactive rather than a proactive mechanism for operational-level issues (Official of the Ministry of Defence of Latvia 2019).

Coordination is also formalised in the aforementioned institutions. In the Saeima, the main committees involved with issues related to external crises and conflicts are: the Foreign Affairs Committee; the Defence, Internal Affairs and Corruption Prevention Committee; and the National Security Committee. Furthermore, ministries have internal structures that are responsible for focusing on internal and external crises and conflicts. For example, in the Ministry of Foreign Affairs, there is a NATO and European Security Policy Division as well as an International Operations and Crisis Management Division (Ministry of Foreign Affairs of Latvia 2019a), whereas there is a Crisis Management Department in the Ministry of Defence (Ministry of Defence of Latvia 2019).

Informal mechanisms, such as those between the ministries of Foreign Affairs and Defence, are functioning fairly well. Since the number of persons working on the respective issues is not vast, officials often participate in the same exercises and jointly coordinate their draft legislation, policy or operational issues (Official of the Ministry of Defence of Latvia 2019; Official of the Ministry of Foreign Affairs of Latvia 2019).

Engagement with civil society actors regarding external crises and conflicts, however, is unbalanced. Experts from thinktanks and universities are involved in consulting with the authorities on external affairs in general terms, while non-governmental organisations are involved in consulting on and implementing development-cooperation activities (Cabinet of Ministers of Latvia 2016). At the same time, non-governmental actors do not have any significant impact on major decisions regarding external crises and conflicts, such as whether Latvian troops should be deployed on international missions or operations abroad. To be fair, such decisions regarding participation have not been widely contested by civil society, apart from forms of activism regarding the Second Iraq War.

4 | How does your country operationalise a WGA?

Latvia's contribution to preventing and managing external crises and conflicts consists of providing political support and/or development and humanitarian aid to certain countries in addition to participating in military and civilian operations and missions.

Latvia's most notable efforts in terms of external political engagement in crises and conflict situations have been providing assistance to Georgia and Ukraine following their respective conflicts with Russia. Countries in the EU's Eastern Partnership (including the aforementioned Georgia and Ukraine) and in Central Asia have been priority areas of Latvia's development policy, along with areas where Latvian troops and civilian experts are deployed. Such assistance, though limited, has been provided in various spheres. The development aid, along with political support and other activities, has helped Latvia to maintain a decent level of visibility in both Ukraine and Georgia as well as in Central Asia.

Another instrument of engagement is Latvia's participation in military operations abroad. To date, the highest number of troops has been sent to operations led by NATO and the US: the Implementation Force (IFOR) and Stabilisation Force (SFOR) in Bosnia-Herzegovina; the Kosovo Force (KFOR); the International Security Assistance Force (ISAF) in Afghanistan; and Operation Iraqi Freedom (National Armed Forces of Latvia 2019). Latvia's current military operations include: the EU-led operations NAVFOR ATALANTA, EUNAVFOR MED Sophia and EUTM MALI; the UN-led operation MINUSMA (also in Mali); and the NATO-led operation Resolute Support Mission in Afghanistan (which currently has the largest contingent of Latvian troops, or 42). The current number of troops on operations – 63 (Ministry of Foreign Affairs of Latvia 2019b) – is significantly lower than it used to be, down from more than 300 in the 2004–2012 period (National Armed Forces of Latvia 2019).

Latvia also contributes its experts to civilian missions. At present, 16 Latvian experts have been contributed to the EU-led operations EUMM Georgia and EUAM Ukraine as well as to the OSCE-led SMM Ukraine (Ministry of Foreign Affairs of Latvia 2019b). However, the pool of experienced and qualified experts who can be sent abroad is small, and they are also needed at home, though the Ministry of Foreign Affairs is striving to increase the current number (Official of the Ministry of Foreign Affairs 2019).

Latvia has also contributed to other missions and operations. For example, Latvia's border guards have participated in operations of the European Border and Coast Guard Agency (FRONTEX) aimed at supporting the protection of the EU's southern external border (cf., e.g. State Border Guard of Latvia 2010).

5 | Conclusions

Overall, even though it has not been an objective per se, the whole-of-government approach has been running well in Latvia. Having all relevant institutions involved in policymaking has been a standard practice. No known significant decisions on external crises have been taken unilaterally.

The main advantage of Latvia's system is its smallness and the frameworks set by its international alliances. The former factor means a relatively compact public administration in which the relevant players interact with each other frequently and across a broad spectrum of issues. The latter factor – i.e. membership in both the EU and NATO for 15 years (which is longer than the period between gaining independence and joining these alliances) – has fostered the transposition of a mostly modern, post-Cold War-era approach to preventing and managing crises and conflicts. Operations and missions led by the above-mentioned organisations as well as by the United States have been the focus of Latvia's external engagement, along with the development aid and civilian missions to countries in the EU's Eastern Partnership (Georgia and Ukraine, in particular) and Central Asia.

The drawbacks of the Latvian approach are the lack of strong political initiatives and insufficient resources devoted to streamlining the whole-of-government approach as well as engagement with external crises and conflicts. To make Latvia's external engagement and the national mechanisms underpinning it work better and more boldly, the following can be suggested: to enhance training for and funding of a better-integrated whole-of government approach and external engagement in general; to increase funding for development aid and to thereby expand the scope of activities in crisis and conflict regions; to increase the number of Latvian troops and civilian experts deployed to missions and operations abroad; to launch bolder political initiatives aimed at preventing and managing crises and conflicts abroad – and to thereby enable Latvia to hit above its weight.

6 | Reference list

Cabinet of Ministers of Latvia (2016). "Par Attistibas sadarbibas politikas pamatnostadnem 2016.-2020. gadam." 14 September 2016. https://likumi.lv/ta/id/284775-par-attistibas-sadarbibas-politikas-pamatnostadnem-20162020-gadam.

Cabinet of Ministers of Latvia (2019). "Deklaracija par Artura Krisjaņa Kariņa vadita Ministru kabineta iecereto darbibu." www.mk.gov.lv/sites/default/files/editor/kk-valdibas-deklaracija_red-gala.pdf.

Ministry of Defence of Latvia (2019). "Kontakti." www.mod.gov.lv/lv/kontakti.

Minister of Foreign Affairs of Latvia (2018). "Arlietu ministra ikgadejais ziņojums par paveikto un iecereto darbibu valsts arpolitika un Eiropas Savienibas jautajumos. 2018. gads." www.mfa.gov.lv/images/ministrija/Arpolitikas_zinojums_2018.pdf.

Ministry of Foreign Affairs of Latvia (2019a). "Arlietu ministrijas talruņu saraksts." 16 July 2019. www.mfa.gov.lv/ministrija/kontakt informacija/arlietu-ministrijas-talrunu-saraksts.

Ministry of Foreign Affairs of Latvia (2019b). "Latvijas daliba starptautiskajas misijas un operacijas." 1 March 2019. www.mfa.gov.lv/images/uploads/infografiki/lv_misijas_2019.jpg.

National Armed Forces of Latvia (2019). "Ieprieksejas operacijas." www.mil.lv/lv/aktualitates-un-macibas/starptautiskas-operacijas/ieprieksejas-operacijas.

OECD (Organisation for Economic Co-operation and Development) (2018). "Net ODA." https://data.oecd.org/oda/net-oda.htm#indicator-chart.

Official of the Ministry of Defence of Latvia (2019). Interview by the author of the chapter. 17 April 2019.

Official of the Ministry of Foreign Affairs of Latvia (2019). Interview by the author of the chapter. 16 May 2019.

Saeima (2000). "Nacionalas drosibas likums." 14 December 2000. https://likumi.lv/doc.php?id=14011.

Saeima (2011). "Par Nacionalas drosibas koncepcijas apstiprinasanu." 10 March 2011. https://likumi.lv/doc.php?id=227460.

Saeima (2015). "Par Nacionalas drosibas koncepcijas apstiprinasanu." 26 November 2015. https://likumi.lv/ta/id/278107-par-nacionalas-drosibas-koncepcijas-apstiprinasanu.

Saeima (2016). "Par Valsts aizsardzibas koncepcijas apstiprinasanu." 16 June 2016. https://likumi.lv/ta/id/282964-parvalsts-aizsardzibas-koncepcijas-apstiprinasanu.

Saeima (2017). "Par videja termiņa budzeta ietvaru 2018., 2019. un 2020. gadam." 23 November 2017. https://likumi.lv/ta/id/295595-par-videja-termina-budzeta-ietvaru-2018-2019-un-2020-gadam.

State Border Guard of Latvia (2010). "Valsts robezsardzes speki piedalas starptautiska operacija." 8 July 2010. www.rs.gov.lv/index.php?id=1031&top=-6&rel=1369.

Lithuania

Dovile Jakniunaite

1 | Introduction

To date, Lithuania has not introduced a formal whole-of-government approach (WGA) system to deal with external conflicts and crisis. In other words, it has yet to map out a system for how to provide a coherent response to such events in a coordinated manner. However, this does not mean that Lithuania does not have any foreign policy coordination. In fact, a range of mechanisms and procedures that allow for coordination and cooperation among various governmental institutions and actors in crisis situations has been established and is in use. In addition, over the last two years, the government has started planning how to introduce what it refers to as an 'integrated crisis coordination system'. Thus, it is evident that efforts are underway to move the country towards a more formalised WGA. That said, one must add that the plans developed so far are fairly general, and that the steps taken to date have only been incremental.

One can identify at least four reasons why Lithuania does not yet have a complete and coherent WGA system. First, the country's foreign policy is coordinated through a range of formal, semi-formal and informal mechanisms, and they have been used when needed so far. However, having yet to encounter any major disaster or failure, there has not been any external pressure on the government to establish a more coherent system. Second, Lithuania is a small country and does not have a huge government apparatus of personnel working in foreign affairs and security policy. Most of the players involved know each other, the chains of command and hierarchy structures are not long, and it is usually not difficult to mobilise the responsible people in a crisis situation. Third, since Lithuania regained its independence in 1990, the idea that the country needs to have a coherent system to coordinate and manage crisis situations has always existed. But this idea has not become reality yet due to the absence of clear political leadership at a sufficiently high level of the government and owing to the lack of will and resources to implement such a system. What's more, inter-institutional competition regarding which body should be in charge of such coordination has also compounded this lack of will. Over the last decade, the Office of the President's dominant role in foreign policy matters has also rendered a formal system unnecessary, as the office has coordinated most of the needed responses informally and assumed what appears to be a dominant position. Finally, while Lithuania's foreign policy is concentrated on the country's national security and the Russian threat, most efforts related to security and defence policy focus on domestic crises and threats. For this reason, it is assumed that any serious response to an external crisis should be undertaken either by bigger states or through consultations in the context of the EU and/or NATO and using their fairly developed instruments.

2 | What policies have been developed to further policy coherence?

As mentioned earlier, Lithuania has yet to develop a clear framework for strengthening the integration, coordination and effectiveness of foreign, security and developmental policies, or what might be called a coherent WGA framework. However, there are several policy-coordination instruments and mechanisms to ensure policy coherence on the strategic level as well as some systems in place on the tactical level. First, there is the State Defence Council, a constitutional body for debating and making decisions about the most important national security matters. Second, there are two legally binding national security documents that are updated frequently and define the main focus areas of national security efforts. Third, there is a generally strong consensus in Lithuania on the most important foreign policy questions, which obviates the need to discuss which external crises the country should focus on and on which level. In what follows, I will provide more details about these three points.

As noted above, the State Defence Council (SDC) is a special body devoted to coordinating national security issues on the national level. This entity is mentioned in Article 140 of the Constitution of the Republic of Lithuania (adopted in 1992), which states that the main issues of national defence are considered and coordinated by the State Defence Council. The council consists of the president, the prime minister, the speaker of the Seimas (parliament), the minister of national defence, and the commander of the armed forces. The SDC is convened and headed by the president. The Law on the State Defence Council (adopted in 1997) (Seimas of the Republic of Lithuania 1997) adds that the council deliberates on foreign and domestic policy questions related to national security and territorial integrity as well as to the main principles of security policy, supplies recommendations on international treaties and defence agreements, coordinates the activities of state institutions working on national security, provides guidelines on strategic crisis management and the defence budget, and coordinates the activities of the intelligence agencies. According to the law, the chairperson of the Seimas National Defence Committee, the director of the State Security Department, and the minister of the interior are to be invited to SCD meetings. As a rule, the minister of foreign affairs has also been invited.

Although neither the constitution nor the law designates the SCD as the main body for strategic planning and guidance, in practice the body is also used to debate and decide on any challenges related to national security and/or foreign policy. Thus, it can be viewed as the main national body devoted to WGA on the national strategic level. However, it should also be noted that the council does not meet very often. In fact, the president usually convenes the council when he or she wants to reach or demonstrate institutional/governmental consensus on some national security question. For example, such a demonstration of consensus agreement was needed when the first debates on the Lithuanian international military missions started (in 2005/2006) as well as when the decision was made to reintroduce military conscription in response to the crisis in Ukraine (in 2014). In the context of external crises and conflict prevention, the SCD would convene and hold debates if there were a military crises close to Lithuanian borders. But, in all likelihood, other external crises would be tackled by other instruments and/or institutions (as is further discussed below).

Regarding documents related to national security and foreign policy, Lithuania has two legal documents that systematically define its foreign and national security policies on a strategic level (e.g. the main goals, objectives, threats, risks and responsible institutions), and that provide some ideas about a system for managing and coordinating crises. The first one is the Law on the Basics of the National Security (originally adopted in 1996, but amended 28 times between then and 2018) (Seimas of the Republic of Lithuania 1996). The law indicates that the government must create and develop a crisis-management system to monitor, prevent, foresee and react to threats, and it stipulates that the Crisis Management Committee headed by the prime minister should be the main coordinating body in this. According to the law, a 'joint coordination centre' is to be set up for each crisis, if needed, to coordinate and manage the response. The law also talks about the integral crisis-management plans that each ministry and other governmental institutions should have (on the actual functioning of these institutions, see below).

The second strategic policy document is the National Security Strategy adopted in 2017 (Seimas of the Republic of Lithuania 2017). This is the fourth such strategy, following previous versions adopted in 2002, 2005 and 2012. It defines national security interests, threats, risks, and both long- and short-term objectives.

In addition to these two documents, Lithuania's foreign policy community has a long, informal tradition of seeking and reaching consensus on strategic foreign and security matters and positions among the main political parties of Lithuania by publicly signing the agreement on strategic foreign, security and defence policy commitments. Such agreements – which are considered binding, though legally they are not – were made in 2004 and 2008. These two documents are the Strategic Guidelines for the Foreign, Security and Defence Policy of the Republic of Lithuania for 2014–2020 (signed in 2014) (Seimas of the Republic of Lithuania 2014) as well as the Lithuanian Defence Policy Guidelines (signed in 2018) (Seimas of the Republic of Lithuania 2018). Finally, from time to time, the Seimas also adopts resolutions on foreign policy directions, most recently in 2016 (Seimas of the Republic of Lithuania 2016).

Such agreements and resolutions seek to demonstrate strategic consensus on the main questions and directions of foreign and security policy. These policies, in turn, are supposed to provide guidelines for the day-to-day activities related to making and implementing foreign policy decisions, including ones related to responding to external crises. Such guidelines also specifically indicate which external crises should be considered important and why.

Finally, in order to understand the (currently) minimal need to have a coordinated system in Lithuania for responding to external crises, it is useful to keep in mind the main foreign policy priorities of the country. Lithuania is strongly focused on its own security and on maintaining a secure environment around its borders, i.e. in its 'neighbourhood'. Thus, all thinking about external conflicts and crises is dominated by self-interest and regional interests. At present, Russia is the main security threat and adversary – and Lithuanians generally consider this not only to apply to themselves, but also to Europe as a whole. Indeed, Russia is viewed as an expansionist state that seeks to control its own neighbourhood as well as one that destabilises the region whenever these goals are not achieved, as has happened in Georgia and then Ukraine. In fact, Russia is not only a military threat, but also militarily threatening. In other words, in addition to being prepared and ready to use force, it is also willing to do so. And this also includes via non-military means, such as through energy policy, false information campaigns and cyberattacks. Although neighbouring Belarus is not directly mentioned often in security and foreign policy discussions and documents, perceived threats do arise from the fact that it is viewed as somewhat of a Russia satellite. However, Belarus' new nuclear plant in the border city of Astravyets, which is scheduled to enter into operation in 2020, has led it to be viewed in recent years as a threat due to safety concerns.

Given these concerns about its neighbours, all strategic documents and papers emphasise the vital importance of Lithuania's memberships in the EU and NATO, which are both considered the primary guarantors of the country's security. Accordingly, the viability and unity of NATO and the EU, as well as the degree of solidarity within both organisations, are of paramount interest to the country. Regarding NATO, the main focus is on collective defence commitments and the importance of maintaining strong transatlantic ties (i.e. on keeping American forces in Europe and keeping Americans interested in the continent). In order to counter Russia's efforts to destabilise and exert influence in Eastern Europe, Lithuania strongly supports more closely integrating Georgia, Moldova and Ukraine into to the EU (and eventually offering them membership) and having a strong Eastern Partnership (EaP) in addition to inviting these countries to join NATO.

Instability in other parts of the world is acknowledged, and the negative consequences for the international community of problems in regions further away are recognised. However, unless some EU instrument is activated and there is a need for a national position, little more is done in terms of strategic deliberations on the national level. Thus, in Lithuania, there is not much in terms of systematic and comprehensive thinking on external crisis management, conflict prevention or conflict resolution if these are not taking place in nearby regions (e.g. Belarus, Georgia or Ukraine). In such cases, general remarks about solidarity and strengthening international security and stability are usually made. Furthermore, Lithuania acknowledges that its security depends on countering challenges to the south of Europe, where prolonged conflicts, unstable states and security vacuums are creating conditions for terrorism, uncontrolled migration, organised crime and humanitarian crises – all of which present a huge challenge to EU unity. But the country's focus and urgency to react is usually only reserved to a limited number of external security threats.

3 | Who are the main actors involved in cooperating in a WGA?

There are four main institutions that would usually be involved in coordinating a reaction to an external crisis in some WGA-like fashion: the Ministry of Foreign Affairs (MFA), the Ministry of National Defence (MND), the Prime Minister's Office and the President's Office. Depending on the issue at hand, other institutions might be involved, such as: the State Security Department; the so-called Second Investigation Department under MND, a military intelligence unit; the Ministry of the Interior; or the Ministry of Economy and Innovation.

In times of external crisis, coordination and cooperation would take place in more or less the following way, which is based on a mixture of formal and informal practice. In general, the government has a pretty clear system of disseminating information during a crisis situation. This is done via a messaging system and/or telephone, and there is a system for who gets informed, about which matters, how the level of urgency is determined, and who should be contacted next. In a second step, a decision is made about whether to react and, if so, about whether those in the circle of already-informed bodies should respond to the problem or the response efforts should be taken to a higher, if not the highest, level. After the initial decision on the nature of the situation, the type of subsequent communication depends on the type of crisis (internal, external, both) and the sector impacted by the crisis (security, defence, foreign, interior, energy, cyber, etc). In serious situations, the initial decision about whether to react would usually be made in the President's Office, which would then contact the MFA. However, the opposite can also happen, with the MFA taking this decision and then contacting the President's Office. If the crisis has security- or defence-related aspects, the MND would also be involved. Given the external nature of the crisis, Lithuania's permanent representative to the EU and/or NATO (depending on the type of question) would also be brought into the communication loop and then assist in coordinating subsequent consultations. Since Lithuania is a small country, the communication chain is usually short and quick. But the success of this procedure depends a lot on how good the working relations and/or personal contacts between the President's Office and the ministries are.

For a long time, even though the Prime Minister's Office coordinates the Crisis Management Committee and the newly created National Security Commission, the office and the prime minister him- or herself have been rather marginal actors in this system. Moreover, the National Security Commission is just beginning to function, so its role among the actors has yet to be defined, and the Crisis Management Committee has never become functional and has only been activated a few times, all of which have involved domestic crises.

4 | How does your country operationalise a WGA?

Despite Lithuania's lack of a single, coherent WGA framework, there are procedures and mechanisms in place regarding what is and should be done in times of crisis. One part of the existing system (information-sharing) and how it functions among actors in various institutions have already been described above. In what follows, the additional elements are discussed.

As things now stand, plans for having a more integrated and coordinated system of managing crises are being proposed and discussed. This indicates that more systemic efforts are being made to move towards something more similar to a WGA. As discussed earlier, even though Lithuanian laws have established various crisis-management structures, to date they have either been ineffective or virtually non-functional. The Law on the Basics of National Security (Seimas of the Republic of Lithuania 1996) mentions the Crisis Management Committee, which is headed by the prime minister and consists of the responsible ministers and the chancellor of the government. The committee is supposed to help the government with crisis management and coordination. For example, it has to propose a strategy, develop a system of crisis management, and be the institution in charge should a crisis occur. However, this committee has never become fully functional, it has not had any supporting institutions to organise its meetings and activities, and it has usually only convened when a (domestic) crisis has arisen.

Another body, the Crisis Management Center in the MND, existed until 2010. Although this institution was also tasked with creating some kind of crisis-management system, it did not produce any significant results and was silently dissolved. Furthermore, it should also be noted that there are legal acts, procedures and sometimes even plans regarding crisis management on the governmental and ministerial levels. Nevertheless, the biggest challenge here is that not every minister has had trainings or participated in crisis simulations, which means that not everyone in the system would know what to do in an actual crisis.

Recently, the MFA and the MND, the two ministries that would deal with most external crises, have begun testing and checking their crisis-response systems and procedures. The mechanism in these two ministries for working and coordinating with EU institutions is also well established, as it is the same mechanism used for non-crisis situations. The leading actors are the MFA and Lithuania's Brussels-based permanent representatives to the EU and NATO, who regularly also contribute to coordination efforts. The president contributes to the formation and representation of EU policy issues that are discussed in the European Council, but his or her involvement in the coordination process depends on the political and strategic salience of the issue. The Permanent Representation of Lithuania to the EU represents the country's official positions in EU institutions, contributes to the formation of national positions, and disseminates information about EU initiatives. Thus, the representation is the main hub through which coordination and communication with EU institutions takes place, and its communication channels and procedures with the MFA are also well established. The biggest challenge is a matter of resources (mainly human, but also financial), so there must be scrupulous prioritisation regarding which issues to focus on (as discussed earlier in the section on Lithuania's foreign policy priorities).

Regarding initial steps to establish an integrated crisis-management system, the programme of the current government (which assumed office in late 2016) mentions the goal of putting in place an integrated crisis-management and hybrid threat-prevention system by the end of 2020. The idea is to establish a functioning system that would be prepared to respond to hybrid threats. This would involve creating, among other things, a coordinating body, a mechanism for crisis prevention, an information-exchange system and an early warning system.

The current government began working on establishing a more defined mechanism for crisis coordination among the ministries by creating a new structure in late 2017. The Governmental National Security Commission aims to become the main institution coordinating threat-monitoring and -prevention measures, and it would also serve as the main body responding to a security-related crisis (as mentioned earlier, the State Defence Council would retain responsibility for military threats). The new commission also aims to have a working crisis-communication system between ministries and other responsible agencies. The 'working' part here is meant to acknowledge that such a system already exists on paper, but nobody knows whether and how it would work in an actual crisis situation. The commission, chaired by the prime minister, consists of the heads of several ministries (Economy and Innovation, National Defence, and the Interior), a representative of the President's Office, and the directors of the State Security Department and the Second Investigation Department under MND. The commission is supposed to generally meet on a monthly basis and to be responsible for coordinating the whole crisis-management cycle, including threat identification and evaluation, crisis prevention and crisis management. At present, it mostly discusses strategic questions and preventive measures, but it is also considered to be the main institution in charge of organising responses to emergencies.

The Office of the Government, as the Prime Minister's Office is also known, is divided into groups, one of which is the Threat Management and Crisis Prevention Group. It currently serves as a secretariat for the above-mentioned National Security Commission (NSC) and the Crisis Management Committee (CMC). However, the CMC will cease to exist if the new amendments to the Law on the Basics of National Security are adopted. On paper, the NSC partly duplicates the work of the CMC. For this reason, the proposed amendments would eliminate the CMC and shift its responsibilities to the NSC, thereby expanding the latter's functions. The new commission has been formed, but without the supporting higher-level legal acts. These provisions were being discussed in parliamentary committees at the time of writing (June 2019).

One of the related plans is to create a body responsible for supporting the work of the revised National Security Commission, called the Joint Threat Management and Crisis Prevention Group (not to be confused with the above-mentioned group with the almost exact name), which would comprise representatives of the relevant ministries and other governmental agencies. In this way, the complete institutional crisis-management system would be established: The NSC would handle coordination on the strategic level; the joint group would execute coordination efforts and facilitate information-exchange among institutions; the group in the Prime Minister's Office would coordinate the work of the NSC and joint group; and the ministries would have their own crisis-management structures.

At the moment, the whole system only exists on paper as a draft. However, initial steps and existing plans indicate that a concerted effort is being made to move towards a more systemic and coherent WGA. If these plans are implemented, one could say that Lithuania has developed (at least on paper) a WGA system for crisis management. Still, even under the proposed system, the focus would remain on internal crises and domestic security issues. But, implicitly, the system is also supposed to work for the majority of major external crises.

5 | Conclusions

After reviewing the efforts over the years to coordinate foreign and security policy in Lithuania both in crisis and normal situations, the first thing that needs to be mentioned is the fact that Lithuania is focused on its own national security, and that thinking about crisis management is oriented internally. Given these circumstances, the majority of the crisis-management mechanisms that exist or are in the planning stage mainly focus on domestic crises or threats. When asked directly if the existing or future mechanism for crisis management will be applicable to external crises, most officials working on such matters would say 'yes', though they would likely add that this dimension of crisis management is rarely the focus. Instead, EU and/ or NATO institutions, mechanisms and procedures are usually considered to be more appropriate and suitable structures for implementing a comprehensive approach to external crises.

The external crises that Lithuania's foreign policy establishment tends to react to and to try to produce a coordinated response to concern Russia and countries in the EU's eastern 'neighbourhood' (e.g. Belarus, Georgia, Moldova and Ukraine). For example, the crisis in Ukraine has definitely prompted a coordinated and systematic response in which a range of institutions have been involved, projects have been coordinated, and a related budget has been systemically and consistently allocated. Other external crises are usually considered 'not for us to solve', and the principles of either solidarity or non-involvement are invoked. Accordingly, for a long time, there was no need to develop a systematic WGA framework for managing external crises and preventing conflict. Thus, despite the efforts to establish an integrated crisis-management system, most crisis communication is now done via a mixture of formal, informal and ad hoc ways.

As some efforts to establish an integrated crisis-management system are underway and some previous experience in crisis management exists, it is possible to pinpoint several factors that would contribute to the success of a WGA system. The first – and, it seems, the most crucial – is the role of leadership. Leadership matters in at least two senses: in understanding the need and reasons for a WGA, and in showing the will to create such a system. The second factor is the ability to take advantage of the smallness of the country, which would result in a less complicated governmental structure, quicker decision-making and having a rather small number of people involved. The third necessary factor is a willingness among the relevant players to implement reforms. The current partly formal-partly informal system seems to be working, so there must be strong incentives for and enthusiasm about establishing a more formal and legalistic system (even if the backers of a more flexible or creative approach might view this as a hindrance). Finally, external pressure and/or vigorous recommendations (AKA nudging) from the EU and/or NATO could provide additional stimulus to Lithuania to start implementing a working WGA system. All in all, if at least all four of the factors listed above were present, it would not be overly presumptuous to claim that Lithuania would be on a much quicker road to having a formal WGA system in place that would enable coordinated, coherent and long-term responses to external conflicts and crises.

6 | Reference list

Seimas of the Republic of Lithuania (1996). Law on the Basics of the National Security. No. VIII–49. https://e-seimas.lrs.lt/portal/legal Act/lt/TAD/TAIS.34169/asr.

Seimas of the Republic of Lithuania (1997). Law on the State Defence Council. No. VIII–209. https://e-seimas.lrs.lt/portal/legalAct/lt/ TAD/TAIS.38353/asr.

Seimas of the Republic of Lithuania (2014). Accord between the Political Parties Represented in the Seimas of the Republic of Lithuania on Strategic Guidelines for the Foreign, Security and Defence Policy of the Republic of Lithuania for 2014–2020. www.lrs.lt/sip/port al.show?p_r=10140&p_k=2&p_t=144957.

Seimas of the Republic of Lithuania (2016). Resolution Concerning the Consistency and Continuity of the Foreign, Security and Defence Policy of the Republic of Lithuania in 2016–2020. No. XIII–9. www.lrs.lt/sip/getFile3?p_fid=2595.

Seimas of the Republic of Lithuania (2017). National Security Strategy. No. XIII–202. www.e-tar.lt/portal/lt/legalAct/TAR.2627131DA 3D2/asr.

Seimas of the Republic of Lithuania (2018). Agreement among the Political Parties Represented in the Seimas of the Republic of Lithuania on the Lithuanian Defence Policy Guidelines. 10 September 2018. http://ministraspirmininkas.lrv.lt/uploads/ministraspirmininkas/documents/files/Partij%C5%B3%20susitarimas%20d%C4%97l%20Lietuvos%20gynybos%20politikos%20gairi%C5%B3%20EN.pdf.

Luxembourg

Patrick Heck

1 | Introduction

In the late 1990s, with the lessons learned in the Yugoslav Wars, Luxembourg policymakers and politicians realised the need to put in place a 3D (diplomacy, development, defence) approach. Many factors led to a more integrative approach, such as the need to seek synergies between the ministries concerned, the need to pool limited human and financial resources in order to have a bigger effect and better coordination, the need to eliminate waste and duplications, the need to eliminate competition between government departments, the growing realisation that internal security is very much linked to external security, the evidence that development and cooperation aid can actually prevent crises, and the important realisation that post-conflict situations can only be stabilised using non-military resources.

The government that came into office in June 1999 first stated in its government programme its desire to establish a 3D approach and cross-government whole-of-government approach (WGA) in the fields of foreign and security policy. In 1999, the Ministry of Foreign Affairs (MFA) and the Ministry of Defence (MOD) bureaucracies were merged following the creation of a political-military committee between the ministries in April of that year, which itself represented a recognition of the need to bring these two communities together.

While the bureaucracies were merged, there remain two members of the government with a distinct political responsibility for defence and foreign affairs, respectively. A Directorate for International Aid and Development already existed within the MFA (which is now called the Ministry of Foreign and European Affairs, or MFEA). Once foreign affairs, defence and international development aid were brought together into a single institution, all three elements of 3D were under the same roof, so to speak, which made cooperation much easier.

Thenceforth, in terms of shaping policy, 3D became more and more of a reality. In Kosovo, in Afghanistan and, later, in Africa, the 3D approach was actively pursued through this 'joint bureaucracy', which jointly elaborated various policies for decision-makers. Such decisions could relate to a wide range of issues, such as deploying troops abroad, funding development and cooperation packages, and engaging diplomatically with and on behalf of countries in crisis.

The joint bureaucracy worked together, exchanged information, developed policies and exploited synergies. This enabled the three sectorial policies to be better informed of their respective plans and policies, and it facilitated joint decision-making. In other words, when the defence department was thinking about deploying troops to country X in crisis, it would inform the other two departments in the 3D nexus. These other two departments could then decide to also develop a policy in support of country X, which the defence department was preparing to support with military resources. The 3D 'bureaucracy' also makes it easier to implement decisions reached at an international level through national 3D or WGA processes.

The 3D approach is a good fit for Luxembourg's specific characteristics. It is a small country with a small bureaucracy (in absolute terms). Communication lines are short and (generally) fast. Information circulates well between agencies. The level of transparency between ministries involved in crisis management is good. At the level of senior civil servants, people knew each other and understood the need to keep each other informed. Given these circumstances, putting a 3D approach in place came (fairly) easily and naturally after 1999.

Luxembourg's financial resources are small (in absolute terms). Combining efforts and pooling budget articles through a 3D approach yields bigger amounts for a 'bigger bang'. Indeed, 3D made sense from a political point of view (from the vision perspective), from a practical point of view (better effect, better efficiency, better control, better coordination, better implementation), and from a budgetary point of view. With the growing visibility of this 3D approach both at home and abroad, WGAs have been adopted across government, i.e. beyond just the fields of foreign and security policy. What's more, civil servants have generally come to have a positive mindset about it. In view of its positive experience with 3D, Luxembourg is actively supporting such approaches at the international level. The only missing piece, of course, is a detailed, spelled-out strategy.

2 | What policies have been developed to further policy coherence?

While there is no stand-alone WGA strategy or policy paper in Luxembourg, 3D or integrated approaches appear in many sectorial policy papers. For example the country's defence guidelines for 2025 and beyond (MFEA 2017: 13), notes that Luxembourg "supports national and international peace and stability efforts in a holistic and coherent approach combining diplomacy, development cooperation and defence (known as the '3D approach')", adding that its military "is also a component of Luxembourg's foreign policy which, in conjunction with traditional diplomacy and development-cooperation policy, contributes to conflict prevention and post-conflict reconstruction." The country's most recent development-cooperation strategy (Luxembourg Aid & Development 2018: 1) states that Luxembourg "considers development cooperation as a key pillar of its foreign policy's 3D approach (diplomacy, development and defence) and therefore actively engages with multilateral organisations, while supporting ongoing reforms in the international development system and promoting global efforts towards poverty eradication, environmental sustainability and human rights." The MFEA's mission statement (MFEA 2019) says that the ministry "endeavours to promote a coherent approach towards diplomacy, defence, development and immigration." And, most recently, Foreign Minister Jean Asselborn's speech to parliament on 13 March 2019 on Luxembourg's foreign policy (Asselborn 2019) underlined that: "Luxembourg is committed, both through a multidimensional approach (i.e. the '3D' approach of diplomacy, development and defence) and through a multilateral approach, to help concretely to build peace, security and prosperity where everyday life has hitherto been marked by conflict and poverty."

The 3D approach has also paid off for Luxembourg. For example, it has enabled improved circulation of information; allowed for a more thorough preparation of decisions, actions, policies; and made possible more efficient monitoring of implementation. The institutional merger of the core ministries (diplomatic service, defence and development aid) dealing with internal crisis management and the creation of multiple inter-ministerial working groups has not only generated a more coherent and efficient foreign policy, but also fostered the formation of WGAs across the government. Most importantly, it has instilled a cooperative WGA mindset.

Furthermore, the 3D approach has led various government stakeholders to strongly embrace a coherent, common and integrated WGA, especially in the field of international crisis management, where Luxembourg's small territorial size can only be compensated for by pooling its national resources and expertise. Indeed, nowadays, references to 3D, to WGA, to integrated approaches or to multidimensional approaches can be found in a wide variety of government documents related to crisis management, including cybersecurity, military mobility, hybrid threats, human rights, sustainable development and climate change.

3 | Who are the main actors involved in cooperating in a WGA?

Luxembourg has a WGA when it comes to implementing international norms, decisions and agreements. It is most pronounced in the field of international peace and security in the widest sense possible, of which I will provide four examples. First, an inter-departmental working group chaired by the MFEA's director-general for political affairs brings together all relevant ministries and oversees the formulation of the national plan of action for implementing the Sustainable Development Goals of the UN's 2030 Agenda, both at home and through Luxembourg's development-cooperation efforts abroad. This working group regularly reports to the government on progress made, and it prepares the reports to the UN's high-level political forum on sustainable development. Second, the Interministerial Committee on Human Rights – again, using a WGA – oversees the reporting to the UN treaty bodies as well as to the Council of Europe in addition to holding frequent consultations with civil society by convening regular meetings, exchanging information and soliciting feedback. Third, a national Inter-ministerial Committee for Development Cooperation was set up by law in 1996 and is under the MFEA's Directorate for Development Cooperation and Humanitarian Affairs. And, fourth, a Political-Military Committee was established by ministerial decree in April 1999.

The drivers/chairs of these joint institutions are the MFEA's Directorate of Political Affairs, Directorate of Defence, and Directorate of Development Cooperation. Other participants include the Prime Minister's Office, the Ministry of Home Affairs, the Ministry of Justice, the Ministry of Health, the High Commission for National Protection, the army staff headquarters and the national police.

These institutions meet officially at the levels of ministers and senior officials, and they work on the basis of a formal invitation, formal agenda and formal report. Daily contacts and interaction exist between desks and/or experts. Officials from embassies or permanent representations (e.g. to the EU, NATO and the UN) can be included in the formal meetings via digital conferencing. When preparations are being made for Luxembourg personnel to formally participate in an international peacekeeping operation, the Chamber of Deputies, as the parliament is known, has to be consulted as a matter of law. This is because, by law, the parliament's Committee on Internal Security and Defence has to vote on whether to give favourable advice for such actions. It should be noted that defence used to be part of a committee called the Committee on Foreign and European Affairs, Defence, Cooperation and Immigration, which comprised all three 3D elements. Although the new coalition government formed in late 2018 decided to split defence and foreign affairs, this should in no way be interpreted as a rethinking of the 3D policy, to which Luxembourg remains firmly committed. The splitting occurred because the parliament wanted to exercise better oversight over defence policy as the defence budget and structures are growing to meet Luxembourg's so-called '2 percent commitment' to NATO. Furthermore, although the government is not bound by the parliament's vote, it has always followed the committee's vote. Moreover, the 1992 law that provides for this consultation procedure is now being updated to make decision-making faster and more reactive so as to be in line with the tempo of international crises.

Above, I have listed the various interdepartmental bodies and committees or working groups that ensure the functioning of a WGA in Luxembourg. Of these, the merger of the three key bureaucracies in 1999 has been the key enabler. The Political-Military Committee is the operational arm of this integrated structure. It operates a permanent review of issues related to international crisis management in addition to making recommendations on policy and decisions. This committee meets at regular intervals, holding at least five ordinary meetings per year, and is chaired by the director general for political affairs. It reports to the three members of government (i.e. the MFEA's minister of foreign and European affairs, minister for development cooperation and humanitarian affairs, and minister of defence), and it involves the embassies when called for by its agenda.

At the political level, when in session, the Government Council reviews international affairs on a weekly basis under a dedicated agenda item. Once a crisis exists and crisis-management measures have been taken by the EU or NATO, the High Commission for National Protection (HCNP) is activated and implements the declared crisis measures on a national level.

This Government Council has working groups that are activated depending on the particular nature of the crisis. These working groups are under the authority of the High-level Council of National Protection (CSPN), an inter-ministerial committee chaired by the HCPN. The composition of the working groups varies depending on the nature of their areas of competence. During a crisis, both the Political-Military Committee and the HCNP report to the government through the minister for foreign affairs and the prime minister, respectively. This WGA enables the committees to have full situational awareness of all elements of a crisis, which in turn helps them make better-informed decisions.

One should note that, as a purely advisory body, the above-mentioned Inter-ministerial Committee for Development Cooperation is not involved in the daily (i.e. operational) management of an international security crisis. However, it reviews the lessons and/or needs from existing or past crises when defining its policies, priorities and budgets, together with representatives from the ministries of Foreign and European Affairs, Defence, Home Affairs and Justice, who are members of this committee by law.

Through these integrated structures, Luxembourg has been able to make timely, integrated contributions to the EU's missions and operations, to NATO's operations, to various international trust funds, and to peace initiatives. To list a few examples, Luxembourg has contributed to UN operations in Croatia and Bosnia-Herzegovina (UN-PROFOR); to EU missions in Mali (EUTM) and Somalia (EU NAV-FOR Operation Atalanta); and to several NATO efforts, including ones in Bosnia-Herzegovina (SFOR), Kosovo (KFOR), Afghanistan (ISAF and the Afghan National Army Trust Fund), Lithuania (Operation Resolute Support) and Central Asia (demining and demilitarisation trust funds).

5 | Conclusions

While Luxembourg lacks a detailed, spelled-out and written WGA/3D strategy, it is fair to say that such integrated approaches have become the default setting of the bureaucracy. Furthermore, despite the absence of an explicit WGA strategy or policy, the bureaucracy has been restructured based on the needs of a WGA. The WGA/3D strategy, which has generated concrete instruments, development-aid policies and joint efforts, enjoys strong political, public and bureaucratic support across the government. In fact, there is a great deal of enthusiasm for the 3D approach, especially because it has made the country more visible at the international level. For example, in recognition of Luxembourg's contributions to international peace and security, it was made a non-permanent member of the UN Security Council in 2013 and 2014.

The objective of the 3D approach is to have a concrete impact on international peace and security through a concerted, integrated and pooled contribution to international crisis management. Luxembourg has realised the need to act through a WGA to make more, better and more consistent contributions to international peace, security and stability. This, in turn, has generated visibility for the country as a useful and credible net contributor to international security.

On the national level, Luxembourg's WGA has helped to establish and bolster a mindset across the government that the various bodies and institutions need to act in concert to make the country a more credible player on the international level. Apart from the traditional foreign policy and security actors in Luxembourg, a WGA has enabled other government departments and national stakeholders to see their usefulness in contributing to peace and security. Indeed, the WGA has helped to show to other ministries that they, too, have an interest in and can contribute to international peace and security.

Furthermore, Luxembourg's WGA has been extremely helpful in terms of avoiding duplication and competition among departments. Now there is a sense of coherence, solidarity and coordination among the national players. All actors feel compelled to pitch in to help make Luxembourg a more efficient and more visible international player. The reward for all these efforts has been a sense of satisfaction and pride in the minds of the actors who participate in the national structures described in this contribution. There is a sense of accomplishment and of having made a difference by using an integrated approach to contribute to resolving international crises.

6 | Reference list

Asselborn, Jean (2019). Speech of Foreign Minister Jean Asselborn to Parliament on 13 March 2019. https://maee.gouvernement.lu/cont ent/dam/gouv_maee/minist%C3%A8re/d%C3%A9clarations-de-p olitique-%C3%A9trang%C3%A8re/2019/FR-Declaration-de-politi que-etrangere-2019.pdf.

Luxembourg Aid & Development (2018). Luxembourg's General Development Cooperation Strategy: The Road to 2030. https://coopera tion.gouvernement.lu/dam-assets/politique-cooperation-action-hu manitaire/documents-de-reference/strat%C3%A9gie/Strat%C3% A9gie-MAEE-EN.pdf.

HCNP (High Commission for National Protection). Remit. https:// hcpn.gouvernement.lu/en/service/attributions.html.

MFEA (Ministry of Foreign and European Affairs) (2017). Luxembourg Defence Guidelines for 2025 and Beyond. https://defense. gouvernement.lu/dam-assets/la-defense/luxembourg-defence-gui delines-for-2025-and-beyond.pdf.

MFEA (2019). Mission Statement. Updated 4 April 2019. https://maee. gouvernement.lu/en/le-ministere.html.

Malta

Roderick Pace

1 | Introduction

Malta has not developed a whole-of-government approach (WGA) regarding external conflicts and crises, and there are several likely reasons for this. The first is that the concept is new in the sense that, until recently, international crises have been seen as falling almost exclusively in the domain of foreign affairs, with the result that they were primarily handled by diplomatic bodies. During its entire post-independence period, Malta was mainly preoccupied with its own security and building its statehood. Malta's small size, its population of less than half a million (Eurostat 2019), its limited resources and its policy of neutrality and non-alignment during the Cold War further accentuated this approach of standing on the sidelines, so to speak. However, since becoming an EU member state, new opportunities have arisen for Malta to participate in regional and global efforts. Historically, it has tended to become more involved (though to varying degrees) in crises occurring in the Mediterranean region and whose consequences have a direct impact on its security and well-being. An example of this was Malta's role during the 2011 civil war in Libya. In general, Malta prefers to act through EU-led initiatives (e.g. CSDP missions) rather than through UN-led ones, as exemplified by its participation in UNIFIL (Lebanon) and the Organization for Security and Co-operation in Europe (OSCE).

2 | What policies have been developed to further policy coherence?

As noted above, Malta has not developed an explicit WGA for responding to international crises. However, the fact that some official documents refer to a WGA indicates that this concept is not entirely unknown in the public service. For example, an Armed Forces of Malta strategy paper covering the 2016–2026 period (AFM 2016: 6) says: "While a significant institution in its own right, the Armed Forces of Malta does not act in isolation. It contributes to the whole-of-government approach that is required to address the serious security challenges being faced in today's world." A WGA is also mentioned in passing in other official documents, such as the 2018–2020 strategy of the Malta Information Technology Agency, which discusses a "One-Government" approach (MITA 2017: 17) and then goes on to define "One-Government or Whole of Government" as "An integrated approach to public service delivery moving away from an isolated silo approach" (ibid.: 56). Furthermore, in the last two decades (and mostly as a result of EU membership), the culture of Maltese public affairs has increasingly avoided the silo mentality, which separates key aspects of decision-making into compartments that hardly communicate with each other. Indeed, by now, an 'inter-ministerial' approach to confronting multi-dimensional issues that touch on several policy areas has become well established within the Maltese public service.

In the absence of an explicit WGA policy, one can look for signs of an implicit one by assessing whether the authorities and national decision-makers understand the need for and efficacy of a WGA. In international affairs, Maltese decision-makers appreciate the importance of leaning on a varied array of policies in sequence or all together in a coordinated approach. Malta participates in several peacekeeping missions aiming to stabilise crisis situations. While prioritising CSDP missions (see Fiott 2015), it has committed less to the UN, the Partnership for Peace (PfP) and the Organization for Security and Cooperation in Europe (OSCE) (Cauchi Inglott 2018). However, this does not imply that it is unaware of the other non-military tools (e.g. development policy and humanitarian aid) that are required to properly respond to and manage international crises.

3 | Who are the main actors involved in cooperating in a WGA?

In most cases, decision-making of a WGA-type in Malta involves public officials, the heads of the armed forces (AFM), and government ministers. In the most serious cases of crisis, the prime minister is also involved. In the past decade, only one international crisis has brought out all the characteristics of a WGA, namely, the 2011 civil war in Libya, which threatened to spill over into Malta, particularly if thousands of war refugees were to reach Maltese shores in a disorganised manner.

Malta ensures policy coherence at EU level by establishing a number of interconnected national decision-making bodies that bring all segments of government, parliament and civil society together. These structures have almost eliminated the problem of operating in separate silos. The protagonists in the decision-making process know each other, and their offices are often located within walking distance of each other. The smallness of the public service and the relatively few layers of bureaucracy (compared to those of larger states) facilitate horizontal cooperation and centralised decision-making. In fact, together with the UK and Ireland, Malta is among the most centralised EU countries (Thijs, Hammerschmid and Palaric 2017: 10).

Briefly, the national EU-related decision-making process works as follows: First, all ministries have set up an EU Directorate or the equivalent to deal with all EU issues falling under the particular ministry's remit. Officials in these directorates participate in the EU's comitology. Second, a new Ministry for European Affairs and Equality (MEAE) was established in 2013, effectively separating EU affairs from foreign policy. It was this ministry that led preparations for Malta's presidency of the Council of the EU in 2017 (Harwood, Moncada and Pace 2018). Third, within the public service, an EU Co-ordination Department has been established to replace the EU Secretariat. Fourth, there is an Inter-Ministerial Committee that includes all the permanent secretaries (i.e. heads of ministries), which meets and reports to the cabinet. Fifth, above these stands the cabinet (of ministers), which is headed by the prime minister, approves the national position, and takes all final decisions. Civil society, NGOs and lobbyists are consulted through the Malta-EU Action and Steering Committee (MEUSAC), and their views are relayed to the key bodies within the national structure. When viewed in its totality, one sees that this national decision-making system has a WGA-like structure.

One can also mention a number of WGA-like cooperations. First, Malta has participated in one UN operation, the United Nations Interim Force in Lebanon (UNIFIL). At first, its forces were part of the Italian contingent. But, in 2019, the UN listed Malta as providing 11 peacekeepers independently (UNIFIL 2019). Second, in accordance with the Vienna Document (OSCE 2011), Malta deploys military officers as guest evaluators/inspectors with arms control agencies of other European countries. Third, although Malta is not a member of NATO, it did re-join the alliance's Partnership for Peace (PfP) in 2008, and its individual programme focuses on non-military activities of the partnership (NATO 2018). Lastly, in 2019, Malta joined two of NATO's Science for Peace and Security (SPS) projects (Inside Quantum Technology 2019). The first aims to establish and implement post-quantum cryptographic solutions and protocols to guarantee a secure solution for cryptographic computerised communications used to protect sensitive information. The second aims to establish a communication channel between Italy and Malta using underwater optical fibres. In the long run, this project aims to help protect critical infrastructures in Malta and to pave the way for quantum communications to be used between Malta and Italy.

4 | How does your country operationalise a WGA?

There are several examples of a WGA in the Maltese public service, although they do not go by that particular name. They consist of consistent patterns of action as well as inter-ministerial structures. Some of the latter (e.g. the one related to the EU) are permanent, while others have been set up in an ad hoc manner to implement certain policies or strategies in response to specific challenges, such as tackling poverty, fostering inclusion, combatting climate change and drafting the new version of the security strategy (The Malta Independent 2019). Both formal and informal patterns of interaction are discernible among the main decision-makers in times of crisis. What is important to highlight in the case of a small state like Malta is that decisions during crisis often reach the highest echelons of the political order.

The case of the 2011 Libyan conflict is instructive, as it had many dimensions: a diplomatic/political dimension, as Malta enjoyed strong relations with Libya; an economic dimension due to Maltese investments in the country; and a military/security dimension because of the probability that some military action would also impact Malta and the sovereignty of its territory, including its territorial waters. What's more, Malta's only runway and international airport – i.e. its non-maritime lifeline – was also vulnerable to a possible military attack or accident.

In response to the crisis, the director of defence set up a national crisis centre based within the Office of the Prime Minister (OPM), which at the time was responsible for national defence. This centre brought together and networked several ministries and national agencies and services (e.g. transport, trade, the armed forces, and security-service and diplomatic staff) to confront the crisis. At the political level, there were frequent consultations with the parliamentary opposition, and the government made statements in parliament to ensure that it remained apprised of events as they unfolded. This was a de facto WGA, although the national crisis centre gradually stopped operating once the crisis subsided. What's more, there is no indication that a permanent structure of the same type or a similar WGA strategy is being planned.

Together, the experience gained in handling the Libyan crisis and the public service's coordinated inter-ministerial cooperation provide a strong basis for the emergence of a Maltese WGA to international crises. Although maintaining a permanent structure might be considered too costly, a strategy for and a protocol on the steps to be taken to set a WGA in motion during times of crisis could serve as a useful alternative.

Given the fact that Malta is a small island country with limited resources and modestly sized armed forces, as well as considering its pacifist foreign policy, it is paradoxical that participation in external crises has almost entirely focused on the deployment of members of the armed forces in CSDP missions even though Malta has a lot of potential for contributing to non-military efforts to respond to international crises (e.g. human rights education, transitional justice, training of border-control officials, civilian control of the military, development assistance, humanitarian assistance and development aid). Granted, the involvement of the Maltese soldiers as peacekeepers does not go against the concept of neutrality or pacifism. But the non-military resources at the disposal of small states can also be mobilised during times of crisis.

The Maltese bodies and resources that can be mobilised in the service of a WGA include: several institutions of learning in the country; medical staff, including paramedics and physicians, to provide health services; several NGOs to assist with migrants and development projects overseas; and legal experts, especially those who have worked in international organisations. The country's pubic service also employs several engineers and architects as well as an array of other professionals. In short, there are several sectors of Maltese society that – if coordinated, trained and organised to pursue a WGA – could be mobilised in the same manner as the members of the armed forces and deployed in times of crisis. For a small country that is short on trained military resources but rich in civilian assets, this could be an approach for boosting its involvement in responding to crises by participating in multinational missions, such as those led by the EU.

5 | Conclusions

In analysing Malta's case, one must unfortunately start by noting that there is neither a WGA strategy nor a permanent structure for assuming a WGA to international crises. However, on closer inspection, one can conclude that WGA-like structures and approaches do, in fact, exist. What's more, as discussed with the case of the 2011 civil war in Libya, the country also has experience at quickly and successfully setting up ad hoc WGA-like structures.

Looking forward, the factors (or 'enablers') that could lead to a more permanent and explicit WGA are the following: First, the fact that Malta has already had positive experiences with inter-ministerial cooperation may make it more likely to embrace the approach on a more permanent basis. Second, the relatively small size of Malta's bureaucracy would make it easier to establish an explicit WGA. Indeed, this works in both a horizontal and vertical fashion in Malta, as upper-level politicians and government officials are already used to exercising hands-on leadership on crucial issues, and most public officials already have personal ties to their counterparts both within and among ministries, agencies and other bodies.

The main disablers include the facts that international crises are all unique in their own way and often require types of specialised knowledge which are hard to obtain in small states, and that the information-gathering capabilities of small states are relatively meagre despite the importance of having such information. What's more, small states also suffer from a lack of resources and may also encounter difficulties in the implementation and follow-up stages.

As discussed above, an example of a WGA applied to international crisis is Malta's handling of the 2011 civil war in Libya. There are various positive factors that help explain the successful management of this crisis at the national level: First, public servants in small countries tend to have to be generalists rather than specialists in order to be able to grapple with a broad array of circumstances and decisions. Since they are not normally restricted to specialised silos and can therefore take a bird's-eye view of events, they tend to cultivate a much broader view of how to act in certain circumstances as well as to have the needed range of tools and services at their disposal. Second, Malta's smallness results in few bureaucratic layers, facilitating ease of communication. Indeed, if Maltese public servants opt not to use modern systems of instantaneous communication, they usually only have to walk a short distance to meet face-to-face with their counterparts in other parts of the government apparatus. Third, the proximity that political decision-makers enjoy in terms of both physical space and bureaucratic layers helps them to project their leadership more easily and directly. In fact, seeing and meeting with their minister on a regular or even daily basis is nothing out of the ordinary for most senior officials, and politicians at the highest level of government often participate in deliberations and decision-making with the lower-level officials who are directly responsible for the issue at hand. Fourth, even though this is not the case for other areas of governance, when it comes to responding to international crises, there has consistently been the horizontal and vertical consultation – among political elites, between the government and parliament, and between the government and the opposition – needed to secure the necessary political consensus. This, in turn, helps in efforts to mobilise public support for the approach agreed for responding to the particular crisis.

Despite these advantages, small states like Malta also face several challenges to responding to international crises. First, though they may have a voice in decision-making and access to information (e.g.

through EU institutions), they have limited resources and 'punching weight' to influence proceedings in international fora, organisations and institutions. Second, they are often reliant on external sources to provide the information they need to take good decisions. Third, the fact that small states have fewer diplomats, embassies and consulates overseas makes it more difficult to nurture contacts and gather information. Fourth, smallness also often results in a lack of expertise in some situations and a reliance on generalists (or external resources). Fifth, despite what many might (perhaps romantically) imagine, small states are not immune to the internal political and societal cleavages of larger states. In fact, party politics, political competition and bureaucratic rivalries are often just as present and crucial in small states as in large ones.

In the case of small states like Malta, it is fairly reasonable to expect that they will be more interested in crises which are closest to them in a regional context and which could have a strong negative spillover effect on their societies, and that distant crises will appear remoter to them than for larger states, especially if the benefit of resolving such a crisis is relatively smaller for them in any case. However, if the distant threat (e.g. piracy in the Persian Gulf) could impact their trade or economic well-being or if they are viewed as potentially leading to some other negative trends (e.g. mass emigration) that could directly impact them, they are naturally more interested in them. Furthermore, smaller states often have greater incentives (and needs) than larger states to work through multilateral institutions or organisations, such as the EU, the UN and the OSCE.

Lastly, it should be noted that, despite their small size and limited resources, states like Malta can nevertheless supply invaluable assets to international crisis management.

AFM (Armed Forces of Malta) (2016). Strategy Paper 2016–2026: Press Brief. https://homeaffairs.gov.mt/en/media/Policies-Documents/Documents/The%20Armed%20Forces%20of%20Malta%20Strategy%20Paper%202016-2026.pdf.

Cauchi Inglott, Martin (2018). "Neutrality and EU defence: conflict or opportunity?" *Times of Malta* 11 November 2018. https://timesof malta.com/articles/view/neutrality-and-eu-defence-conflict-or-opp ortunity-martin-cauchi.693995.

Eurostat (2019). Population on 1 January. https://ec.europa.eu/euro stat/databrowser/view/tps00001/default/table?lang=en.

Fiott, Daniel (2015). "Being Small Acting Tall? Malta and European Defence." *In The Common Security and Defence Policy: National Perspectives,* edited by Daniel Fiott. Egmont Paper 79: 93–96. http://aei.pitt.edu/64766/1/ep79.pdf.

Harwood, Mark, Stefano Moncada and Roderick Pace (eds.) (2018). *Malta's EU Presidency: A Study in a Small State Presidency of the Council of the EU.* Institute for European Studies. Msida: Malta University Publishing. www.um.edu.mt/library/oar//handle/1234 56789/35431.

Inside Quantum Technology (2019). "NATO Is Supporting Two Quantum Tech Projects to Secure Digital Communications." www.in sidequantumtechnology.com/news/nato-supporting-two-quantum -tech-projects-secure-digital-communications/.

MITA (Malta Information Technology Agency) (2017). MITA Strategy 2018–2020. https://mita.gov.mt/en/Documents/MITA%20STRAT EGY%202018-2020.pdf.

NATO (2018). Relations with Malta. www.nato.int/cps/en/natohq/top ics_52108.htm.

OSCE (Organization for Security and Co-operation in Europe) (2011). Vienna Document 2011: On Confidence- and Security-Building Measures. Vienna: OSCE. www.osce.org/fsc/86597?download=true.

The Malta Independent (2019). "Evaluation plan to improve country's security on the agenda of inter-ministerial meeting." 25 February 2019. www.independent.com.mt/articles/2019-02-25/local-news/Plans-for-Home-Affairs-Ministry-on-the-agenda-of-inter-ministeri al-meeting-6736204202.

Thijs, Nick, Gerhard Hammerschmid and Enora Palaric (2017). A comparative overview of public administration characteristics and performance in EU28. European Commission Directorate-General for Employment, Social Affairs and Inclusion Directorate F – Investment. https://publications.europa.eu/en/publication-detail/-/publication/3e89d981-48fc-11e8-be1d-01aa75ed71a1/laguage-en.

UNIFIL (United Nations Interim Force in Lebanon) (2019). UNIFIL Troop Contributing Countries. https://unifil.unmissions.org/unifil-troop-contributing-countries.

Netherlands

Erik de Feijter

1 | Introduction

Dutch policy to ensure coherence between the political, security, humanitarian, development and economic dimensions of foreign policy goes back to the early 1990s. The 1993 policy paper 'A World in Dispute' (Ministry of Foreign Affairs 1993) noted that conflicts had become more complex in the post-Cold War era and required an integrated response of the instruments of foreign, defence and development policy, which in turn required these ministries to cooperate more closely. In 1994, this led the Ministry of Foreign Affairs to decide to reorganise and integrate the departments that had previously worked specifically for the minister of foreign affairs or the minister for development cooperation. This process of integration was taken one step further in 1997 when the Homogenous Budget for International Cooperation (HGIS) was created, which brought together the foreign affairs budgets of all relevant ministries into one budget overview in order to formulate a coherent, integrated foreign policy and stimulate inter-ministerial cooperation.

The concept of the integrated approach was further developed in subsequent policy documents in the late 1990s and particularly in the early 21st century. For example, there was a 2003 document on civil-military cooperation and a 2005 document on reconstruction after violent conflicts. The Advisory Council on International Affairs also produced 'Failing States: A Global Responsibility' (AIV 2004), a report which led to the establishment of the Stability Fund. This fund combined ODA and non-ODA budgets to allow for flexible financing in the security sector in fragile countries, and it became an important instrument for bridging the gap between development and security support.

However, an important driver of the practical development and operationalisation of the integrated approach were the significant military deployments in Iraq (2003–2005) and in Afghanistan (2003–present) and, more specifically, the deployment of provincial reconstruction teams (PRTs) to Baghlan and Uruzgan provinces. The deployment of PRTs under the International Security Assistance Force (ISAF) in Afghanistan led to the Dutch '3D' (development, diplomacy and defence) policy as a way to develop and operationalise the poorly defined PRT concept. Although other countries were developing similar policies, 3D became something of a Dutch brand, as the Netherlands pushed the integration of military and civilian personnel further than most others. Politically, the 3D policy was also a useful instrument in that it allowed the different political parties in the Dutch coalition government to stress different aspects of the mission.

Eventually, 13 civilians were deployed with the mission in Uruzgan at any given time under a civilian representative who shared responsibility for joint civilian-military efforts with the military commander. Although the 3D label was eventually dropped, it has had an important legacy. First, it put the integrated approach to the test under difficult circumstances. Different perspectives that could be papered over in the abstract had to be confronted in the field, and pragmatic ways of deconflicting and coordinating with NGOs and IOs had to be worked out. The high political profile and the joint reporting to parliament by the relevant ministers necessitated compromises and common language. Detailed aspects of the integrated approach were discussed in parliament on a regular basis.

Second, it also meant that a significant number of diplomats, military and police personnel, and aid workers had first-hand experience of working with counterparts from other departments and thereby often gained mutual understanding and appreciation. After taking this experience back with them into the relevant ministries and organisations, they were subsequently instrumental in further developing the integrated approach both at a national and international levels.

2 | What policies have been developed to further policy coherence?

The Dutch government generally prefers the term 'integrated approach' when referring to the framework for delivering coherent interventions and support to countries in crisis or conflict, while a whole-of-government approach (WGA) is considered a means to this end. As outlined above, the relevant policies can be traced back to at least the early 1990s, but the most relevant current policy document is the 'Guidelines on the Integrated Approach' (Ministry of Foreign Affairs 2014). The guidelines set the conceptual framework and specify government structures and procedural steps for implementing this approach in addition to providing the framework for a WGA.

The integrated approach is operationalised in the Integrated International Security Strategy (IISS) 2018–2022 (Ministry of Foreign Affairs 2018a), and the 'Investing in Global Prospects' note (Ministry of Foreign Affairs 2018b), which outlines Dutch policy on foreign trade and development cooperation. References to an integrated approach are generally found in most government documents regarding foreign and security policy.

Also worth mentioning is the formal framework (Toetsingskader) for assessing foreign military deployments. Although this framework does not formulate policy as such, it sets the framework for government and parliament regarding decision-making on possible military deployments. The framework dates back to 1995, but since its most recent updates (2009, 2014), it takes into account the political context in which a military deployment takes place as well as the way in which a military intervention would support or facilitate aspects of stabilisation, human security and development. The framework therefore ensures an integrated approach and involves relevant ministries from the earliest stages of planning a military deployment.

The policy documents build on years of experience, and their quality is generally high. The documents have been shared with parliament and, certainly since the Dutch engagement in ISAF, the integrated approach has gained familiarity and broad support in the parliament. This, in turn, translates into broad support for ambitious policies and strategies in multilateral settings. It also means that references to the integrated approach are found in almost all policy papers regarding foreign and security policy.

The 2014 guidelines were drafted as overall principles and working methods and, as such, they are applicable in any conflict-affected country or region. The guidelines provide a step-by-step plan in six phases that tries to capture all aspects of a conflict, from early warning and early action through stabilisation, peacebuilding and reconstruction. It builds on experience with (elements of) the integrated approach in various countries and regions, such as Afghanistan, Burundi, the Horn of Africa, Mali and Syria, but acknowledges that there are no blueprints that will apply everywhere as well as that a country-specific approach will always be required to find the right mix of instruments and interventions to have an impact. In principle, the guidelines are system-wide in that they reference the importance of using all available instruments and entry points, including economy and trade, and of engaging all relevant stakeholders, including international organisations and civil society. However, the practical focus (also in terms of structures and procedures) is of a medium scope, with most attention being devoted to cooperation between diplomacy, development cooperation, military intervention and support for the rule of law.

The IISS and the 'Investing in Global Prospects' note have operationalised the guidelines and applied them to the priorities of the current government. In geographical terms, the IISS prioritises the countries and regions of instability and insecurity around Europe (the so-called 'ring of instability'), particularly to its east and south, as well as those that are close to the Dutch overseas territories in the Caribbean. It sets out a number of goals that include (conflict-)prevention, combatting the root causes of terrorism and migration, and strengthening the international legal order. It also links issues related to security, climate change and sustainable development.

The 'Investing in Global Prospects' note focuses on instability in regions such as West Africa and the Sahel, North Africa, the Middle East and the Horn of Africa as well as on (the root causes of) irregular migration. The note formulates its goals regarding just and peaceful societies in a chapter on stability and poverty reduction. It specifically mentions strengthening the rule of law and legitimate governance, supporting peace processes and preventing radicalisation. The integrated approach is seen within the broader policy framework of foreign trade and development cooperation, and its scope is in that sense system-wide.

In practical terms, the integrated approach is explicitly applied and debated when the government notifies the parliament in a so-called Article 100 letter that it intends to deploy military personnel abroad. This formal notification will have been drafted in accordance with the evaluation framework (Toetsingskader) and usually signed by all relevant ministers (Defence, Foreign Affairs, Foreign Trade & Development Cooperation and, when applicable, Justice & Security). Parliament will scrutinise the government's justification to determine whether the military deployment is credibly embedded in a broader integrated approach.

3 | Who are the main actors involved in cooperating in a WGA?

The key actors that cooperate in the context of the integrated approach are: the prime minister and the ministers of foreign affairs, defence, development cooperation & foreign trade, and justice & security. The term 'whole-of-government approach' is therefore a bit of a misnomer, as other ministries may sometimes provide specific expertise or information, but they are rarely substantially involved in formulating and implementing of policy regarding external conflicts and crises.

At the political level, the Council of Ministers has a number of sub-councils. Most relevant in this context are the Council for Defence and International Affairs (RDIA) and the Council for Security and Intelligence (RVI). The RDIA deals with issues regarding foreign and defence policy as well as foreign trade and development cooperation. The RVI deals with developments regarding national and international security, including terrorism and cybersecurity, but also participation in military missions. Senior officials of the military, intelligence services, police and public prosecutor, as well as the national coordinator for security and counterterrorism, may attend sessions, as required.

At the senior official level, the Steering Group Missions and Operations (SMO) is the most senior coordinating body. It meets weekly and includes representatives (generally at the level of director-general or director) of the Prime Minister's Office and the ministries of Foreign Affairs, Defence (both civilian and military), and Justice & Security. Its focus is on Dutch participation in military and civilian missions within an integrated approach, and it advises the relevant ministers. The role of the SMO is crucial in that it anchors a range of inter- and intra-departmental working groups on relevant issues and provides a forum for discussing developments and resolving issues at the most senior official level.

Although these ministries form the core of the integrated approach, they do not operate in isolation. The implementation of the civilian aspects of an integrated approach is to a large extent done by international organisations and NGOs through funding of their programmes or projects. Through a number of 'knowledge platforms', the Ministry of Foreign Affairs engages academics and NGOs on themes related to foreign and development policy. Particularly within the Security & Rule of Law knowledge platform, there is an exchange of information that is relevant to an integrated approach to specific crises and conflicts.

In the field, the Netherlands has made arrangements to deconflict, coordinate and cooperate with NGOs that are active in the same areas where Dutch military or civilian personnel are deployed. The local embassy or embedded diplomats are generally involved in these coordination mechanisms with the added aim of ensuring coherence with bilateral programmes and projects in the same areas.

More generally, the Netherlands does not implement an integrated approach in a country or region on a bilateral basis. As mentioned above, as a strong believer in multilateralism, the Netherlands supports and advocates for UN-led coordination efforts, particularly in fragile countries. Where possible, the Netherlands will channel financial support through multi-donor trust funds or support policy priorities that have been drafted by or with the government of the country concerned. Deployment of military and civilian staff will usually take place in the context of missions or operations of, among others, the UN, the EU, NATO and the OSCE or sometimes in ad hoc coalitions of like-minded countries. It follows that the Netherlands is actively engaged in policy discussions in these multilateral frameworks on the integrated approach.

Finally, the Dutch parliament provides oversight and is actively engaged in debates regarding the integrated approach, and will sometimes provide guidance to the government through motions. Different parties generally prioritise different aspects of the integrated approach, and NGOs will often have their own interactions with parliament to call attention to specific concerns that they may have.

4 | How does your country operationalise a WGA?

At an institutional level, the Netherlands has taken a number of steps to ensure policy coherence. In 1994, the Ministry of Foreign Affairs was restructured and the departments that worked specifically for the minister of foreign affairs or the minister for development coordination were de-compartmentalised ('ontschotting'), creating regional and thematic departments working for both ministers. In 2012, the portfolio for foreign trade was transferred from the Ministry of Economic Affairs to the Ministry of Foreign Affairs under a minister for foreign trade and development cooperation. This means that the instruments for foreign policy, development cooperation and foreign trade have been integrated into a single department under two ministers.

On the ministerial level, decision-making on crisis management and deployment in fragile states takes place in the weekly Council of Ministers. Sub-councils, on the other hand, only meet when required, are chaired by the prime minister, and have a composition that depends on the specific sub-council, but can include the ministers of defence, foreign affairs, development cooperation & foreign trade, and security & justice.

On a more operational level, the Steering Group Missions and Operations (SMO) meets weekly and brings together the most senior military and civilian officials of these same ministries. At the working level, there are a number of inter-departmental working groups, such as the Working Group Civilian Missions, the Inter-Agency Working Group Early Warning & Early Action, and working groups for countries or regions with a significant degree of Dutch engagement, such as Afghanistan, Libya and the Sahel. Relevant embassies and representations will join meetings of these working groups by videoconference. Besides the formal working groups, which have clear reporting lines, compositions and meeting schedules, there is a range of more informal groups that may be formed to deal with a specific issue for a limited period of time and will include relevant colleagues from various departments.

Policy is formulated in integrated notes to parliament, which are then presented by the relevant ministers. Annual or multi-year plans, which include input from the relevant departments, are drawn up for specific countries and regions.

In financial terms, the Homogenous Budget of International Co-operation (HGIS) was created in 1997 to combine the foreign affairs budgets of the relevant ministries into a single budget overview. This principle was taken one step further in 2013 with the creation of the International Security Budget (BIV), which covered the costs of contributions to international security in a broad sense. The ministers for foreign affairs, defence, and foreign trade & development cooperation and, when appropriate, the minister of security & justice made joint decisions on the allocation of BIV funds to ensure that the various ministries' interests and perspectives were weighed and that joint context analyses were taken into account while preparing decisions. Although this decision was partly reversed in 2017, when parts of this budget were reallocated to the relevant ministries, a common budget of EUR 190 million was retained for the financing of international deployments.

On a more operational level, since 2004, the Ministry of Foreign Affairs has had a specific financial instrument, the Stability Fund, to finance activities at the nexus of security, stability and development cooperation. This fund, with a current budget of EUR 90 million, is made up of both ODA (EUR 55 million) and non-ODA (EUR 45 million) funds, which allows for greater flexibility to finance activities in the security sector. It is jointly managed by the Stabilisation and Humanitarian Aid Department and the Security Policy Department.

In terms of personnel management, a number of steps have been taken to facilitate exchange and cooperation. The integration of development cooperation and foreign trade into the structures of the Ministry of Foreign Affairs has meant that no separate personnel structures exist, and that staff can move and bring expertise from one area to another. Furthermore, since 2007, the ministries of Defence and Foreign Affairs have been exchanging advisers who contribute to relevant planning and decision-making processes.

In 2004, a list of individuals who could serve as volunteer foreign policy advisers (POLADs) to be embedded in military missions and operations was drawn up. These POLADs have been deployed on a range of missions, and have been complemented with development and cultural advisers to help ensure an integrated, holistic perspective in the field. In the context of ISAF, this concept was expanded with the deployment of a civilian representative alongside the military commander of the mission in Uruzgan. The Ministry of Foreign Affairs also keeps a roster of external civilian experts (the 'Civilian Missions Pool') who have been pre-selected for secondment to international missions, such as ones of the EU, the UN, NATO and the OSCE. If a candidate is selected by the organisation in question, he or she is then offered a temporary contract with the Ministry of Foreign Affairs for the duration of the deployment and then seconded to the relevant mission. Experts may be active in the non-governmental or private sector, but they can also be active judges, prosecutors or civil servants from the Ministry of Justice & Security. At present, some 50 experts from this pool are deployed each year, although the ministry aims to increase this number.

The police organisation and the Royal Netherlands Marechaussee (gendarmerie) manage their own rosters of volunteers for deployment to international missions, particularly for the purpose of capacity-building. The inter-departmental working group Civilian Missions ensures coherence among the relevant departments. There is no overarching Dutch structure for training or exercises. The police and Marechaussee generally organise pre-deployment training for their own staff. The Ministry of Foreign Affairs provides so-called hostile environment awareness training (HEAT) to diplomats who are to be deployed in high-risk areas, and it will also provide its staff and the volunteers on the roster for civilian missions with access to training and courses provided by others bodies, such as the European Security and Defence College.

The first 'Common Effort' exercise was organised in 2010 by 1 German/Netherlands Corps as a civilian-military exercise based on a realistic scenario and involving diplomats and representatives from the UN and NGOs, among others. These exercises have been held annually since 2014.

5 | Conclusions

It is fair to say that the Netherlands is relatively advanced in the realisation of a WGA if one considers its explicit formulation of policy and its implementation at headquarters level and in the field. Whether this has been a success in practice is harder to establish. The two most prominent examples of the country's integrated approach – Afghanistan and Mali – have hardly been resounding successes in terms of international interventions. However, on a smaller scale, the Dutch approach has been successful in ensuring greater policy coherence between the different ministries and departments as well as in building trust and confidence by having military and civilian personnel engage in real-world cooperation.

There are a few reasons that can be identified for this relative success. On the political level, there has been commitment to an integrated approach since the early 1990s, particularly among successive ministers for development cooperation. Integrating development cooperation into the Ministry of Foreign Affairs in 1994 meant that joint policies had to be developed to demonstrate the added value of this concept. That, in turn, meant that there was already a solid foundation in terms of policy when the ambitious deployment in Afghanistan put the integrated approach to the test. For the coalition government of the time, the so-called 3D approach to the provincial reconstruction teams (PRTs) in Baghlan and Uruzgan was useful, as it allowed the coalition parties to stress different aspects of the mission (cf. van der Lijn 2011). The high political profile of the mission meant that there was great pressure from the prime minister on down to make the integrated approach work. Structures were created, compromises were made, and a common language was settled on to make this happen. The frequent debates with parliament meant that the details of the integrated approach were familiar to parliamentarians across the political spectrum, and the importance of this approach became almost axiomatic. Although the Netherlands certainly wasn't alone in developing this kind of approach, the 3D policy became something of a Dutch brand thanks to the innovative and ambitious way in which it was implemented.

On a working level, the role of the Steering Group Missions and Operations (SMO) was crucial. It allowed for day-to-day management at the highest official level as well as for the resolution of conflicts and friction between the various departments involved. Under the SMO, a range of both inter- and intra-departmental working groups were formed to manage specific aspects of the integrated approach. These working groups – sometimes having a formal mandate and sometimes being more ad hoc in nature – normalised day-to-day contacts with colleagues from other ministries and the cooperation across silos.

In the field, the deployment of significant numbers of diplomats, development experts and police personnel along with a military contingent meant that they had to determine how to apply the integrated approach to practical issues under difficult circumstances. Although this undeniably led to friction and frustration, it also built trust and mutual appreciation. In addition to taking this experience back into their departments and helping to further develop policy, these men and women formed an informal network across ministries and organisations. The value of this practical cooperation is hard to quantify, but it has undoubtedly been important to the internalisation of the integrated approach.

One downside, which can mainly be attributed to the Afghanistan deployment, is that the integrated approach is now strongly associated with military missions. This can potentially be a handicap now that the Netherlands no longer has an ambitious military deployment with an integrated civilian component. Currently, the potential for an integrated approach seems to be most obvious around the nexus of internal and external security – and particularly with the issue of irregular migration. This is mostly a matter of cooperation between different civilian agencies and departments with little military involvement. The existing frameworks for a WGA will therefore need to be adapted in response to these developments.

Looking ahead, the real test of a Dutch whole-of-government approach may be in dealing with the hybrid threats from Russia and the challenges posed by China. These will require a coherent response by a much broader spectrum of ministries and agencies than has been needed in dealing with the external crises and conflicts of the past two decades.

6 | Reference list

AIV (Advisory Council on International Affairs) (2004). *Failing States: A Global Responsibility*. The Hague: AIV.

Ministry of Foreign Affairs (1993). *A World in Dispute*. The Hague.

Ministry of Foreign Affairs (2014). *Guidelines on the Integrated Approach*. The Hague.

Ministry of Foreign Affairs (2018a). *Working Worldwide for the Security of the Netherlands: An Integrated International Security Strategy 2018–2022*. The Hague.

Ministry of Foreign Affairs (2018b). *Investing in Global Prospects, for the World, for the Netherlands*. The Hague.

van der Lijn, Jair (2011). *3D 'The Next Generation': Lessons learned from Uruzgan for future operations*. The Hague: Clingendael Institute. www.clingendael.org/sites/default/files/pdfs/20111130_cscp_rapport_lijn.pdf.

Poland

Adam Balcer

1 | Introduction

If the UK leaves the EU, Poland will become the fifth-most populous country in the EU, and it will boast its fifth-biggest economy (measured in GDP PPP) thanks to having the fastest pace of GDP growth among the major EU economies. What's more, it will have the fifth-highest military expenditures among EU states. In fact, these expenditures are increasing rapidly and are supposed to reach 2.5 percent of GDP by 2030.

These factors help to explain why Poland drafted a few strategic documents developing the idea of a whole-of-government approach (WGA), although they sometimes are rather selective and superficial. In theory, such economic, demographic and military potentials, combined with elements of strategic thinking and a holistic approach, make Poland one of the key stakeholders of potential cooperation within the WGA among EU member states. However, one should mention several caveats. First, Poland has been more of a follower than a leader when it comes to operationalising a WGA for responding to foreign conflicts and crises. Second, substantial Polish military and police deployments abroad tend to not include a strong civil (including diplomatic) component, and receive completely negligible assistance from development-cooperation bodies or organisations. Third, countries whose security is of strategic importance to Poland (e.g. Ukraine) occasionally do not receive sufficient financial and organisational support from Poland.

These shortcomings when it comes to operationalising a WGA in foreign affairs can be attributed to structural problems, such as insufficient formal cooperation between various national institutions. Instead, such cooperation is overshadowed by informal relations, political interference and the 'insularity' of state structures (not to mention the unnecessary rivalries between them). Moreover, the situation has deteriorated decisively since the parliamentary elections of 2015, which represent a turning point in the most recent history of Poland. The election saw the establishment of the first single-party government (de jure, a single electoral list) since the fall of communism. After the elections, the Law and Justice Party (PiS), a soft Eurosceptic and national-populist party, implemented a comprehensive political programme. Titled 'Good Change', the programme is transforming Poland from a liberal democracy that is based on the rule of law and protects individual and minority rights into a majoritarian and 'national' democracy with authoritarian elements. The governing party's virtual capture of the state has been accompanied by an exceptional rise in the number of informal networks working behind the scenes. There has been a major decrease in the transparency of the decision-making process as well as in the oversight and efficiency of state institutions. The rivalry between various PiS factions constitutes another serious impediment to embracing a WGA because each of them controls different institutions or departments.

Furthermore, Poland's rather close cooperation with key EU members states and EU institutions in pursuing a WGA to foreign conflicts and crises has grown considerably more difficult in recent years. The PiS views any efforts to further integrate the EU with suspicion and, in fact, advocates for a radical reversal in such trends and efforts. The Polish government has also nurtured very close ties with the United States and particularly with the Trump administration. Meanwhile, the dismantling of the rule of law in Poland has resulted in an unprecedented deterioration of relations between the Polish government and key EU member states and EU institutions.

2 | What policies have been developed to further policy coherence?

In recent decades, Poland has drafted quite a few documents promoting the idea of a WGA that also applies to externally directed activities. At present, a Strategy for Responsible Development for the period up to 2020 (Ministry of Investment and Development 2017) constitutes the most important and comprehensive official document concerning a WGA. At almost 420 pages, the strategy, which was adopted by the Polish government in February 2017, covers a wide range of fields, including security, economic external expansion and energy. The strategy particularly focuses on establishing an integrated system for managing hard and soft security. Mention of a WGA related to external activities can also be found in other official documents, such as laws or decrees on a national framework for cybersecurity policy for the 2017–2022 period (GCS n.d.), the multiannual development-cooperation programme for the 2016–2020 period (MFA 2018), an ordinance on the inter-ministerial team on Poland's resource policy (Government of Poland 2016), and Poland's defence concept (MoD 2017).

The quality of the above-mentioned documents is relatively high, but they also have some considerable shortcomings. For instance, the Strategy for Responsible Development (Ministry of Investment and Development 2017) aims to be holistic, but it is sometimes too vague in practice, such as by assuming that more concrete solutions will be worked out in the future, and it also neglects to cover some important issues (e.g. ODA, China and Russia).

Poland's WGA related to foreign affairs should be viewed in the context of its relations with the UN, especially as far as official development aid (ODA) is concerned. The Strategy for Responsible Development (ibid.) declares its compatibility with a number of UN documents, such as the 2030 Agenda for Sustainable Development and the UN Guiding Principles on Business and Human Rights. Poland's multiannual development-cooperation programme for 2016–2020 (MFA 2018) also treats the 2030 Agenda for Sustainable Development as a point of reference.

However, in practical terms, the implementation of a Polish WGA in the UN context faces serious obstacles. For example, according to the above-mentioned UN documents, Poland is obliged to increase its ODA to 0.33 percent of GNP by 2030. Achieving this goal will be very challenging, and Poland doesn't even have a comprehensive long-term plan for how to reach that level. In 2018, Polish ODA accounted for just 0.14 percent of Polish GNP. Polish ODA increased in 2015 (from 0.10% of GNP), but it has stagnated again in recent years (OECD 2019).

In the 2000s, Poland's engagement in UN missions was very limited, and it was much more involved in NATO- and EU-led missions. The situation has recently changed to a certain degree because Poland started its two-year term as a non-permanent member of the UN Security Council on 1 January 2018. In consequence, Poland decided in autumn 2019 that around 200 Polish soldiers would join the United Nations Interim Force in Lebanon (UNIFIL).

Hard security occupies a considerably more important place in the Polish WGA in comparison to those of many EU member states owing to Poland's geographic location on the Eastern flank of the EU and NATO as well as to Russia's increasingly aggressive foreign policies in Eastern Europe. The Strategy for Responsible Development (Ministry of Investment and Development 2017), the defence concept (MoD 2017: 30–32) and other security-related laws identify NATO (and particularly the US in the case of the defence concept) as Poland's main partner for security-related issues. Furthermore, Warsaw was an active participant in NATO's discussions about a WGA strategy. However, concrete linkages between the WGA of NATO and that of Poland are not explicitly mentioned in the official documents drafted by the Polish administration.

Due to NATO's importance to Polish security, Polish deployments abroad have usually come as part of NATO- or US-led missions, such as those in Afghanistan, Iraq and Kosovo. However, it should be noted that the PiS government has dramatically increased security-related cooperation with the US since 2015, and that this bilateral cooperation has seemingly taken precedence over working in a multilateral (i.e. NATO) framework. This strengthening of bilateral cooperation between Poland and the US is presented by both sides as being based on ideological affinities between US President Donald Trump and the PiS.

The EU does not constitute a key point of reference for Poland's WGA as it relates to foreign conflicts and crises. Generally speaking, the EU is mentioned rather rarely in Polish documents referring to its WGA. For instance, the EU Global Strategy of 2016 did not influence or inspire Polish documents regarding the national WGA, and it is not mentioned at all in the above-mentioned strategy and concept documents. Admittedly, one could say that some of them had been issued before the EU Global Strategy was even announced. But, if desired, these documents could have also been amended to include references to the Global Strategy.

In Polish documents especially focused on security, NATO occupies a much more prominent place than the EU. In contrast, when it comes to issues related to foreign affairs or ODA, the EU plays a more significant role as a point of reference for Poland's WGA. For instance, the country's multiannual cooperation development programme (MFA 2018: 44) states that "Poland will take care about the cohesion and complementarity of ENP with the development policy." Of note here is the fact that the European Neighbourhood Policy (ENP) is part of the Global Strategy. Moreover, almost 60 percent of Poland's total ODA is transferred to the EU budget (Polish Aid n.d.). However, Polish NGOs and public institutions are only involved to a very limited degree in efforts to implement projects co-funded by the EU.

In practice, Poland's cooperation with EU institutions and key EU member states in the WGA sphere results in a mixed picture and faces structural challenges and problems related to the most recent internal political developments in Poland. On the one hand, Poland is substantially engaged in EU-led missions in Georgia, Moldova, Ukraine and the Western Balkans. However, Polish involvement in other EU missions is minimal or, more often, nonexistent. Furthermore, Polish deployment in EU missions operating outside of Europe has substantially declined in recent years. In consequence, Poland did not launch special WGA initiatives within the CSDP missions. In fact, since the decisive victory of the PiS in the parliamentary elections of October 2015, the domestic policies of the current Polish government have resulted in an unprecedented deterioration of Poland's relations with EU institutions and key EU member states, making WGA-based cooperation with them in the international arena more difficult than before.

3 | Who are the main actors involved in cooperating in a WGA?

Poland has established an institutional setup that is tasked with elaborating and implementing the national WGA related to foreign affairs. Institutionally, the Chancellery of the Prime Minister occupies a central place in the WGA. As relates to the international dimension of the WGA, particularly prominent roles are played by the Ministry of

Foreign Affairs, the Ministry of the Interior and Administration, and the Ministry of National Defence.

The way in which the Strategy for Responsible Development (Ministry of Investment and Development 2017: 5) was elaborated represents a good example of the WGA at the preparatory stage. This process involved officials from almost all ministries and agencies in addition to outside experts. They were divided into 12 inter-ministerial theme-based teams, such as ones dedicated to energy, transport and environment, security, economic expansion abroad and the efficiency of spending EU funds. Although the entire process was conducted under the auspices of the prime minister, individual ministries occasionally assumed a temporary role as the main coordinator of efforts to prepare concrete strategies.

The Government Centre for Security (GCS) is a software of the state, so to speak, on issues related to security, and it represents a key component of a comprehensive emergency-management system. It is headed by a director appointed by and subordinate to the prime minister. The mission and the main task of the GCS is to assess both threats (including external ones) and possible responses to them on the basis of data received from a range of sources, including international partners. The GCS also oversees cooperation with international partners or organisations related to emergency management. In the case of external conflicts and crises, this usually involves NATO and/or the EU.

The National Coordinator for International Development Cooperation serves as a proxy for the minister of foreign affairs in efforts to coordinate development aid and chairs the Development Cooperation Programme Board. The tasks of this opinion-making and consulting body include making proposals regarding geographical and thematic priorities of development cooperation, issuing opinions on drafts of the multiannual development-cooperation programme and annual plans, issuing opinions on annual reports related to the implementation of development-cooperation tasks by state administration authorities, and drafting government documents related to development cooperation (MFA 2018: 3). The board consists of 21 members representing various state institutions and civil society organisations (e.g. ministries, the parliament, NGOs, academia and the business community) (OECD n.d.: 2). However, at the end of 2017, the Department for Humanitarian Aid was created in the Chancellery of the Prime Minister. It is still unclear what the impact of this new entity will be on the effectiveness of Polish development cooperation, and the department's competencies overlap the activities of the MFA in the field of humanitarian aid. Furthermore, one should also note that ODA projects related to a WGA to foreign affairs sometimes also involve local governments, especially big cities and voivodeship (province) assemblies.

For many years, Poland has been struggling with the so-called 'silo' character of its state administration. Ministries and agencies have often operated as closed units. Insufficient consultation and co-ordination as well as rivalry both between and within ministries has constituted an impediment to the decision-making process regarding a Polish WGA to foreign affairs. Moreover, the informal networks of politicians and their interference in theoretically technocratic processes has a bigger impact on the functioning of state institutions and on the relations between them in Poland than in other states in Northern and Western Europe.

However, under the PiS government, parallel networks and informal actors in state institutions have gained unprecedented influence. For example, even though Jaroslaw Kaczynski, the president of the PiS, does not occupy any public post apart from being a member of parliament, any significant decision requires his approval. On the lower level, close and trusted allies of his have been inserted into state institutions, sometimes as éminences grises, where they play a similar role. Granted, in such a system, certain key decisions are taken more quickly if Kaczynski or his close associates are convinced of their importance and urgency. However, sometimes decision-makers do not take procedures or even laws into consideration. What's more, decisions regarding foreign affairs are often endorsed without consulting independent, genuine experts, but rather on the basis of political calculations and prejudices. This assessment is confirmed by internal confidential or secret reports and private correspondence between officials that have been leaked to the public.

The rivalry between factions within the ruling elite, which also plays out between and within state institutions, represents another challenge to the functioning of Poland's WGA. In order to maintain control of the party and state institutions, Kaczynski and his political nominees use the principle of divide and conquer, playing various factions within the elite against each other, which increases the unpredictability of the decision-making process and heightens tensions between state structures. However, since the 2015 elections, the polarisation of the political landscape, which was already intensive, has deepened radically. This trend constitutes a grave impediment to the development of the WGA in foreign affairs.

4 | How does your country operationalise a WGA?

General and structural challenges to the operationalisation of a WGA increased greatly in Poland after the sweeping victory of the PiS in the parliamentary elections of 2015. The degree to which the ruling elite captured state institutions is unprecedented in the modern history of Poland. Many thousands of civil servants, diplomats and officers were fired, forced or persuaded to retire early, suspended or demoted to lower posts. Many officials, diplomats and officers were marginalised. Among officials who experienced this kind of mistreatment, individuals with more professional experience, including positions held abroad and close contacts with foreign partners, were overrepresented. At the same time, many diplomats, officials and officers were hired or promoted solely on the basis of their political sympathies or loyalties instead of according to meritocratic principles.

The operationalisation of the Polish WGA in foreign affairs faces other challenges in addition to the above-mentioned structural problems, such as a lack of sufficient diplomatic presences in countries with the biggest Polish military deployments, very limited support from civil society institutions, and insufficient dedicated financial resources. The internal political polarisation in Poland discussed above has also started to exert a negative influence on the Polish WGA regarding foreign affairs, and it may also be undermined by bilateral problems with countries in which it operates.

The conflict in Ukraine definitely represents the most important challenge to Polish security. For this reason, Ukraine constitutes the main area for the operationalisation of Poland's WGA regarding foreign conflicts and crises. Poland has strengthened its engagement in Ukraine, such as with ODA and by deploying monitors, advisers and border guards. For example, Poland is involved substantially in international missions of the EU and the OSCE operating in Ukraine or on its borders. Polish General Slawomir Pichor manages the European Union Border Assistance Mission to Moldova and Ukraine (EUBAM), whose headquarters are located in Odessa (Ukraine). The Polish contingent in the mission is one of the biggest: 18 police officers and border guards, or almost 10 percent of its staff. A maximum of 10 Polish police officers and civil servants are engaged in the European Union Advisory Mission (EUAM) Ukraine, which was established in 2014. And 35 Polish officials participated in the OSCE Special Monitoring Mission to Ukraine. However, given Ukraine's significance to Poland, one can says that Poland's WGA in Ukraine has had serious shortcomings, such as insufficient institutional coordination, bilateral problems between both countries, and levels of ODA and resource deployment that are both below Poland's potential and incommensurate with Ukraine's importance to Poland.

Poland's performance concerning ODA after the 2014 revolution in Ukraine, known as the Revolution of Dignity, also gives a rather mixed picture. After Euromaidan, Poland did not substantially increase its ODA allocated for Ukraine until 2017, when it was boosted by 250 percent over the previous year (although this did not even exceed USD 60 million in absolute terms). Whereas Poland's ODA in 2016 only made up 1.5 percent of the total ODA received by Ukraine, this figure rose to 5 percent in 2017 as a result of the increase.

The steep increase in Polish ODA allocated for Ukraine in 2017 largely resulted from the growing engagement of local Polish governments (e.g. provincial assemblies and the governments of larger cities) and civil society organisations (NGOs). Until the autumn 2018 elections, the vast majority of the institutions of local government were under the control of the opposition and were in sharp conflict with the central government. One should also note that the Polish government also takes a negative view of many Polish NGOs operating in Ukraine because they do not support its internal policy. Taken together, this political polarisation has complicated efforts to coordinate the activities of various Polish development-cooperation actors in Ukraine. Furthermore, clashes related to politics of history and identity, which have been fanned by the PiS, have led to an unprecedented deterioration of bilateral relations between Poland and Ukraine, which in turn has represented another challenge to the operationalisation of Polish ODA in the country.

Poland's development aid allocated to Ukraine focuses on supporting good governance, human capital, entrepreneurship and the private sector. In its efforts to ensure a more effective response to the protracted crisis in Ukraine, Poland has officially adopted an approach of mutually reinforcing humanitarian and development measures, including and particularly ones targeting internally displaced persons from the eastern region of Donbass. However, there has been a huge gap between words and deeds, as Poland only transferred slightly more than USD 2 million of its total humanitarian aid to Ukraine in 2017, and around 35 percent of that amount went to international agencies active in Ukraine.

At present, Poland's largest foreign deployment is in Kosovo, where more than 400 Polish police officers, soldiers and civil servants are operating. Up to 300 of them are soldiers serving in the NATO-led KFOR mission, and there are almost 100 Polish police officers serving in the EU-led EULEX mission. These police officers constitute the largest single contingent in that mission, accounting for around 30 percent of all servicemen (MFA n.d.). However, Poland's capacity to implement a WGA in Kosovo is limited due to a lack of diplomatic representation and Poland's very low level of interest in contributing to the development of Kosovo. Indeed, although Poland already recognised the independence of Kosovo in 2008, it is the only one among the EU countries to do so that has not yet established diplomatic relations with Pristina. This extremely lukewarm stance has been motivated by internal political calculations. For example, the fact that a majority of Poles and certain politicians were opposed to or at least sceptical about Kosovo's independence led Kosovo to be viewed as only a marginal item on the agenda of Polish foreign policy. What's more, Poland's ODA allocated to Kosovo is extremely low and has not surpassed USD 500,000 on average in recent years (Polish Aid n.d.).

Poland has deployed members of its armed forces in the Middle East (Iraq, Jordan, Kuwait and Qatar), but they are not engaged in military operations. The contingent operating in Iraq is composed of more than 115 soldiers and civil servants (MFA n.d.), who particularly focus on training Iraqi soldiers while operating within the US-led Operation Inherent Resolve and NATO Mission Iraq (NMI). One possible criticism of Poland's WGA in Iraq is that there is minimal engagement in fields other than hard security. For instance, the Polish ODA allocated for Iraq between 2014 and 2017 roughly amounted to only USD 5 million (ibid.). Moreover, during the September 2014 offensive of the Islamic State, Poland closed its embassy in Baghdad (and only reopened it after two years) even though the main EU and NATO member states did not take such a drastic step.

Poland also has a military contingent in Afghanistan operating within NATO's Resolute Support Mission. Composed of a maximum of 350 soldiers and civil servants (MFA n.d.), it is responsible for providing Afghan police and soldiers with training on strategic planning and operational activities. As in the case of Iraq, a criticism of Poland's WGA in Afghanistan is that it only has minimal engagement in fields other than hard security and, in fact, even less than in Iraq. Furthermore, Poland closed its embassy in Afghanistan in 2014, and Polish ODA transferred to Afghanistan has been minimal in recent years (Polish Aid n.d.).

5 | Conclusions

Poland's considerable economic, diplomatic and military potential led it to elaborate official documents dedicated to a WGA to foreign conflicts and crises. However, the operationalisation of the WGA in foreign affairs has been only moderately success. Poland's particular preoccupation with hard security has prompted it to deploy Polish soldiers, monitors, police officers, advisers and border guards abroad, but these resources receive very limited civil assistance, lack a supporting diplomatic presence on the ground, and are insufficiently reinforced by Polish ODA.

Poland's WGA regarding foreign affairs also suffers from the general and structural deficiencies of Polish state institutions, such as the unsatisfactory coordination between them, institutional rivalries and the strength of informal networks. In fact, Poland's WGA regarding foreign affairs represents an exceptionally interesting case at present, as the capabilities of the state structures engaged in the WGA are rapidly deteriorating. This negative trend stems from the fact that Poland has been experiencing a structural transformation of its political system since the national elections of 2015 from a liberal democracy based on a division of powers towards a 'majoritarian' democracy with authoritarian elements that is dismantling the rule of law. What's more, due to the high level of factionalism within the ruling elite, its opaqueness and its inclination to reject technocratic and meritocratic criteria, the unprecedented scale of capture of state institutions that has occurred in the wake of the 2015 elections has injected more unpredictability into decision-making processes and more volatility into efforts to coordinate activities within and between state institutions.

The exceptional polarisation of Poland's political landscape (e.g. between the government and the opposition) is also contributing to a weakening of the operationalisation of the WGA regarding foreign affairs, especially when it comes to ODA. In consequence, even though the PiS government is continuing to develop new comprehensive strategies promoting the WGA, successfully implementing them has become much more difficult than in the past. In fact, the Strategy for Responsible Development (Ministry of Investment and Development 2017), which includes a robust external component, largely remains just a strategy on paper more than two years after its announcement.

Moreover, the negative trends related to Poland's WGA to foreign crises and conflicts may strengthen considerably in the years ahead. The PiS won the national elections in October 2019 and re-established a single-party government. Most probably, the process of de-democratisation and, by default, the PiS's capture of the state will substantially accelerate and will further aggravate tensions with EU institutions and key EU member states. In accordance with its 'sovereigntist' vision of Europe, the PiS government is also likely to pursue its policy of distancing itself from the EU mainstream. Such a scenario will further hamper the operationalisation of Poland's WGA related to foreign affairs.

6 | Reference list

GCS (Government Centre for Security) (n.d.). International Cooperation. https://rcb.gov.pl/en/international-cooperation/.

Government of Poland (2016). Ordinance on the Inter-ministerial Team for Resource Policy of the State. 17 May 2016. https://bip.kprm.gov.pl/kpr/bip-rady-ministrow/organy-pomocnicze/organy-pomocnicze-rady/3662,Miedzyresortowy-Zespol-do-spraw-Polityk i-Surowcowej-Panstwa.html.

MFA (Ministry of Foreign Affairs) (n.d.). Operacje NATO i UE. www.msz.gov.pl/pl/polityka_zagraniczna/polityka_bezpieczenstwa/ope racje_nato_i_ue/.

MFA (2018). The multiannual development cooperation programme for 2016–2020. www.gov.pl/attachment/d6da9192-10ab-4abb-8242-87f1d3b33b98.

Ministry of Investment and Development (2017). Strategia na rzecz Odpowiedzialnego Rozwoju do roku 2020 (z perspektywą do 2030 r.). www.gov.pl/documents/33377/436740/SOR.pdf.

MoD (Ministry of National Defence) (2017). The Defence Concept of the Republic of Poland. https://archiwum2019-en.mon.gov.pl/p/pliki/dokumenty/rozne/2017/07/korp_web_13_06_2017.pdf.

OECD (n.d.). Poland. www.oecd.org/governance/pcsd/Poland.pdf.

OECD (2019). "Development aid drops in 2018, especially to neediest countries." 10 April 2019. www.oecd.org/newsroom/development-aid-drops-in-2018-especially-to-neediest-countries.htm.

Polish Aid (n.d.). Polish help in numbers. www.polskapomoc.gov.pl/Polska,pomoc,w,liczbach,15.html.

Portugal

Francisco Seixas da Costa and Patricia Magalhaes Ferreira

1 | Introduction

From its intermediate geographic position between the Atlantic and Mediterranean regions and between Europe and Africa, as well as owing to its recent history, Portugal is keenly aware of the importance of building bridges and the notion that only together can we respond in a more effective way to multidimensional and complex global (security, political, developmental) challenges. The commitment to multilateralism, including support for multilateral action and coordinated responses to crises and conflicts, is therefore an important feature of Portugal's foreign policy.

As a small country with limited resources, Portugal's external actions have always stressed the importance of multilateral responses based on a wider international effort, perceiving the EU, NATO and the UN as complementary rather than competing frameworks. In this context, at the national level, Portuguese governments have viewed sharing collective responsibilities and participating in international efforts aimed at fostering peace and security (e.g. participation in all EU CSDP missions) as an instrument for strengthening the country's external reputation and credibility.

It should be noted that Portugal was struggling to fulfil its commitments during the financial/economic crisis and the so-called Adjustment Programme (2011–2014), a period in which there was a political decision to reduce participation in international missions to a minimum and even to halt participation in EU missions. In the last few years, however, there has been an effort to increase participation in and contributions to international security efforts. For example, at present, 11 percent of Portugal's armed forces are engaged in international missions (a total of 19 missions in 2019), with the largest headcounts being in the Central African Republic and Afghanistan.

The perception of participating in international efforts as an instrument for strengthening Portuguese external action necessarily implies increased coordination among policies, instruments and actors. In this context, there is an increasing awareness of the need to improve coherence and joint approaches (particularly between the diplomatic and defence axes, which implies the reformulation of legal instruments and strategic documents) as well as to increase coordination between different instruments, actors and institutions in what is often referred to as a whole-of-government approach (WGA). Despite this awareness, these efforts are not being implemented in a very structured way in practice, and there is some resistance to them from institutional structures and cultures.

Most strategic guidance related to a WGA is linked to Portugal's foreign policy priorities, which have not changed for many years and rest on four main pillars: the Atlantic, including relations with the United States; the European Union and the European integration process; the Portuguese-speaking world (with special attention being paid to Portuguese-speaking African countries (PALOP) and the Community of Portuguese Language Countries (CPLP)); and Portuguese communities abroad.

On the one hand, particularly regarding external action related to defence and security, Portuguese strategic documents mainly highlight the country's participation in NATO and in external missions of the European Union. On the other hand, Portuguese action in response to external crises and conflicts is very much linked to Portugal's focus on the most vulnerable and fragile countries as well as related security, diplomatic and development efforts. Some of the main partners of Portuguese development cooperation are fragile and/or affected by situations of fragility (e.g. East Timor, Guinea-Bissau, and São Tome and Príncipe), and supporting them – through both bi- and multi-lateral cooperation – is of particular importance to Portugal.

At the bilateral level, Portugal's development-cooperation attaches particular importance to peacebuilding and statebuilding, including institutional strengthening and capacity development in key areas, such as governance, the rule of law, security and the provision of essential services. This is also linked to Africa as a foreign policy priority, which is reflected in Portugal's participation in EU CSDP missions and in its diplomatic stances regarding the importance of Africa to EU external relations. For example, there are the past Africa-EU summits and the Joint Africa-EU Strategy (JAES); the new European Peace Facility and its stress on the need for increased commitments to Africa; and, most recently, the negotiations surrounding a post-Cotonou framework. Focusing on Africa will also be a major priority when Portugal holds the rotating presidency of the Council of the EU in 2021.

2 | What policies have been developed to further policy coherence?

Although Portugal does not have a defined overall WGA strategy regarding its response to external conflicts and crises, the need for greater coordination and coherence is outlined in several strategic documents and policies, among which the following are noteworthy: First, in 2009, the Council of Ministers approved the National Strategy for Security and Development (Government of Portugal 2009). The strategy, which was the result of a much-needed debate among stakeholders engaged in defence/security and development cooperation, was regarded as a natural extension of a stronger stance in Portugal's responses to fragile situations and aimed to "promote greater coherence and coordination in the external global action of the Portuguese state regarding security and development". However, ownership was not ensured, and the strategy did not have visible concrete results, partially because it failed to establish clear responsibilities in the implementation of follow-up mechanisms.

Second, in 2013, the Council of Ministers adopted the Strategic Concept for National Defence (Government of Portugal 2013). This guiding framework analyses the major threats and establishes national priorities at both the domestic and international levels, with the latter focusing on Portugal as a security provider. However, since this overarching framework is very much focused on the armed forces, it does not define any follow-up mechanisms and also tends to be hindered by a fragmented framework in practice. A related document, the National Defence Law (as amended in 2014) (Republic of Portugal 2009), states that the national defence policy includes the public-sector policies that are relevant to safeguarding the strategic interests of

Portugal, and specifically mentions inter-ministerial coordination as well as cooperation between the armed forces and the security/police forces. Nevertheless, some have argued that there is a need for an overarching national strategy on security that would allow for a more comprehensive approach towards security by going beyond the defence sector and the armed forces. This is made difficult, however, by legal constrains linked to a juridical/constitutional dimension of the security concept.

Third, in February 2014, the Council of Ministers adopted the Strategic Concept of Portuguese Development Cooperation 2014–2020 (Government of Portugal 2014) to be the guiding document for the country's development policy. In addition to firmly establishing development policy as an element of Portuguese foreign policy, this document prioritises the link between peace, security and development by reinforcing coordination among actors and instruments of external action according to the 3D (diplomacy, defence, development) principle.

Fourth, in 2015, the Council of Ministers approved the Operational Strategy for Humanitarian and Emergency Aid (Government of Portugal 2015), which focuses on providing practical guidance to increase coordination and coherence in responses to emergency situations. The objective is to enhance this integrated response both within government departments and institutions engaged in humanitarian responses as well as when they coordinate with non-state actors. However, it does not have much political leverage, and awareness of its existence should be increased.

Returning to the issue of defence documentation, it should also be noted that a new cycle of programming is currently being defined regarding Portugal's defence policy (2019–2022), which is supposed to be able to respond to emerging threats and new challenges in a more coherent and comprehensive manner. This will hopefully include an update of old but still valid legislation from the 1980s and 1990s that covers several aspects of defence policy-related external actions, including defence cooperation with partner countries. The need to update these instruments as well as to revise other strategies, such as the Strategic Concept for National Defence (Government of Portugal 2013), is explicitly stated in a decree of the Ministry of National Defence from April 2018 (Ministry of National Defence 2018).

At present, strategic documents regarding defence and security only mention civil-military coordination, particularly the need for increased coordination among all the security forces involved in external missions (i.e. the narrow scope of a WGA). The most recent documents also mention the priorities of maritime security and cybersecurity, which will also require greater civil-military coordination. What's more, the extension of Portugal's continental shelf is also a reason for civil and military organisations to enhance coordination and share equipment. Of course, Portugal's armed forces are supposed to fulfil the state's international commitments in the military field, to participate in humanitarian missions and international peacekeeping operations, to cooperate in civil protection missions, and to engage in technical-military cooperation in the broader context of the country's cooperation policy (which is now called 'defence cooperation'). Nevertheless, documents on security strategies make almost no reference to other actors beyond those in the security-defence axis, and development stakeholders are completely overlooked.

Turning now to the EU level, Portugal has actively participated in discussions to develop comprehensive approaches to external conflicts and crises. The Portuguese agenda in the negotiations surrounding the Global Strategy was centred on advocating for a stronger focus on Africa (e.g. regarding the development of a regular high-level political dialogue that goes beyond development cooperation and is not limited by the migration agenda) as well as on the Mediterranean and the EU's southern neighbourhood.

Portugal pushed its agenda during its 2007 presidency of the Council of the EU. For example, the first Council of the EU joint session of defence and development ministers was held, the new European Consensus on Development and the European Consensus on Humanitarian Aid were approved, the Joint Africa-EU Strategy was endorsed, and the process of developing an action plan related to fragile states and situations was initiated. Portugal also pressed for a EU ESDP mission in Guinea-Bissau (2008–2010), which was the first ESDP mission conducted in an integrated manner by involving the entire security sector (defence, justice and police) as well as the first mission fully planned and controlled as part of the Civilian Planning and Conduct Capability (CPCC) for civilian operations of EU crisis management. However, most member states showed little interest in contributing to and being actively engaged in this mission, which in turn contributed to its shortcomings.

At the international (non-EU) level, Portugal is generally seen in multilateral forums as an honest broker that pays special attention to the voice of the least developed and most fragile countries (which struggle to find a voice even within their development groups) and, therefore, as a useful partner for building bridges and consensus. It has strongly advocated for the inclusion of the 'peace, justice and strong institutions' global goal (Goal 16) during the negotiations surrounding the 2030 Agenda for Sustainable Development, and it is involved in several discussions at the UN and the OECD on peacebuilding and statebuilding approaches in countries prioritised by Portuguese external action, such as the Portuguese-speaking countries.

3 | Who are the main actors involved in cooperating in a WGA?

Portugal's participation in international missions and launching of such external-action defence initiatives has a well-structured coordination process when it comes to the military component. The minister of foreign affairs and the minister of national defence make a decision, and then they take this decision and the related forces planning to the Supreme Council of National Defence (CSDN), which is the coordination entity for advising the president of the republic on national defence issues. The CSDN then issues an opinion on the participation of Portuguese military forces in external missions arising from Portugal's international commitments. This structure includes military and political actors: the prime minister; the ministers of defence, foreign affairs, internal administration and finance; the ministers responsible for the industry, energy, transports and communications sectors; the top commanders of the armed forces; representatives of the autonomous regions (i.e. the Azores and Madeira); and representatives of the national parliament.

There are other coordination mechanisms between the Ministry of Foreign Affairs (MFA) and the Ministry of National Defence (MND) that contribute to increasing coherence. These include: holding regular councils of defence and security (MFA+MND); having a diplomatic officer working in the cabinet of the minister of national defence; having a representative of the armed forces (from the cabinet of the chief of the general staff of the armed forces) working in the MFA's Director-ate-General for Foreign Policy; maintaining regular and open com-munication channels between the MND and Portugal's permanent representation to the EU in Brussels (which also has a military officer to coordinate with diplomats). However, articulation between political and military sensibilities is not always easy, even within the MND.

From a more comprehensive perspective, the Interministerial Commission for European Affairs and the Interministerial Commis-sion for Foreign Policy (both under the MFA) have regular meetings that are attended by representatives of several ministries and aim to increase the coherence of Portugal's external actions. The CFSP is dis-cussed at the Inter-ministerial Commission for Foreign Policy, which has political meetings and then technical meetings dedicated to spe-cific topics.

The role of the EEAS and the rise of new structures and institu-tional linkages at the EU level geared towards responding to external crises and conflicts have also prompted some changes in Portugal aimed at better adapting to these new dynamics. This is taking place within the MFA as well as between the MFA and the MND, but it mainly involves adding competencies to the already-existing institu-tions rather than creating new structures or strategies. Some achieve-ments resulting from the Global Strategy have motivated Portugal to develop specific policies and measures. This is the case, for example, with PESCO, for which a national implementation plan and a 'project participation monitoring group' for following up on PESCO activities (GAPP-PESCO) were created in 2019. The latter's members include several representatives from the defence establishment (e.g. from the Directorate-General of National Defence Policy, the cabinet of the chief of the general staff of the armed forces, and the individual branches of the military).

The National Authority of Emergency and Civil Protection (ANEPC), which is responsible for emergency civil planning in cases of disasters, crises or war, has both domestic and external competen-cies, according to its organic law published in 2019 (Republic of Portu-gal 2019). On the external level, it can participate in foreign assistance missions (by order of the Ministry of Internal Administration) and is responsible for coordinating with the MND efforts that are related to civil emergency planning under the NATO framework. One should note, however, that there is some discontent regarding this arrangement stemming from a lack of clarity regarding responsibilities. While the ANEPC is the authoritative body when it comes to coordinating and participating in civil-protection missions and actions, the ANEPC does not always have the necessary skills and knowledge to spearhead civil emergency planning, which is an activity of a military nature.

When it comes to participation in UN and EU missions, Portugal contributes both military and police personnel. Regarding UN efforts, Portuguese soldiers are serving in stabilisation missions in the Central African Republic (MINUSCA), Mali (MINUSMA) and Colombia (UNMCOL), and Portuguese police officers are participating in joint efforts in Colombia (UNVMC), South Sudan (UNMISS), Guinea-Bissau (UNIOGBIS), Haiti (MINUJUSTH), Kosovo (UNMIK) and Darfur (UNAMID, a hybrid UN-AU mission). Regarding EU efforts, Portugal currently contributes soldiers to missions in Somalia (EUNAVFOR ATALANTA and EUTM SOMALIA), Mali (EUTM MALI), the southern-central Mediterranean (EUNAVFOR MED) and the Central African Republic (EUTM RCA), the last of which is led by a Portuguese officer and includes some 200 Portuguese soldiers. At the police level – which includes members of the Public Security Police (PSP), the National Republican Guard (GNR), and the Foreigners and Borders Service (SEF) – Portugal has officers (though sometimes as few as one) deployed on EU missions in Mali (EUCAP), Georgia (EUMM), Niger (EUCAP), Kosovo (EULEX), Ukraine (EUAM), Somalia (EUCAP), the Central African Republic (EUTM RCA), the Palestinian territories (EUPOL COPPS), and Bosnia-Herzegovina (EUFOR ALTHEA).

Portugal faces some difficulties in its efforts to coordinate between security/police forces and political institutions. The large number of internal security forces (e.g. the PSP, the GNR, the SEF, the Judicial Police and the Maritime Police) complicates coordination, there is still a lack of clarity regarding certain roles and responsibilities, and certain procedures and practices (e.g. on information-sharing and data collection) have yet to be harmonised. Whereas the military has an established annual budget for participating in international missions (approved within the state budget), the participation of security forces in international missions involves decisions that are made on an ad hoc, individual basis. For instance, if Portuguese police institutions receive a call for proposals or job posting from the EU (via the permanent representation in Brussels), each police force makes its own assessment regarding whether it is suited to participate rather than making a joint assessment or analysis at the strategic level.

The role of parliament, known as the Assembly of the Republic, has both relevant aspects and shortcomings. The parliament has specific permanent (i.e. standing) committees with representatives drawn from several parliamentary groups (e.g. the European Affairs Committee and the Committee on Foreign Affairs and the Portuguese Communities). Since 2010, the parliament has also selected priority EU-related issues to receive monitoring and follow-up. For example, in 2018, these priority issues included implementing the EU Global Strategy and fostering greater efficiency and coherence in CFSP implementation. Nevertheless, the parliamentary commissions frequently conduct their work in an isolated manner, and the quality of the debate on different sectoral issues is often undermined by parliamentarians' lack of knowledge on specific issues or technical aspects.

Regarding external action, and specifically pertaining to the EU, the interactions between Portugal's government and parliament include regular debates with government representatives (e.g. before and after meetings of the European Council), regular reporting to parliament on policies and measures, and consultation processes. Government representatives also attend parliamentary hearings if requested to do so by the parliament. To name a recent example, in January 2019, at the request of the parliamentary Committee on Foreign Affairs and the Portuguese Communities, the minister of defence and the minister of foreign affairs participated in a hearing dedicated to discussing the implementation of the EU's Global Strategy and PESCO. However, when it comes to participation in international missions, the parliament is only informed of a decision that has already been taken at the government and military levels.

Although civil society organisations in Portugal would like to have a stronger voice in influencing public policies and WGAs related to external actions, they basically play no role in drafting or implementing WGAs. There are exceptions, however, when it comes to activities related to the development-cooperation sector, as members of civil society organisations attend some meetings and participate in the Coordination Unit for Humanitarian and Emergency Aid in the framework of the Strategy for Humanitarian and Emergency Aid, which is overseen by Camoes – Institute for Cooperation and Language, the Portuguese development agency.

In term of administrative structures and processes to operationalise a WGA, Portugal's MFA has established information-sharing mechanisms (e.g. with the embassies and the permanent representation in Brussels), and the MND has internal reporting mechanisms. However, information-sharing within other institutions and between sectors is mainly done on an informal basis. Information is mainly gathered within the individual institutions or sectors, and there is no aggregation of data (e.g. regarding military and police participation in EU and international peace missions). What's more, poor information-sharing can sometimes also result from squabbling over competences and attempts to gain more visibility.

There can also be a lack of coordination within individual sectors. For example, as mentioned above, the profusion of different forces in Portugal's security sector leads to multiple political authorities and, in some cases, overlapping responsibilities and conflicts of jurisdictions. Within the development sector, there are some structures for coordination, such as the Inter-ministerial Commission for Cooperation (CIC). However, in practice, these mainly result in information-sharing, and the system remains fragmented – including in budgetary terms – owing to the plethora of actors and actions. Both of these sectors would benefit from improved intra-sectoral coordination, which would then allow for efforts aimed at improving inter-sectoral coordination between the security and development sectors. It should also be noted that, as in most countries, dialogue and coordination between security and development actors is impacted by different views, languages, mandates and approaches.

At the same time, Portugal has had some success at creating specific WGA-like structures to coordinate external action related to a specific issue. For example, the Portuguese Commission for Supporting the Transition in East Timor (CATTL) was created at the national level to coordinate external action, and Portugal was involved in diplomatic efforts in the transition process on a multilateral basis led by the UN (e.g. UNTAET, UNMIT) as well as several international peace missions (e.g. ones regarding the Portuguese language and capacity-building in several sectors as well as bilateral agreements on police cooperation and training). Another example is Portugal's actions in the 2008–2010 period in Guinea-Bissau, which simultaneously included diplomatic efforts; participation in an EU ESDP mission on security-sector reform combining defence, justice and police; and development-cooperation actions. In practice, East Timor and Guinea-Bissau are examples of the diverse fields of action in which Portugal has been engaged. Nevertheless, there is still a lack of discussion of the results of initiatives like these, from which lessons learned could be extracted so as to improve future planning and action.

More recent examples of implementing a WGA can be found in the framework of foreign policy. One good example is the nomination of an ambassador for the Sahel, as Portugal did not have this specifically regional approach beforehand in terms of human resources. Another example is Portugal's actions related to Venezuela, which comprises diplomatic efforts (i.e. bilateral political dialogue and coordination within the EU) and aid (i.e. financing the EU/ECHO joint pool fund for NGOs working inside Venezuela and also through bilateral aid to the refugees in Colombia).

A specific thematic structure that could bring about some positive results is the Coordination Unit for Humanitarian and Emergency Aid, a unit chaired by Camoes – Institute for Cooperation and Language, the Portuguese development agency. Despite some practical difficulties in coordinating participating actors, this coordination structure has been functioning since approximately 2017. Its members include representatives of Camoes (as the MFA's proxy) as wells as of the ministries responsible for the national-defence, internal-administration, health and social-protection sectors, who have regular biannual meetings as well as extraordinary meetings (e.g. when Hurricane Idai ravaged Mozambique in March 2019). The unit's creation has recently sparked a process of clarifying concepts, understanding the language of different stakeholders, and debating issues on the humanitarian agenda, all of which were not done beforehand. Although this process is still in its infancy, it represents a concrete step towards a more coordinated WGA in this area.

It should also be noted that coordination within international structures and missions is mostly vertical. Regarding humanitarian/emergency missions and aid, the central coordinating role is played by the UN through OCHA and sectoral or thematic clusters (e.g. WFP for food aid or WHO for health), and Portuguese support and related organisations are included in those clusters. In the UN or EU missions in which Portugal participates, both at the planning and operational stages, coordination takes place vertically between the Portuguese contingent (whether civil, military or police) and the EU or UN mission (since they are included in a defined command/structure and division of work) rather than horizontally (between Portuguese forces or officials).

Coordination between ministries and several actors is particularly difficult when an emergency arises and prompts a Portuguese external intervention that is not within an EU or international framework. This was the case with the recent response to Hurricane Idai in Mozambique, where there was a prompt response and deployment capacity but a certain lack of clarity regarding mandates between political responsibilities and humanitarian responses (military and civil) as well as difficulties in coordinating efforts in the field. It should be noted, however, that such difficulties in coordination are common to most EU countries.

5 | Conclusions

The level of commitment to comprehensive approaches in responding to external conflicts and crises ranges very widely in Portugal. On the one hand, most strategic-level documents include what are mostly general and non-binding commitments, which in turn have to be translated into concrete policy documents and operational mechanisms. On the other hand, successful implementation frequently relies on multiple interlinked factors, such as political will, individual commitment to moving forward on certain issues (e.g. the knowledge, agenda and capabilities of a minister or high-level official), leadership both at the political and institutional level, a suitable institutional framework, ownership by most relevant actors, and the recruitment/ deployment of necessary human resources.

At the strategic level, the existing framework is very much focused on sectoral approaches rather than WGAs. Within the security/defence sectors, the legal framework is incomplete, outdated in some cases and fragmented. However, there is an awareness of the need to modernise and update these strategic frameworks in order to promote more comprehensive and integrated approaches, and some progress has been made towards these goals in the last few years. In addition, the channels of coordination with and participation in EU structures and policies are multiple, and there is a general perception within Portugal's MFA that coordination within the EU has improved with the creation of the European External Action Service (EEAS).

Development is clearly the weakest link in the defence-diplomacy-development nexus, as it is neglected in Portugal's efforts to promote its WGAs, which are mainly focused on the interactions of diplomacy/foreign policies and security/defence policies (which are, incidentally, much needed in the case of Portuguese participation in European/international missions and structures). Within the defence sector, references to coordination are mainly at the domestic/internal level, either among the military or between civil and military aspects, and there are shortcomings in training on aspects that go beyond military issues (e.g. diplomatic/negotiation skills and even knowledge of languages).

There are some strategic documents that reflect a wider WGA perspective at the strategic level, such as the National Strategy for Security and Development (Government of Portugal 2009) and the Operational Strategy for Humanitarian and Emergency Aid (Government of Portugal 2015). However, the success of their implementation has been mixed, as it depends on the existence of political will, leadership, leverage and other domestic factors.

Such political leadership is influenced by the mandate (i.e. term in office) of each government, as there is a change in the high-level officials every four years that includes but is not limited to ministers and secretaries of state. In addition, this reshuffling includes directors and political appointees who are also very relevant for leadership within public institutions and administrations. Indeed, in a context in which most of the general WGA commitments are non-binding and where most coordination and coherence mechanisms between sectors is of an ad hoc nature, political will and institutional leadership are key and can vary significantly depending on individual levels of commitment, knowledge, motivation and skills.

A dimension that is not sufficiently addressed is the participation of Portuguese officials in international functions, organisations and missions who have valuable experience and knowledge. For example, there are not enough mechanisms to enable effective knowledge-sharing and the analysis of lessons learned. Instead, in most cases, the knowledge remains with the individual, and the opportunity to use that experience to improve Portuguese policies and actions is not exploited.

Ownership is also an important issue, because even where there is political will, if most actors are not engaged in the process and there are no clear structures for implementation, strategies tend to be just words on paper. One obvious example is the National Strategy for Security and Development (Government of Portugal 2009). This strategy resulted from clear political guidance and coordination of the relevant ministries at a high level, but the appropriation of human resources from both sectors was not ensured, the coordination mechanisms for implementation were not in place, and it was not considered a priority by the new government from 2011 onwards (which also corresponds to a period of financial crisis). The combination of these factors led the strategy to be completely forgotten. Thus, one can say that a combination of several factors – and ones that go beyond the existence of strategies, structures and mechanisms – determine whether some governmental/political documents with WGA aspects and approaches will make some progress towards achieving their objectives, while others are simply not implemented and fail to achieve any or all of their intended goals.

6 | Reference list

Government of Portugal (2009). National Strategy for Security and Development. Council of Ministers Resolution No. 73/2009. https://dre.pt/application/dir/pdf1sdip/2009/08/16500/0560305608.pdf.

Government of Portugal (2013). Strategic Concept for National Defence (CEDN). www.idn.gov.pt/conteudos/documentos/CEDN_2013.pdf.

Government of Portugal (2014). Portuguese Concept of Development Cooperation 2014–2020. www.instituto-camoes.pt/images/cooperacao/conctestratg_eng_v2.pdf.

Government of Portugal (2015). Operational Strategy for Humanitarian and Emergency Aid. Council of Ministers Resolution No. 65/2015. https://dre.pt/home/-/dre/70128396/details/maximized?p_auth=v6yb9gAl.

Ministry of National Defence (2018). Decree No. 4101/2018 on the Defence External Action and Programming Cycle for Military Defence. https://dre.pt/home/-/dre/115147958/details/maximized.

Republic of Portugal (2009). National Defence Law, with changes made by the Organic Law 5/2014 of 29th August.

Republic of Portugal (2019). Decree-Law on the National Authority for Emergency and Civic Protection, Decree-Law No. 45/2019. 1 April 2019. https://dre.pt/application/conteudo/121748967.

Interviews carried out at the Ministry of Foreign Affairs, the Ministry of National Defence, the National Republican Guard, and Camoes – Institute for Cooperation and Language.

Romania

Oana Popescu-Zamfir and Ana Maria Teaca

1 | Introduction

The first time that a whole-of-government approach (WGA) was introduced and operationalised in Romania was in 2002, when the country's Supreme Council of National Defence (CSAT) was founded. The CSAT is an independent body working under the leadership of the president of Romania and accountable to the parliament, and it is responsible for elaborating the country's strategic vision as well as for providing oversight of and for coordinating all security- and defence-related policies and decisions. Its members are the president of the country; the prime minister; the ministers of foreign affairs, national defence, internal affairs, justice, economy and public finance; the heads of the domestic and foreign intelligence services; the chief of the general staff; the presidential adviser for national security; and the secretary of the Supreme Council of National Defence (CSAT). This wide-ranging composition ensures coordination and coherence in both decision-making and implementation.

Since Romania's constitution also makes the president the country's highest representative for foreign and security policy, the commander of the armed forces, and the person who sits on the European Council, this institutional setup ensures coordination with the EU level, as well. Results of this coordination are then passed down the hierarchy to all other institutions represented in the CSAT.

The CSAT has a permanent secretariat that keeps tabs on the calendar of tasks assigned to each institution in pursuit of the goals outlined in the annual programme and any other strategic document. It holds regular meetings and also discusses and plans ahead for the coming year.

As mentioned above, the founding of the CSAT preceded the 2016 EU Global Strategy (EUGS) in terms of institutional setup, but the publication of the EUGS has been hugely instrumental in adding further substance to Romania's pre-existing institutional framework. For example, it has brought more coherence and coordination between the EU level and member states in addition to requiring the same level of coordination among line ministries in cases where the responsibility for various tasks lies with different EU affairs departments. The high profile of the EUGS and the related communication efforts (as well as outreach events organised in preparation for its release) have also led institutions across the legislative and executive spectrum (e.g. ministries and parliament) as well as civil society organisations to become more familiar with it.

Apart from permanent structured cooperation, topics that are of strategic or high importance generate their own set of inter-institutional instruments for cooperation and implementation. For example, the issue of military mobility involves cooperation among multiple ministries, including the Ministry of National Defence (MND), the Ministry of Foreign Affairs (MFA), and the Ministry of Transport. Other examples include the Three Seas Initiative (with its own inter-ministerial working group), Romania's (now failed) candidacy for a non-permanent seat on the UN Security Council, and its efforts to become an OECD member (with a working group at the government level). Previously, the Danube Strategy and the national strategy for the Black Sea region played a similar role.

Prior to the EUGS, it was NATO-related issues that generated the highest level of coordination and cooperation, from endeavours aimed at meeting various obligations to participation in missions abroad. To some extent, Romania's NATO and EU accession roadmaps, with their clearly set goals in coordination with the supranational policies of both bodies, and the benchmarks to achieve those goals helped to create a culture of cooperation among all levels and sectors of the administration.

However, Romania's presidency of the Council of the EU in the first half of 2019 marked the real coming of age, with the country achieving full maturity in its exercise of EU membership in the course of preparations for the presidency in 2018 as well as before that and during this presidency itself. The complexity of this exercise has made even personnel who had not previously been involved in EU-related coordination much more familiar with the workings of EU institutions and with the Brussels framework. One should also note that since even before these efforts to prepare for the presidency, Romania has had a European Affairs Coordination Council, which brings together all persons responsible for EU affairs in the line ministries in regular meetings.

In a nutshell, Romania's focus on security and its WGA have their roots in its strategic culture. This culture sees the country's position on the south-eastern border of the EU and NATO, close to historically hostile and revisionist regional powers and to turbulent nearby regions both to its south and its east, as an existential threat. The paradigm shift that it underwent thanks to its accession to NATO (in 2004) and the EU (in 2007) not only resulted in a clear foreign policy option, but also brought about internal reform (e.g. regarding the rule of law, pluralism, and checks and balances). These changes, in turn, have made many aware that strategic stability is the cumulative result of foreign policy options and internal action in various sectors. What's more, the current WGA and integrated approach can probably be attributed to these realisations.

2 | What policies have been developed to further policy coherence?

Romania's WGA policies date back to the establishment of the National Defence Supreme Council (CSAT), whose stated purpose in its founding law of 2002 (Parliament of Romania 2002) is to be "the autonomous authority invested, by the Constitution, with the unitary organisation and coordination of activities pertaining to national defence and security." The more recent National Security Strategy (for the period 2015–2019) (President of Romania 2015) plays a similar role and reiterates, under the signature of the president, that the document aims to "integrate organically the foreign and security policy, so that it may defend and advance national interest". The Strategy is, according to the Constitution and to Law 473/2004 regarding defence planning (Parliament of Romania 2004), "the main instrument underlying national defence planning and ensuring the strategic framework for unitary coordination and organisation of the activities pertaining to national defence and security, through the CSAT." However, beyond these explicitly formulated policies, Romania's domestic and external cooperation efforts are based on a number of other coordination mechanisms.

Of particular significance is the 2016 EU Global Strategy (EUGS). Romania's MFA and other line ministries were heavily invested in the elaboration of the EUGS under the coordination of the MFA's Policy Planning Department. As such, several outreach events were organised, and various branches of the administration were involved throughout the process. One of the reasons for the depth of engagement is that Romania had by then already started preparing for the its presidency of the Council of the EU in early 2019. In fact, Pillar 3 ("Europe, as a stronger global actor") of the four on which Romania's presidency was based was almost entirely dedicated to supporting the implementation of the EUGS. Thus, every relevant sector has grown familiar with the EUGS and the associated tasks deriving from it, including the parliament and some thinktanks. At the same time, various formal or informal inter-institutional working groups were created. Since the EUGS provides a framework for longer-term goals, cooperation is structured, ongoing and involves regular meetings.

Romania has also tried (with mixed success) to streamline its development aid coordination. Romanian development aid used to be channelled through a special unit in the MFA, while some other elements of it (e.g. university scholarships for students from priority countries) were under the Ministry of National Education. In 2016, the Romanian Agency for International Development Cooperation (RoAid) was created, and its mission is to act as the single independent body coordinating development aid (as part of Romania's EU obligations). Its mission statement sounds ambitious, as it claims to unite the "work of the Romanian public institutions, the civil society and private sector towards the global efforts of sustainably alleviating extreme poverty and supporting stronger democratic institutions in developing countries." However, the strategic planning unit remains in the MFA, the budget is also allocated by the MFA, and input is collected via consultations with other ministries and agencies (including UNICEF, e.g., regarding development aid meant to improve children-related policies in target countries). Priority areas do not frequently change (with the neighbourhood and MENA being permanent target recipient regions), and annual planning is carried out. Given the rather recent nature of this initiative to streamline policies and the related funding, it still works better in theory than in practice. Among the reasons behind the remaining shortcomings is the fact that external aid has never been a priority area for either the MFA or the government.

When it comes to defence policies, Romania's WGAs related to military mobility and the EU's Permanent Structured Cooperation (PESCO) are examples of WGAs born out of the immediacy of certain topical issues. The policy is of high priority to Romania in light of its being host to several US and NATO bases and military facilities and of the general emphasis on interoperability, defence and security (not to mention its pledge to allocate 2% of GDP to defence in accordance with NATO commitments). This issue spans the ministries of Foreign Affairs, Defence, Internal Affairs and Transport as well as the intelligence services. In line with NATO's seven lines of action in the field of domestic resilience, Romania supported the European Commission's 2017 joint communication on resilience in the EU's external action (European Commission 2017) and tabled the joint proposal (with the other two members of the current EU Council presidency trio, Finland and Croatia) of a Council horizontal working party on countering hybrid threats, whose mission is to improve the resilience of the EU and its member states against hybrid threats and to support action to strengthen the crisis resilience of societies. Again, these are EU- and NATO-level policies that have triggered an integrated response mechanism in Romania. The MFA took active part in preparatory debates on the joint communication in Brussels, but the parliament has also published its own communication as a follow-up, which reinforces the recommendations in the EU document. By nature, hybrid threats are complex challenges that span multiple domains. Implementation therefore involves the Ministry of Internal Affairs, the MND, the intelligence services, the general secretariat of the government, and the presidential administration.

In terms of the EU's Common Security and Defence Policy (CSDP), Romania has been an active contributor to NATO-, OSCE-, UN- and US-led missions abroad (e.g. in Afghanistan, Africa, the Balkans and Iraq). Its interest in civil-military cooperation (CIMIC) has therefore been longstanding. What's more, it has developed its CIMIC dimension in several ways (e.g. via the National Defence University and by participating in joint trainings and exercises with allies), and it continues to do so. One can also say that EU-level policies (e.g. those prescribing precise responsibilities to member states regarding their contributions to EU efficiency, deployment, pools of civilian experts, etc) have played an integrating role in Romania. What's more, they have been eagerly embraced owing to their potential to further structure this inter-institutional coordination and to give more weight to the civilian sector, which is currently less developed than the military one, such as by improving the legal framework, training, recruitment and financial instruments.

Furthermore, Romania has always been supportive of an approach that sees the EU's crisis-prevention role as being complementary to NATO, as opposed to EU collective defence, which is seen as overlapping. There have been ongoing efforts to use the EU's crisis-management and relief framework as an anchor to further develop both external (i.e. with other countries) and internal cooperation. Although Romania already has quite a lot of experience in this field (including in emergency services infrastructure, capacity of intervention, etc), it still needs to consolidate it. Among the government bodies involved, the MFA currently plays the coordinating role (because it has also been coordinating EU civilian missions abroad). The Ministry of Internal Affairs is the main contributor to such efforts, but some specialised tasks are also assigned to the Ministry of Justice, the MND and the intelligence services, especially when they involve cybersecurity, strategic communications and hybrid threats. Furthermore, the European Defence Fund (EDF) provides a good concrete anchor to help boost cooperation between the MND, the Ministry of Economy, and the domestic defence industry (i.e. private entities). The Ministry of Public Finance, which co-funds this cooperation, and the Ministry of Education (for the R&D part) are also a part of it.

When it comes to maritime security, Romania's security assessment views the Black Sea as a particularly vulnerable soft spot. For this reason, the country places emphasis on maritime security and has coordinated and cooperative policies regarding related goals. As an overarching principle, Romania allocates a lot of importance to NATO-EU cooperation. It sees its security interests best represented by NATO, which, from the country's perspective, was also the first supranational organisation into which it was integrated, in 2004, which was followed by EU accession in 2007. Furthermore, Romania is involved in the Three Seas Initiative and the EU's Danube Strategy in addition to having its own strategy for the Black Sea region. It has joined these framework initiatives in the hopes of throwing the weight of cooperation on a number of civilian fields in the pursuit of strategic and often security-driven goals. Some of them have not produced much in terms of outcomes, and some of them (e.g. the Three Seas Initiative) are still in their infancy. Nevertheless, efforts are being made to bring relevant actors together to create a permanent form of cooperation.

Romania's strategic partnership with the United States, which has pretty much developed in parallel to the country's NATO contribution, has also helped to integrate policies, since the dialogue with the US comprises not just military operations, but also a number of other issues, such as ones related to taxes, immunities and litigation. At the same time, however, the administration sees the EU as the political body with the highest potential to generate frameworks that are immediately transferrable into national policies and mechanisms (much like the adoption of the acquis in the pre-accession period), and that, through subsidiarity, encourage cooperation with the local authorities and society at large. This is especially the case given the fact that these cooperation mechanisms with local authorities, which determine questions such as who is in charge of what, have been all but lost since the end of the Cold War. Therefore, all policies that have both an EU and NATO dimension translate quite quickly into WGAs, and a security-related mini-infrastructure exists among the relevant ministries.

3 | Who are the main actors involved in cooperating in a WGA?

In most cases of dealing with external and internal conflicts and crises, Romania's Ministry of Foreign Affairs (MFA) represents the focal point of coordination and cooperation at the national level, as it is uniquely equipped to integrate both the EU and NATO paradigms. The Ministry of Defence (MND) and the Ministry of Internal Affairs are also regular participants in the WGAs. The presidential administration and the Supreme Council of National Defence (CSAT), as the highest coordinators and decision-makers, represent the highest level of integration and the bearers of the political message in addition to supervising the strategic planning documents, such as the National

Defence Strategy (President of Romania 2015). Other bodies that often play a role are the ministries of Transport (infrastructure), Energy, Economy and Education; the intelligence services; and the general secretariat of the government (as an integrator, making sure that the prime minister has a 360-degree view of important issues at stake).

The parliament (Chamber of Deputies) has been slower to catch up owing in part to its lack of an autonomous strategy and analysis capacity. Despite its nominal mission of exercising oversight of government policies, the relevant professional support of the parliament most often will simply request the necessary information from the line ministries, which obviously will not process that information in a critical way. However, there are exceptions (which have increased in frequency with the exercise of the presidency of the Council of the EU), such as in the cases of the Committee on European Affairs and the Committee on Foreign Affairs. However, these exceptions have to do with the quality of the parliamentarians and advisers involved rather than with any institutional facilitating conditions. In addition, most governments have traditionally passed a significant (and most often unjustified) number of emergency ordinances, thereby bypassing the formal legislative process and decreasing the importance and influence of parliament. Last but not least, parliamentarians are seldom qualified or eager to understand international affairs, which is a job they prefer to leave to the MFA.

Civil society has functioned as an echo chamber for the establishment for a long time, having been deliberately structured as such since the beginning of its development. As the country was nearing NATO membership, it had not yet developed a functional civil society with healthy debate around security issues, as per NATO requirements. To fulfil this condition, the security establishment of the time (especially the intelligence agencies) created supposedly 'independent' thinktanks and NGOs, but in reality they were almost exclusively populated with offshoots of the system (e.g. retired staff, former diplomats and political cronies) tasked with reiterating the messages of the main institutions. This has made it very difficult for other truly independent outlets to emerge and gain in substance and influence, as donors are also few and virtually no public money is allocated to them. However, as the complexity of issues has increased, the need to reach out to partners that can make a real contribution has made at least some of the previously reluctant institutions much more open to consultation and cooperation.

One area of external action that is sometimes (though more indirectly) linked to the prevention of conflicts and crises as well as to post-conflict reconstruction is economic diplomacy. A WGA has permanently functioned much less here than in other fields, partly owing to persistent disagreements over whether the primary stakeholder should be the MFA or the Ministry of Economy. As a result, the inter-institutional structures have faced constant change as well as the complications that inevitably come with being subordinate to two ministries. With few exceptions, the diplomats in charge of economic diplomacy have had little if any training in trade, economics or business. As a result, the success of Romania's economic diplomacy, including as an instrument contributing to stability and peace, differs from country to country depending on the individual diplomats' talents and capacity to learn and understand the needs of bilateral business and economic relations.

4 | How does your country operationalise a WGA?

Romania has several administrative structures and processes that facilitate WGAs. First, there is the group comprising the presidential administration, the Supreme Council of National Defence (CSAT), and the MFA as focal points and overall coordinators and integrators of horizontal and vertical cooperation as well as of strategic planning. The second group is made up of the inter-ministerial committees and working groups focused on issues of strategic importance. The general secretariat of the government, as the integrator of policies overseen by various ministries, provides an additional umbrella for coordination. Last but not least, the EU affairs departments of various ministries reflect the setup at the EU level and translate it to their own institutions. It is worth mentioning that during Romania's presidency of the Council of the EU, the MFA's Presidency Coordination Unit was the one that played a crucial role in streamlining consultations and cooperation among various institutions.

In terms of how the country operationalises its WGA and with what degree of success, there has been overall continuity with regard to Romania's strategic orientation as well as to its foreign and security policies. Perceptions and political/societal consensus have not changed much over the years, and strategic political objectives have also received widespread support from society. The process of socialisation into the Western system of values and institutional framework that took place during Romania's integration into NATO (in 2004) and then the EU (in 2007) has helped to build an institutional culture of sharing major goals and means, which is now instrumental in maintaining coordination and continuity. Even in more recent times, in which consensus on the country's general strategy has been wavering under governments with populist and revisionist inclinations, the same elements have contributed to bottom-up pressure and continued coordination. What's more, the 'cooperation reflexes' of professionals in the state apparatus have helped to prevent a discontinuation of this kind of integrated policymaking.

Furthermore, although Romania is admittedly an agenda-taker (which is not always a good thing), the EU framework is at least reflected in its domestic institutional framework, which in turn leads to internal coordination. Continuity at the top is also helped by the crucial role of the president, who, according to the constitution, has a five-year term in office and has traditionally won a second term, which means that there are usually 10-year spans of policy and staff continuity. There is also continuity in the composition of the MFA, the MND, the Ministry of Interior, and the intelligence services. Although professionals do come and go, there are many who circulate within the system of related institutions. One should mention, however, that even if this does provide for continuity, it can also cause major problems in terms of transparency, meritocracy and talent mobility. Indeed, since Romania's public administration as a whole is rather cloistered and non-transparent, it has few sources of fresh ideas and is plagued by groupthink.

In Romania, WGAs are very often the result of bottom-up pressure from the various levels of the administration. In other words, when there is a perception that cooperation is necessary, the administration will request that the management of the institution reach out to the other relevant institutions. Alternatively, given that the level of representation on the EU Affairs Coordination Council is that of state secretary and director general, but that the heads of the EU affairs/external relations departments also participate, the middle-management level has direct access to coordination discussions and can directly interact with counterparts in various other ministries.

In comparison, there are fewer instances of continuity at the top (political) levels. This is not necessarily a result of disagreements over agendas or strategic orientation. In fact, such disagreements have only been present with the current ruling coalition, and Romania has otherwise enjoyed broad cross-party agreement on its foreign and se-curity policy for decades. This can be attributed to the so-called 'Sna-gov Agenda', a negotiated consensus at the beginning of the NATO and EU accession processes that had all political forces subscribe to the 'red lines' of political infighting to prevent domestic policy disa-greements from spilling over into the realm of foreign policy. Instead, the main reasons for discontinuity at the top levels is political instabil-ity, frequent changes in government, a lack of institutional memory, or the absence of the kind of continued multistakeholder dialogue that would ensure a common understanding of the issues at stake.

Given these circumstances, the level of coordination very much depends on the particular organisational culture of one institution or another. Cooperation and coordination are also greatly facilitated by European or other external programmes that require (and train) stra-tegic planners to perform a number of related tasks, such as to coordi-nate, to do multi-annual budgeting and to set multi-annual priorities. Again, much more happens at a theoretical level and less is translated into practice, but the organisational culture is almost always built around external programmes, where they exist.

Some of the enablers of a WGA are the above-mentioned EU pro-grammes and trainings that help prepare personnel; EU and NATO frameworks reflected in the domestic setup; UN, multilateral and US strategic partnership frameworks providing incentives and mecha-nisms (including fixed calendars and benchmarks) for cooperation; continuity and training of personnel in the spirit of cooperation; and continuity of consensus on the strategic orientation of the country and the priorities of its foreign, security and development policies.

On the other hand, the disablers are an insufficient formalisation of institutional mechanisms (e.g. auditing, monitoring, evaluation, multi-annual planning and budgeting); inadequate formal institu-tional memory; political incoherence and irresponsibility; de-profes-sionalisation both within politics and the state administration; crony-ism within the state administration, where civil servants enjoy relative impunity and there are few instruments for accountability; a lack of openness to civil society; the absence of a capacity for self-regulation; a lack of (human and financial) resources; and poor management.

5 | Conclusions

Overall, Romania has a well-articulated WGA in terms of legislation, regulations and its institutional setup. This WGA has been in place for a long time, which has generated quite a remarkable culture of co-operation, coordination and integrated policymaking – sometimes fully formalised, sometimes rather informal, but with quite a high degree of continuity.

The main success factors have been the umbrella provided by the Supreme Council of National Defence (CSAT), the country's NATO and EU integration processes, and the framework of a well-articulated strategic orientation with across-the-board political consensus and widespread societal support. Permanent coordination with the EU and NATO (coming from the perception that satisfactory performance within these two organisations has high added value for the country and the potential to raise Romania's profile) have also been helpful because the internal setup has mimicked the supranational one. The intensive training programmes that have also come with EU accession have contributed to the education of personnel in the same spirit of coordination and cooperation. These skills were more recently honed in the run-up to and during Romania's presidency of the Council of the EU in the first half of 2019, which has allowed for the genuine, massive, collective exercise of the theoretical framework learnt during the first years of integration.

Overall, therefore, Romania's WGA works quite well at the input level. In contrast, the output level has been less satisfactory and efficient in practice, mostly because of generally poor management, a lack of accountability and resources within the state administration, de-professionalisation, cronyism, and insufficient formalisation of institutional mechanisms (e.g. regarding auditing, monitoring, evaluation, multi-annual planning and budgeting), which results in an inadequate formal institutional memory. We can add to this political instability and irresponsibility, political short-sightedness and 'short-termism', a lack of high-level guidance and leadership, and reluctance to be open to civil society and other stakeholders that could offer incentives for self-regulation. This has lowered the level of ambition and placed the focus on delivery rather than on stewardship and initiative-taking.

Compared to other countries, the number and level of responsibilities that Romania has taken on is not modest for a country with recent experience in navigating the EU environment – and the degree of coordination that has been achieved is quite good.

6 | Reference list

European Commission (2017). Joint Communication: A Strategic Approach to Resilience in the EU's External Action. https://ec.euro pa.eu/europeaid/sites/devco/files/joint_communication_-a_strate gic_approach_to_resilience_in_the_eus_external_action-2017.pdf.

Parliament of Romania (2002). Law No. 415 of 27 June 2002 on the organisation and functioning of the National Defence Supreme Council. www.sie.ro/legislatie_Legea_nr.415-2002.html

Parliament of Romania (2004). Law No. 473/2004 on defense planning.

President of Romania (2015). National Defence Strategy 2015–2019: A Strong Romania within Europe and the World. www.presidency. ro/files/userfiles/National_Defense_Strategy_2015_-_2019.pdf.

Interviews: Lt. Col. Constantin Balan (head of the MoD press office); Bogdan Dima (former adviser on constitutional law, Presidential Administration); Cosmin Dobran (adviser on horizontal coordination, Permanent Representation of Romania to the EU); Corina Popa (child protection expert with UNICEF); Anca Stoica (former UNDP country coordinator for Romania); Ana Tinca (MFA Director for Security Policies); Olivia Toderean (MFA Director for Policy Planning); Codru Vrabie (independent expert on constitutional law and anti-corruption)

Slovakia

Tomas Valasek

1 | Introduction

Slovakia is edging rather than racing towards embracing a whole-of-government approach (WGA). Several forces are driving this (slow) progress. The 2016 EU Global Strategy (EUGS) has been influential in general terms, and the 2017 provisional update of the Slovak Security Strategy (Government of the Slovak Republic 2017) specifically names the EUGS as one of its guiding lights. However, Slovakia's participation in EU missions has been even more instrumental. Since the EU calls for all kinds of contributions (i.e. not just military), and since Slovakia generally strives to please when the EU calls for assistance, the country has found itself pulled towards a more comprehensive kind of engagement.

The influence of the Ministry of Defence (MoD) has historically been important, and Slovakia initially lagged behind other EU member states in bringing non-military resources to crisis-management contributions. The MoD has found itself frequently asked to contribute forces to EU (and NATO) missions in order to uphold Slovakia's reputation and credibility in those institutions, but without ever receiving additional resources. The MoD came to see these requests as basically foreign policy through other means and implemented at the expense of other defence priorities. In response, beginning in the early 1990s, it began to pressure the Ministry of Foreign Affairs (MFA) to do its fair share by sending non-military experts abroad. Eventually, it took until December 2011 for the country to pass the necessary legislation (National Council of the Slovak Republic 2011) and build a list of reserves capable and willing to deploy abroad, but at least the option now exists. However, it has been used very sparingly to date, and only a handful of civilian experts from the MoD have been posted to Ukraine and Georgia since the law's passage.

These days, the MFA is the key driver of Slovakia's WGA, although it has enjoyed only limited success. Inter-party rivalry impedes cooperation with the MoD, which is in the midst of an arms-modernisation drive and is therefore reluctant to dilute its focus and resources – of civilian or military forces – by expanding existing deployments or committing to new missions. The MFA controls development aid and, in principle, should be well positioned to ensure that this aid is used in a manner that is aligned with the overall goals of the country's foreign and security policies. But this happens too little in practice. Moreover, the MFA does a poor job of narrowing the list of priorities down to a meaningful (i.e. manageable) number. For example, the 2019 statement of foreign policy priorities (MFEA 2019) lists everything from energy security to cultural diplomacy as a priority. The net effect is that such documents give poor guidance to the departments managing security policy and development aid, respectively, in addition to giving them few reasons to actually collaborate. To complicate matters further, the upper echelons of the MFA leadership are not involved in pushing for a comprehensive approach to crisis management abroad, as the issue is not a priority and development aid is often spent with little reference to Slovakia's participation in crisis-management missions abroad.

One should note, however, that things have not always been this way. For example, Slovakia has tried to match its contribution to the NATO-led International Security Assistance Force (ISAF) in Afghanistan through small development projects with NGOs, and it applied the same logic to its participation in the EU's Operation Althea in Bosnia-Herzegovina. But budgetary pressures have caused the MFA to primarily refocus foreign aid on meeting UN priorities to bolster the country's role as chair of the UN General Assembly (in 2018).

2 | What policies have been developed to further policy coherence?

There are no explicitly formulated WGA policy documents in Slovakia. The closest the country comes to this is in the form of the

National Security Strategy of 2005 (National Council of the Slovak Republic 2005b), but even its guidance is cursory and somewhat incongruous. The strategy lists the armed forces and foreign service as the main security tools, adding that police, fire-brigade and other forces are also very important. However, it is clear from the context that the 'security' in question here is internal security rather than crisis management abroad. Elsewhere, the document states that in managing "failing states", Slovakia will also deploy development aid and will seek to mobilise civil society, as well. Although this is admittedly more in line with mainstream WGA thinking, the reference is cursory and the strategy does not establish any mechanism for implementation.

The 2017 provisional update of the 2005 Security Strategy (Government of the Slovak Republic 2017) provides fresh details on which fields of action for EU crisis-management missions Slovakia prioritises (e.g. building resilience in the European neighbourhood, preventing state failure and upholding responsibility to protect), but without specifying the means for accomplishing these goals or calling for a WGA in deploying those means. Incidentally, the 2017 update of the strategy received cabinet approval but stalled in the parliament, although it is technically binding on the current government. Furthermore, the 2005 Defence Strategy (National Council of the Slovak Republic 2005a) mentions the need for a comprehensive approach to crisis management in general, but without explaining whether and how this applies to Slovakia's contributions to such missions.

In addition to the aforementioned strategies, Slovakia has a law on the books that mandates inter-agency coordination when civilian experts are deployed abroad (National Council of the Slovak Republic 2011). The law also establishes a coordination council composed of representatives of the ministries of Foreign Affairs, Justice, Interior, Finance and Defence. However, rather than to create a WGA effect, the council's mandate is merely to "exchange information, agree on modalities of the deployment of civilian experts, review their reports and agree on the financing of their deployment". Strangely, there is no formal requirement on the books for inter-agency coordination regarding military deployments which would mirror the one that applies to the deployment of civilian experts.

While Slovakia has no overall strategy/concept document for a 'comprehensive approach' or WGA as such, a potentially similar document (i.e. a security system concept) is currently in the drafting stage. Its purpose is to foster a better WGA mindset on security issues. However, it appears to predominantly focus on crises within the country's borders rather than those abroad. What's more, at the time of writing (October 2019), the concept had not been passed yet and elections for a new government had not been held yet. In any case, the draft's fate in the next government is uncertain.

3 | Who are the main actors involved in cooperating in a WGA?

The Ministry of Foreign Affairs (MFA), the Ministry of Defence (MoD), and the Ministry of Interior play the key roles in cooperating in a WGA-like fashion. Here, one should note that Slovakia's development aid is administered by an agency within the MFA, so there is no equivalent to a department for international aid and development. Furthermore, the country's National Security Council plays only a marginal role in crisis intervention abroad in addition to having no right of initiative and no real coordination role. Even when it does debate deployments, instead of genuinely pressing for a WGA effect, it merely serves to clear up any differences among the various ministries involved regarding the modalities of deployment.

In practice, fairly intense but informal consultations – mainly between the MoD and the MFA – usually precede deployments of armed units (as is discussed in more detail below). These consultations serve to discuss whether and how the proposed deployment serves Slovakia's foreign policy priorities and sometimes to inspire other departments to get involved, as well. In theory, the aforementioned coordination council that manages the deployment of civilian experts abroad could serve to bring about a more comprehensive approach to crisis management. However, according to insiders, it does not do so in practice. Instead, the ministries tend to decide on their own who they want to deploy and where, and they merely use to council to gain the pro forma approval of other ministries.

In the absence of a unifying WGA strategy, coordination mechanisms or top-down pressure, individual initiative and informal cooperation have produced the few limited examples of a comprehensive approach that Slovakia can point to. The country has a small but fairly tight-knit security community made up of roughly two dozen individuals who move relatively freely between the offices of the president and the prime minister, the MoD, the MFA and, to a lesser extent, the parliament. There is some but relatively little turnover within the community by virtue of the low availability of qualified personnel, and there are not very many newcomers into the system. Also, unlike the Baltic states, Romania or Poland, Slovakia does not have any immediate security threats on its borders, meaning that security issues attract relatively little following or 'fresh blood'. Instead, those who focus on the issues tend to stay active in them for a long time and to generally remain unchallenged.

Interactions within this security community often stand in for formal WGA structures and policies. When the policy director in the MoD has good relations with his or her counterpart in the MFA (i.e. the security policy director), they will often meet to debate, among other things, a more comprehensive approach to crisis-management missions abroad. Some of the deployments of civilian MoD experts on EU- or NATO-led missions, such as to complement Slovakia's diplomatic or military efforts in the same theatre, have originated in this way. In other words, these deployments have not happened as a result of top-down pressure, with the prior knowledge of superiors, with EU prodding or with any real reference to any official strategy. Instead, they happened simply because they made sense.

The downsides of such a heavily informal system are as evident as the advantages. First, while the members of the security community do tend to stay put for a long time, when some retire, change posts or are shuffled between departments, they often leave a void that may or may not be filled. Since a WGA is not a top concern, the department that has lost a contact point may not be concerned for years that it no longer enjoys good coordination with its sister departments. What's more, since so much of the inter-agency interaction is dependent on individual initiative rather than on formal coordination mechanisms, the absence of the right counterpart can degrade or halt coordination for long periods of time.

Second, while the informal security community includes individuals in some senior positions (e.g. advisers to the president or prime minister), its members more often than not operate without official sanctioning or even much interest from the top echelons of the government. They are allowed to coordinate rather than encouraged or urged to do so. This works fine in most instances, but not when decisions need to be made that involve cabinet or, even worse, parliamentary approval. The security expertise at the ministerial or parliamentary level is extremely sparse, interest in the issue is low, and efforts by members of the informal security community to forge better inter-departmental coordination often fall apart when they run up against inter-personal politics and polemics in the upper echelons.

The impact on the WGA is that even if the lower-ranking officials, using informal ties and their familiarity with one another, agree and propose a coordinated inter-agency approach to crisis management to their superiors, the latter often demur or let the suggestion die out of disinterest. Here, one should briefly note that this disinterest in security issues at the top levels also explains why the Slovakia's key conceptual documents (e.g. the National Security Strategy or the security-sector concept under development), which by definition require multi-stakeholder endorsement and implementation, tend to take so long to get approved or updated.

What also often works against a WGA to EU crisis management is the relatively insular mindset of the defence and interior ministries. While the MFA, by virtue of its mandate and the circulation of personnel between Brussels and Bratislava, tends to be rather immersed in EU policies and to follow the latest thinking, the same cannot be said of the other two departments involved. In fact, members of the defence and interior ministries tend to regard EU or NATO missions as something of a luxury as well as something that one only does after urgent domestic priorities have been met. However, one should note that even if this increasingly is the case for the MoD, the Ministry of Interior is gradually becoming less insular and more active abroad. What's more, mindsets are not the only hindrance to EU- and NATO-related WGAs. Since human and financial resources are always tight, participation in the missions of these international organisations is often the first to get the axe.

It has not always been this way. In days when WGAs were a relatively new phenomenon, the MoD was the entity egging on the interior and foreign ministries to get involved in crisis management abroad. This championing of a WGA was born of first-hand experience, as the MoD had uniformed personnel in EU- and NATO-led operations even before Slovakia's 2004 accessions, and was long the exclusive provider of personnel for such missions. What's more, it saw that other countries had started to contribute in ways other than by supplying military personnel, and felt that Slovakia should, too, if only to reduce the pressure on the MoD budget (i.e. to spread the pain). But the last several defence ministers have brought a far more domestic mindset to their job, and the MoD has gone from being the driving force behind a WGA to an often-reluctant participant.

5 | Conclusions

Slovakia's successes with WGAs have been few and far between. Conceptually, a WGA is nearly invisible, save a passing and somewhat incongruous reference in the National Security Strategy (National Council of the Slovak Republic 2005b) and a limited application of inter-agency coordination to the act of deploying civilian experts overseas. Institutional coordination does take place (e.g. in the aforementioned case of civilian experts or when decisions on crisis-management participation come up in the National Security Council), but it rarely produces a WGA effect. Top-down pressure from ministers or other senior officials for departments to approach crisis management in a comprehensive fashion is basically nonexistent. Those successes that have been scored (e.g. the shift from contributing armed forces exclusively to deploying policy and civilian defence experts as well, though not necessarily alongside each other in the same missions) have resulted from individual initiative, EU nudging or budgetary pressures (e.g. when the MoD leaned on the MFA to start sending its own experts to missions in order to lighten the load on the defence budget).

One area in which Slovakia performs particularly poorly (and regrettably always has) is in aligning its trade activities with the other tools of a WGA. Indeed, it has managed to deploy all of its other resources – soldiers, police officers, civilian defence experts, diplomats, aid workers – in crisis management abroad (even if not always all on the same missions and admittedly often only in symbolic amounts), but the trade bit has eluded Slovakia almost completely. There are two main reasons for this: First, the country does not have very many companies or entrepreneurs with the resources and mindset to invest in risky locations – which are, by definition, the places to which the EU tends to deploy crisis-management missions. Diplomats and defence officials struggle to find the right business counterparts, and the government does not have the option of leaning on managers of state-owned companies to participate. The fact is that, with the narrow exception of slices of the defence industry, Slovakia has privatised virtually all other sectors of the economy.

The second reason why business remains impervious to opportunities that may present themselves in the framework of Slovak crisis-management missions abroad is the low level of trust in government. Public procurement, in particular, has seen a number of corruption scandals. As a result, the business community has come to think of the public sector as self-serving and crooked. This mainly concerns tenders within Slovakia's borders, but public-private interaction abroad has not always gone well either. In fact, stories circulate within the business community about diplomats who exact a percentage of the profits in exchange for helping Slovak companies place their products or services on foreign markets – the latter being part of diplomats' job description. As a result, few companies are willing to participate in WGAs out of fear that their reputation will suffer.

6 | Reference list

Government of the Slovak Republic (2017). The proposed Security Strategy of the Slovak Republic. 29 September 2017. https://rokovan ia.gov.sk/RVL/Material/22364/1.

MFEA (Ministry of Foreign and European Affairs of the Slovak Republic) (2019). Evaluation of Foreign and European Policy Priorities of the Slovak Republic in 2018 and their focus on 2019. February 2019. www.mzv.sk/documents/10182/2686701/2019+Hodnote nie+prior%C3%ADt+zahraničnej+a+európskej+politiky+Slovensk ej+republiky+v+roku+2018+a+ich+zameranie+na+rok+2019.pdf.

National Council of the Slovak Republic (2005a). The Defence Strategy of the Slovak Republic. 23 September 2005. www.mod.gov.sk/data/files/794.pdf.

National Council of the Slovak Republic (2005b). The Security Strategy of the Slovak Republic. 23 September 2005. www.mod.gov.sk/data/files/795.pdf.

National Council of the Slovak Republic (2011). Law No. 503/2011 on the secondment of civilian experts to perform work in crisis management activities outside the territory of the Slovak Republic and on amendments to certain acts. 22 December 2011. www.slov-lex.sk/pravne-predpisy/SK/ZZ/2011/503/.

Slovenia

Milan Jazbec

1 | Introduction

Established after the end of the Cold War, the Republic of Slovenia is a small state with a multicultural identity of Central, South-eastern, Mediterranean and Western European influences. It proclaimed independence in June 1991 and received international recognition in January 1992. The first democratic elections took place in spring 1990, and the opposition coalition Demos was sworn in that May. It is very important to note that the 1974 Yugoslav Constitution granted its republics certain statehood prerogatives as constituent parts of the federation. As a result, the first formal structure for the conduct of international cooperation was established. The Republic Committee for International Cooperation was a formal structure and served as a structural and organisational foundation for the formation of the Ministry of Foreign Affairs (MFA) of the independent Slovenia. This primarily means that the administrative/governmental approach of cooperation and coordination – or a so-called whole-of-government approach (WGA) – has a tradition stretching back almost half a century in Slovenia.

During the first decade and a half of its independence, Slovenia was engaged in a unique series of multilateral projects. It was a non-permanent member of the UN Security Council (1998–1999); it became a member of NATO and the EU (2004); it has held the chairmanship of the OSCE (2005), of the Human Security Network (May 2005–May 2006), and of the IAEA Board of Governors (Autumn 2006–Autumn 2007); and it has held the presidency of the Council of the EU (first half of 2008) and the chairmanship of the Committee of

Ministers of the Council of Europe (May–November 2009). Two challenges that it faced during its presidency of the Council of the EU were Kosovo's proclamation of independence and the conclusion of the partnership and cooperation agreement (PCA) between the EU and the Russian Federation.

From this, one can draw three basic conclusions that can help one gain a better understanding of the behaviours and structures of Slovenia's foreign policy. First, from the beginning, Slovenia has been an active member of the international community, and by successfully combining bi- and multi-lateral diplomatic approaches, it has had unique 'soft power' policy output. Second, the most important products of this approach are the Bled Strategic Forum, the International Trust Fund for Demining, the Centre for European Perspective, the Centre for Excellence in Finance, and the Centre for International Cooperation and Development, all of which are important tools for conceptualising international development cooperation as one of the priorities of Slovene foreign policy. Third, from the organisational point of view, these activities were managed by intra- and inter-ministerial task forces that were formed on an ad hoc basis and pursued a relatively loose network approach. In other words, they were formalised bodies with targeted purpose that only existed for the duration of a single project.

These policy characteristics are the basic premises for understanding how Slovenia conducts its international relations as well as how it conceptualises and manages related projects and processes. This was most clearly illustrated by Slovenia's presidency of the Council of the EU. This extremely important – and complex – project is also the background for understanding and analysing Slovenia's stance towards and experience with a WGA. Indeed, these experiences enhanced the country's institutional/organisational mindset and conceptualisation, although they were not explicitly formalised within structures as a WGA. However, a WGA can be implicitly detected in Slovenia's strategy related to international operations and missions (Government of the Republic of Slovenia 2009). At the same time, there are some structures (e.g. intra-governmental bodies, working groups and permanent commissions) that use the goals of a WGA – namely, to be comprehensive, coordinated, goal-oriented and integrated – as a policy guideline.

2 | What policies have been developed to further policy coherence?

Slovene policy documents do not explicitly formalise a WGA. However, as mentioned above, there are some examples of clear implicit references, such as in the strategy for activities related to international operations and missions (Government of the Republic of Slovenia 2009). What's more, taken together, there are a number of documents that de facto present and form Slovenia's WGA-like framework. From the Parliament of the Republic of Slovenia, there is a resolution on the country's foreign policy (2015a), the foreign policy strategy itself (2015b), a resolution on the country's national security strategy (2010b), a strategy on international development cooperation and humanitarian aid (2018b), and a declaration on the Western Balkans (2010a). From the Government of the Republic of Slovenia, there is an action plan regarding the fight against human trafficking (2019a), an action plan regarding the Western Balkans (2019b), and a strategy on migration policy and coordinating related activities (2019c).

The documents are focused, of a high quality, and geared towards the nation as a whole. There is a clear guidance approach in these and related operational documents. What's more, there are various action plans in place to spell out the specific aspects of implementing the various strategies.

In these documents, one will find a combination of an explicit (binding) approach and an implicit (suggested) approach. For example, paragraph 21 of the resolution on development cooperation (Parliament of the Republic of Slovenia 2017) says that the government has to regularly inform the parliament about the progress of implementing this resolution, while the binding aspect is found in paragraph 19. Seven months later, the parliament adopted the related law on development cooperation (Parliament of the Republic of Slovenia 2018a).

The related fields of action are numerous and broad. They include humanitarian aid and development cooperation, stabilisation, crisis management, peacebuilding and post-conflict transformation, all of which are backed up by economic efforts. They form an integrated, complementary set of activities whose thematic priorities have been specified in policy documents or decisions of the government and/or parliament.

In thematic terms, Slovenia's humanitarian-aid and development-cooperation efforts focus on two sets of priorities. First, they aim to foster inclusive and sustainable economic growth, full and productive employment, and decent work for all. Second, they promote the sustainable management of natural resources and the fight against climate change. Third, Slovenia pays special attention to children and women, particularly in armed conflicts, as well as to providing them with post-crisis rehabilitation and psychosocial assistance. For example, these priorities prompted Slovenia to launch the International Trust Fund for demining and the social rehabilitation of the victims of landmines in 1998.

In geographical terms, Slovenian priorities for development-cooperation and humanitarian-aid efforts encompass the Western Balkans, the so-called 'European neighbourhood' and sub-Saharan Africa. The priority issues here are environmental protection and social inclusiveness.

In terms of stabilisation activities, among other things, Slovenia has launched the Brdo-Brijuni Process and has contributed a police contingent to North Macedonia. Its collaborative peacebuilding efforts include contributions to KFOR and UNIFIL. And it has contributed to post-conflict transformation efforts in Afghanistan and Iraq.

The EU Global Strategy has both inspired and influenced policy thought in Slovenia, especially regarding the formation of EU-related policies and what kind of EU Slovenia would ideally like to see (in this case, one that is strong and united). Since Slovenia views integration as being in its strategic interest, it would like the EU to become more cohesive and stable. With these goals in mind, Slovenia has influenced and supported the EU's Global Strategy in discussions and by participating in various fora at different levels.

Furthermore, the UN Millennium Goals decisively paved the way for Slovenia's strategy and specific policies related to development cooperation and humanitarian aid (Parliament of the Republic of Slovenia 2018a). In addition, to a large extent, all Slovene national strategies take into consideration and draw from documents of the UN, the OECD and the OSCE. In the Slovene documents, foreign policy is conceptualised as a whole. Rather than explicitly setting out a WGA, such an approach is implicitly obligatory for the most part, since it appears in policy formulations in various documents and thereby paves the way for a possible future formalisation of a WGA.

Slovenia also supports further development of the EU's Common Security and Defence Policy (CSDP) in all its dimensions: operations, institutions and capabilities. It participates in CSDP operations in Bosnia-Herzegovina, Kosovo, and Chad/Central African Republic. It also took part in the CSDP operation in the Democratic Republic of the Congo and joined EU efforts to support the African Union in Sudan/Darfur. Together with the European Commission, Slovenia also launched the Positive Agenda for the Youth in the Western Balkans initiative in April 2015.

Management of the 2015/2016 migration crisis stands out as the clearest example of a WGA-like effort by Slovenia. With his November 2015 letter to EU and World Bank leaders, then-Prime Minister Miro Cerar set the framework for solving the crisis. The Slovene government formed a special task force with members drawn from various ministries and agencies, who collaborated in a de facto WGA manner and produced successful results. During its chairmanship of the OSCE in 2005, Slovenia published the Slovene translation of the IOM's Dictionary of Migration (IOM 2006) to aid understanding of the issue. Slovenia also initiated efforts to strengthen regional cooperation aimed at preventing radicalisation and stemming the recruitment efforts of foreign terrorist organisations.

Other soft policy initiatives include water diplomacy, membership in the so-called 'Green Group' of countries advocating action to slow the pace of climate change, and participation in Responsibility to Protect (R2P) activities. During its 2005 chairmanship of the OSCE, Slovenia also launched a project to increase children's knowledge of human rights, which has been recognised as an important tool for almost 15 years.

Generally speaking, there are explicit elements as well as strong hints of a WGA in various documents and policies. When circumstances call for an ad hoc WGA, it is goal-oriented, goal-driven and well-articulated. Hence, there should be a planned push towards contextualising those policies as a WGA whose scope is system-wide, encompassing foreign, security, development-cooperation, humanitarian-aid, economic and trade policies in cooperation with the NGO sector.

Slovenia has a long tradition of acting in a WGA-like fashion. Presently, it could be understood as a unique combination of several outstanding multilateral projects from the first decade and a half of Slovenia's existence as well as from the experiences from the last decade. Although Slovenia has experienced political turbulence during the latter period, it has continued to be an active player in the international arena.

After Slovenia became a member of the EU and NATO, in-country cooperation and coordination in dealing with external conflicts and crises increased in terms of both momentum and scope. Cooperating and coordinating with the Brussels-based structures and member states of the EU became part of routine procedures. This has broadened the scope and enriched policy results, while preserving both formal and informal methods and processes. This enrichment significantly has to do with the adoption of a WGA in both practical and pragmatic ways, even though it has not been formalised.

There are a number of formal governmental bodies and structures that produce coherent and integrated policy approaches. Some of the most important are the Government Committee for Policy Affairs, the Government Committee for Economic Affairs, the National Security Council and its secretariat, the Strategic Council for Foreign Policy, the Permanent Coordination Group for International Development Cooperation, and the Ministry of Foreign Affairs as the supreme formal coordinating body for the whole field of development cooperation. These bodies coordinate policies and approaches between government departments as well as with the relevant EU bodies (as well as NATO, depending on the issues at hand). At the same time, they also coordinate their activities with relevant parliamentary bodies, and such efforts are well established and formal, producing policy output on areas relevant to a WGA. Some of the most important formal parliamentary bodies here are: the Parliamentary Committee on Foreign Policy, the Parliamentary Committee on European Union Affairs, the Parliamentary Committee on the Defence, and the Parliamentary Commission for Supervision of Intelligence and Security Services.

In addition, most of the ministries employ senior officials who deal with parliament and its bodies for this purpose, while some of them also have small task forces that permanently nurture these relations. What's more, the secretary general of the government has a special team dedicated to looking after government-parliament relations. Within the ministries, bodies can be formed on an ad hoc basis to help coordinate policy, but their organisational approach, practical activities and duration of activity vary from case to case.

Coordination and cooperation with EU institutions and actors are primarily handled by Slovenia's permanent mission to the EU, although some governmental bodies maintain direct contact with their EU counterparts on policy issues. As far as foreign policy, security and development cooperation are concerned, the MFA is the main formal coordinating/cooperation body within the government as well as for important international actors, such as the UN, NATO, the OECD-DAC and the OSCE. Although Slovene permanent missions are the 'point' players for these international organisations, some government and other bodies also have direct communication with them. In addition, an important aspect of Slovenia's cooperation with the UN is the Ljubljana-based International Institute for Middle East and Balkan Studies (IFIMES), which has had a special consultative status with the United Nations Economic and Social Council (ECOSOC) since 2018.

Various formal and informal groups in different ministries are also responsible for coordination/cooperation with civil society groups. Among the most important are the Government Coordination Group for Civil Society and the Permanent Coordination Group for International Development Cooperation. Ad hoc meetings with senior governmental representatives also take place occasionally, as was the case with the MFA regarding crises in Yemen and South Sudan. An important part of policy cooperation is handled by the MFA's Policy Planning and Research Department.

Last but not least, strong informal coordination and cooperation has been driven by a group of highly experienced members of the previous and current governments. This has included two ex-prime ministers as well as ministers of defence, of economic development and technology, of education and of justice.

The cooperation/coordination activities discussed above are both horizontal and vertical, taking place both within and between various government departments, as well as with the parliament, civil society organisations, the EU and other important international actors. This broad and flexible web of formal and informal activities amounts to a de facto WGA that is goal-oriented, goal-driven and well-articulated when circumstances arise. Indeed, although it is not formalised, Slovenia's WGA works very efficiently on its current informal basis.

4 | How does your country operationalise a WGA?

Generally, the main part of the structural shifts that support the WGA-like policies and approaches were introduced into Slovene policymaking after it became a member of the EU and NATO in 2004 as well as when it held the rotating presidency of the Council of the EU in 2008, both of which deepened, enhanced and formalised many elements of its policymaking structures and processes. It was also influenced by experiences of taking temporary leadership roles for other multilateral projects and institutions, as discussed above.

These memberships and leadership roles have triggered many changes that reflect Slovenia's commitment to an integrated WGA-like approach. For example, after Slovenia joined the EU, its former Ministry for EU Affairs was transformed into the Government Office for Development and EU Affairs (GODEA). In the meantime, the main change within the MFA involved the introduction of the position of a director general and corresponding directorates as well as the position of a political director.

The MFA's Directorate for EU Affairs has four departments: the Department for European Affairs, the Department for European Countries (i.e. EU and EEA members), the Department for European Countries (which are all EU members), and the Department for General and Institutional Affairs. The position of its director general is merged with that of the political director, as experience showed that this was the best solution for policy integration in practice. The main principle for defining departments consists of geographical and topical criteria, which is in keeping with the practice of the EU's organisational units. The MFA has a Directorate for Common Foreign and Security Policy (CFSP), and the Department for Development Cooperation and Humanitarian Aid is located in the Directorate General for Economic and Public Diplomacy.

The related changes in structures, approaches and policy efficiency have primarily been driven by practical needs. They are most noticeable in the MFA and the MoD as well as in the organisational arrangements and changes in the Office of the Prime Minister, but also in some other ministries, such as the Ministry of the Interior. They focus on adopting and implementing policies and their organisational modus operandi as well as on pragmatic approaches related to the activities of various international actors.

On the whole, one can say that, even though they are not formally defined as a WGA, these adapted structures do produce integrated, comprehensive and coordinated approaches to policy issues and their implementation. They have also functioned at between an average and excellent level. For example, in times of an emergency or crisis, these bodies and structures have been able to respond in an effective and high-quality manner. One outstanding example of this is the efficiency with which Slovenia (in close cooperation and coordination with the EU bodies as well as on their behalf) managed the process related to Kosovo's proclamation of independence while Slovenia held the presidency of the Council of the EU in the first half of 2018.

Currently, the strongest motivator for further effectiveness and quality of the process leading to a formalised WGA is Slovenia's forthcoming presidency of the Council of the EU in the second half of 2021. Its preparations are mainly focusing on policy, political, financial, organisational and personnel-related aspects. If its efforts to foster collaboration, coordination and synergy succeed in Brussels, it would only strengthen the argument and push for formalising a WGA back home.

One should also note that there are no special financial resources dedicated to WGA-like activities in Slovenia. They are therefore covered at present by the 2020–2021 national budget, which is also focused on the forthcoming presidency of the Council of the EU. Budgetary means for processes related to responding to international crises and emergencies are taken from the MFA, the MoD, the Ministry of Interior, and other resources. A recent example of this involved the management of the 2015/2016 migration crisis. Although there were no explicit resources in the budget for this purpose, the government's response was efficient and had the needed financial and personnel resources. Regarding the latter, one should add that there are also no explicit human resources (HR) policies related to WGA-like activities in Slovenia. However, the Ministry for Public Administration seeks out individuals who have the experience and abilities needed to conceptualise and implement integrated, comprehensive policy approaches and solutions.

Within the government structure, there are not any formal leadership positions that would push for a WGA. However, clear elements of such an approach are evident in the activities of the current government, which was appointed by the National Assembly on 13 September 2018. Indeed, working under the determined prime minister, these veteran officials have brought a WGA-like method of leadership to this government's activities. These individuals include the minister of foreign affairs and the minister for infrastructure, both of whom are former prime ministers. There is also the current minister of defence, who is serving his second term in this position and is the longest-serving of all the ministers, having also been the minister of foreign affairs for seven years and the minister of the environment for three years. And there are also the minister of economic development and technology, the minister of education, and the minister of justice, all of whom are also serving in their second terms.

The effectiveness and quality of this political/administrative leadership when it comes to enabling a WGA can be assessed as average to excellent, depending on the issue at hand. This way of coordinating and implementing political issues can primarily be attributed to the vast political experience of the above-mentioned members of the government. Indeed, their style of governmental decision-making reflects a de facto WGA – and one that could rather easily be transformed into a deliberate, formalised WGA, a move for which there is noticeable support.

5 | Conclusions

Although Slovenia does not have a formal WGA, it has a de facto one in practice. Behind this are three main drivers. First, the tradition of cooperating and integrating policy issues in political management in Slovenia has a long tradition. This stems from the fact that, in accordance with the Yugoslav Constitution of 1974, Slovenia established the Republic Committee for International Cooperation as the first formal structure for managing its efforts related to international cooperation. Following Slovenia's independence in 1991, this served as a basis for the Slovene Ministry for Foreign Affairs in both structural and organisational terms. In other words, an administrative governmental notion of cooperation and coordination has a long and proven track record in the country.

Second, being engaged in a series of outstanding multilateral projects in the first decade and a half after its independence enabled Slovenia to develop very early on a special policy sense for taking a soft-power approach in multilateral efforts, on the one hand, and to frequently set up ad hoc structures capable of producing integrated, comprehensive and coordinated policy results, on the other.

Third, Slovenia's first-ever holding of the rotating presidency of the Council of the EU in 2008 has been the strongest push to date towards transforming its informal WGA into a formalised one. The main WGA-related challenges it faced during the presidency involved taking an integrated, comprehensive and coordinated approach (within the Slovene government as well as within the structures of the EU, with its member states and with other international actors) towards Kosovo's proclamation of independence and the conclusion of a partnership and cooperation agreement (PCA) with the Russian Federation. The presidency also influenced important structural changes in the organisational setup of Slovenia's public administration (especially of the Office of the Prime Minister and the ministries of Foreign Affairs and Defence). Structural changes were also introduced as a result of responding to the 2015/2016 migration crisis as well as of holding the presidency of the UN Human Rights Council in 2018.

Another important characteristic of Slovenia that contributes to its informal WGA is its administration's high level of flexibility when it comes to adapting to structural challenges. Indeed, whether it involves foreign policy, defence, development cooperation or closely related areas, Slovenia's de facto WGA has been able to swiftly, flexibly and efficiently respond to concrete challenges and produce successful results.

One can already say that Slovenia's de facto WGA works well in practice, efficiently producing high-quality policy outcomes. It is backed by various policy statements in a wide range of documents (strategies, declarations, action plans), and it rests on numerous, primarily ad hoc structures.

Given these experiences, structures, characteristics and documents – and the fact that there are many leaders who recognise the need for an integral, coordinated and comprehensive approach –

Slovenia's de facto WGA could be easily and smoothly upgraded from an ad hoc approach to a formalised, institutionalised and policy-backed WGA.

In addition to the experiences Slovenia has gained while developing its policies (as discussed above), there are three success factors that could underpin such a transformation. First, the current government has a strong, informal group made up of a determined prime minister and highly experienced ministers who are used to working together in a WGA-like manner and could back and assist with a formalisation effort. Second, since Slovenia held the presidency of the Council of the EU in 2008, there has been continuous (though admittedly not very visible) policy planning support for activities and decisions related to foreign policy. Third, there are the two important drivers of Slovenia's foreign policy ambitions: outside policy influence and encouragement combined with internal policy decisions. For example, the fact that Slovenia was the first of the group of countries that became EU member states in 2004 resulted from both initiative within EU circles in Brussels and Slovenia's political ambitions, which increased as a result of having already successfully managed multilateral projects, such as while holding the OSCE chairmanship in 2005. It also had a successful presidency of the UN Human Rights Council in 2018, and its forthcoming presidency of the Council of the EU in the second half of 2021 offers an excellent opportunity for Slovenia to articulate a formal WGA in terms of structures and policies.

6 | Reference list

Government of the Republic of Slovenia (2009). Cooperation strategy of the Republic of Slovenia in international operations and missions. www.pisrs.si/Pis.web/pregledPredpisa?id=STRA58.

Government of the Republic of Slovenia (2019a). Action Plan of the Intergovernmental Working Group for Fight Against Human Trafficking for the Period 2019–2020. 10 January 2019. www.gov.si/assets/vladne-sluzbe/UKOM/Boj-proti-trgovini-z-ljudmi/Dokumenti/Akcijski-nacrti/Akcijski_nacrt_2019-2020.pdf.

Government of the Republic of Slovenia (2019b). Action Plan for the Western Balkans. www.gov.si/assets/ministrstva/MZZ/Dokumen ti/skupna-zunanja-in-evropska-politika/siritev-in-JV-evropa/2cc1a 22125/ANC-ZB-za-2019.pdf.

Government of the Republic of Slovenia (2019c). The Governmental Strategy for Migration Policy and for the Coordination of Activities in this Area. www.gov.si/assets/ministrstva/MNZ/SOJ/STR17072 019.pdf.

IOM (International Organization for Migration) (2006). Glosar Migracij. Geneva: IOM.

Parliament of the Republic of Slovenia (2010a). Declaration on the Western Balkans. http://pisrs.si/Pis.web/pregledPredpisa?id=DEK L29.

Parliament of the Republic of Slovenia (2010b). Resolution on National Security Strategy of the Republic of Slovenia. www.pisrs.si/ Pis.web/pregledPredpisa?id=RESO61.

Parliament of the Republic of Slovenia (2015a). Declaration on the Foreign Policy of the Republic of Slovenia. www.pisrs.si/Pis.web/ pregledPredpisa?id=DEKL37.

Parliament of the Republic of Slovenia (2015b). Foreign Policy Strategy. www.gov.si/assets/ministrstva/MZZ/Dokumenti/javne-obja ve/strateski-in-programski-dokumenti/3b680c3f05/strategija_ZP. pdf.

Parliament of the Republic of Slovenia (2017). Resolution on the International Development Cooperation and Humanitarian Aid of the Republic of Slovenia. www.pisrs.si/Pis.web/pregledPredpisa?id= RESO117.

Parliament of the Republic of Slovenia (2018a). International Development Cooperation and Humanitarian Aid of the Republic of Slovenia Act. www.pisrs.si/Pis.web/pregledPredpisa?id=ZAKO7602.

Parliament of the Republic of Slovenia (2019). The Governmental Strategy for migration policy and for the coordination of activities in this area. www.gov.si/assets/ministrstva/MNZ/SOJ/STR17072 019.pdf.

Parliament of the Republic of Slovenia (2018b). Strategy of the International Development Cooperation and Humanitarian Aid of the Republic of Slovenia till 2030. www.gov.si/assets/ministrstva/M ZZ/Dokumenti/multilaterala/razvojno-sodelovanje/5d79681620/S trategija_MRSHP.pdf.

Spain

Felix Arteaga

1 | Introduction

Until the 1980s or 1990s, Spain did not participate in crisis-management operations either alone or with third parties. This limited record
of international engagement helps to explain the lack of national
whole-of-government approach (WGA) instruments. Spain's first involvement with the WGA concept came during the Multinational Experiments series organised by NATO member states in the first decade of the new century to improve crisis-management procedures.
Within that framework, Spain put together an interdisciplinary team
comprised of diplomats, military officials and thinktank members to
explore the potential of using an integrated approach to crisis management. Then, in June 2018, Spain's national delegation presented a
first-ever assessment of Spain's WGA during the Comprehensive Approach to Crisis Prevention and Management Seminar (CAS) held in
Helsinki (Rintakoski and Autti 2008: 168–172).

Later, when NATO and the EU developed their own WGA concepts, Spanish diplomats and military officials involved in the crisis-
management systems of both organisations were familiarised with a
WGA. Spain's Ministry of Defence and its Ministry of Foreign Affairs,
the European Union and Cooperation (MAUC) soon imported this
practice into their vocabulary and, since then, the number of mentions of a WGA ('enfoque integral' in Spanish) have proliferated in official documents. The first reference to a WGA appeared in the Spanish Security Strategy of 2011. The team tasked with elaborating this
strategy was led by Javier Solana, who had become familiar with the
WGA concept as the EU's high representative for common policy and

security policy from 1999 to 2009. Believing that the WGA model offers advantages in terms of managing national security, the team incorporated it into the document. In fact, they even called for the creation of an External and Integrated Response Unit (Unidad de Respuesta Integrada Exterior, URIE), although subsequent governments have not acted upon this explicit recommendation.

Unfortunately, subsequent administrations and governments have not thought (or perhaps cared) about strengthening inter-agency coordination. The national administration continues to be divided into watertight departments that very zealously guard their competences and display little openness to the idea of inter-agency cooperation. The president of the government (as the prime minister is known) could theoretically call for the National Security System to be re-designed to deal with international crises in a WGA mode by reinforcing its resources and competences. However, the management of external crises remains without presidential leadership and without any single authority able to impose a WGA upon all actors involved. For this reason, there are no binding guidelines to develop WGA or WGA-like concepts in Spain.

The MAUC's Strategy for External Action of 2015 acknowledges this shortcoming and highlights the "need to improve the integral approach in the management of crises, combining civil and military mechanisms more effectively", but it does so without identifying the proper measures to bring such an improvement about (MAUC 2015: 64). Indeed, the lack of WGA implementation reveals a gap between the high degree of importance that Spain assigns to the WGA concept and its limited real-world impact on governmental structures and procedures. Paradoxically, the theoretical success of the concept has created the virtual perception that national structures and procedures have been adapted for its implementation. For instance, the National Security Council (DSN) recommended in 2017 that the WGA model of crises management be imported into the sphere of national security, writing (DSN 2017: 82): "It is, therefore, a priority to further develop and adapt the comprehensive crisis management model within the framework of the National Security System in order to provide effective and timely responses to today's threats and challenges."

2 | What policies have been developed to further policy coherence?

Official documents acknowledge Spain's commitment to managing international crises and conflicts. Among others, the strategies for national security and external action include references to the WGA concept as the preferred way to accomplish the country's goals when it comes responding to multidimensional crises. Nevertheless, Spain's contribution to WGA commitments is heavily influenced by the country's strategic culture and its preference for working within multilateral frameworks.

First, Spain's strategic culture determines the level of ambition it has about using force in international commitments because decision-makers and the public tend to disapprove of the use of military power for historical and political reasons (cf. Arteaga 2013). This, in turn, makes it difficult for Spanish governments to carry out tasks within the more demanding part of the military spectrum of WGA operations. For the same reason, regardless of its actual relevance, they tend to overemphasise the humanitarian dimension of international commitments in order to prevent potential social or political opposition to Spanish military interventions.

Indeed, legitimation matters because Spanish governments must acquire the authorisation of the Congress of Deputies before deploying troops abroad. Securing legitimation is easier when the specific WGA operations fall under a wider European umbrella, as this allows governments to emphasise the EU's role as a global actor and the need for Spain to do its fair share to help Europe live up to its supposed responsibility to provide security worldwide, even in military terms. In this regard, unlike other international constellations that have carried out international crisis-management operations without obtaining legal authorisation from the United Nations Security Council, the EU is perceived as a reliable legitimiser.

That said, Spain's strategic culture will continue to influence its military commitments. For instance, Spanish governments are reluctant to transfer their authority over Spanish military contingents to foreign commanders without caveats (whether to avoid combat operations or so-called 'mission creep'). This bias will also impact Spain's contribution of troops to EU military initiatives even though it would be easier under a Common Security and Defence Policy (CSDP) framework than under any other multinational framework.

Returning to the second major influence on Spain's contribution to WGA efforts, one can say that Spain generally prefers to contribute to international crisis management within the framework of international organisations, such as the EU, NATO or the UN. This preference for multilateral frameworks results from two factors: the aforementioned need to legitimise the military operations and the lack of national capabilities to conduct unilateral crisis-management operations. Indeed, acting within a multinational group helps Spanish governments to legitimise their military and civilian commitments because it is easier to justify them in terms of 'international responsibility' than of 'national interest'.

Furthermore, Spain understands that national contributions are needed to achieve 'effective' multilateralism, such as the one called for in the European Security Strategy of 2003. For this reason, Spain has accompanied the development of the European WGA concept and supported the elaboration of the European Security and Foreign Policy strategies, the development of external security instruments for the CSDP, and the effort towards EU strategic autonomy to act with others partners whenever possible or alone if necessary. Spain has also supported every initiative to develop the EU's crisis-management structures, including an operational headquarters (currently the Military Planning and Conduct Capability for non-executive missions), and its commitment has been more visible in the core of the development of the Permanent Structured Cooperation (PESCO), together with France, Germany and Italy.

In terms of contributions of manpower, Spain is the top-ranking contributor to CSDP operations and missions. In fact, over the last decade, it has provided roughly 30 percent of all the men and women in uniform serving in EU-flagged operations and assumed a dozen mission commands, and Spain is the only country to have supplied troops to all EU military missions and operations since 2003 (Gómez Castro 2018: 33). Spain also takes part in the rotations of the EU battlegroups, assumes the command of naval operations (Atalanta at this moment), and contributes to the paramilitary forces of the Euro Gendarmerie Force by providing members of the Guardia Civil for CSDP missions and operations. Finally, Spain is contributing to the

CSDP missions and operations in Africa, where the WGA is being implemented.

Regarding humanitarian and development aid, Spain is the fifth-largest contributor to the European development-cooperation funds. In the 2013–2017 period, it provided USD 5.273 billion, or 43 percent of the total funds (USD 12.405 billion). After being accredited in July 2011 as an executive agency of the European Commission, Spain's Agency for International Development Cooperation (AECID) has been managing EU funds associated with the Common Foreign and Security Policy (delegated cooperation). Spain allocates 30 percent of these funds to Africa, 23 percent to the Americas, 15 percent to Eastern Europe, and 14 percent to Asia under EU programmes (Olivie and Perez 2019: 2–5).

Africa is Spain's preferred setting for applying a WGA to prevent and manage international crises and conflicts. Its national security strategies have identified North Africa and the Sahel as the areas posing the greatest risk to its national security, and the MAUC's 2019 plan for Africa (MUAC 2019b) highlights the need to address the migration and security challenges in sub-Saharan Africa. Since Spain does not have the capacity to develop a unilateral WGA in these regions, it must contribute to the CSDP missions and operations in those areas and, as noted above, even boxes above its weight in these efforts. Outside these areas, Spain only carries out bilateral military, humanitarian or development-aid projects, devoting the greatest individual effort to Latin America (37%) and Africa (20%), roughly reversing the order of its contributions to EU-funded projects: 30 percent in Africa and 23 percent in Latin America.

Despite its support for and contributions to the European WGA, Spain faces serious obstacles to developing a national WGA. Without a centralised crisis-management system under the presidency of the government, ministries and agencies must use their own means to fulfil international commitments, and they do not receive any common funding or additional resources for WGA from the government. Limited resources, in turn, make ministries and agencies reluctant to take part in WGA missions and operations. What's more, in addition to financial resources, they also encounter difficulties finding human resources for such efforts. In the military sphere, the problem has to do with the increasing cost of maintenance and operations (around 20% of defence expenditures). In the civilian sphere, the government can neither force officials to participate in WGA missions nor does it have the necessary funds to recruit external experts. Given these circumstances, it is easier for Spain to contribute to the European model of WGA management than to develop its own model, as other European powers (e.g. France and the UK) have done.

3 | Who are the main actors involved in cooperating in a WGA?

In Spain, management of external crises has traditionally been a competence of the executive branch. The legislative branch only became involved in the decision-making process after Spain's controversial participation in the invasion of Iraq in 2003. Two years later, the National Defence Act introduced the requirement that the Congress of Deputies provide its authorisation before Spanish troops are deployed abroad. At present, lawmakers are more active in terms of launching CSDP missions than in monitoring or evaluating them. Their contribution is limited to periodically receiving information from the ministers of defence and foreign affairs, and they play no active role in the crisis-management system.

The daily management of external conflicts and crises is mainly handled by the ministries of Defence and Foreign Affairs. There are not any formalised coordination structures or procedures with other ministries or agencies, although the presidency of the government may have a hand in management efforts. When the National Security System was created in 2013, the Council of National Security (DSN) was formed to be a new stakeholder with the appropriate WGA design to conduct crisis management. However, the DSN has focused its priorities to date on managing domestic crises rather than on external crises and conflicts, which has put any strategic management for CSDP missions into a kind of political-administrative limbo. As a result, responsibility for WGA coordination at the strategic level remains with Brussels-based governmental representatives of the ministries of Defence, Foreign Affairs and Interior who are involved in crisis management.

The president of the government delegates the management of external crises to the defence and foreign ministers without any structured or binding system of coordination. Thus, the model of WGA-like coordination for crises is the same as for the rest of the bilateral affairs between both ministries, and there is no specific bilateral mechanism other than the quarterly meetings with or without representatives of the presidency. Within the Ministry of Defence, the Armed Forces, the Guardia Civil and the National Intelligence Center may contribute to a WGA effort. Their members have experience with EU missions and operations, and they receive training to become familiar with implementing the WGA concept. Their potential contribution to national WGA management became clear in the Canary Islands in 2006, when the Ministry of Interior led the multidimensional response of the Armed Forces, Frontex, the search and rescue agencies, local authorities and NGOs to a migration crisis.

The Armed Forces and the Guardia Civil, in particular, have expanded their basic responsibilities (i.e. defence and security, respectively) to include new dimensions related to the WGA. These include, among others, maritime security, border control, search and rescue, surveillance and technical assistance. Both forces also contribute to the ministerial programmes for international cooperation, which enhances their expertise for WGA contributions. For example, the ministries of Defence and Foreign Affairs jointly organise a 'defence diplomacy' programme.

For its part, the MAUC also contributes to developing the WGA concept. The diplomats and officials of the Foreign Service contribute to EU crisis management from national or common positions, while the MAUC's secretary of state for the European Union works as the point of contact between national and EU affairs. They contribute with traditional diplomatic instruments, except in the case of humanitarian and development aid, which is handled by Spain's Agency for International Development Cooperation (AECID). Although the AECID has ties to the MAUC, the fact that it enjoys full autonomy makes it very difficult to incorporate these dimensions into the national WGA. The organisation's autonomy can be attributed to humanitarian agents' traditional suspicion that the government will try to use development aid as a leveraging tool in their foreign policies, or that humanitarian aid will potentially be politicised if it overlaps with other development, peace and security agendas (MAUC 2019a: 16).

However, this distrust might be diminishing as a result of two factors: first, the AECID's participation in programmes to reform the EU security sector; and, second, Spain's contribution to the financing of the EU's African Peace Facility via the European Development Fund

(EDF), which supports peace operations led by African partners themselves (MAUC 2019b: 34). This change of mind is also due to the prominence that security is given as a goal in the UN's 2030 Agenda for sustainable development as well as to the linking of development and security in the EU's Global Strategy on Foreign and Security Policy, as Spain's most recent master plan for cooperation acknowledges (AECID 2018: 10). In both the MAUC's plan for Africa and the AECID's master plan for cooperation (the two documents cited above), Spain acknowledges the need to support the so-called 'security-development nexus' in order to improve the security of people and to reinforce the resilience of countries.

The ministries of Interior and Justice also support the development of the WGA in the EU, especially when it comes to the police, justice and penitentiary components of the CSDP's civilian missions. They contribute by providing experts from the National Police Corps, the Guardia Civil, or the justice and penitentiary institutions to carry out tasks related to security-sector reform, crime prevention and training local security forces, judges, prosecutors and the like. Their individual contributions are limited by the difficulties they face in recruiting civil servants to participate in such efforts for the reasons mentioned above. To help mitigate these limitations, civil servants have developed their own International and Ibero-American Foundation for Administration and Public Policies (FIIAPP), which has full autonomy to decide where, how and when to collaborate in the fields of development and governance. The FIIAPP acts as mediator between EU-funded programmes and the leading organisations, primarily as an agency for recruiting national experts. As an authorised executive agency of the European Commission since 2011, the FIIAPP manages community funds (delegated cooperation) to finance one third of its projects, and it is a key player in EU projects related to technical cooperation both within Europe and between the EU and Latin America (FIIAPP 2017: 1).

Since the role of the ministries of Interior and Justice is limited to authorising the mediation of the FIIAPP, they cannot take advantage of individual contributions to develop their own WGA experiences, structures and doctrines. Their limitation is higher in the field of external security because the contribution is limited to members of the Guardia Civil, who are the only individuals with the military education and authorisation to take part in gendarmerie-type missions within the CSDP. This handicap prevents many agencies from taking part in wider WGA actions despite their potential to add value. Another difficulty comes from the lack of funding to externalise the recruitment of national experts. Individual citizens are not eligible for CSDP missions because they cannot be contracted either as international seconded members for the EU or as 'freelancers' for the Spanish government. For these reasons, there are neither clusters of experts nor civil servants available for manning CSDP missions, which in turn affects Spain's contribution to WGA efforts.

4 | How does your country operationalise a WGA?

All in all, and despite the above-mentioned obstacles, Spanish actors have improved the operationalisation of their WGA capability within the EU framework. Having representatives from the various ministries in Spain's permanent mission to the EU in Brussels (REPER) facilitates strategic coordination in a WGA-like mode. Their colleagues back in Madrid, on the other hand, do not have daily contact with the WGA management. The operational and tactical levels of coordination remain within the intra-ministerial chains of command, both in the capital and on the ground. Their interaction remains limited by the low number of genuine WGA missions and operations at the EU level involving multiple dimensions as well as by the lack of national-led ones.

Spain contributes to the EEAS crisis system mechanism in several phases on a timeline ranging from early warning to response. It provides the available national information to the EEAS's secretary general or to its deputy secretary general for CSDP and crisis response (DSG-CSDP) regarding the identification and assessment of a crisis or the related collection of data. It may also request that the DSG-CSDP pay attention to a potential crisis. The monitoring of the crisis is conducted at the national level in Madrid in close contact with the REPER in Brussels in order to foresee possible immediate actions. This process provides early warning and situational awareness, and it also facilitates any adjustments to advance and contingency planning on the strategic and operational levels.

Once a crisis-management concept has been approved in Brussels, Spanish military, diplomatic and civilian representatives assess the impact of strategic options for military and civilian actors. This assessment regarding a Spanish contribution is very close to the desired WGA way of management, and it goes from the national representatives in Brussels to their ministerial departments in the capital in order to nurture feedback within Brussels.

The presidency is informed about the situation, and any final decisions on CSDP missions are adopted by the government within the Council of Ministers. A contingency fund in the national budget provides funds for the deployment of troops under CSDP missions. The use of this extraordinary source of funding has been criticised for political and budgetary reasons, and the Armed Forces are facing further financial obstacles to participating in future CSDP missions and operations. Given these circumstances, it would be desirable for the EU's WGA to increase the amount of common funds available for military operations (via the so-called 'Athena' mechanism) in order to keep the contribution of Spanish troops at its current level.

The civilian costs are covered better via various EU mechanisms, and their amount is too small to cause financial troubles for the Spanish agencies. Common funding ensures that Spain will continue providing humanitarian and development aid as part of EU-led projects. However, one should always keep in mind the reluctance of humanitarian actors to see security and development efforts mixed. In fact, in response to this resistance, the Spanish government has a state-owned construction company (TRAGSA) to participate in reconstruction tasks, which is another national asset for WGA actions.

The WGA model is being exported to fields other than that of external crisis management. After the creation of the European Defence Fund and the European Defence Action Plan, public and private stakeholders in Spain agreed that there is a need to come up with new institutional arrangements for cooperating with EU institutions and action plans. For example, there has been the establishment of an inter-agency working group including representatives of the ministries of Defence, Foreign Affairs, Industry and Finance, of the key industrial associations, and of other organisations.

The outcome of this WGA coordination has been very relevant so far. It has allowed various stakeholders – including those in the defence sector – to see the opportunities and risks involved in EU initiatives, and it has contributed to raising public awareness about the need for a European Industrial and Technological Base (EDITB). Another example is the creation of a WGA model for preventing disinformation during electoral periods. Spain had already joined the Helsinki-based European Centre of Excellence for Countering Hybrid Threats, and it created a model based on the division of labour among the National Intelligence Centre (Ministry of Defence), the Centre for the Protection of Critical Infrastructures (Ministry of Interior), and the Cyber Defence Command (Ministry of Defence) under the leadership of the secretary for communications of the presidency of the government. Although it is too early to access the effectiveness of this new WGA-like arrangement, the relevant issue is that the presidency has realised the need to manage complex crises using a WGA model. Given this acknowledgement, it is possible that a WGA could be applied to Spanish responses to external crises in the future.

5 | Conclusions

The success of a WGA in Spain is contingent upon several factors. The national strategic culture and the preference for multilateral frameworks of action in foreign and security policy have prevented the development of a national WGA instrument to deal with external crises and conflicts. The preference for playing a supporting role reduces the level of ambition for a Spanish WGA. The lack of explicit documents and doctrines on WGA reveals that a WGA is viewed as a best practice for management but mainly for EU affairs. Although Spain contributes by having Spanish actors who are familiar with WGA procedures participate in CFSP/CSDP projects, it is not able or willing to develop its own WGA system.

A growing familiarity with WGA procedures and the creation of the National Security System could change Spain's level of ambition about adopting a WGA, but it will require political leadership. Indeed, strong political backing will be necessary for Spanish participation in CSDP missions and operations, especially if they go against the dominant strategic culture and could potentially impact political or social situations. Of course, the need for hard decisions on CSDP missions and operations is very limited at the moment, but it could change in the future if the EU increases its strategic autonomy and operational level of ambition.

A lack of national leadership is both the cause and effect of Spain's lack of a crisis-management system for responding to external crises and conflicts at the level of the president of the government (as the prime minister is known). Granted, the basic elements – structures, procedures and regulations – of a WGA-like model of management already exist, but they are mainly geared towards internal crises or situations impacting national security. The jump to a genuine WGA at the presidential level could happen sooner than expected given the progressive acknowledgment within the National Security System that complex crises are better coordinated at the supra-agency level. However, it will be very difficult for the National Security System to displace ministries and agencies from the management of external crises and conflicts unless a person with strong leadership skills and a desire to alter this situation holds the presidency. Meanwhile, all other factors being equal, the de facto delegation of the national WGA system to the European one will continue to work reasonably well.

The rivalries among potential WGA actors in Spain are both the cause and effect of the lack of an inter-agency culture of coordination. As explained above, these actors do coordinate their contributions to CSDP missions and operations, but they do so without set procedures to facilitate the development of a WGA culture. However, their reluctance to cooperate could diminish if the government or the EU were to provide the proper funding to CSDP missions and operations instead of exhausting the agencies' limited budgets. That said, if there is a feeling that the burden-sharing is unfair, it may increase their resistance to contribute to national commitments.

Material resources are not the only obstacles to developing a culture and practice of WGA in Spain. The administrative difficulties faced in recruiting civil servants or independent experts to participate in a WGA will also affect Spain's contribution to CSDP efforts, such as the development of the EU's 'Civilian Compact' to reinforce its capacity to deploy civilian expertise. For these and other reasons, the failure to establish a connection between national and EU WGA cultures – which has actually been a strategic goal of Spanish governments – puts the 'effectiveness' of the European multilateral framework at risk. In fact, the absence of an effective multilateral WGA management in the EU could reverse the trend towards the convergence of WGA cultures and practices towards having national and ad hoc ones. Without such convergence, the Spanish push for an EU-versus-national WGA model of coordination may fail, and Spain would find itself without any national or collective procedure to manage international crises and conflicts.

Transparency and accountability also matter for WGA systems. The evaluation of the CSDP missions and operations must include the WGA procedures, as well, in order to gauge their contribution to final outcomes. Given the current lack of oversight and transparency, this best practice would permit Spanish lawmakers and members of its academic community to monitor the management of external crises and conflicts by both national and European WGA practitioners.

6 | Reference list

AECID (Agency for International Development Cooperation) (2018). V Plan Director de la Cooperacion Espanola 2018–2021. Madrid: MAUC. www.exteriores.gob.es/Portal/es/PoliticaExteriorCoopera cion/CooperacionAlDesarrollo/Documents/V%20Plan%20Direct or%20de%20la%20Cooperaci%C3%B3n%20Espa%C3%B1ola.pdf.

Arteaga, Felix (2013). "Spain." In *Strategic Cultures in Europe: Security and Defence Policies Across the Continent,* edited by Heiko Biehl, Bastian Griegerich and Alexandra Jonas. Potsdam: Springer VS: 333–342.

DSN (Council of National Security of Spain) (2017). National Security Strategy 2017. Madrid: Government of Spain. www.dsn.gob.es/ sites/dsn/files/2017_Spanish_National_Security_Strategy_0.pdf.

FIIAPP (International and Ibero-American Foundation for Administration and Public Policies) (2017). Memoria de Actividades 2015. Madrid: FIIAPP. www.fiiapp.org/wp-content/uploads/2017/07/Me moria-FIIAPP.pdf.

Gómez Castro, Elena (2018). "PESCO: CSDP reaches the age of majority." *European Defence Matters* Issue 15. Brussels: European Defence Agency. www.eda.europa.eu/webzine/issue15/cover-story/ pesco-drivers-the-floor-is-yours.

MAUC (Ministry of Foreign Affairs, the European Union and Cooperation) (2015). Estrategia de Accion Exterior. Madrid: MAUC.

MAUC (2019a). Estrategia de Accion Humanitaria. Madrid: MAUC.

MAUC (2019b). III Plan Africa. Madrid: MAUC.

Olivie, Iliana, and Aitor Perez (2019). "Donde esta la ayuda espanola?" *Analysis of the Elcano Royal Institute* No. 49 (May). www.realinstitutoelcano.org/wps/portal/rielcano_es/contenido?WCM_GLOBAL_CONTEXT=/elcano/elcano_es/zonas_es/cooperacion+y+desarrollo/ari49-2019-olivie-perez-donde-esta-la-ayuda-espanola.

Rintakoski, Kristiina, and Mikko Autti (2008). Comprehensive Approach. Trends, Challenges and Possibilities for Cooperation in Crisis Management. Annex 2. Helsinki: Ministry of Defence. www.defmin.fi/files/1316/Comprehensive_Approach_-_Trends_Challenges_and_Possibilities_for_Cooperation_in_Crisis_Prevention_and_Management.pdf (executive summary only).

Sweden

Lars Niklasson

1 | Introduction

When it comes to a whole-of-government approach (WGA), Sweden has taken three relevant actions. In 2003, there was the introduction of a general policy for global development, which aims to be a cross-cutting coordinating device (Regeringens proposition 2003). This was followed in 2007 by a strategy for international military-civilian operations (Regeringens skrivelse 2007a). The latter strategy is in line with the scope of this study, while the broader policy of 2003 is often seen as a role model for policy coherence in external policies, providing a background for the 2007 strategy. As discussed below, the policy and the strategy have hardly lived up to the high ambitions they set.

In addition, in 2002, an agency was set up to support international civilian peacebuilding missions by coordinating their Swedish and non-Swedish participants. The agency, which was partly based on pre-existing programmes, was named the Folke Bernadotte Academy. Whereas the proper name refers to an early Swedish peace negotiator, the term 'academy' indicates that one of its major goals is to educate people for these missions.

Returning to take a deeper look at the policy introduced in 2003, we see that it is linked to separate EU and UN initiatives. The UN Millennium Development Goals (MDGs) were introduced just before the Swedish policy was introduced, and the EU also introduced its principle of coherence in development policy at around the same time. The Swedish policy was later linked to the UN Sustainable Development Goals (SDGs), with the minister for international development cooperation being put in charge of related issues on the international level and the minister for public administration being tasked with handling related issues on the domestic level. What's more, a number of policies were introduced around the same time to pursue cross-cutting issues and to be advanced by all ministries. Other examples are an elaborate set of environmental goals, regional coordination of national policies, and a general policy of gender mainstreaming.

In general, however, the 2003 policy and its focus on coherence only make sense when viewed in the context of Sweden's particular constitutional structure, which prioritises governing by consensus. To quote The Oxford Handbook of Swedish Politics (Persson 2016: 637): "Almost all government decisions [in Sweden] are made collectively – a marked contrast to the situation in most other countries, where ministers make most decisions independently. The strong commitment of the Swedish government to collective decision-making is institutionalized through a joint preparation procedure (gemensam beredning) [...]. Moreover, it is common practice to circulate all government bills among ministries [...]. These procedures ensure that all government decisions are prepared jointly and that all relevant ministries are involved."

In other words, Sweden's constitution simply doesn't allow theme-based groups of ministries to work together on an issue. In fact, this strong principle of consensus-based decision-making actually makes it difficult to integrate policies across ministerial boundaries, as no ministries can be excluded. The available option is to introduce general policies, often giving weak powers to the lead ministry, which is what the other ministries accept (Niklasson 2007, 2011, 2015; Niklasson and Barr 2015).

Complicating matters further, there are two highly independent agencies involved in these issues that operate under different ministries (foreign affairs and defence, respectively). The Swedish International Development Cooperation Agency (SIDA) enjoys a strong international reputation and is involved in long-term development aid as well as short-term humanitarian aid. The other agency is the armed forces, which have gone through a period of fundamental change, shifting their focus from national defence to international operations (and, more recently, back to national defence). The 2003 policy and the 2007 strategy aim to coordinate cooperation among these agencies and other agencies involved in international operations.

The documents described above were introduced by different governments and have survived several changes of government, which indicates that their content has been embraced by most political parties. But the policies have also been revised, partly to send political messages and partly to deal with the strong criticism from the two national audit bodies regarding the weak design of the policies.

2 | What policies have been developed to further policy coherence?

The 2003 policy on global development was an early example of WGA and very similar to the EU principle of policy cohesion in development policy. The government bill describes the global situation, states a set of general aims for Swedish policies related to global development, and outlines 11 policy areas to be involved. However, the most specific part of the text is an outline of the Swedish policy for international development cooperation (aid), i.e. one specific policy area.

The government bill and the stated ambitions in the various areas are in themselves instruments for coordination, especially the statement that the policies must be consistent with each other. In addition, the bill proposes a 'coordination function' in the Government Offices, as the cabinet office is called, and additional work to establish an 'evaluation function' for this policy. The bill proposes continued support for international work to develop an index of cohesion, and argues that conflicts of interest across policy areas should be explicitly stated and acted upon. However, it fails to mention where this should be stated and by whom. In fact, there is no evidence of such a discussion in the official documents, and the bill merely states that the administrative instruments are to be further developed.

The 2007 strategy (Regeringens skrivelse 2007a) was introduced in a report to parliament, which is technically a piece of information on something already enacted by the cabinet, rather than as a proposal for a future policy to be decided on by parliament. After restating the general goals of the 2003 policy, it provides further elaboration on the specific area of international military-civilian operations by spelling out what the relevant military and civilian capabilities are. The strategy also discusses international and national coordination, with the latter being an encouragement (i.e. mandate) for the relevant agencies to improve coordination among themselves.

The agency set up in 2002 to support international civilian peace-building missions is interesting as an instrument for coordinating fieldwork. Its mandate is to contribute directly to the goals of the (narrow) policy of international development cooperation (aid) and indirectly to the broader cross-cutting goals.

However, as discussed earlier, these policies need to be seen in relation to existing barriers to and other mechanisms for cooperation in the Swedish context. A more general mechanism for policy coherence is the consensus decision-making in the cabinet office. As discussed earlier, the constitutional principle of consensus decision-making is carried out through mandatory consultations across the ministries (gemensam beredning). Since all proposals must be agreed by all other ministries beforehand, each ministry effectively has a right of veto. A typical example is when ministries protect 'their' agencies from participating in joint initiatives. The outcome is coherence by the least common denominator. In practice, though, the Ministry of Finance has a stronger position due to its power over the budget, and the Prime Minister's Office also enjoys a stronger position, especially over the legislative agenda.

Furthermore, the consensus-based model also means that all formal instructions to agencies are given by the cabinet as a whole rather than by individual members of the government. As a result, individual ministers are generally not held accountable for what happens in 'their' agencies. In other words, the agencies have (on paper) a high level of independence from the cabinet office. In reality, informal instructions are accepted, which creates the odd situation that the formal instructions are agreed by all ministries, while the informal instructions are only given by the closest ministry.

It should also be noted that a large number of strategies are issued by the Ministry for Foreign Affairs, mainly to guide the implementation of programmes by the international development-cooperation agency (SIDA), which results in a very complex structure of instructions (Statskontoret 2011). Hence, there are several other strategies that relate to general ambitions yet add little to this analysis. These include the follow-up on the 2008 Policy for Global Development (Regeringens skrivelse 2007b), the Policy for Security and Development in Swedish Development Cooperation 2011–2014 (Regeringskansliet

2010), the 2014 Platform for Development Cooperation (Regeringens skrivelse 2014), the 2016 Policy for Development Cooperation and Humanitarian Assistance (Regeringens skrivelse 2016), the 2017 National Security Strategy (Regeringskansliet 2017b), and the Strategy for Sustainable Peace 2017–22 (Regeringskansliet 2017a).

3 | Who are the main actors involved in cooperating in a WGA?

Sweden's WGA-related policies state general ambitions of coordination while specifically listings which agencies (policy areas) are required to participate. The government bills are the outcome of negotiations in the Government Offices over who must be involved, which has further consequences for instructions, budgets and other matters. In other words, the policies are examples of high-level coordination to be supported by the previously mentioned working groups.

In addition to development cooperation (aid), the 2003 strategy (Regeringens proposition 2003) mentions 11 policy areas considered to be part of the broader and more general policy for global development: law enforcement, defence, trade, migration, health and social care, finance, education, agriculture and fishery, culture, environment and commerce. The 2007 strategy (Regeringens skrivelse 2007a), on the other hand, speaks more narrowly of military and civilian capabilities. A number of agencies are mentioned as examples of civilian recruitment to international missions: the police, the prosecutors, the courts, the jails, the agency to support the fire brigades, the agency for international cooperation, and the Folke Bernadotte Academy. In any case, there are very few studies about coordination or cooperation at the operational level.

4 | How does your country operationalise a WGA?

There is a long tradition in Sweden of what is now called multi-level governance.

Sweden's WGA-related coordination mainly takes place at the top levels of the agencies and the ministries. Unfortunately, very few studies about coordination on the ground exist, with the study on the

Swedish mission to Afghanistan between 2002 and 2014 (SOU 2017) being a notable exception.

The area of external conflicts and crises can be expected to be different from domestic policy areas, where coordination from the bottom-up is sometimes very pronounced (although it is rarely uniform across the country). Much domestic collaboration is driven by a desire to deal with overlapping missions and funding streams across ministries and levels of government (Niklasson 2007, 2011, 2015; Niklasson and Barr 2015). This is often rooted in a desire to provide efficient services.

In the international context, the agencies provide complementary competencies, while international missions are relatively new to most of them. The agencies probably see a need for collaboration in the field, but it may be difficult to arrange this at home due to bureaucratic inertia or even turf wars.

Coordination-related procedures mainly take place at the ministerial level within the Government Offices. The 'coordination function' for this area has evolved over time. It is mainly an informal group to complement other, more formal procedures as well as an instrument to make the ministries more willing to contribute to a common goal (i.e. to avoid exercising their right of veto).

At one point, the coordination function was the responsibility of a single civil servant in the Ministry of Foreign Affairs. Criticism led to the setup of a group at the head-of-department level, together with a working group dealing with the issues in a more hands-on fashion. This was merged in 2018 with the group tasked with coordinating the implementation of the UN Sustainable Development Goals.

There is some integration with and within parliament on these issues. For example, a joint committee for defence and foreign affairs formed in 2001 deals with issues pertaining to both committees. In addition, every committee can ask for input from another committee. There is also some informal coordination to decide where an issue belongs.

A 'council' of nine agencies was introduced in 2013, which includes the nine agencies in the 2007 strategy (listed above) in addition to the coast guard and the armed forces. The ambition was to encourage cooperation and to find synergies across these agencies' operations. The council is an informal partnership, which is a format applied in several areas where the government wants to encourage inter-agency collaboration.

Since 2016, there has also been a joint funding mechanism for this area. The relevant agencies receive a joint instruction on how to use some of the funds allocated in the budget, while no mandate is delegated to the agencies to decide on who gets what. More specifically, it refers to a section of the aid budget to be used by the police, the agency for prosecutors, the agency for jails, the agency for courts, the agency for civilian emergencies, and the Folke Bernadotte Academy. While the funding itself is already divided by the government into specific amounts for each agency, the use of a joint instruction underlines the need to take other agencies' operations into account. It is an atypical instrument in the Swedish context, where, as noted, the autonomy of each agency is a constitutional principle (Niklasson 2007, 2011).

This high degree of autonomy often becomes a barrier to coordination from the top, and the instruments designed to overcome this fragmentation are often weak. Instead, the government often encourages bottom-up coordination in the form of local or regional partnerships. In the area of external conflicts and crises, there is little mention of such instruments, whether they are encouraged by the government or introduced by the agencies themselves or their staff.

5 | Conclusions

Sweden's WGA-related policies have been severely criticised. The 2003 policy was investigated by the Agency for Public Management (APM) in 2014, which argued that the goals are too visionary and fail to specify what should be done and by whom. Furthermore, the APM concluded that the policy is too much of a statement on aid policy rather than on a broader spectrum of policies and instruments – in other words, that it isn't really an example of a genuine WGA. The APM suggested that the other ministries should report on how their policies relate to the common ambitions and how they can contribute further to their achievement. In addition, it said that the inter-ministerial working group has an unclear mission, especially in relation to the home ministries, and it argued that the promotion of certain values in and the development of other countries need to be further supported via standard mechanisms of domestic coordination (which, for example, are more focused on short-term funding). Lastly, the APM noted that more resources must be devoted to fostering better coordination. At the time of writing, the Ministry for Foreign Affairs had one civil servant tasked with coordinating a number of ministries. The coordination function was redesigned in 2015 and 2018, and the biannual reports to parliament were structured along the lines of the SDGs in 2016 and 2018 (Statskontoret 2014).

The 2007 strategy (Regeringens skrivelse 2007a), on the other hand, was investigated by the National Audit Office (NAO) in 2011. This agency argued that the strategy's goals are too general in that they only indicate which missions Sweden should contribute to rather than what they should achieve. Furthermore, the NAO argued that there should be a comprehensive report on what the missions accomplish that relates to the strategy, noting that it is reasonable to expect the same level of analysis as the government demands for its aid policy. The funding streams are fragmented, the NAO continued, which makes it difficult to control costs. Other criticism were: that only parts of the military-related costs are reported and decided by parliament; that it is unclear what the government expects from collaboration; that the format is insufficiently defined; and that a lack of coordination in the Government Offices leads to a situation in which field officers are left with the task of performing any needed coordination themselves. Lastly, the NAO argued that the Folke Bernadotte Academy has insufficient resources to perform its ambitious mandate (Riksrevisionen 2011).

In 2011, the Agency for Public Management also carried out a general evaluation of the instruments used by the Government Offices to guide its agencies in the area of international development cooperation. The evaluation's general finding was that there were too many overlapping strategy documents, and that this reduces the overall effect of the messages sent by the cabinet (Statskontoret 2011). Some of the problems have been noted in other reports on the situation in Sweden (see, e.g., Veron and Sheriff 2018; Prontera 2016).

In sum, one can say that Sweden's instruments of coordination are generally weak compared to the forces for the autonomous pursuit of the goals of individual organisations. These include, for example, the constitutional autonomy of the agencies and the ministries, the results-based management of each organisation, and the lack of staff rotation across ministries and agencies.

Niklasson, Lars (2007). Joining-up for regional development. How governments deal with a wicked problem, overlapping policies and fragmented responsibilities. Statskontoret Rapport 2007:2. www.statskontoret.se/globalassets/publikationer/2007/200702.pdf.

Niklasson, Lars (2011). "Strategies to join up resources across levels and sectors of government: A twelve country comparison." In *Policy, Performance and Management in Governance and Intergovernmental Relations: Transatlantic Perspectives*, edited by Eduardo Ongaro, Andrew Massey, Marc Holzer and Ellen Wayenberg. Cheltenham: Edward Elgar Publishing Ltd: 143–155.

Niklasson, Lars (2015). "Challenges and reforms of local and regional governments in Sweden." In *The Oxford Handbook of Swedish Politics*, edited by Jon Pierre. Oxford: Oxford University Press: 399–413.

Niklasson, Lars, and Jonathan Barr (2015). *Employment and skills strategies in Sweden. OECD reviews on local job creation*. Paris: OECD.

Persson, Thomas (2016). "Policy Coordination under Minority and Majority Rule." *In The Oxford Handbook of Swedish Politics*, edited by Jon Pierre. Oxford: Oxford University Press: 634–649.

Prontera, Andrea (2016). "Subsystem politics and policy coherence in development cooperation: Evidence from four EU Member States." *Comparative European Politics* (14) 3: 298–318.

Regeringens proposition (2003). Gemensamt ansvar: Sveriges politik for global utveckling. 2002/03:122. Stockholm: The Government Offices.

Regeringens skrivelse (2007a). Nationell strategi for svenskt deltagande i internationell freds- och sakerhetsframjande verksamhet. 2007/08:51. Stockholm: The Government Offices.

Regeringens skrivelse (2007b). Sveriges politik for global utveckling. 2007/08:89. Stockholm: The Government Offices.

Regeringens skrivelse (2014). Bistandspolitisk plattform. 2013/14:131. Stockholm: The Government Offices.

Regeringens skrivelse (2016). Policyramverk for svenskt utvecklingssamarbete och humanitart bistand. 2016/17:60. Stockholm: The Government Offices.

Regeringskansliet (2010). Peace and Security for Development Policy for Security and Development in Swedish Development Cooperation 2011–2014. Stockholm: The Government Offices. www.gove rnment.se/49b74d/contentassets/036c986985e04c32beee05a913bc c91e/peace-and-security-for-development-policy-for-security-and-d evelopment-in-swedish-development-cooperation-2011-2014.

Regeringskansliet (2017a). Strategy for Sustainable Peace 2017–2022. Stockholm: The Government Offices.

Regeringskansliet (2017b). Nationell sakerhetsstrategi. Stockholm: The Government Offices.

Riksrevisionen (2011). Svenska bidrag till internationella insatser, RiR 2011:14. Stockholm: Riksrevisionen.

SOU (Statens offentliga utredningar) (2017). Sverige i Afghanistan 2002–2014. Betankande av Afghanistanutredningen. 2017:16. Stockholm: The Government Offices.

Statskontoret (2011). Styrning av svensk bistandspolitik. En utvardering. Rapport 2011:25. Stockholm: Statskontoret.

Statskontoret (2014). Politik for global utveckling. Regeringens gemensamma ansvar? Rapport 2014:1. Stockholm: Statskontoret.

Veron, Pauline, and Andrew Sheriff (2018). Supporting peacebuilding in times of change: Case Study Sweden. Maastricht: ECDPM.

United Kingdom

Laura Cleary

1 | Introduction

The United Kingdom (UK) was one of the first countries to launch a whole-of-government approach (WGA) in pursuit of its foreign and security interests. It was former Prime Minister Tony Blair (1997–2008) who was the first to demand that the British government "speak with one voice" on foreign and security issues, calling for "joined-up government". In the intervening years, those efforts have been advanced by successive governments, which in turn has resulted in formal institutional, policy and financial arrangements.

The establishment of a WGA in the UK coincided with the government's pursuit of an agenda of liberal interventionism, which evolved in response to lessons learned in successive military campaigns in the Balkans, Sierra Leone, East Timor, Afghanistan and Iraq (MCDC 2014; Stepputat and Greenwood 2013). More recently, the drivers for the furtherance of WGA have been related to the policy of austerity and the requirement across government to achieve economies of scale wherever possible.

Despite political declarations that austerity is at an end (May 2018b), the UK is unlikely to reverse its WGA. The forecasted economic consequences of leaving the European Union, and the consequent need and/or desire to demonstrate that Great Britain remains a global player of note, will require departments of state to act in a coordinated and consistent fashion.

The ability of departments to act in this way will be dependent on the extent to which civil servants adhere to existing policies and procedures. It seems unlikely that there will be any radical changes to foreign and security policy whilst the political agenda is consumed by the process and implications of leaving the EU. In the absence of direct political engagement on security issues, it has fallen to civil society organisations to outline the framework for future policies. One recently published paper advocated the further consolidation of WGA as a means to ensure a "global Britain" in the 21st century (Seely and Rogers 2019). The authors proposed a national strategy council, a national global strategy, integration of departments, establishment of joint effects teams, and the assessment and recalibration of development assistance.

At this juncture, it is better to anticipate modifications to the existing WGA rather than a complete reversal. Those changes are likely to affect institutional and financial arrangements as efforts are made to operationalise the new Fusion Doctrine, which was unveiled in the National Security Capability Review in 2018 (HM Government 2018). There are indications that the Department for International Development (DFID) will be brought more fully under the direction of the National Security Council (NSC), and that the types of projects that receive funding from the GBP 1.2 billion Conflict, Stability and Security Fund (CSSF) will be reviewed. These are, however, refinements to what is a well-established method of working to resolve and prevent conflict.

2 | What policies have been developed to further policy coherence?

The initial steps in the establishment of WGA in the UK were taken with the publication of the Strategic Defence Review (SDR) in 1998 (Ministry of Defence 1998). Both the process of that review and the objectives set within it were viewed as means through which the newly elected Labour Government could reposition itself in terms of defence and the UK could assert itself within the post-Cold War order. Historically, the Labour Party had been perceived as weak on defence, given that it wished to withdraw from NATO and dismantle the nuclear deterrent. Tony Blair, as leader of New Labour, was an internationalist who sought to revise the party's image. In successive speeches and in the party's manifesto, he stressed the importance of the UN, NATO and the EU, and Britain's leadership role within them, for stability and peace in Europe and the world (Labour Party 1997; Kampfner 2003).

Although produced within the Ministry of Defence (MOD), the SDR was very clearly foreign policy led. The ministry, then led by Secretary of State George Robertson, had adopted a more open and consultative approach during the review process, conferring with other departments of state, allies, CSOs, service personnel and thinktanks. As a result, strategic priorities were derived from and set within a broader strategic context, rather than solely being determined by costs and affordability. It was recognised that national security and prosperity were dependent on the promotion of international stability, freedom and economic development. The government declared its intention that the British Armed Forces should be a "force for good in the world" (Ministry of Defence 1998).

The review acknowledged that Britain no longer faced an existential threat, but that state fragility and conflict in other parts of the world could impact on its security. Thus, if the Armed Forces were to achieve their aim, they would need to act in concert with the Foreign and Commonwealth Office (FCO) and the Department for International Development (DFID), which had been newly established in 1997. As will be discussed below, a number of pragmatic institutional reforms were taken to encourage WGA, however the overarching national policy framework under which that occurred remained the 1998 SDR and its 2002 update titled 'Strategic Defence Review: A New Chapter' (Ministry of Defence 2002).

The publication in 2008 of the UK's first National Security Strategy (NSS) (Cabinet Office 2008) marked a step change in terms of the way in which the UK conceptualised, assessed and provided security. While previous government policies had acknowledged the changed threat environment post-Cold War and the requirement for interagency cooperation for effective response, the 2008 NSS made that case far more explicit. It recognised that globalisation and greater political, financial, social and technological interconnectedness made it increasingly difficult to differentiate between purely domestic and foreign policy.

If individuals rather than states are the referent objects of security, then a fundamentally different approach to providing that ultimate public good is required. The 2008 NSS outlined a more systematic approach to the assessment and management of risk, and it argued that partnerships across government and between government and the private and third sectors would be necessary to ensure national security.

The 2008 NSS reflected lessons learned over a decade. Specifically, it acknowledged the growing complexity of the global security environment and noted that if the UK wished to tackle problems at source, then it would have to operate in coalition with others and employ WGA. Afghanistan had illustrated that stabilisation operations had a higher chance of success if a comprehensive approach was adopted. That approach would need to draw on the full range of capabilities across government and within NGOs. Two key enablers were to ensure that activities were demand- rather than supply-led and that there were links between the strategic, operational and tactical levels of a campaign (Baumann 2010).

Having waited 10 years to update the WGA policy framework, subsequent changes occurred quite rapidly. In 2009, following the start of the global financial crisis, the government published an update to the NSS titled 'Security for the Next Generation' (Cabinet Office 2009). This document outlined in greater detail the risk assessment process being employed, looking at "threat drivers, threat actors and threat domains". Again, the importance of WGA was acknowledged, but in this instance the government went beyond referencing the big three (MOD, FCO and DFID), acknowledging the contribution of the intelligence services, Home Office, cabinet committees and cabinet secretary to the delivery of security at home and abroad. The 2009 NSS detailed which ministries would lead in responding to which threats and outlined how parliament would conduct oversight of these activities through the establishment of a new Joint Committee on National Security Strategy.

This process of creeping centralisation was given further impetus when the coalition government published its own NSS in 2010 (HM Government 2010). Widely criticised at the time for being a rushed affair in which inadequate consultation took place, the 2010 NSS is viewed as significant because of the legal and institutional changes that accompanied it.

Prime Minister David Cameron sought to address perceived strategic deficits by creating a standing National Security Council (NSC), formalising the National Security Risk Assessment (NSRA), establishing a Joint Forces Command (JFC) and ensuring that, in the future, quinquennial strategic defence and security reviews (SDSRs) would align with the five yearly general election cycle (Thompson and Blagden 2018). In so doing, the coalition government sought to formalise the approach to security, avoiding the accusations of adhocism, adventurism and creeping incrementalism made against the preceding government's conduct of operations in Afghanistan and Iraq. The aim was to ensure that the government pursued an evidence-based, strategic and comprehensive approach in the future.

Although this was the aim, it has not been fully achieved in practice. Political posturing in advance of the 2015 NSS and SDSR (HM Government 2015) placed in question the extent to which discussions were held across government on strategic priorities (Thompson and Blagden 2018). Subsequent events have raised further doubts regarding the UK's strategic priorities. The 2016 Brexit referendum, Prime Minister Cameron's resignation, the succession of Theresa May, and her decision to call a snap election in 2017 played havoc with the newly established fixed-term parliament and quinquennial security review. The government's response was to publish a National Security Capability Review in 2018 (HM Government 2018), which assessed the capabilities without addressing the National Security Risk Assessment (NSRA).

The development of a WGA within the UK has been primarily driven by internal considerations regarding operational and cost effectiveness. A desire to promote peace on a global stage and a firm belief in the utility of the comprehensive approach have led the UK to champion the adoption of this method within the UN, NATO and the EU. It has done so by leading debates in the UN Security Council on how to improve the coordination and effectiveness of assistance to countries emerging from conflict. Further, as an advocate for the universal adoption of the Sustainable Development Goals of the UN's 2030 Agenda, the UK has been keen to demonstrate the application of WGA at home and abroad.

Within the EU, the UK sought to accelerate the conceptualisation of and planning for a comprehensive approach through the provision of support from the Development, Concepts and Doctrine Centre, the Permanent Joint Headquarters and the Stabilisation Unit, all of which were also engaged in knowledge transfer with NATO (House of Commons Defence Committee 2010). As one of the 'Big Three' foreign policy leads in the EU, a member of the UN Security Council, and the holder of the Deputy Supreme Allied Commander Europe (DSA-CEUR) post in NATO, the UK has been able to influence the agenda in these institutions so that they are mutually reinforcing (Lehne 2012). In turn, the evolution of WGAs within international organisations has led to further refinements of the UK's own approach. This demonstrates that the more one engages in multinational operations, the greater the potential to learn and improve.

3 | Who are the main actors involved in cooperating in a WGA?

The British WGA has evolved over time as well as in response to the ideological preferences of the government of the day and changes within the broader strategic context. The year 2010 marked a watershed year in the development of the WGA because it saw the transition from the Labour- to the Conservative-led coalition government and a more formalised approach to the management of the WGA.

Under the Labour governments of Tony Blair and Gordon Brown (1997–2010), the three principal ministries were the Foreign and Commonwealth Office (FCO), the Department for International Development (DFID), and the Ministry of Defence (MOD). The focus on these three ministries was reflective of two key drivers. First, the end of the Cold War and the collapse of the Soviet Union had fundamentally changed the perceived threat environment. Indeed, according to the Strategic Defence Review of 1998, Britain no longer faced a state-based existential threat (Ministry of Defence 1998).

Second, there was growing global recognition that the way in which developed states engaged with less developed or under-developed states needed to change. The publication of the Brandt Report in 1981 had an impact on the way in which North-South relations would subsequently be framed. The Labour government's establishment of DFID in 1997 was reflective of that change.

The significance of these two drivers was that although the traditional functions of diplomacy, aid and arms were at the forefront of UK engagement in the world, the balance between them had changed. Initially, there was a significant power struggle between the three ministries, both in Whitehall and overseas. As Her Majesty's representatives overseas, ambassadors felt themselves to be primi inter pares. The Armed Forces, as represented by defence attachés, felt that they could provide the most effective access to the security services and, thus, to decision-makers in conflict and post-conflict states. The DFID, however, had the money and was able to spend it. Competing organisational cultures led to competing agendas. Formal mechanisms were thus required to harness the three ministries.

One of the ways in which the government sought to operationalise its WGA was through the establishment of a series of delivery units that were staffed by personnel seconded from the three principal ministries and the Home Office. The most significant and enduring of these has been the Stabilisation Unit (SU), which was established in 2007. Staffed by a core team of personnel drawn from across government and with the capacity to deploy experts (government civil servants and consultants), the mission of the SU is to "support the integrated co-ordination of UK government activities in fragile and conflict-affected states by being a centre of expertise on conflict, stabilisation, security and justice" (SU n.d.).

Political direction for, and coordination of, overseas engagements was provided by the Cabinet Office's National Security Committee, chaired by the prime minister. Support was provided by the National Security Secretariat under the direction of a security and intelligence coordinator. The coordination of intelligence and security risk assessments was undertaken by the Joint Intelligence Committee. The Cabinet Office Briefing Room (COBR) was responsible for responding to emerging security situations. The Defence Council was responsible for coordinating military activity.

In 2010, then-Prime Minister David Cameron chose to overhaul this structure in response to the increasing complexities of ongoing operations in Afghanistan and the post-Iraq security environment, concerns over the lack of emphasis placed on national security by his predecessor, and what was perceived to be a diminished ability to make a coherent national security strategy. In response, Cameron created a cabinet-level National Security Council (NSC) with a supporting secretariat and a national security adviser. A formalised national security risk assessment (NSRA) process was established to support the publication of the National Security Strategy (NSS). The government also established a Joint Forces Command to further integrate operational military activity.

These structural changes necessitated a review of how parliament ensured accountability. Prior to 2010, foreign, defence intelligence and development activities had been reviewed by relevant committees within the House of Commons. Post-2010, the parliament added a select committee to monitor the NSC.

As the risk of international terrorism has increased and it has become ever more apparent that interventions abroad have direct consequences for security at home, a growing number of ministries and agencies have been incorporated into the UK's WGA. The promulgation of the country's Fusion Doctrine – as set out in the National Security Capability Review of 2018 (HM Government 2018) – and the explicit linkage made between economic, security and influence activities are illustrative of that wider change. All ministries now need to demonstrate how they are contributing to the attainment of the three national security objectives: protect our people, project our influence, and promote our prosperity (HM Government 2015). One should note, however, that there has been some criticism that explicit measurement of performance against national security objectives risks securitising development assistance.

Concern has also been expressed about the implications of Brexit for national security. In her speech to the Munich Security Conference in February 2018 (May 2018a), then-Prime Minister Theresa May acknowledged that European and British security would remain closely interlinked post-Brexit and that, consequently, the government would wish to "continue this co-operation" in the EU's Common Security and Defence Policy (CSDP) missions and operations in the future. To date, British contributions to CSDP missions have been limited in terms of the number of personnel (2.3% of member state contributions), but significant in terms of effect. Britain's parliament has recognised that "CSDP missions and operations have made a significant contribution to UK foreign policy priorities and been an important channel of UK influence – from tackling piracy to promoting the rule of law to peacebuilding in post-conflict states" (House of Lords 2018: 3). Britain's principal contribution to these operations has been strategic guidance during their planning and review. Concern has been expressed that a failure to address the nature of a future relationship with the EU may mean that the UK is called upon to provide assets without having a say in how they are used – a position with which none of the political parties would feel comfortable.

4 | How does your country operationalise a WGA?

In an article on 'joined-up government' published in 2002 (Ling 2002), Tom Ling suggested that there were four critical success factors for what was then called 'inter-agency cooperation'. These were: new ways of working across organisations evidenced by shared leadership, pooled budgets, merged structures and joint teams; new types of organisations with the concomitant requirement to establish new cultures and values, information and training systems; new accountabilities and incentives which would require the establishment of shared outcome targets, performance measures, regulations and systems of accountability; new ways of delivering services which will require joint consultation/involvement, shared client focus and shared customer interface. At various stages in the evolution of the UK's WGA, each of these critical success factors has been in evidence.

When the policy of 'joined-up government' was first promoted, there were clear tensions between the FCO, the MOD and the DFID, with each ministry feeling that its autonomy was being undermined. In order to promote greater cross-departmental collaboration, the government decided in 2001 to pool the resources of the three ministries in order to "develop a more formal, collective approach to addressing conflict prevention" (Cleary 2011: 45). Two funding pools were established: the Global Conflict Prevention Pool (GCPP) and the African Conflict Prevention Pool (ACPP). The three ministries agreed that any proposed project submitted to the pools should contribute to one of the following three aims (Ministry of Defence 2003: 13): first, to strengthen international and regional systems' capacity for conflict prevention, early warning, crisis management, conflict resolution/peacemaking, peacekeeping and peacebuilding; second, to contribute to global and regional conflict-prevention initiatives, such as curbing the proliferation of small arms and the diversion of resources to finance conflict; and, third, to promote initiatives in selected countries, including indigenous capacity-building, to help avert conflict, reduce violence and build sustainable security and peace.

Over time, those two pools would merge into one. In 2015, the government announced the establishment of the Conflict, Stability and Security Fund (CSSF) worth GBP 1.2 billion. That fund was described in the 2018 NSCR as enabling the government "to use the optimum combination of development, diplomacy, defence and security assistance rapidly and flexibly in countries at risk of conflict and instability" (HM Government 2018: 44). Its establishment is credited with enhancing the agility of response to crises, incentivising the joined-up use of capabilities, and funding assessed contributions to multilateral peacekeeping operations (ibid.).

It is the National Security Council that sets the strategic priorities of the CSSF, which are demonstrably linked to the national security objectives. Prior to 2015, the allocation of funds was achieved on the basis of agreement between the FCO, the MOD and the DFID. Research conducted by the author (Cleary 2011) has indicated that the FCO and the DFID were generally more successful at getting their projects funded because they tended to send more senior personnel capable of taking decisions to the deliberative committees.

The establishment of a series of operational delivery organisations, including the Security Sector Development Advisory Team, the Post-Conflict Reconstruction Unit and, later, the Stabilisation Unit, are all examples of the government's seeking to establish joint teams for the delivery of effect. Each of these organisations has been staffed in a similar way, with personnel seconded from the FCO, the MOD, the DFID and the Home Office. Each has relied on its ability to draw additional resources from other government departments as well as from consultants. And each has struggled in the first instance with engendering a shared culture among its seconded staff.

The 2010 establishment of a National Security Council is evidence of an attempt to create a new institution, but assessments of its effectiveness have been mixed. Given the way the conceptualisation of national security has changed, the establishment of an NSC is viewed as a welcome alternative to the previously informal attempts at inter-ministerial coordination. Those most closely associated with the NSC, however, suggest that it is falling short of its stated objectives, and that it could do more to set national strategy. Specifically, it could seek to "present a unifying national aim, especially in times of international crisis, and to further enhance inter-departmental coordination" (Thomson and Blagden 2018: 581).

This last point is particularly important given the conclusions of the Chilcot Inquiry into Iraq (Committee of Privy Councillors 2016). Published in July 2016, the Chilcot Report details the decision-making process that led to the UK's commitment of forces in Iraq in 2003. It made a number of criticisms of that process, stating that the assessment of risks and the capabilities required to address them was not as robust as it could and should have been, that there was insufficient coordination across government, and that ministries struggled to work across organisational boundaries.

Since the publication of the Chilcot Report, ministries have been at pains to demonstrate that they have taken on board the recommendations it made. This has led to efforts to improve oversight and accountability within ministries. For example, in 2017, the MOD published the Good Operation Handbook (Ministry of Defence 2017), which provides a checklist for the planning, delivery and review of an operation. It encourages personnel to bring critical thinking to bear and to resist groupthink. At a national level, the NSC is seeking to hold ministries to account by asking them to demonstrate how their individual and collective activities contribute to the attainment of the national security objectives. Their performance is also reviewed by a number of select committees within the House of Commons as well as by the National Audit Office.

Taken collectively, these efforts seek to inculcate a culture in which consultation and collaboration become the norm. Although there may be criticism of the formal structures that have been established, they have encouraged informal networking (see, e.g., Thomson and Blagden 2018). Civil servants in different ministries are discussing issues, generating scenarios and seeking to determine joint positions prior to ministerial meetings. This is a fairly significant cultural development and one that can lead to the generation of more effective doctrine for stabilisation operations (Ministry of Defence 2016). It is also of the utmost necessity to ensure a degree of policy continuity during periods of political crisis, such as that currently being experienced.

5 | Conclusions

In his book Exporting Security, Derek Reveron defined 'interagency' as "an adjective to describe a process of bringing together elements from across the government and not a noun to describe an organization that brings solutions" (Reveron 2010: 181). That process should be viewed as an iterative one – or, in other words, government should learn by doing.

As this report has highlighted, initial efforts at establishing a WGA in the UK were blighted by a number of fairly predictable occurrences. Different organisational cultures led to a competition over status, agendas and resources. This competition was reduced, although not completely eliminated, through the provision of clear political direction. In the first instance, ministries were forced to work together owing to the fact that their funding was pooled. The establishment of formal committee structures to determine the allocation of resources and the co-location of personnel from the FCO, the MOD, the DFID, and other ministries and agencies in overseas missions led to improvements in informal networking, which in turn led to further adjustments being made in the formal architecture.

The responsiveness and resilience of any system is only demonstrated when that system is placed under stress. UK operations in Iraq and Afghanistan certainly provided a test for the system, and elements of it were deemed to have failed. Since the publication of the Chilcot Report in 2016 (Committee of Privy Councillors 2016), all political parties and government ministries have declared their desire to learn from the mistakes of the past, which has led to the establishment of new institutions and accountability mechanisms as well as the adoption of new doctrines. Thus, one can conclude that a critical enabler for a successful WGA is to encourage an organisational culture that is reflective and capable of learning from mistakes.

Another key enabler is the provision of a unified purpose. The introduction of an NSS in 2008 (Cabinet Office 2008) and its subsequent linkage to a Strategic Defence and Security Review in 2010 (HM Government 2010) have succeeded in providing a conceptual framework for security from which all relevant ministries subsequently derive their purpose.

Britain's assessment of its strategic context has changed dramatically since 1989. In the initial post-Cold War period, there was no apparent existential threat. Operational commitments in Sierra Leone and the Balkans were relatively contained. However, 9/11 and the subsequent wars in Afghanistan and Iraq fundamentally altered how the UK viewed its security. From 2002 onwards, the risk posed by international terrorism would increasingly dominate the security debate within the UK. The London bombings in July 2005 painfully demonstrated that interventions overseas could have dire consequences for domestic security. The case for a WGA was firmly made.

As of 2019, the United Kingdom has a formal and centralised system that provides direction and coordinates activity across government. There is an established system for assessing global trends and security risks. There is a process for the regular review and revision of the National Security Strategy and associated doctrines. Internal and external accountability mechanisms are being continuously refined, and substantial funds for conflict response and development assistance have been set aside and ring-fenced.

The publication of the NSCR in 2018 (HM Government 2018) and its unveiling of the Fusion Doctrine demonstrate that WGA has now become the cultural norm. Government officials acknowledge that the promotion of a WGA has contributed to the development of a wider perspective on issues, reduced the extent of competition among ministries, improved the delivery of security, and ensured greater cost-effectiveness. It has, however, taken over 20 years to achieve that. The final lessons are that it takes time to develop a WGA, and that it will always be subject to further revision.

The 2018 'Global Britain' agenda (House of Commons Foreign Affairs Committee 2018) reflects the UK's determination to remain a global player, upholding the rules-based international system and contributing to the furtherance of global prosperity, peace and security. While the UK's future relationship with the EU remains in question, the desire to work on a multilateral basis to resolve conflict is not. In all the pronouncements on security that have been made in the last three years, there is a consistent recognition of the value of WGA, and that if the UK is to be a force for good in the world, then its overseas operations will need to be multi-phased, multi-dimensional, multi-level and multi-lateral. Given the consistency in policy prescriptions, we should expect to see modifications to WGA, specifically with reference to institutional and financial arrangements, as the British government seeks to operationalise the Fusion Doctrine. Now more than ever, the government needs to speak with one voice on security.

Bauman, Andrea Barbara (2010). "The UK's Approach to Stabilisation: the Comprehensive Approach in Action?" London: Chatham House. www.chathamhouse.org/publications/papers/view/109394.

Cabinet Office (2008). National Security Strategy of the United Kingdom: Security in an Interdependent World. London: Crown Copyright.

Cabinet Office (2009). National Security Strategy of the United Kingdom: Update 2009, Security for the Next Generation. London: Crown Copyright.

Cleary, Laura R. (2011). "Triggering Critical Mass: Identifying the factors for a successful defence transformation." *Defence Studies* (11) 1: 43–65.

Committee of Privy Councillors (2016). The Report of the Iraq Inquiry HC 264. London: Crown Copyright. https://webarchive.nationalarchives.gov.uk/20171123122743/http://www.iraqinquiry.org.uk/the-report/.

HM Government (2010). A Strong Britain in an Age of Uncertainty: The National Security Strategy. London: Crown Copyright.

HM Government (2015). National Security Strategy and Strategic Defence and Security Review: A Secure and Prosperous United Kingdom. London: Crown Copyright.

HM Government (2018). National Security Capability Review. London: Crown Copyright. www.gov.uk/government/uploads/system/uploads/attachment_data/file/705347/6.4391_CO_National-Security-Review_web.pdf.

House of Commons Defence Committee (2010). The Comprehensive Approach: the point of war is not just to win but to make a better peace. Seventh Report of Session 2009–2010. HC 224. 9 March 2010.

House of Commons Foreign Affairs Committee (2018). 6th Report Global Britain. HC 780. 12 March 2018.

House of Lords EU External Affairs Sub-Committee (2018). Brexit: Common Security and Defence Policy Missions and Operations. HL 132. 14 May 2018. https://publications.parliament.uk/pa/ld201719/ldselect/ldeucom/132/132.pdf.

Kampfner, John (2003). *Blair's Wars*. London: The Free Press.

Labour Party (1997). "New Labour because Britain deserves better." www.labour-party.org.uk/manifestos/1997/1997-labour-manifesto. shtml.

Lehne, Stefan (2012). *The Big Three in EU Foreign Policy*. Washington, D.C.: Carnegie Endowment for International Peace.

Ling, Tom (2002). "Delivering joined-up government in the UK: Dimensions, issues and problems." *Public Administration* 80: 615–642.

May, Theresa (2018a). Speech at the 2018 Munich Security Conference on 17 February 2018. www.gov.uk/government/speeches/pm -speech-at-munich-security-conference-17-february-2018.

May, Theresa (2018b). Speech to the Conservative Party Conference in Birmingham on 3 October 2018. www.politicshome.com/news/uk /political-parties/conservative-party/news/98760/read-full-theresa-mays-speech-2018.

MCDC (Multinational Capability Development Campaign) (2014). Understand to Prevent: The military contribution to the prevention of violent conflict. https://assets.publishing.service.gov.uk/go vernment/uploads/system/uploads/attachment_data/file/518617/ 20150430-U2P_Main_Web_B5.pdf.

Ministry of Defence (1998). Strategic Defence Review. London: Crown Copyright.

Ministry of Defence (2002). Strategic Defence Review: A New Chapter. London: Crown Copyright.

Ministry of Defence (2003). Delivering Security in a Changing World: Supporting Papers. Norwich: TSO. www.voltairenet.org/IMG/pdf/ es-volume2.pdf.

Ministry of Defence (2015). Policy Paper: 2010–2015 Government Policy: international defence commitments. www.gov.uk/govern-ment/publications/2010-to-2015-government-policy-international-defence-commitments/2010-to-2015-government-policy-internati onal-defence-commitments.

Ministry of Defence (2016). JDP 05 Shaping a Stable World: The Military Contribution. London: Crown Copyright.

Ministry of Defence (2017). The Good Operation Handbook. London: Crown Copyright.

Reveron, Derek (2010). *Exporting Security: International Engagement, Security Cooperation, and the Changing Face of the US Military*. Washington, D.C.: Georgetown University Press.

Seely, Bob, and James Rogers (2019). "Global Britain: a Twenty-First Century Vision." London: Henry Jackson Society. https://henryj acksonsociety.org/wp-content/uploads/2019/02/HJS-Global-Britai n-%C2%AD-A-Twenty-first-Century-Vision-Report-A4-web.pdf.

SU (Stabilisation Unit) (n.d.). About Us. www.gov.uk/government/or ganisations/stabilisation-unit/about (Accessed August 2019).

Stepputat, Finn, and Lauren Greenwood (2013). "Whole of Government Approaches to Fragile States and Situations." Copenhagen: Danish Institute for International Studies Report 2013:15. www. diis.dk/en/research/whole-of-government-approaches.

Thompson, Catrina P., and David Blagden (2018). "A Very British National Security State: Formal and informal institutions in the design of UK security policy." *British Journal of Politics and International Relations* (20) 3: 573–593. https://journals.sagepub.com/doi/ pdf/10.1177/1369148118784722.

The big picture:
Towards a whole-of-Europe approach to external conflict management

Loes Debuysere and Steven Blockmans

In recent years, efforts to implement a whole-of-government approach (WGA) to better coordinate responses to conflicts and crisis situations outside the EU's borders have increasingly taken centre stage in Europe. This volume has cast light on how the EU's institutions and member states have sought to conceptualise and operationalise such approaches to crisis response at the headquarters level. While labels to designate WGAs vary from one administration to another – ranging from a 'comprehensive' or an 'integrated' approach to a 'global' or a 'networked' approach – the goal is the same: to bring together the relevant policies, actors and tools into one holistic approach in order to increase the coherence of crisis responses abroad.

Based on the answers collected by the 28 country experts, this chapter seeks to make a comparative analysis of the various WGAs of the EU's institutions and member states. The four WGA enablers that have been identified in organisational literature and were outlined in this volume's introduction provide a framework for comparative analysis. These enablers include: (1) adaptations in institutional setups and structures (e.g. the creation of specific units or interdepartmental structures of coordination); (2) the presence of WGA-specific human resources (e.g. specialised staff or resources and WGA-related trainings); (3) the presence of political and administrative leadership that actively pushes for WGAs; and (4) the establishment of WGA instruments and tools (e.g. joint financial instruments, early warning, country/regional/sectoral strategies, joint analysis, and guidelines or rules of procedure informing the WGA conduct). Furthermore, the conclusion draws on the EU and country reports collected in this volume as well as the accompanying semi-structured surveys that inquired into conceptual, institutional and procedural changes at the headquarters level. Some survey questions included a simple scaling system (cf. Annex), on which the graphs and tables in this chapter are based.

To shed light on the core research question of whether institutional practices (deeds) have lived up to WGA commitments (words), the conclusion first looks into how different countries conceptualise WGAs by studying the scope and quality of country-specific WGA policies. Then, it compares how the relevant actors at all levels coordinate and cooperate in an effort to forge and execute a coherent conflict response. The next section provides an overview of some key success factors and obstacles that the country experts identified as being relevant when implementing a WGA in the realm of external crisis management. Finally, this concluding chapter ends with a WGA typology of EU member states, which sheds light on potential gaps between political rhetoric and institutional practice. Importantly, rather than attempting to rank EU member states, the typology simply classifies member states according to certain commonalities and differences.

WGA rhetoric in policy documents

The country reports and the surveys on which these are based underline that almost all member states have accepted that having a WGA is necessary if one wishes to tackle new and complex security challenges. Indeed, most EU member states have made either explicit or implicit policy commitments to a WGA to external conflict and crisis (cf. Figure 1). In almost two-thirds of the member states (64%), there are governmental documents that specifically address the concept of a WGA in external crisis management. In these countries, either one core WGA document (e.g. in Belgium, Denmark and the Netherlands) or a number of more sector-specific WGA policies (e.g. in Germany and Sweden) exist. Countries without an explicit WGA document (32%) generally have other policy documents (e.g. national security strategies) that contain one or more references to comprehensive action in the realm of external conflict and crisis.

National WGA documents have come into being at very different moments in time over the past two decades. Denmark, the UK and the Netherlands can be identified as pioneers in terms of developing an integrated or comprehensive approach to external crisis management, as they adopted a WGA policy as early as in the 2000s in the wake of the 1992 publication of UN Secretary-General Boutros Boutros Ghali's 'An Agenda for Peace' report and the peacebuilding debate at the level of the United Nations. Some other countries, such as Belgium and Croatia, have only adopted a WGA in recent years. In these latter countries, the 2016 EU Global Strategy (EUGS) served as an important source of inspiration for drafting a national WGA policy. In addition to the EUGS, WGA documents and practices of intergovernmental organisations have generally provided much inspiration to EU member states to adopt a WGA. For example, the UN's 2030 Agenda for Sustainable Development (e.g. in Belgium, Finland, Greece, Luxembourg and Poland), the guidelines of the OECD's Development Assistance Committee (OECD-DAC) (e.g. in Austria, Finland, France and Poland), or NATO's operational planning in Afghanistan (e.g. in Austria, the Czech Republic, Germany, Italy and Spain) have been of particular importance in spurring on the drafting of national WGAs to external conflict.

Figure 1: Is there a WGA framework for coordination and cooperation at the national level?

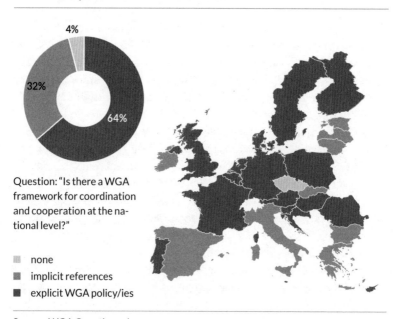

Question: "Is there a WGA framework for coordination and cooperation at the national level?"

- none
- implicit references
- explicit WGA policy/ies

Source: WGA Questionnaire

Overall, when taking into account both explicit and implicit commitments of all EU member states, the scope of WGA policies varies widely (cf. Table 1). While a relatively small group of member states have committed themselves to a narrow WGA (i.e. one that principally pushes for civilian-military coordination in conflict response and resolution), other countries seek to coordinate a wider approach combining the so-called three D's: development, defence and diplomacy. Increasingly, the latter is being expanded to a system-wide approach that encompasses all dimensions relevant to conflict management, including trade, justice and internal affairs. This is in line with the EU's multidimensional 'integrated approach' to external crisis and conflict as outlined in the 2016 EUGS. An interesting finding is that bigger and more populous member states do not automatically adopt a system-wide approach to external conflict and crisis. For example, the WGA policies of Spain and France have a more limited scope.

Table 1: What is the scope of the national WGA policy?

System-wide	Belgium, Croatia, Denmark, Germany, Greece, Latvia, Netherlands, Slovenia, UK
Medium to system-wide	Austria, Estonia, Finland, Poland, Romania
Medium	France, Hungary, Ireland, Italy, Lithuania, Luxembourg, Slovakia, Sweden
Narrow to medium	Cyprus, Portugal
Narrow	Spain
N/A	Bulgaria, Czech Republic, Malta

narrow = civil-military coordination; medium = diplomacy, security, development and humanitarian aid; system-wide = also including economy and trade
Source: WGA Questionnaire

A number of caveats should be taken into account when assessing the data in Table 1. First, many member states with a relatively narrow WGA policy at the national level do take part in comprehensive WGA missions organised by the EU or other intergovernmental organisations. Indeed, a lack of national resources for external conflict management is often remedied by active support and involvement in, for example, CSDP missions. Moreover, adopting a system-wide approach on paper does not necessarily mean operationalising a system-wide approach in practice. Paper commitments are often more ambitious than actual WGA implementation at the headquarters level (cf. infra). What's more, the scope of a WGA may shift from narrow to system-wide depending on the nature of the specific crisis or conflict that is being addressed by the member state.

When looking into the geographical focus that member states adopt in their WGA policies, small to medium-sized countries (e.g. Croatia, Cyprus, Greece, Latvia, Lithuania, Malta and Romania) generally focus their WGA-related attention on neighbouring countries and regions that may pose a direct threat or lead to negative spillover on the domestic level. Similarly, the thematic focus of these countries' WGAs is often in line with the specific type of 'threats' they face (e.g. maritime crises for Cyprus and Malta, migration flows for Slovakia and Slovenia, or hybrid threats for the Baltic states). On the other hand, the WGA remit of the above-mentioned 'pioneering' and bigger EU member states tends to extend worldwide, with African, Pacific and Caribbean countries often figuring as priority areas for former colonial powers (e.g. France, Italy and the UK). These WGAs often encompass actions related to the whole conflict cycle, ranging from prevention to stabilisation to peacebuilding.

Where they do exist, WGA documents are generally considered of high quality and a matter of good governance. However, most country experts identified the actual paper-to-praxis transition of these WGAs as a crucial challenge, with many member states lacking concrete and binding guidelines on how to implement and enforce WGA policies. The next sections look into how WGA policies are operationalised at the headquarters level.

WGA operationalisation and institutional practice

One would expect that operationalising a WGA to external conflict and crisis requires sufficient coordination and cooperation among the relevant actors (cf. Table 2). In most EU member states, inter-ministerial cooperation (e.g. between the ministries of foreign affairs and defence) is generally quite formalised and well-established. The same holds true for coordination with relevant EU actors and other international organisations, such as the African Union, NATO, the OSCE and the UN. Much less formalised or sometimes wholly absent is cooperation with parliament and civil society. In part, this has to do with the fact that parliaments are rarely a key (f)actor in responses to conflicts given the typically fast-paced nature of the latter. Nevertheless, parliaments often hold significant budgetary powers and the final say over the deployment of military personnel to conflict areas.

When assessing the data collected in Table 2, it is important to keep in mind that more formalised coordination does not necessarily imply more successful WGA practice. Country experts for some member states, such as the Czech Republic and Ireland, argue that informal WGA practice suffices to bring the relevant actors together in an effective way. Moreover, formalised and informal coordination often go hand in hand and complement one another. This applies to the EU as well, where crisis (platform) meetings are convened both via WhatsApp as well as via the formal meeting requests of geographical desk officers of the EEAS. While Table 2 shows the most prevalent form of coordination in the member states, it is not meant to indicate that other forms of coordination or cooperation do not exist in any given country.

Table 2: Percentage of EU member states that have fostered certain types of coordination/cooperation which may contribute to the operationalisation of a WGA to external conflict and crisis

Type of coordination/ cooperation	Well-established, formalised coordination	Some kind of coordination, often more informal	No cooperation
Inter-ministerial	71%	29%	0%
Intra-ministerial	57%	43%	0%
Intra-parliamentary	50%	32%	18%
Between executive and parliament	43%	50%	7%
With civil society	29%	61%	11%
With EU institutions and actors	75%	25%	0%
With NATO, OECD-DAC, OSCE, the UN	71%	29%	0%

Source: WGA Questionnaire

Figures 2–5: Percentage of EU member states with administrative structures and procedures changed to implement WGA policies (Source: WGA Questionnaire)

Figure 2: Institutional changes and setup

Question: "Is there a set of special structures or arrangements in place to make a WGA happen?"

Figure 3: Leadership

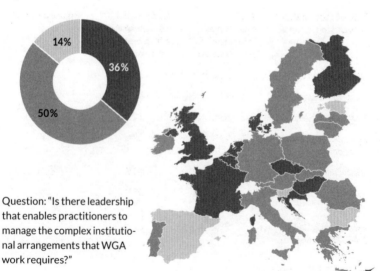

Question: "Is there leadership that enables practitioners to manage the complex institutional arrangements that WGA work requires?"

Figure 4: (Non-)financial instruments and tools

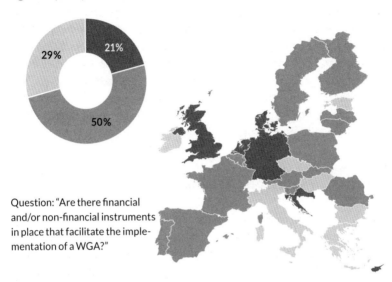

Question: "Are there financial and/or non-financial instruments in place that facilitate the implementation of a WGA?"

Figure 5: Human resources

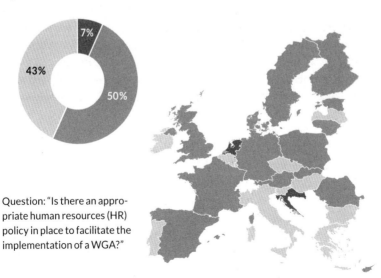

Question: "Is there an appropriate human resources (HR) policy in place to facilitate the implementation of a WGA?"

In addition to effective coordination and cooperation between the relevant actors, WGA-related literature also identifies that (1) adaptations in the institutional setup and structures, (2) WGA-targeted human resources, (3) the presence of WGA leadership, and (4) joint tools and instruments facilitate the implementation of a WGA. The figures above (Figures 2–5) provide an overview of the presence of these four enablers in the member states. It shows how the EU member states have mainly relied on changes in the institutional setup of their administration to foster a WGA (with almost 90% of the member states having made either minor or significant changes in that realm), while a specific human resources policy adapted to implementing a WGA is much less prevalent (with just over half of the member states featuring some changes in this realm).

Identifying WGA success factors

These four institutional WGA enablers have been present to varying degrees and with varying degrees of success in the EU and its member states. First, in terms of adaptations to the institutional setup and structures, WGAs to external conflict and crisis are often facilitated by formal inter-ministerial steering groups, joint crisis-management centres or national security councils. The key players and drivers behind these structures are generally the ministry of foreign affairs and/or the ministry of defence. More ad hoc or informal ways of WGA operationalisation can also be found, sometimes even in addition to formal structures. For instance, ad hoc crisis coordination happens through gatherings or temporary centres that deal with one particular crisis theatre, such as the Sahel region (e.g. in the Czech Republic and France) or Libya (e.g. in Malta).

The extent to which these formal and informal bodies are effective in fostering coordination varies significantly. Some of the member states with the most robust WGAs in place have highly formalised WGA structures. The presence of a central crisis hub, for example, which is in charge of facilitating a WGA to external crisis response, can help in facilitating inter- and intra-ministerial cooperation. Examples of crisis hubs, beyond those in the pioneering countries, include the crisis management centre in Cyprus, the steering group of the comprehensive approach in Belgium, a newly designated department in Germany's Federal Foreign Office, and the new Directorate ISP at the EU level. Another way of facilitating a successful WGA is through the introduction of a WGA mandate for the ministry of foreign affairs. In countries such as Belgium, Hungary, Italy, Luxembourg and the Netherlands, the ministry of foreign affairs is also responsible for the portfolios of development, international cooperation and/or international trade. This fosters better synergies between different dimensions (trade, development, defence) of external crisis management.

However, drawing from experiences in other member states, the presence of a specific WGA policy and/or formalised WGA structures do not appear to be a conditio sine qua non for effective coordination or cooperation in the realm of external crisis management. In fact, there are countries that coordinate quite well among relevant actors without having one specific WGA policy document in place (e.g. the Czech Republic, Ireland and Luxembourg). Similarly, a number of countries (e.g. the Czech Republic, Ireland, Malta and Slovenia) manage to operationalise their WGA in an informal and/or ad hoc way without having established formal and/or permanent structures and processes.

Second, leadership that provides clear political WGA direction is identified as being crucial for enabling a WGA. Successful leadership can take the form of top-down political steering (e.g. in France), while what matters most in other cases is the positive role that individual personalities play within the administration (e.g. in Italy and Malta). A combination of both political and administrative leadership is perceived as being ideal for the operationalisation of a WGA. However, the country case studies also illustrate how leadership may actually hamper effective WGA coordination and cooperation. Indeed, leadership that is particularly centralised and authoritarian, such as that in Hungary and Poland, may undermine transparency and multilateral cooperation, both of which are key for a successful WGA.

Third, WGA tools and instruments (e.g. WGA guidelines, joint lessons learned procedures and mechanisms for information sharing) are generally not (yet) very institutionalised in EU member states, except in the pioneering countries. Overall, many country experts noted that there is a high risk of losing institutional knowledge over time. To remedy this problem, a process of joint lessons learned is needed as well as the development of designated bodies, accountability mechanisms and doctrines. Moreover, while joint budgets are identified as being a key tool to successfully operationalise a WGA to external conflict and crisis, most member states have not (yet) set up such pooled funding mechanisms.

There are, however, a number of positive exceptions. Denmark has a 'Peace and Stabilisation Fund' managed by an inter-ministerial secretariat, which includes representatives from the Prime Minister's Office and the ministries of Foreign Affairs, Defence and Justice. The 'Conflict, Stability and Security Fund' in the UK pools finances across the Treasury, the Foreign and Commonwealth Office, the Ministry of Defence, and the Department for International Development. The Netherlands has two joint budgets for coordinated international crisis management: the 'International Security Budget', which is based on inter-ministerial decisions, and the more operational 'Stability Fund', based in the Ministry of Foreign Affairs. The 'Enable & Enhance Initiative' in Germany is another example of a budget that is financed and administered jointly by its Federal Foreign Office and Ministry of Defence.

Fourth, most member states have not set up a specific human resources policy to improve the administration's WGA to external crisis response and conflict management. Exceptions include some countries that organize joint trainings (e.g. France, Germany and Sweden) or secondments and rotation schemes that foster inter-ministerial and inter-organisational staff exchanges (e.g. Finland, Germany, the Netherlands and Slovakia). The latter also applies to the secondment of secretarial staff from the European Parliament to the EEAS. Human resources that foster WGAs are often identified as a realm in need of improvement.

Apart from these four enablers, the country case studies also shed light on a number of additional success factors that are relevant in the realm of external crisis management. Recurrent in many country reports is the positive influence of the WGAs of various international organisations – whether the EU or other multilateral bodies (e.g. the OECD, NATO and the UN) – on the development of national WGAs. Indeed, many national WGAs have been patterned after WGA documents of the EU and other multilateral organisations. Moreover, direct political exposure to the EU institutions has also driven further development of national WGAs. For example, the fact that a Cypriot once served as EU Commissioner for Humanitarian Aid and Crisis Management facilitated the setup of Cyprus' WGA to external crisis management. Similarly, the first Slovene presidency of the Council of the EU, in early 2008, provided the strongest push for developing Slovenia's WGA.

Table 3: Overview of WGA success factors

- ► Adaptations to the institutional setup and structures
  - • A central crisis hub
  - • A WGA mandate for the ministry of foreign affairs
- ► Leadership
  - • Top-down political leadership
  - • Administrative leadership
- ► WGA tools and instruments
  - • Joint lessons learned procedures
  - • Pooled budgets
- ► WGA human resources
  - • Trainings
  - • Staff rotation schemes and secondments
- ► Positive influence of existing WGAs of international organisations
  - • Inspiration from multilateral policy documents
  - • Active multilateral participation
- ► Country-specific success factors
  - • Smaller-sized administrations
  - • Geostrategic location
  - • Conducive national culture and history

Source: WGA Questionnaire

There are also a number of more country-specific success factors. The size of a country may impact the country's success in implementing a WGA. Smaller member states (e.g. Estonia, Ireland, Luxembourg and Malta) tend to have smaller administrations that facilitate frequent exchanges and personal ties between policymakers, a plus for a successful WGA culture. Indeed, the absence of a huge bureaucratic hierarchy makes communication easier and the distance between leadership and public servants smaller. Conversely, while small-sized countries may find it easier to set up effective coordination between and within different ministries, they also often lack sufficient financial and human resources to effectively implement a WGA system. A lack of (non-)financial resources is more generally identified as being a key obstacle to successful WGA implementation.

Another country-specific success factor constitutes the geostrategic location of a country, which may foster the political will to implement WGAs to external threats. By way of example, the flow of refugees and migrants stemming from the Middle East have put the issue of a comprehensive approach to this 'crisis' higher on the political agenda in, for example, Cyprus and Greece. A country's national culture and history is a final factor that may impact the implementation of WGAs. For example, in some countries (e.g. Austria, Germany and Sweden), constitutional provisions aimed at preventing concentrations of power by allocating leadership responsibilities to multiple parties as well as at fostering negotiation and compromise in the political process also affect the implementation of WGAs.

Gaps between rhetoric and practice: a typology

While almost two-thirds of EU member states have one or more WGA policies in place, the track record of actually implementing and operationalising a WGA at the headquarters level is much more mixed. A tentative typology based on an assessment of the above-mentioned variables in the EU member states differentiates between five groups of states with varying gaps between political rhetoric and institutional practice.

A first, marked group consists of the WGA pioneers – Denmark, the Netherlands and the UK – which have already been developing their WGA to external conflict and crisis for a generation. These countries have one core WGA policy document in place that features an ambitious, system-wide scope. Their WGAs are operationalised in a formal and centralised way as well as facilitated by a joint budget instrument. These countries are generally perceived as having a high-quality performance in both WGA policy and practice.

A second group consists of smaller member states with rather successful WGA coordination in the realm of external conflict and crisis. This group includes countries such as Belgium, Cyprus, Croatia, the Czech Republic, Ireland and Luxembourg, which have very different levels of explicit/implicit WGA policy and formal/informal WGA practice. For example, while Belgium and Cyprus have one core WGA policy document with fixed institutional structures that facilitate a WGA, Ireland and the Czech Republic lack a WGA policy and formalised structures but still function in a coordinated way, albeit in a more informal and ad hoc manner. The small size of these countries is generally perceived as facilitating coordination and cooperation between and within different ministries and services (with the exception of Belgium, with its institutional complexity). This group of member states is often inspired by the integrated or comprehensive approaches of the EU and/or other multilateral organisations.

A third group, which includes France and Germany but also the EU, are key players in external crisis management with an ambitious yet inconsistent WGA record. While they differ greatly in terms of their practical implementation, these players have WGA policies with broad geographical ambitions. And even if there are formal structures in place to implement these policies, the 'siloed' culture between the different services and ministries is difficult to overcome. Leadership plays a key role in driving a WGA forward.

A fourth group consists of small and medium-sized member states that, despite having some WGA policies and commitments in place, still face shortcomings in terms of WGA implementation. This group includes countries such as Austria, Finland, Portugal, Romania, Slovenia and Sweden. One sub-category within this group are member states with strong (authoritarian) leadership, such as Hungary and Poland. While a power vertical may help in taking coordinated WGA decisions, a culture of 'divide and rule' and a lack of transparent institutions may simultaneously undermine effective cooperation.

Finally, there is a group of countries with national WGA policies and structures that are not very developed. This group includes both bigger member states (e.g. Italy and Spain) and smaller to medium-sized member states, including countries in the Baltic region (e.g. Estonia and Lithuania), in Central and Eastern Europe (e.g. Slovakia), and in Southern Europe (e.g. Greece and Malta). Due to limited resources, either in general or specifically allocated to external crisis management, these countries generally lack formalised structures to operationalise a WGA. However, in recent years, some of these countries have been trying to upgrade their WGA performance in external crisis response and conflict management, principally within a broader EU framework.

All in all, it is clear that WGAs to external conflict and crisis have become more and more sophisticated over the years in both the EU and its member states. Several factors – including institutional adaptations, decisive leadership, pooled budgeting and multilateral exchanges – have helped to translate paper commitments into actual WGA practice at the headquarters level. Despite the many shortcomings that still exist, a whole-of-Europe approach to external conflict and crisis management is – at least at the headquarters level – slowly in the making.

About the Authors

EU | *Loes Debuysere*

Loes Debuysere is a Researcher in the Foreign Policy Unit of the Centre for European Policy Research (CEPS), a Brussels-based thinktank. Her expertise and publications are situated at the intersections of conflict studies, democratisation theories and gender politics. She has worked extensively on the EU's integrated approach to external conflict and crisis, for example as a Researcher in a H2020 project on the EU's conflict sensitivity in external crisis response. Loes was previously a Schuman Trainee at the DG for External Policies of the European Parliament and holds a PhD in Conflict and Development Studies from the University of Ghent.

EU | *Steven Blockmans*

Steven Blockmans is Head of the Europe in the World programme at the Centre for European Policy Research (CEPS), a Brussels-based thinktank, and Professor of EU External Relations Law and Governance at the University of Amsterdam. He is the author of Tough Love: the EU's Relations with the Western Balkans (Asser Press, 2007) and The Obsolescence of the European Neighbourhood Policy (Rowman & Littlefield, 2017) in addition to having published widely on the EU's integrated approach to external action. He served as the Leading Rapporteur of task forces on 'More Union in European Defence' chaired by Javier Solana (2015) and 'Regroup and Reform: Ideas for a More Responsive and Effective European Union' (2017). Steven is a frequent media commentator and regularly advises governments of countries in wider Europe and in Asia on their relations with the EU. Before joining CEPS in 2012, he was Head of Research at the Asser Institute, an international law centre based in The Hague. From 2010 to 2014, he was a special visiting professor at the Law Faculty of the University of Leuven. Steven holds a PhD in International Law from Leiden University.

Austria | *Cristian Strohal*

Christian Strohal is a senior Austrian diplomat. After having served from 2013 to 2016 as Austria's Permanent Representative to the Organization for Security and Co-operation in Europe (OSCE) in Vienna, he was nominated to be Special Representative for Austria's OSCE Chairmanship in 2017. Since retiring, he has been a Senior Adviser to the current Slovak OSCE Chair-in Office and a non-resident Fellow at the Liechtenstein Institute on Self-Determination (LISD), which is affiliated with Princeton University. From 2008 to 2013, Christian represented Austria at the UN Office, the Conference on Disarmament and other international organisations in Geneva. From 2003 to 2008, he was Director of the Office for Democratic Institutions and Human Rights (ODIHR) of the OSCE. Between 2007 and 2012, he also served as an alternate Member of the Management Board of the EU Fundamental Rights Agency. Earlier functions include Ambassador for the 1993 Vienna World Conference on Human Rights; Director for Human Rights at Austria's Ministry for Europe, Integration and Foreign Affairs; and Ambassador to Luxembourg. Christian was educated in Vienna, London and Geneva and holds a Dr.iur. from the University of Vienna. He has also held lecturing positions at various institutions and published a number of articles.

Austria | *Ursula Werther-Pietsch*

Ursula Werther-Pietsch works in Austria's Ministry for Europe, Integration and Foreign Affairs, served as Senior Visiting Fellow at the National Defence Academy, and is one of the founders of Austria's 3C approach. She is Professor of International Law and International Relations and teaches at various academic institutions, including the Diplomatic Academy of Vienna, the National Defence Academy and the Bundeswehr University Munich. Prior to that, she was Head of Unit at the Bureau of the Legal Adviser and the Constitutional Service at the Federal Chancellery. Before entering into public service, she was an Assistant at the universities of Graz and Vienna. Ursula is an Adviser to the master's degree programme of the Academic Forum for Foreign Policy and a Member of the Scientific Commission of the Ministry of Defence. She is founder of the journal Juristische Ausbildung und Praxis and has published widely, including the books Human Rights and Inclusive Societies (2014), International Crisis and Conflict Management (2017), Women as Drivers for Peace (2019), and The Collective Security System of the UN (forthcoming). Ursula studied Law, Architecture and French, and holds a PhD in Law from the University of Graz.

Austria | *Markus Gauster*

Markus Gauster has been a Senior Researcher at the Institute for Peace Support and Conflict Management (IFK) of Austria's National Defence Academy since 2004. He holds a master's degree in Law and a doctorate in Political Science from the universities of Graz and Vienna, and earned a certificate in Broadcast Journalism from the Danube University Krems. He was also active in the private sector and is a Reserve Officer in the Austrian Armed Forces. His research areas include conflict transformation in Afghanistan, civil-military interaction in peace operations, and innovative concepts for international crisis management (e.g. whole-of-nation approaches for coherent action in situations of conflict and fragility). Gauster undertook fact-finding missions in Afghanistan and its strategic environment, including as a long-term Election Observer for the European Union. He has written various articles and publications, and is a member of the International Society of Military Sciences as well as of the executive board of the Vienna-based Austria-Afghanistan Society.

Austria | *Hans Lampalzer*

Colonel Hans Lampalzer currently works at the Institute for Peace Support and Conflict Management (IFK) of Austria's National Defence Academy in Vienna. After graduating from the Theresian Military Academy in 1991, he held various posts in the Austrian Armed Forces in addition to studying Translation Studies and Political Science at the University of Vienna. He also earned a doctorate in Intervention Research from the University of Klagenfurt, where his studies focused on the links between intercultural questions and security. Lampalzer has lectured to military and civilian audiences at, among others, the European Security and Defence College, the George C. Marshall European Center for Security Studies, the FHS St. Gallen University of Applied Sciences in Switzerland, and several Austrian universities. He served at the Kosovo Force Headquarters in 2002 and 2003, has experience as an ODIHR Election Observer, and worked part-time from 2008 to 2015 for the Austrian Verification Center, especially in Russia and Belarus. From 2016 to 2017, he was Head of the OSCE High-Level Planning Group under the German and Austrian chairmanship. From May 2018 to March 2019, he served as a Liaison Officer to Austria's Federal Ministry for European and International Affairs. In this position, in the second half of 2018, he served as a National Delegate to the Friends of the Presidency Group for Countering Hybrid Threats while Austria held the presidency of the Council of the European Union. His current research focuses on security-sector reform, and he is also responsible for the implementation of the Ministry of Defence's contribution to the OSCE Armenia Co-operation Programme.

Belgium | *Alain Spoiden*

Alain Spoiden is Honorary Colonel (General Staff) and a former officer in the Belgian Army. He currently is a Counsellor within the Public Centre for Social Welfare in Aubange, Belgium. As a junior officer, he was Battery Commander within an Air Defence Artillery battalion in Germany. After the fall of the Berlin Wall, he held various staff positions in the General Intelligence and Security Service in Brussels, joined the Eurocorps HQ in Strasbourg, and was deployed to Pristina, Kosovo, within NATO's KFOR 3 HQ. After that experience, he was appointed Director of Scientific Research at the Centre of Defence Studies and, later, as Director of the High Defence Studies of the Royal High Institute for Defence (RHID) in Brussels. He was posted as an Intelligence Officer for the UN Strategic Military Cell in New York. Alain ended his career as Military Adviser helping to prepare for Belgium's EU presidency (2010) and, afterwards, at the Belgian Military Representation to the EU in Brussels. He served in the Army Reserve after his retirement as Faculty Adviser at the RHID.

Bulgaria | *Antoinette Primatarova*

Antoinette Primatarova has been Director of the European Programme of the Sofia-based thinktank Centre for Liberal Strategies (CLS) since 2002. She is a Member of the National Advisory Board of the Diplomatic Institute attached to the Ministry of Foreign Affairs of Bulgaria. Prior to joining the CLS, she held various positions within the Bulgarian diplomatic service. From 1993 to 1997, she was based in Stockholm as

Bulgaria's Ambassador to Sweden, Norway and Iceland. From 1997 to 2001, she was directly involved in the process of Bulgaria's preparation for EU accession as Deputy Minister of Foreign Affairs (1997–1999), Ambassador to the European Communities and Head of the Bulgarian Mission to the EC in Brussels (1999–2001), and Deputy Chief Negotiator (2000–2001). Antoinette holds a master's degree in Germanic Studies from the University in Leipzig, and pursued an academic career at the University of Sofia prior to joining the diplomatic service.

Croatia | *Tonci Prodan*

Tonci Prodan is currently working as Director of the private security consulting company Portus Et Navem in Split, Croatia. He is active on several national and international security projects covering a broad spectrum of security issues, such as counter-terrorism and other contemporary security threats. Furthermore, he is also active as an Interim Lecturer at the University Department of Forensic Sciences in Split and two other private institutions. Prior to joining Portus Et Navem, Tonci served as Assistant Director of the Office of the National Security Council of the Republic of Croatia. He has been professionally involved in issues related to national security for a number of years, and this has expanded to international security in recent years. Tonci holds a PhD in Comparative Politics from the University of Zagreb.

Cyprus | *James Ker-Lindsay*

James Ker-Lindsay is Visiting Professor at LSEE-Research on South East Europe, European Institute, London School of Economics and Political Science, and a Research Associate at the Centre for International Studies, Department of Politics and International Relations, Oxford University. His research focuses on conflict, peace and security in the Eastern Mediterranean and Western Balkans, and he has published 14 books. In addition to his academic work, James has served as an Adviser to a number of international bodies, including the United Nations, the Council of Europe, and the Foreign and Commonwealth Office. He is also a regular media commentator on regional affairs. James holds a BSc in Economics from London University and an MA and PhD in International Conflict Analysis from the University of Kent.

Czech Republic | *Vit Dostal*

Vit Dostal is a Research Center Director at the Association for International Affairs (AMO), a non-partisan thinktank based in Prague. He focuses on Czech foreign and European policy, Central European cooperation, and Polish foreign and domestic policy. Vit has worked for AMO since 2006. During that time, he has authored or edited many publications dealing with Czech foreign policy and Central Europe. He completed a PhD programme on European Studies at Masaryk University in Brno in 2017 with a dissertation titled 'Paradiplomacy of Czech Regions – Regions as Actors of International Relations'.

Denmark | *Peter Viggo Jakobsen*

Peter Viggo Jakobsen is Professor at the Institute for Strategy at the Royal Danish Defence College and (part-time) Professor at the Center for War Studies of the University of Southern Denmark. He has acted as an Adviser and Consultant for several governments and international organisations, is frequently asked by Danish and international media sources to be a commentator on defence and security issues, has won awards for his teaching and public dissemination skills, and has written extensively on civil-military cooperation and the integrated approach, coercive diplomacy, Danish and Nordic foreign and security policy, NATO, peace and stabilisation operations, the UN, and the use of military force. Peter holds a PhD in International Relations from the University of Aarhus, Denmark.

Estonia | *Maili Vilson*

Maili Vilson is currently working as a PhD Research Fellow and PhD Programme Coordinator at the Johan Skytte Institute of Political Studies and at the Centre for EU-Russia Studies (CEURUS), both at the University of Tartu (Estonia). She is finishing a dissertation on the Europeanisation of national foreign policy of EU member states. Previously, Maili was involved in UPTAKE, an EU-funded twinning project in the field of Russian and East European Studies, and has served as a Country Expert on Estonia for several thinktanks. She has published on the Europeanisation of foreign policy as well as on the Eastern Partnership. She holds an MA in EU-Russia Studies from the University of Tartu.

Estonia | *Kristi Raik*

Kristi Raik has been Director of the Estonian Foreign Policy Institute at the International Centre for Defence and Security in Tallinn since February 2018. She is also an Adjunct Professor at the University of Turku (Finland). Her previous positions have included being a Senior Research Fellow and Acting Programme Director at the Finnish Institute of International Affairs in Helsinki; an official at the General Secretariat of the Council of the European Union in Brussels; and a Visiting Fellow at the Centre for European Policy Studies in Brussels and the International Centre for Policy Studies in Kyiv. Kristi holds a PhD from the University of Turku. She has published, lectured and commented widely on European foreign and security policy.

Finland | *Juha Jokela*

Juha Jokela is Director of the European Union research programme at the Finnish Institute of International Affairs. He previously worked in the EU Institute for Security Studies as a Senior Associated Analyst and Senior Visiting Research Fellow, as an Adviser in the Ministry for Foreign Affairs of Finland, and as a Research Fellow and Director of the Network for European Studies of the University of Helsinki. Juha holds a PhD from the University of Bristol (UK), and is a member of the board of Trans-European Policy Studies Association (TEPSA). His current research interests include the political implications of Brexit, differentiated integration (in the EU's external relations), and EU sanction policies. His previous projects and publications covered issues including security developments in the Arctic, the political dimension of the EMU re-forms, the EU's role in the G20, the EU's Asia policies, the Europeanisation of foreign and security policy, and Finland's EU policies.

France | *Francois Gaulme*

Francois Gaulme is currently Associate Researcher at the Africa Centre of the Institut francais des relations internationales (IFRI) in Paris. He has specialised in African and fragility-related issues for his entire professional life. Prior to serving in the Globalisa-tion Directorate-General of France's Ministry for Europe and Foreign Affairs and in the French Development Agency (AFD), Francois was a Teacher in Africa and an Edi-tor for the publications Marchés tropicaux and Afrique contemporaine. He holds a PhD in Ethnology as well as a Doctor in Arts from the Sorbonne University in Paris.

Germany | *Stefani Weiss*

Stefani Weiss is currently working as Senior Expert in the Bertelsmann Stiftung's 'Fu-ture of Europe' programme. She is based in Brussels and a Resident Expert on a broad spectrum of European and international relations. She was a Member of the German Federal Government's Advisory Board for Civil Crisis Prevention until 2017, and pub-lished the book Diplomacy, Development and Defense: A Paradigm for Policy Coher-ence. A Comparative Analysis of International Strategies in 2010. Before joining the Stiftung, she was Director of Research on European Law and Policy at the Gustav Stresemann Institute in Bonn (Germany), Assistant to the president of Atlantik-Bruecke e.V. in Berlin, and Lecturer/Project Manager in the Department of Political Science of the University of Bonn. Stefani holds an MA in Political Science, Sociology, and International and Public Law from the University of Bonn.

Greece | *Giorgos Triantafyllou*

Giorgos Triantafyllou is a Research Fellow at the South-East Europe Programme of the Hellenic Foundation for European & Foreign Policy (ELIAMEP) and a Research As-sociate at the Center for Security Studies (KEMEA) of Greece's Ministry for Citizen Protection. Based in Athens, his research interests include international and Euro-pean security, conflict in the Balkans, security and migration, international institu-tions and peace operations, peacebuilding and statebuilding, NATO and the EU. Gior-gos previously worked as a Consultant for the Western Balkans and the Peacebuilding programmes of the New York-based Rockefeller Brothers Fund. From 2008 to 2012, he was an Assistant Lecturer at the University of Kent, where he taught International History, International Relations and International Governance. Giorgos holds a PhD and MA in International Conflict Analysis from the University of Kent, where he fo-cused on the provision of security during peacebuilding operations in the Balkans. He also holds a BA in International and European Studies from Panteion University in Athens.

Hungary | *Gyorgy Tatar*

Gyorgy Tatar, a retired career diplomat, currently serves as Chair of the Board of Trustees of the Foundation for the International Prevention of Genocide and Mass Atrocities of the Budapest Centre for Mass Atrocities Prevention. Prior to joining the Foundation, he was Head of the Task Force for Horizontal Security Issues and Conflict Prevention in the Policy Planning and Early Warning Unit of the EU High Representative for Common Foreign and Security Policy between 2004 and 2010. Between 1977 and 2004, Gyorgy worked in Hungary's Ministry of Foreign Affairs, where his positions included Commissioner of the Minister for the affairs of the Gabcikovo-Nagymaros Water Dam and EXPO'96, Chief of Cabinet of the State Secretary for EU Integration, and Coordinator of the EU Common Foreign and Security Policy. He served in the Hungarian Embassies in Baghdad, Prague and Vienna. Gyorgy is a graduate of the Moscow State University for International Relations. He also holds a PhD in International Economic Relations from the University of Economics in Budapest.

Ireland | *Isaac Bennett*

Isaac Bennett is a second-year PhD Researcher at the UCD School of Politics and International Relations in Dublin. His research focuses on the relationship between advanced military technology and casualty aversion in democratic countries. Prior to this research, Isaac worked as the owner and operator of Bennett Research Services, a political and security affairs consultancy. He was engaged in several projects for lobby groups and individuals, including a large, in-depth analysis of alleged police and judicial corruption in Ireland (2015). Between 2015 and 2017, he worked for the Cork County Council as part of a change management team to improve local government service provision to citizens and to enhance communication links via a new website. Isaac holds a BA in History and Political Science from Trinity College Dublin (2012), and an MA in International Security and Conflict Studies from Dublin City University (2014).

Ireland | *Ben Tonra*

Ben Tonra is Full Professor of International Relations at the UCD School of Politics and International Relations in Dublin. There, he teaches, researches and publishes on European foreign, security and defence policy; Irish foreign, security and defence policy; and the theory of international relations. Outside the university, he has served as Chair of the Royal Irish Academy's Standing Committee on International Affairs and is a Co-leader of a research programme on EU security and defence at the Institute of International and European Affairs (IIEA) in Dublin. In Ireland, he has also lectured for and worked with the Department of Foreign Affairs and Trade, the Department of Defence, and the Defence Forces. Previously, he was a Lecturer at the Department of International Politics of the University of Wales (Aberystwyth) and a Research Associate at the Center for Strategic and International Studies (CSIS) in Washington, DC. Ben is a graduate of the University of Limerick (BA and MA) and completed his doctoral studies at the University of Dublin (Trinity College) in 1996.

Italy | *Luca Giansanti*

Luca Giansanti is a former Diplomat with the Italian foreign service. He is currently based in Brussels, where he deals with European government affairs for a public company. After joining the diplomatic service in 1984, Luca held various positions, including Director General for Political Affairs/Political Director, Ambassador to Iran, Ambassador to the EU Political and Security Committee, Director General for Multilateral Political Cooperation and Human Rights, Deputy Director General for European Integration, and CFSP/CSDP Coordinator. He holds degrees in Political Science from the Institut d'Etudes Politiques (SciencesPo) in Paris and the LUISS university in Rome.

Latvia | *Maris Andzans*

Maris Andzans is currently a Visiting Fulbright Scholar at the Foreign Policy Institute of the Johns Hopkins University School of Advanced International Studies in Washington, DC. He is a Research Fellow at the Latvian Institute of International Affairs and an Assistant Professor at Riga Stradins University. Maris has a decade of experience in the public administration of Latvia, where he served in various positions related to the coordination of EU and NATO issues, security of transport and communications, civil-military cooperation, aviation, electronic communications and postal issues. He has also chaired the National Cyber Security Council of Latvia and the Dangerous Goods Movement Consultative Council of Latvia. Maris holds a PhD in Political Science from Riga Stradins University.

Lithuania | *Dovile Jakniunaite*

Dovile Jakniunaite is Professor at the Institute of International Relations and Political Science of Vilnius University and Head of the Institute's International Relations Department. Her current research focuses on borders in the context of territorial conflicts, mobility studies, and relations between security and identity in contemporary politics. Her fields of expertise also encompass foreign policy analysis, security studies, international relations theory, Russian foreign policy, conflicts in Georgia and Ukraine, de facto states and EU Eastern Partnership policy. She has written books on Russia's neighbourhood policy (2007) and the role of borders in Georgian territorial conflicts (2017), and has edited a book on Lithuania's foreign policy in the 2004–2014 period. Dovile holds a PhD in Political Science from Vilnius University.

Luxembourg | *Patrick Heck*

Patrick Heck is currently Minister Plenipotentiary for Policy Planning and Global Issues in Luxembourg's Ministry of Foreign and European Affairs (MFA). After two years in Customer Relations at the Bank of Sante Fe in New Mexico (USA), Heck joined the MFA in 1995, spending five years as a desk officer responsible for Asia/Oceania and EU Common Security and Defence Policy within the Directorate of Political Affairs. For the next five years, he served as either Deputy Permanent Representative (2000–2005) or Charge d'affaires a.i. (2002–2003) of Luxembourg's Permanent Representation to NATO before spending four years as a legal adviser to the general manager of the NATO Maintenance and Supply Agency (NAMSA) in Capellen, Luxembourg. After joining Luxembourg's National Intelligence Service in 2009 as the Head of the Operations Branch, he served as the organisation's Director for over five years beginning in March 2010. Between January 2016 and April 2019, he served as the Director of the Department of Defence in the MFA. Heck earned an LLM and Master of Public International Law at Robert Schuman University in Strasbourg, France, in 1993. The following year, he earned a national law certificate at the University of Luxembourg.

Malta | *Roderick Pace*

Roderick Pace is a resident full-time Professor at the Institute for European Studies of the University of Malta, where he held a Jean Monnet Chair. His research and teaching cover world politics, the external relations of the EU, Euro-Mediterranean relations and small states in world politics. He has published on Malta in the EU and Maltese politics. Since 2009, he has been on the editorial board of the journal South European Society and Politics, published by Taylor and Francis. He has over 120 academic works, including books, co-edited books, articles, chapters and papers. Pace co-founded and served as the Director of the Institute for European Studies from 1990 to 2016. He holds a BA (Honours) in Philosophy from the University of Malta; an MA in International Affairs from the School of Advanced International Studies (Bologna Center) of the Johns Hopkins University, and a PhD in Politics from the University of Reading (UK). His latest article (2019) is 'Malta and the European Union' in The Oxford Encyclopedia of European Union Politics.

Netherlands | *Erik de Feijter*

Erik de Feijter currently serves as Deputy Head of Mission at the Netherlands' Embassy in Canberra. Before that, he was Deputy Representative of the Netherlands at the Political and Security Committee of the EU; Coordinator for the Horn of Africa and the Great Lakes region and Senior Policy Officer of the Task Force Uruzgan (Ministry of Foreign Affairs); Head of the Political Affairs department of the Netherlands' Embassy in India; Political Adviser to the Dutch Provincial Reconstruction Team in Baghlan, Afghanistan; and Humanitarian Coordinator Sierra Leone, Liberia, Guinea in the Netherlands' Embassy in Ivory Coast. Erik holds an MA in Astronomy from the University of Utrecht.

Poland | *Adam Balcer*

Adam Balcer is a Political Scientist specialising in the area of Central-Eastern Europe, the Black Sea region and Polish foreign policy. He works also as a National Researcher at the European Council on Foreign Relations (ECFR) and a Lecturer at the Centre of East European Studies (SEW) at the University of Warsaw. He cooperates on the permanent basis with the journals Nowa Europa Wschodnia (New Eastern Europe) and the Aspen Review Central Europe as well as the website 'Dialog Forum: Perspektiven aus der Mitte Europas'. He also hosts 'Lechistan', a podcast about Poland's historical relations with the Muslim world in association with the radio station TOK FM. Adam served as an Expert in the Balkan section of the Department of Central Europe (2001–

2009) and Project Leader of the Turkish programme at the Centre for Eastern Studies (2005–2009). He has also been Director of the 'Enlargement and Neighbourhood' programme at demosEUROPA–Centre for European Strategy (2009–2013), a Member of the Advisory Group to the Committee of Foreign Relations of the Polish Parliament (2010–2012), and Adviser at the Presidential Expert Program (2013–2015). In 2015, Adam was Director of the annual conference 'Polish Eastern Policy', the largest event in Poland dedicated to Eastern Europe. In addition to numerous articles and reports, he has authored the books Polska na globalnej szachownicy (Poland on the Global Chessboard), Orzel i Polksiezyc. 600 lat polskiej publicystyki poswieconej Turcji (The Eagle and the Crescent: 600 Years of Polish Publications about Turkey) and Turcja, Wielki Step i Europa Srodkowa (Turkey, the Great Steppe and Central Europe).

Portugal | *Francisco Seixas da Costa*

Francisco Seixas da Costa is a retired Diplomat currently working as a Strategic Consultant and a Member of the Board of several international companies. He is a Member of the Consultative Council of the Calouste Gulbenkian Foundation and a Member of the Independent General Council of the Portuguese public service broadcaster RTP. He is also a newspaper columnist. Francisco was Secretary of State for European Affairs in the Portuguese government, Executive Director of the North-South Center of the Council of Europe, and a Visiting Professor at several Portuguese universities. As a diplomat, after being posted in Oslo, Luanda and London, he was Permanent Representative to the UN, OSCE and UNESCO as well as Ambassador to Brazil and France. He holds a degree in Political Science and has published books on European and international affairs.

Portugal | *Patricia Magalhaes Ferreira*

Patricia Magalhaes Ferreira is an independent Consultant and Researcher on development issues and policies, peacebuilding and fragile states. She has worked as a Consultant for the Portuguese Development Cooperation Agency on several projects and studies; conducted development evaluations in Portugal, Angola, Cape Verde, Guinea-Bissau and Mozambique; and carried out policy-oriented research, studies and assessments for Portuguese NGDOs as well as European thinktanks and organisations. For more than a decade, Patricia served as a Researcher in the Africa Department of the Institute for Strategic and International Studies (IEEI) in Lisbon. She has published several books and papers on development cooperation, development response to fragile situations, and EU-Africa issues. Patricia holds a PhD in African Studies from the ISCTE-IUL in Lisbon as well as a BA in International Relations and an MA in African Studies.

Romania | *Oana Popescu-Zamfir*

Oana Popescu-Zamfir is Director and Founder of GlobalFocus, an independent foreign policy and strategic analysis thinktank based in Bucharest. Previously, she served as a State Secretary for EU Affairs, Foreign Policy Adviser to the President of the Romanian Senate, Programmes Director of the Aspen Institute Romania, and Senior Editor of the Romanian edition of the journal Foreign Policy. In her earlier career, she was a Journalist covering foreign affairs. Her expertise mainly covers geopolitics and security in the EU/NATO neighbourhood, transatlantic relations, global political risk and strategic analysis, EU policies, democratisation and transitions, hybrid threats and shifting models of governance. Oana is an international Consultant and Media Commentator, as well as Writer and Lecturer. She coordinates international research as well as public and expert strategy events in addition to being Editor-in-chief of Eastern Focus, an international affairs quarterly. She was a Fulbright scholar at Yale University, where she studied emerging threats, post-conflict reconstruction and democratisation, with further executive studies in leadership at Harvard University and on terrorism at University of St Andrew. She has an MA in Conflict Analysis from the National School of Political and Administrative Studies, Bucharest.

Romania | *Ana Maria Teaca*

Ana Maria Teaca is currently working as a Senior Research Analyst and Programme Manager at GlobalFocus, an independent foreign policy and strategic analysis think-tank based in Bucharest. She also worked as a Chief of Staff and EU Affairs Adviser to the State Secretary of EU Affairs in Romania's Ministry of Labour. She holds an MA in European Studies from the University of Bath and also spent a semester studying International Relations at Humboldt University Berlin while pursuing this degree.

Slovakia | *Tomas Valasek*

Tomas Valasek is the Director of Carnegie Europe, where his research focuses on security and defence, transatlantic relations and Europe's Eastern Neighbourhood. Previously, Tomas served as the Permanent Representative of the Slovak Republic to NATO for nearly four years. Before that, he was President of the Central European Policy Institute in Bratislava (2012–2013), Director of Foreign Policy and Defence at the Centre for European Reform in London (2007–2012), and Founder and Director of the Brussels office of the World Security Institute (2002–2006). Between 2006 and 2007, he served as Acting Political Director and Head of the Security and Defence Policy Division of the Slovak Ministry of Defence. Tomas is the author of numerous articles in journals and newspapers, including the International Herald Tribune, the Wall Street Journal, and the Financial Times. He has advised the Slovak ministers of defence and foreign affairs, the UK House of Lords, and the Group of Experts on the new NATO Strategic Concept

Slovenia | *Milan Jazbec*

Milan Jazbec has been the Slovene Ambassador to the Republic of North Macedonia since September 2016. He is also Professor of Diplomacy at the University of Ljubljana and teaches diplomacy at the Faculty of International and European Studies of New University in Nova Gorica. Milan served as the Slovene Ambassador to Turkey from 2010 to 2015, and was also accredited to Azerbaijan, Iran, Iraq, Lebanon and Syria. He has been Director of the Policy Planning and Research Department (2006–2010), the Department for European States (2015–2016), and the Consular Department (1996).

He was also State Secretary for Defence Policy at the Ministry of Defence (2000–2004) and the first Slovene Consul in Klagenfurt. He has published more than 50 books in nine languages, one-third of them on diplomacy. He is a Member of the Slovenian Association for International Relations, Editor of the academic journal European Perspectives, and a Member of the Slovene PEN since 2017. In 2019, Milan received the Racin Award for his achievements in literature and, in 2005, the Grand Decoration of Honour in Gold with Star for services to the Republic of Austria.

Spain | *Felix Arteaga*

Felix Arteaga currently serves as Senior Analyst for Security and Defence at the Elcano Royal Institute, a Spanish thinktank based in Madrid. Previously, he was Professor of EU Common Security and Defence Policy at the University of Navarra and the Instituto Universitario General Gutierrez Mellado of the Open University (UNED) and the Ministry of Defence. Before that, he was a Lecturer at the Universidad Carlos III of Madrid, the Universidad Autónoma and the Universidad Complutense, as well as Senior Analyst at the Instituto de Cuestiones Internacionales (INCI) and the Instituto Universitario de Seguridad Interior (UNISCI). Between 1999 and 2001, he directed the European Commission's Security Sector Reform Programme in Paraguay. A former Military Officer (retired), Felix holds degrees in Law (Open University) and Political Science (Complutense University of Madrid), a PhD in International Relations (Complutense University of Madrid), and a diploma in National Security (National Defence University, Washington, DC).

Sweden | *Lars Niklasson*

Lars Niklasson is a Senior Researcher at the Swedish Institute for European Policy Studies (SIEPS) as well as Deputy Professor of Political Science at Linkoeping University. Before joining SIEPS and Linkoeping University, Lars was a Policy Analyst for several Swedish ministries, agencies and consultancies. He is also a National Expert for the OECD. His research focuses on the global role of the European Union, including its relations to Africa and its role in the global implementation of the UN's Sustainable Development Goals. He teaches International Political Economy and Comparative Politics with a focus on global challenges and governance. Lars earned a PhD at Uppsala University in 1992, and has been a Visiting Researcher at a number of European and American universities, as well as at the University of Nairobi. His latest book is Improving the Sustainable Development Goals: Strategies and the Governance Challenge (Routledge 2019).

United Kingdom | *Laura Cleary*

Laura R Cleary is the Director of Oakwood International Security. Prior to establishing her own business in 2019, she was Head of the Centre for International Security and Resilience at Cranfield University. Laura joined Cranfield University in 2002 to head its Defence Diplomacy Education programme 'Managing Defence in the Wider Security Context'. As the programme's Academic Director, she taught 150 nationalities across four continents and acted as a Consultant and Adviser to MODs and parliaments in Asia, Eastern Europe and Africa. A leading expert in the fields of International Defence Engagement (IDE), governance and defence transformation, her research in the field has contributed to British policy formation and strategic planning. In 2017, Laura was shortlisted for a Women in Defence Award for her 'outstanding contribution to British defence'. In 2006 and again in 2019, she was awarded the Director's Commendation for Contributions to the United Kingdom's Defence Relations at the Defence Academy of the United Kingdom. She holds a PhD in Soviet Defence Conversion from Glasgow University and a BA in International Politics and History from Indiana University.

About the Advisory Board

Catherine Woollard

Catherine Woollard currently works as Director of the European Council on Refugees and Exiles (ECRE), a network of 104 NGOs in 41 European countries that work to defend the rights of displaced persons in Europe and in European foreign policy. Prior to joining the ECRE, she worked on peace, security and governance as Director of the European Peacebuilding Liaison Office as well as with a number of NGOs, including Conciliation Resources and Transparency International. She has also worked as a consultant for governments and international organisations and as a university lecturer, gaining international experience across Europe, Africa and Asia. She holds degrees in politics and law.

James Moran

James Moran is an Associate Senior Research Fellow at the Centre for European Policy Studies (CEPS) in Brussels. He has extensive experience in the Middle East and North Africa (MENA). In 2016/2017, he served as the Principal Adviser on the MENA region at the EU's European External Action Service (EEAS). Prior to that, he was Ambassador and Head of the EU Delegation to Egypt between 2012 and 2016. In 2011, he was the EU's Senior Coordinator in Libya during the country's revolution that year. Between 2006 and 2011, he was the EU's Asia Director and served as the chief negotiator for a number of EU partnership agreements with China, Indonesia, Malaysia, the Philippines, Singapore, Thailand and Vietnam. Between 2002 and 2006, he was head of the China division in Brussels. Between 1999 and 2002, he was the EU Ambassador to Jordan and Yemen. Earlier experiences in the 1980s and 1990s included service with the EU Delegations in Jamaica and Ethiopia as well as various assignments in Brussels. Before joining the EU in 1983, he worked for the UK government and in the private sector in London. A UK national, he attended Keele University, Harvard University and the University of London.

Paul Smith

Paul Smith is an expert adviser in strategic planning and capacity-building for reform. He is currently helping the British Foreign & Commonwealth Office develop a human resources management (HRM) strategy to assist a government in the Middle East. Before that, he worked in Iraq as NATO's 'senior civilian' (effectively its ambassador) in

Baghdad, reporting directly to the UN's assistant secretary-general for support operations. This mission included reviewing and restructuring a failing international programme of reform that involved 26 nations and required a complete overhaul to ensure it delivered the agreed objectives in addition to performing a gap analysis to identify required additional support. Since 2000, he has acted in a number of strategic planning and senior management roles for NATO and other international bodies. Prior to this, he held several positions as an officer in the British Army. Smith holds a BSc in Information Management Systems as well as an MSc in Designing Information Systems. He is a graduate of the UK's prestigious Joint Services Command and Staff College, to which he has returned as an instructor, as well as a senior executive coach (Level 7). He is also currently pursuing an Executive Master in Governance & Development Policy at ULB in Belgium.

Poul Skytte Christoffersen

Poul Skytte Christoffersen is Working Chairman of Think Tank EUROPA in Copenhagen as well as Chairman of the European Policy Centre (EPC) in Brussels. In addition, he serves as Senior Adviser at the international executive advisory firm Teneo. Christoffersen's positions have included being Denmark's Permanent Representative to the EU (1995–2003, and 2009), Special Adviser to High Representative of the Union for Foreign Affairs and Security Policy (HRVP) Catherine Ashton in setting up the European External Action Service (EEAS), and Head of Cabinet (Council 1980–1994 and Commission 2006–2009). He holds an MA in Economics from the University of Copenhagen (1972) and a Diploma of Higher European Studies from the College of Europe in Bruges (1973).

Joern Graevingholt

Joern Graevingholt is Senior Researcher in the Transformation of Political (Dis-)Order Programme at the German Development Institute (DIE) in Bonn, Germany, where he heads the 'Forced Displacement and Migration' project. Prior to that, he led or co-led a number of DIE research projects, including 'Supporting Sustainable Peace', 'Transformation and Development in Fragile States', and 'Development Cooperation and Non-State Armed Groups'. He has also conducted research in numerous countries in the post-Soviet world, Asia and Africa. Since 2008, Graevingholt has been a member of the German government's Advisory Council for Civilian Crisis Prevention and Peacebuilding, for which he was the co-chair from 2011 to 2018. His recent publications include The Securitization of Foreign Aid (co-ed. with Stephen Brown, Palgrave 2016) and the data project 'Constellations of State Fragility' (https://statefragility.info). Graevingholt read Political Science, History and Slavonic Studies in Freiburg. He holds an MPhil in European Studies from the University of Cambridge and a PhD in Political Science from Humboldt University Berlin.

Alfredo Conte

Alfredo Conte is a career diplomat with Italy's Ministry of Foreign Affairs and International Cooperation (MFA) who has extensive experience in European foreign policy. In addition to having been a Senior Adviser to a number of Italian foreign ministers, he has held positions in Berlin and Hong Kong (during the time of the handover to China). Between 2008 and early 2018, he was seconded to the EU institutions in Brussels – first to the Policy Unit of Javier Solana, then-high representative for common foreign and security policy, and subsequently to the European External Action Service. In 2011, he was appointed by High Representative of the Union for Foreign Affairs and Security Policy (HRVP) Catherine Ashton to be Head of the EEAS Strategic Planning Division. Under HRVP Federica Mogherini, he has been directly involved in elaborating the EU's Global Strategy for Foreign and Security Policy. Since returning to Italy's MFA in 2018, he has been Special Adviser to the 2018 Italian OSCE Chairmanship in Office. Since November 2018, he has been in charge of overall coordination in the MFA as Head of the Coordination Unit in the Secretariat General. Conte holds a degree (cum laude) in Law from the University of Naples.

Andrew Sherriff

Andrew Sherriff is Head of the European External Affairs Programme at the European Centre for Development Policy Management (ECDPM), a Maastricht-based thinktank at which he has worked since 2008. He has regularly been a part of teams evaluating the implementation of the EU's foreign and development-cooperation policies while on over 30 assignments in Africa, Europe and Asia. Prior to joining ECDPM, he served as an adviser to NGOs, various European foreign ministries and agencies, and EU presidencies. From 1999 to 2004, he worked at the peacebuilding organisation International Alert. In 2019, he edited Investing in the Europe's Global Role: The must-have guide for the negotiations of the Multiannual Financial Framework 2021–2027 (Maastricht: ECDPM). He has authored over 50 policy papers published by thinktanks and research institutes as well as academic articles covering Europe's international relations as well as peace and conflict issues. Originally from Scotland, Sherriff is a political scientist who has studied at Staffordshire University, the University of Limerick in Ireland, and the University of Calgary in Canada. He has also been a visiting professor at American University in Washington, D.C.

Acknowledgments

We are much indebted to the many people who generously gave their time and effort to assist us in this endeavour. First and foremost, we owe sincere thanks to our cooperation partner in the project, the Brussels-based Centre for European Policy Studies (CEPS) and, in particular, its staff members Loes Debuysere and Steven Blockmans, who provided their valuable expertise, guidance and organisational skills throughout. Our Advisory Board was a constant, generous and welcome support. And more than 28 dedicated authors – some on their own and others together with co-authors – answered a detailed questionnaire and composed a report on an EU country, both of which became part of an online platform skilfully fashioned by Dieter Dollacker and Dirk Waldik. Last but not least, our line editor, Josh Ward, bravely soldiered through all sections of the book to make sure that the texts were clear, clean and concise. We thank all these people with all our heart. Without their patient and professional efforts, this ambitious idea of combining voices from across the European Union would not have become a reality.

Annex: Questionnaire on WGA Approaches in the EU and Its Member States

Between April and November 2019, the country experts and the EU experts were asked to fill out the following questionnaire. The experts used their answers to compose the comprehensive country reports and the EU report.

The questonnaire had three sections: "What/Why", "Who" and "How" questions, although the latter two sections partially overlap regarding the institutional setup. A scaling system was included for some questions in order to complement the qualitative assessments made by the experts and to facilitate comparison between country reports. The experts were asked to indicate whether a country or the EU:

> 2: fully meets the statement in the question, with evidence to substantiate this expectation
> 1: falls short of the benchmark response under score 2 in some regard
> 0: does not meet the statement of the question

1. What/Why-Questions: Political and strategic objectives

1.1 National WGA policies on external conflicts and crises

Q1: Is there a WGA framework for coordination and cooperation at the national level?

> 2: There are governmental documents at the national level explicitly outlining a WGA (as special strategy, as part of the national security strategy, in government declarations, in special strategies of certain ministries…)
>
> 1: There are no explicit governmental documents, but implicit commitments can be found in different policy documents.
>
> 0: There is no explicit or implicit mention of WGA in policy documents.

Q2: If the answer to Q1 was yes (score 2 or 1), which countries and regions are covered? And why are these countries and regions particularly relevant for the country?

Q3: If the answer to Q1 was yes (score 2 or 1), what is the scope (narrow = civil-military coordination; medium = diplomacy, security, development, and humanitarian aid; system-wide = also including economy and trade)?

Q4: If the answer to Q1 was yes (score 2 or 1), what are the fields of action (e.g. humanitarian and development aid, conflict transformation, stabilisation and peacebuilding)? Are there particular thematic priorities and, if so, why?

Q5: If the answer to Q1 was yes (score 2 or 1), how would you assess the quality of these documents? For example, how binding are these commitments? Do they contain guidelines for implementation?

1.2 EU framework (Global Strategy)

Q6: Has the Global Strategy 'inspired' or influenced the formulation of national WGA strategies? To what extent have WGA strategies of the EU been setting the framework for developing WGA policies at a national level?

Q7: How much has the member state influenced/supported the EU's Global Strategy? What mutual interactions were/are observable in developing or implementing the Global Strategy?

Q8: Does the member state launch special WGA initiatives within the EU framework (e.g. CSDP missions)?

1.3 International framework

Q9: To what extent have WGA strategies of the UN, NATO, OECD-DAC, OSCE... been setting the framework for developing WGA policies at a national level? How binding are these international organisations' WGAs for the member state?

Q10: How much has the member state influenced/supported the WGA strategies of the UN, NATO, OECD-DAC, OSCE...? What mutual interactions were/are observable in developing or implementing these WGA strategies?

2. Who-Questions: Institutional actors

2.1 In-country cooperation and coordination in dealing with external conflict and crisis

Q12: Is there formal or informal coordination/cooperation between different ministries (inter-ministerial level)? Which ministries and agencies are involved?

- 2: There is well-established and formalised coordination and cooperation
- 1: There is some kind of coordination and cooperation, often informal in nature
- 0: There is no coordination or cooperation taking place

Q13: Is there formal or informal coordination within each ministry (intra-ministerial level)?

- 2: There is well-established and formalised coordination and cooperation
- 1: There is some kind of coordination and cooperation, often informal in nature
- 0: There is no coordination or cooperation taking place

Q14: Is there formal or informal coordination/cooperation within parliament?

- 2: There is well-established and formalised coordination and cooperation
- 1: There is some kind of coordination and cooperation, often informal in nature
- 0: There is no coordination or cooperation taking place

Q15: Is there formal or informal coordination/cooperation between executive and legislative powers?

- 2: There is well-established and formalised coordination and cooperation
- 1: There is some kind of coordination and cooperation, often informal or ad hoc in nature
- 0: There is no coordination or cooperation taking place

Q16: Is there formal or informal coordination/cooperation with civil society actors?

2: There is well-established and formalised coordination and cooperation
1: There is some kind of coordination and cooperation, often informal in nature or ad hoc
0: There is no coordination or cooperation taking place

2.2 EU/international cooperation and coordination in dealing with external conflict and crisis

Q17: Is there formal or informal coordination/cooperation with EU institutions and actors?

2: There is well-established and formalised coordination and cooperation
1: There is some kind of coordination and cooperation, often informal in nature or ad hoc
0: There is no coordination or cooperation taking place

Q18: Is there formal or informal coordination/cooperation with the UN, NATO, OECD-DAC, OSCE?

2: There is well-established and formalised coordination and cooperation
1: There is some kind of coordination and cooperation, often informal in nature or ad hoc
0: There is no coordination or cooperation taking place

3. How-Questions: Degree of interaction and instruments introduced

3.1. Structures

Q20: Concerning WGA at the national level: Is there a set of special structures or arrangements in place to make a WGA happen?

    2: There are significant institutional changes reflecting the country's commitment to WGA at the national level

    1: There are some minor institutional changes being made to enable the country's commitment to WGA

    0: No institutional arrangements or changes have been made

Q21: If the answer to Q20 was yes (score 2 or 1), how would you assess the effectiveness and quality of these institutional arrangements?

Q22: Are there structures or arrangements in place to facilitate policy coherence within the EU framework?

    2: There are significant institutional changes reflecting the country's commitment to the EU's integrated approach

    1: There are some minor institutional changes being made to enable the country's commitment

    0: No institutional arrangements or changes have been made

Q23: If the answer to Q22 was yes (score 2 or 1), how would you assess the effectiveness and quality of these institutional arrangements?

Q24: Are there special structures or arrangements in place to facilitate policy coherence within the international framework (e.g. UN, NATO, OECD-DAC, OSCE and civil society)?

    2: There are significant institutional changes reflecting the country's commitment to WGA with other (international) actors

    1: There are some minor institutional changes being made to enable the country's commitment to WGA with other (international) actors

    0: No institutional arrangements or changes have been made with other (international) actors

Q25: If the answer to Q24 was yes (score 2 or 1), how would you assess the effectiveness and quality of these institutional arrangements?

3.2. Instruments and procedures

Q26: Concerning WGA at the national level: Are there financial and/or non-financial instruments in place that facilitate the implementation of a WGA?

2: There are integrated processes for initiating, programming and implementing a WGA at the national level

1: There are some tools for sharing information and coordinating in place that serve to enable or facilitate a WGA at the national level

0: There are no WGA tools in place at the national level

Q27: If the answer to Q26 was yes (score 2 or 1), how would you assess the effectiveness and quality of these tools in enabling a WGA?

3.3. Human resources

Q28: Is there an appropriate human resources (HR) policy in place to facilitate the implementation of a WGA?

2: There is a strong HR policy in place that favours the implementation of a WGA

1: The HR policy seeks to foster WGA to some extent

0: There is no HR policy in place that is linked to implementing a WGA

Q29: If the answer to Q28 was yes (score 2 or 1), how would you assess the effectiveness and quality of this HR policy?

3.4. Political or administrative leadership

Q30: Is there leadership that enables practitioners to manage the complex institutional arrangements that WGA work requires?

 2: There is clear leadership that enables or facilitates a WGA
 1: There is no outspoken leadership, but some political guidance can be detected
 0: There is no leadership in place that pushes for WGA

Q31: If the answer to Q30 was yes (score 2 or 1), how would you assess the effectiveness and quality of this political or administrative leadership in enabling a WGA?

Abstract

For most of the 20th century, it seemed sufficient for each government ministry or agency to do a good job on the tasks and competences assigned to it. In other words, foreign ministries nurtured friendly relations with other countries, defence ministries ensured national security, health ministries worked to provide good healthcare to the national population, economics ministries promoted trade, and so forth. What's more, there seemed to be no need for greater coherence and coordination between these different policies and the ministries or other bodies responsible for them. However, in today's increasingly interconnected environment, it has become clear that this arrangement is no longer sufficient to have an impact and to achieve the desired policy results.

Especially in the fields of foreign, development and security policy, the many crises and conflicts of the 1990s – such as those in Afghanistan, Africa and the Western Balkans – have shown that this kind of 'siloed' approach is no longer viable. Rather, the complex and interlinked problems of human security, social and economic underdevelopment, and poor governance – factors that underpinned and kept fuelling many of these conflicts – prompted the EU and many of its member states to break new ground in their individual and joint policies for managing crises and conflicts. The general belief behind these efforts has been that greater policy coherence will be rewarded with better results. And to make this possible, the available instruments, which had previously been used individually and for the most part independently of each other – whether in diplomacy, defence or development cooperation – were to be combined into a new approach, and new forms of cooperation between ministries involved in conflict transformation were to be introduced.

This book attempts for the first time to take stock of the development and implementation of such whole-of-government approaches (WGAs) – as they are referred to in organisation theories – to external crisis and conflict management in the EU and all its member states.

The 29 reports – one for each EU member state as well as one on the EU as a whole – examine the policies or strategies that have been developed to adapt to the increasing complex security challenges and to ensure better policy coherence. They deal with the question of how these policy frameworks have been institutionally and organisationally implemented, with the main question being: Do we see that words have been followed by deeds, and that new institutional forms of cooperation and coordination between different actors at the headquarters levels have been introduced both in the EU and its member states?

Methodologically, the research assumes that the organisation of political coherence through a WGA is a necessary though insufficient condition for success in crisis and conflict management. The project is also based on the assumption that any country that claims to have adopted a WGA must necessarily have undergone changes in its method of cooperation – both within and between its institutions on the national level as well as with the EU or other international organisations – and that these changes can be observed and described. The same, with a grain of salt, applies to the EU and its implementation of its 'integrated approach' (or 'whole-of-governance approach'), which was introduced with the 2016 publication of the EU Global Strategy.

The final chapter attempts to provide an initial evaluation and synthesis of where the EU and its individual member states stand in comparison with each other as well as which best practices (or 'enablers') for the successful implementation of a WGA can be identified.

The book will be accompanied by a website offering applications that will enable users to quickly and easily obtain an overview of what has been achieved in the EU and its member states based on the questionnaire on which the reports themselves are based (see Annex). This questionnaire contains 31 questions divided into three sections: 'what/why' questions on political and strategic objectives; 'who' questions on institutional actors; and 'how' questions on the degree of interaction and instruments introduced.